WHAT
WE
SEE

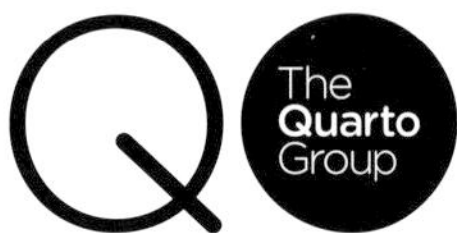

First published in 2023 by White Lion Publishing,
an imprint of The Quarto Group.
One Triptych Place,
London, SE1 9SH,
United Kingdom
T (0)20 7700 6700
www.Quarto.com

A catalogue record for this book is available from the British Library.

ISBN 978-0-7112-7854-7
Ebook ISBN 978-0-7112-7856-1

10 9 8 7 6 5 4 3 2 1

Design by Hannah Naughton

Printed in Bosnia and Herzegovina

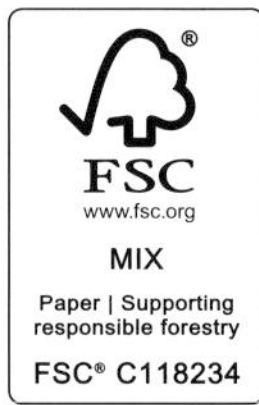

WOMEN PHOTOGRAPH

WHAT WE SEE

Women & nonbinary perspectives through the lens

Curated by **Daniella Zalcman**
& Sara Ickow

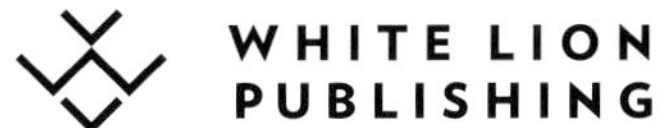
WHITE LION PUBLISHING

Foreword

By Kat Chow

What We See is nothing short of breathtaking. Each of these photographs evoked within me a staggering and visceral response, at times bewildering, at times heartrending. As a journalist who has spent years contextualizing our infinitely complex world, I have witnessed time after time how photographs can illuminate our lives in ways that words and audio simply cannot. *What We See* is certainly no different; I was stunned by how these images drew me into their stories, and how thrilled I was when I recalled that you, too, get to experience this work for the first time. Captured by photographers who are women or nonbinary, these images forge a crucial modern history: one where such perspectives that have historically been ignored – behind the lens and in front of it – are illuminated with care and respect.

The range of these photographs is remarkable. Perspectives from New Delhi, the Weddell Sea, Vava'u in the Kingdom of Tonga, Hong Kong, Cleveland and so many other places, sit alongside one another. They preserve moments of a young woman undergoing surgery to receive the first-ever face transplant, two cholitas in Bolivia mid-fight in a mountain-lined wrestling ring, an examination of Afro-descendants in Mexico, a young woman in Aabey, Lebanon, sitting defiantly in her car following its destruction during a protest in the uprising of 2019.

When I consider what binds the vast array of photos that comprise *What We See*, the word 'intimacy' surfaces. Intimacy, because the emotional connection to each of these photos arrives swiftly, stirring in me – and surely also in you – a deep curiosity about their subjects. Intimacy, because this collection ultimately evokes a sense of support: the stories brought to life here elicit the feeling that we are not alone. And that people are bearing witness to, and capturing, the essential stories that animate our lives.

With deep admiration for these talented photojournalists and the lives they have chronicled, I invite you to sit with, and absorb, these photographs. *What We See* is an impressive feat that will expand your worldview.

Kat Chow *is a journalist and writer. She previously was a founding member of NPR's Code Switch, and her work has appeared in* The New York Times Magazine, The Atlantic, New York Magazine, *among many other places. She is the author of* Seeing Ghosts, *a memoir about family and loss.*

Introduction

By Daniella Zalcman, founder of Women Photograph

Photojournalists are tasked with a unique privilege: teaching others how to see.

We introduce our audiences to people and places they may never otherwise encounter, show them ecosystems, conflicts and communities from every corner of the globe. But for as long as photojournalism has existed as a discipline – built around broadening perspectives – the industry has been dominated by white Western men. That has had a profound impact on our collective visual history: what we choose to document, and why, and how.

It is easy to believe that we, as photojournalists, simply freeze the world around us frame by frame, working as unbiased observers who are fully detached from the events we cover. After all, this is the lie we have told ourselves since the advent of news photography. But, in reality, our identities and lived experiences deeply impact how we access spaces and choose to tell stories. We can only hope to produce nuanced, thorough and respectful journalism with an industry of storytellers as diverse as the communities we document.

I became a photojournalist around 2007 while I was a college student in New York. If I felt the yawning absence of women colleagues and mentors in the press corps at the time, I certainly did not understand how it was impacting my own growth as a photographer. But, by 2016, industry reports were starting to emerge that only 15 to 20 per cent of working news photographers were women and that major news outlets were hiring women photographers at even lower rates. And when interrogated about their assigning practices, editors frequently responded that they just did not know where to find women photographers.

In response, I launched Women Photograph in 2017, a hiring database of women and nonbinary photographers from around the world. Today, our community includes more than 1,600 independent photographers based in 110 countries. And our mission has grown alongside it. We distribute project grants, host annual skills-building workshops, run a mentorship programme that connects early career photographers with editor and photographer mentors, exhibit the work of our photographers at festivals and in galleries internationally, and collect hiring and publishing statistics on the photojournalism industry.

Our long-term objective for the organization is simple: to become obsolete. If Women Photograph is successful in helping the industry achieve true intersectional parity, then the advocacy work at the heart of our organization will no longer be necessary.

Our inaugural book *What We See* is a broad survey that represents the equally broad careers of our members. The goal is not to make any generalizations about the gaze of women and nonbinary photographers – such generalizations are impossible. The directions in which we can expand our traditional understanding of photojournalism are infinite. This book merely begins to hint at the possibilities.

Alongside classic documentary-style images from some of our most acclaimed trailblazers such as Carol Guzy, Susan Meiselas and Lynsey Addario, there is work that defies traditional photojournalistic practice, as in the collaborative images from Koyoltzintli and Charlotte Schmitz, the composite self-portraiture of Haruka Sakaguchi and the constructed images of Sim Chi Yin and Maha Alasaker.

If there is one common thread – and a striking one at that – it is that much of the work in this book feels quiet, even if it was not made in quiet contexts. Anastasia Taylor-Lind's frame of a man in uniform doubled over, next to a bloody stretcher, is a gesture of exhaustion or possibly mourning in the middle of armed conflict. Gulshan Khan's photo of a young woman serenely donning a scarf comes moments before she attends a protest in the wake of Israeli forces' killing 59 Palestinians. Verónica G. Cárdenas' image of a Honduran woman being tenderly resuscitated occurs in the relative calm that follows her near-drowning in the Rio Grande. They are all moments wrapped in grief that still allow for other emotions to seep into our understanding of each picture. There is more than just loss.

This comes in stark contrast to the overwhelming number of noteworthy works in photojournalism that centre violence. We build our history textbooks around war and famine and natural disasters, more or less creating a chronology of the traumas inflicted on and by humans throughout our existence. Journalists are similarly drawn to the worst human experiences – partially because our work often serves as evidence, and partially because many of us do this work to live up to the words of Joseph Pulitzer III, 'We will illuminate dark places and, with a deep sense of responsibility, interpret these troubled times'.

The assembled images in this book do not shy away from those stories. They span war and revolution, terrorism and mass shootings. But the photos themselves often come from the periphery of injustice, or focus on women as the actors in spaces that are so often seen as predominantly male. They remind us of what we miss when visual news media is constructed from a singular perspective.

But the traditional perspective does not only omit narratives, it also imposes them. Historically, the photographer's role has been to record stories as an outsider, often dictating the narrative. As such, photographs are frequently taken without consultation with, or feedback from, those featured. So, there is something revolutionary about photographers like Lola Flash, Golden, Jess T. Dugan and Laurence Philomène turning the camera on themselves to document LGBTQ+ identity, or Tailyr Irvine and Citlali Fabián's portraits of their own relatives in work on modern Indigenous identity.

And while journalism rarely makes proportionate space for the joyful and the ordinary, we wanted to make sure that those photos were included as well: Tanya Habjouqa's photo of a family picnicking on the beach in Gaza or Kendrick Brinson's photo of a synchronized swimming team of retirees.

Whether on the front pages of newspapers or magazines, in school textbooks or tucked away in museum archives, the photography that we have used historically to define and memorialize human history rarely reflects how we collectively see. With this collection of work, we hope to rectify that, sharing a broadened perspective on the stories that define us.

01

Identity

In this selection, photographers honour identity — sometimes by developing a deep bond with a new acquaintance, sometimes, most intimately, by turning the camera on themselves or by sharing their personal visions of the communities to which they belong. Identity can be reflected in our relationships to our own bodies, in our family connections or in the ways in which we exist together and in isolation. Some photos destigmatize an identity, others call attention to what we might otherwise consider mundane. All of them are meant to be declarative: here we are, this is who we are and this is how we want to be seen.

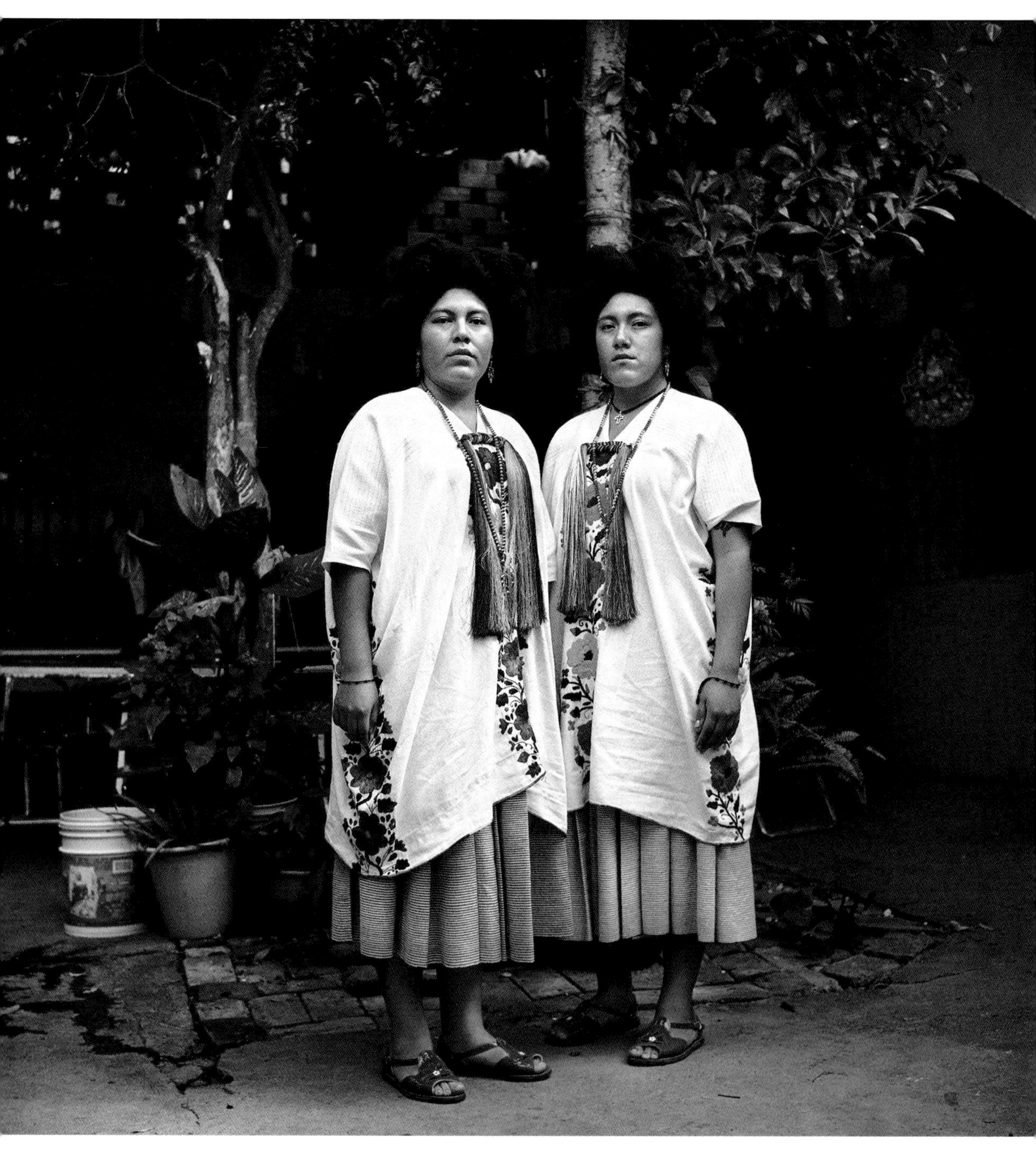

◀

Citlali Fabián

Mexican

My cousins Yessi and Kristel

Oaxaca City, Mexico; 2018

My cousins Yessi and Kristel, daughters of aunt María, granddaughters of uncle Nemo, cousin of my grandma Chencha. That's the thread that connects us as the big family that we are. This image is part of my series Ben'n Yalhalhj (I am from Yalalag), a project I started as a family album by photographing the members of my community who had migrated across Mexico and to Los Angeles, USA. Like many Indigenous youth, I grew up exposed to the exoticization of my reality and at the same time to the lack of authentic representation of our voices. Documenting my community, my Yalalteca diaspora, is a driving force for me as an artist to heal and embrace my identity, and I hope to encourage others to do the same. This project is a family reunion, to bring us together over time and territories, to learn about our experiences, to interconnect us through music and traditions, our migration movements, and to reinforce our bonds and ties to the community. This is my way to honour my ancestors and to see our culture stay alive and withstand colonization processes.

▶▶

Tasneem Alsultan

Saudi Arabian

Leap of Faith

Jeddah, Saudi Arabia; 2016

I wanted to answer a question that many have shared: Do we need marriage to signify that we have love? Do you need a husband to have a significant life? I started this project thinking I only had my personal story to share. I was married at the age of 17 and lived separately as a single parent for the last six years of an unhappy 10-year marriage. Many family members commented that I was foolish to ask for a divorce. Only later, I realized that many Saudi women had similar experiences. I followed the stories of widows, women happily married and divorced women. A common realization among women I photographed was that they all managed to overcome the many hurdles imposed by society or their state. 'Society constrains the definition of a divorcee. What you can or cannot do remains under the control of others. As an independent single mother, I have made peace with the sacrifices I have had to make, but also managed to find happiness on my own.' These are the words of Nassiba, whom I photographed after her first divorce, while she was a single mother to Bilal. Now in her second and happy marriage, and a mother of two sons, I am happy to have been able to document this transition in her life.

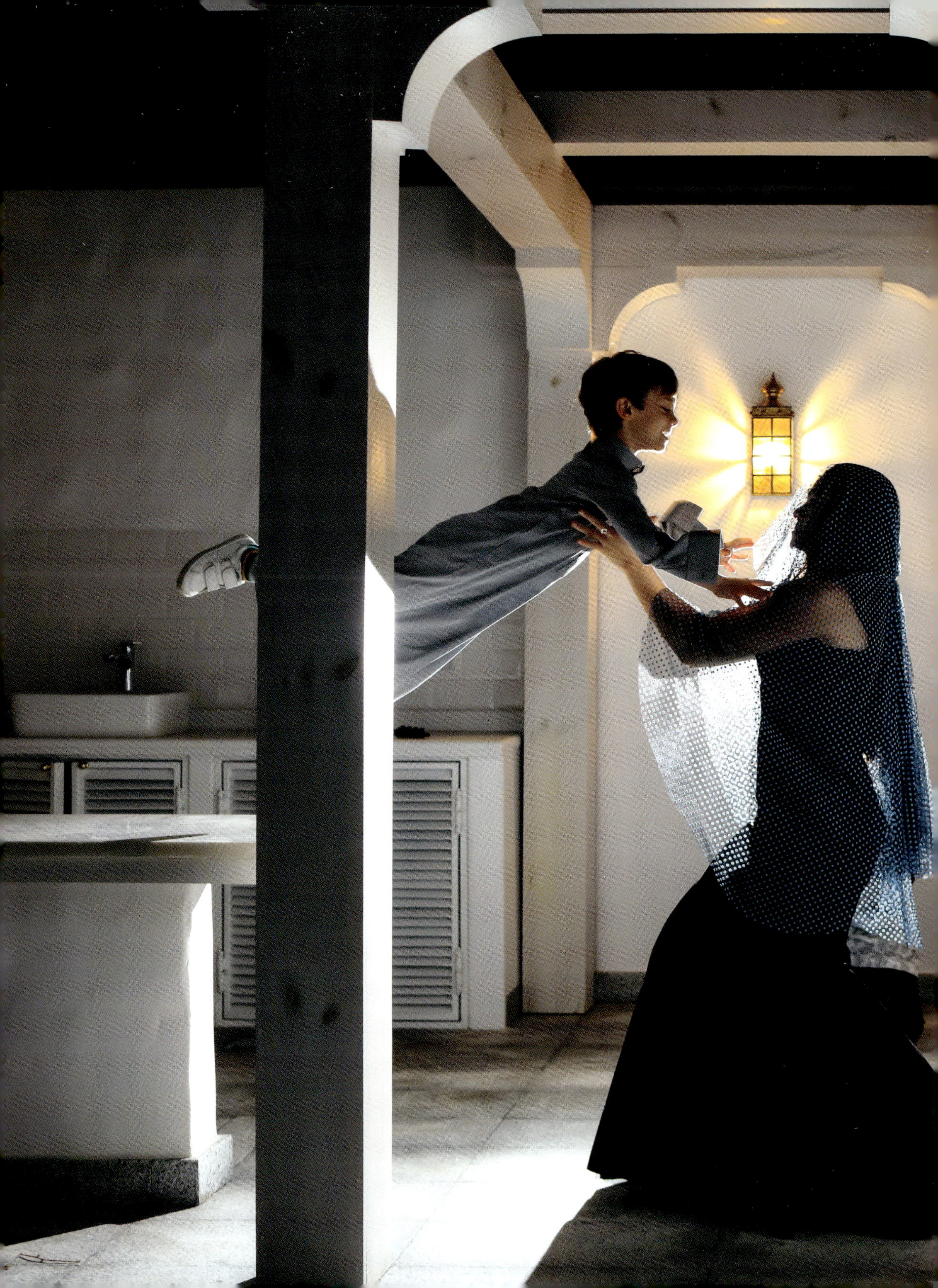

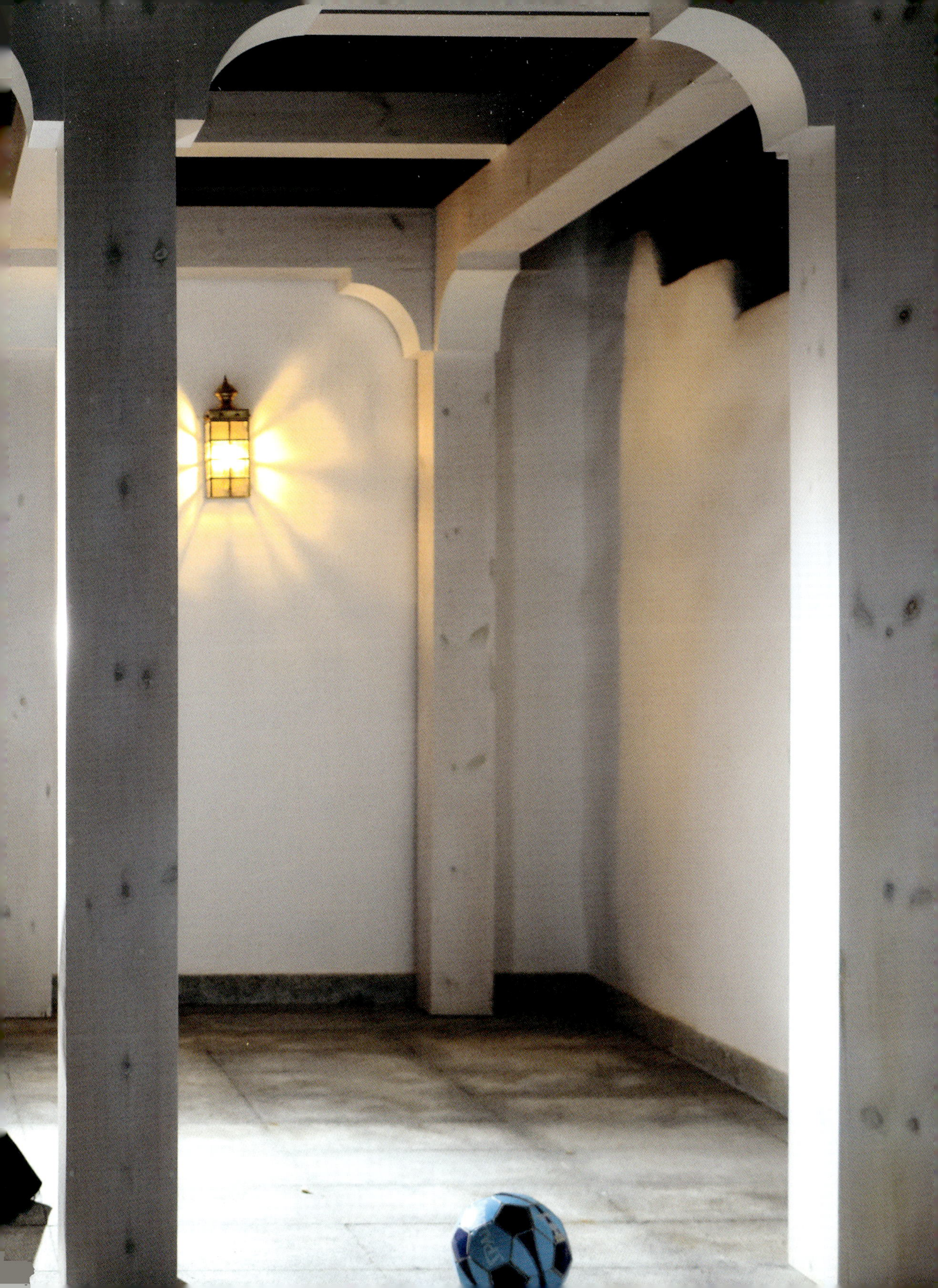

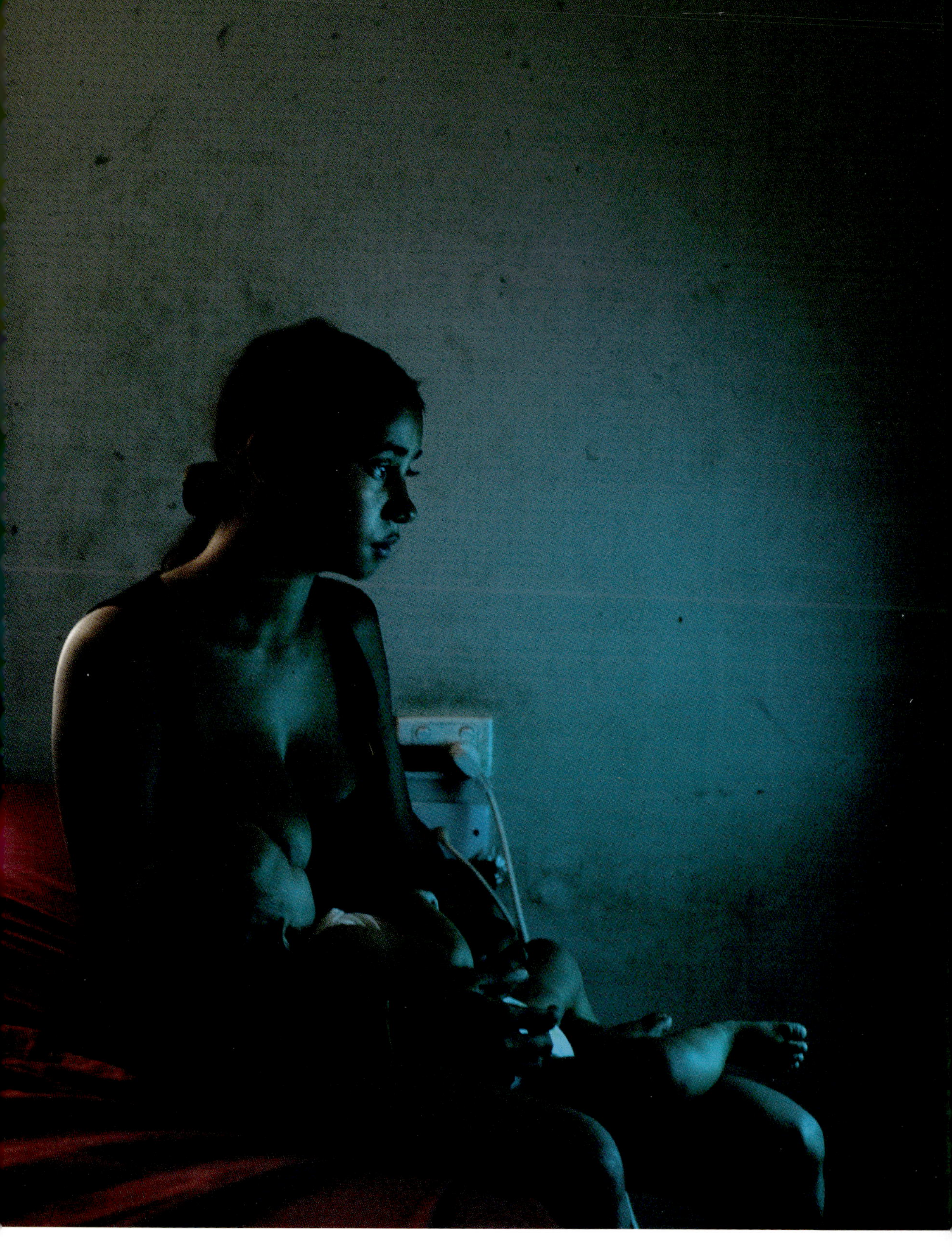

Raphaela Rosella

Australian

Tricia and Ty-Leta

Moree, Australia; 2016

My socially engaged art practice has emerged over 15 years with contributions from several women in my life, with the goal of resisting bureaucratic representations of our lived experiences such as case files and criminal records. These women are my friends, family members and extended kin, whom I now identify as co-creators in my practice. This has resulted in a co-created archive of photographic works, video works, sound recordings, state-issued documents, criminal indexes and ephemera. Using a static television channel as a light source for her bedroom, my friend Tricia breastfeeds her baby daughter Ty-Leta. Tricia's partner Troy was in and out of prison during her pregnancy and was again serving time when this portrait was made. Together we breastfed our babies while we talked about the state's relentless imprisonment of Troy. It is vital to understand prisons, policing and the criminal punishment system in so-called Australia as a continuum of settler colonialism. During this time, Troy had only spent three birthdays outside of prison since the age of nine – he was soon to turn 30. In turn, this image amplifies feelings of intimacy, frustration, kinship and connectedness that circulate between imprisoned people and their loved ones structured through carceral regimes.

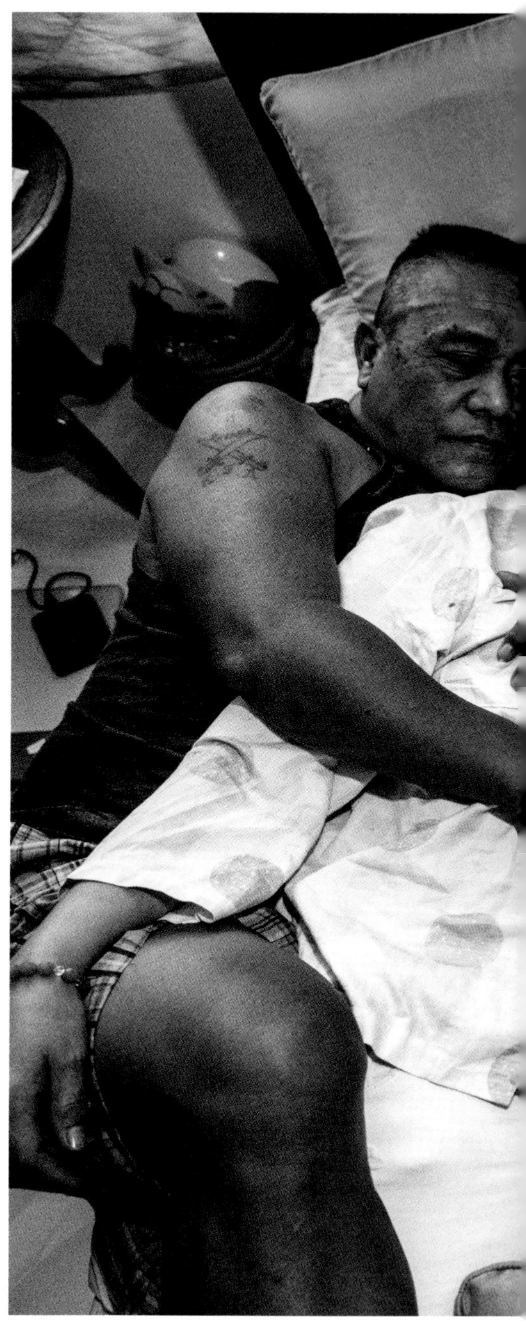

Xyza Cruz Bacani

Filipina

Family Bonding

Philippines; 2017

My father, Villamor, hugs my mother, Georgia, as she spends time with my nieces and sister, Sharila. My mother has been a domestic worker in Hong Kong for more than two decades and only comes home once a year for two weeks. Those two weeks are the happiest I have seen our family. When I took this photo, my family was oblivious to the camera as they were in the moment, enjoying each other. Migration is a big part of our lives, and subconsciously we know that these moments are fleeting. This image is part of We Are Like Air, a body of work focusing on the nuances of migration. My family story is the book's anchor, and photographing my close relatives is one of the most challenging experiences I have had as a documentary photographer. The story is too close, and it opened up many unhealed wounds in our family. Traumas of the separation caused by migration leaked, and forgiveness was a journey we all took together as a family. The process of documenting my own family was cathartic, and it taught me that vulnerability is a gift. The circumstances of our lives made me a survivor but being vulnerable made me a better photographer.

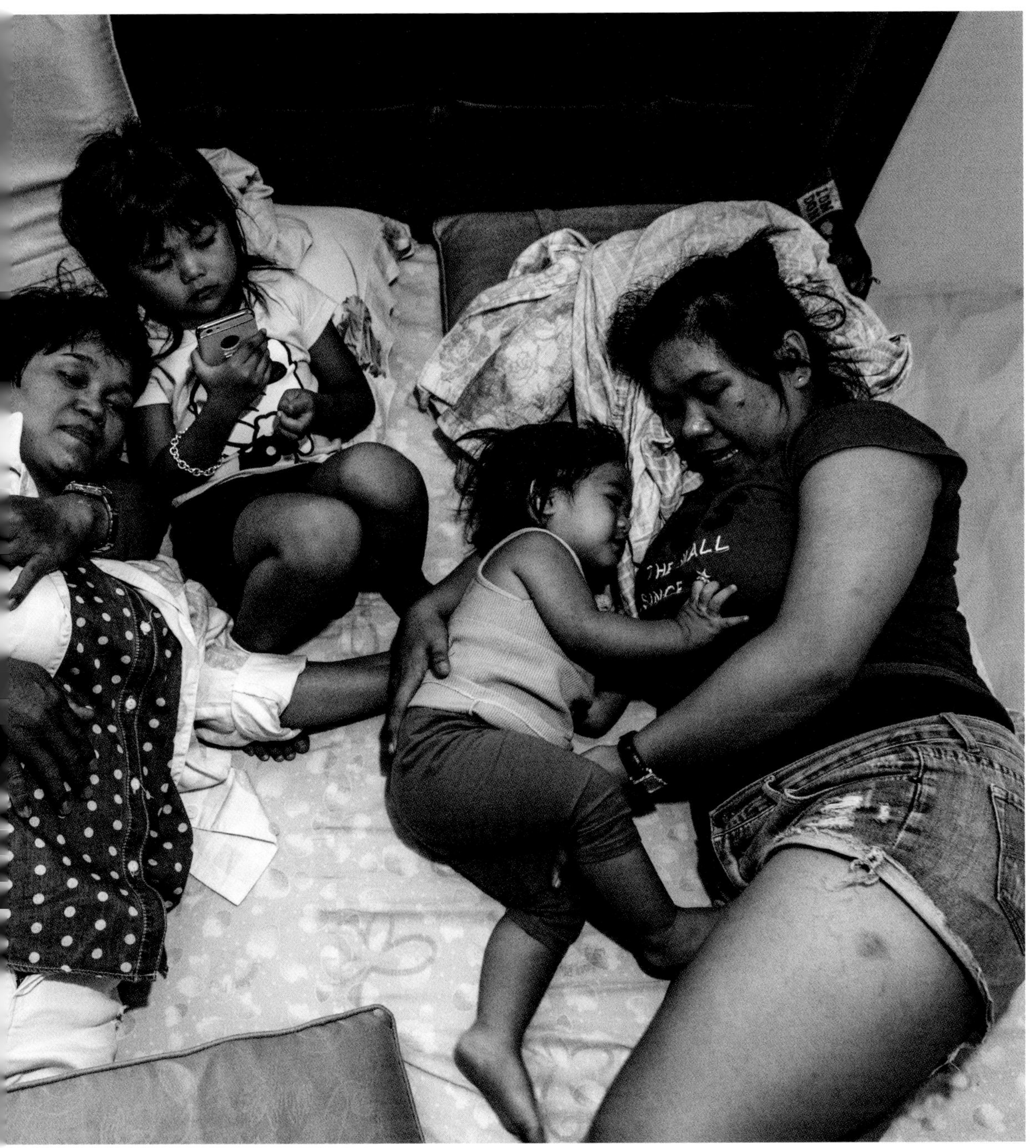

Golden

American

I'm just grateful for niggas in the immediate

Roslindale, Massachusetts, USA; 2022

I'm just grateful for niggas in the immediate is a collaborative portrait of my twin brother, Morgan (he/they), and me (they/them) sitting together in my studio in Roslindale, MA, around New Year's. Like many of the portraits featuring Twin and me in my self-portraiture series On Learning How to Live, which documents Black trans life at the intersection of surviving and living in the United States, this photo presents a still moment amid the chaos of living. Just a few days after Twin recovered from COVID, after learning most of our immediate family members had caught COVID too and our Pop Pop wasn't doing too well. Just a few days after a long drive home, back from our hometown (Hampton, VA), where I stopped to see my older brother in Dover, DE, and picked up Twin in New York City. After hours of playing in closets, deciding what colors match our mood, which make-up marvels our mugs, which poses perfect our frame, we arrive here – hand in hand, legs in limbs again, like once in the womb. Just grateful to have someone to witness the weather with, to say *We are not alone.*

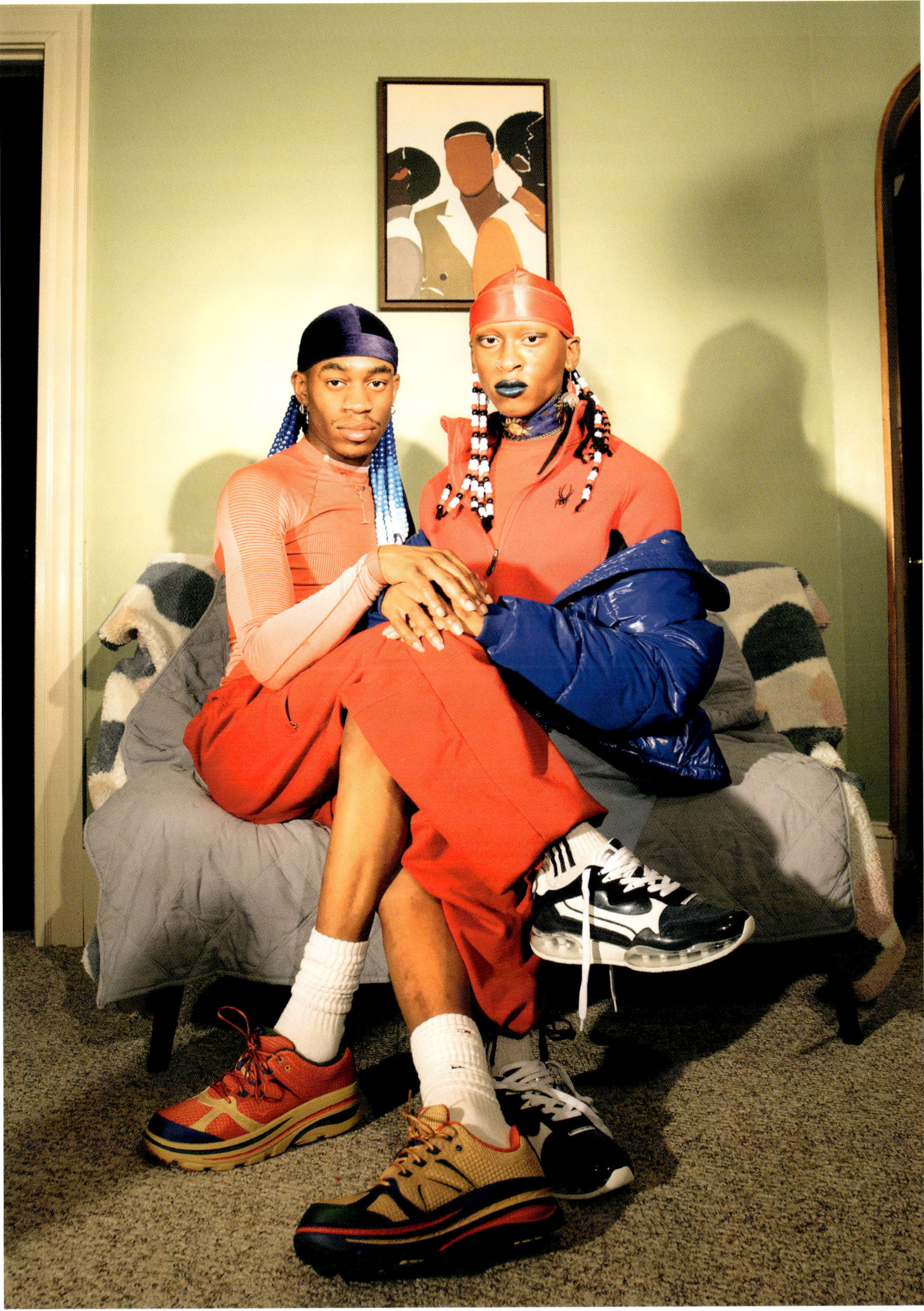

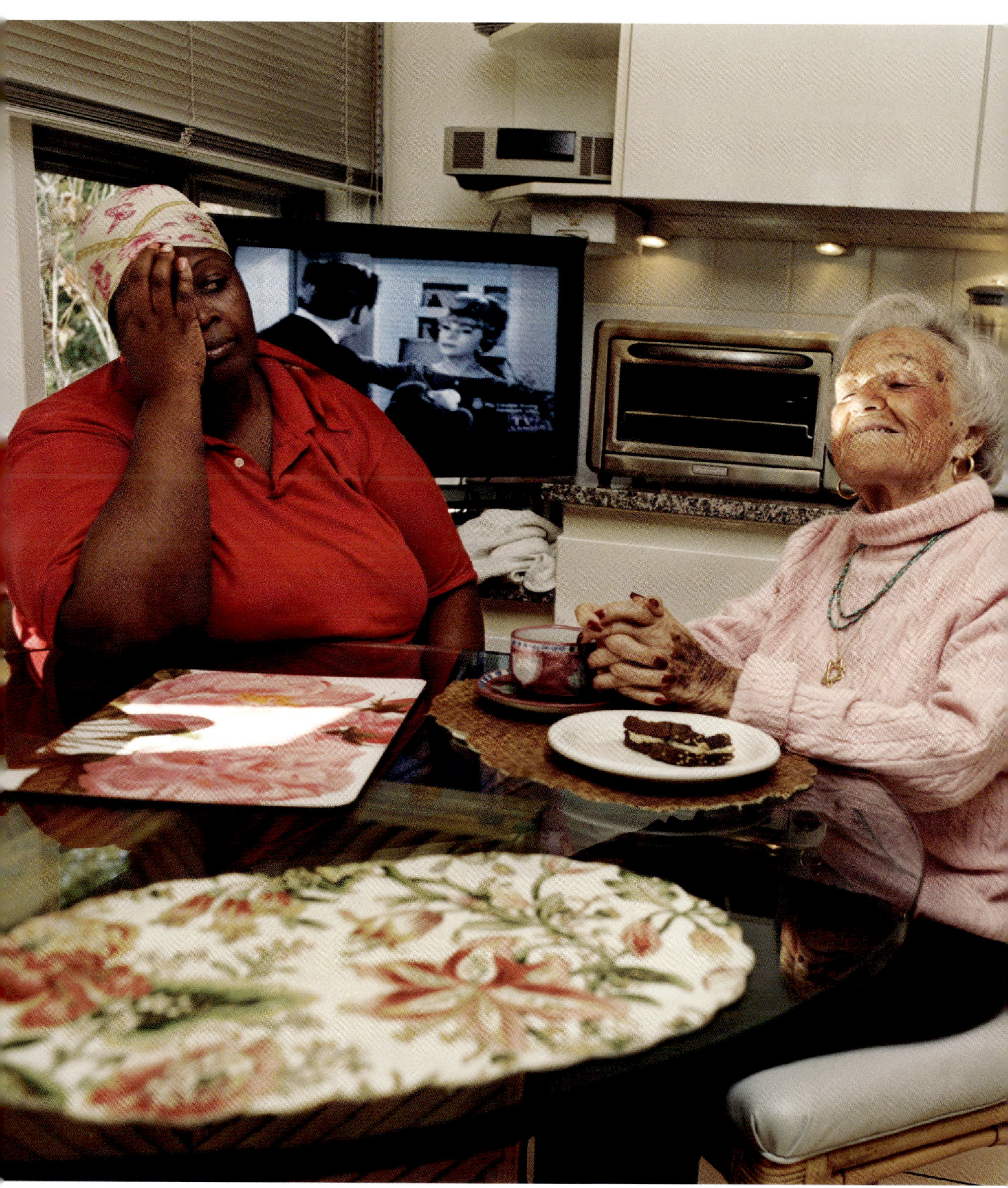

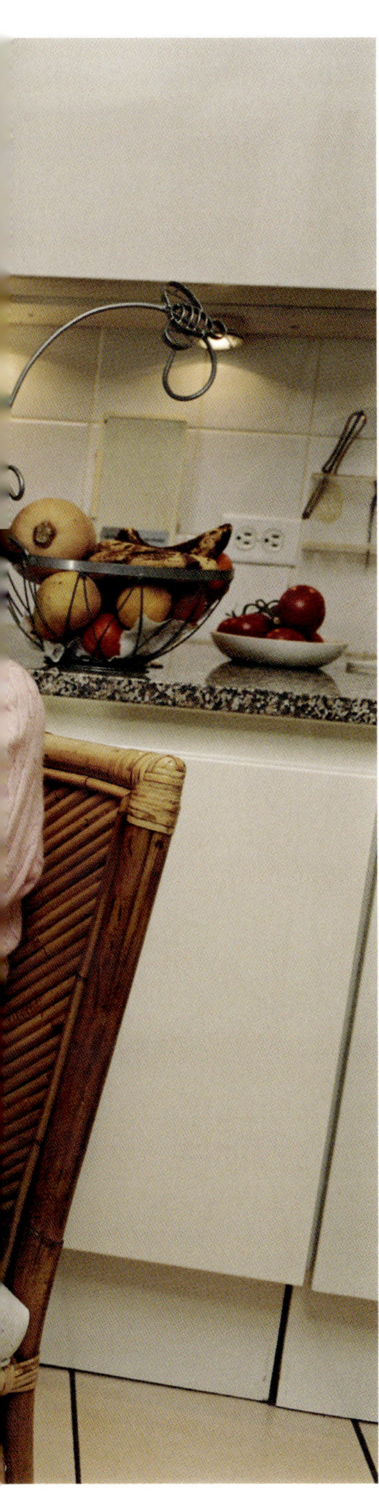

Gillian Laub

American

Grandma's Kitchen

Mamaroneck, New York, USA; 2010

Grandma's Kitchen is an image from Family Matters, a more than two-decade-long project confronting issues of privilege, class and other fissures in the American dream. In 2016, when my parents and I found ourselves on opposing sides of the most contentious issues in recent US history, what I was experiencing with my family felt like a microcosm of a larger fractured America. In this image, my grandmother is pictured with her full-time caregiver, Dorothy, in her kitchen; they would argue every day until she finished her lunch. As I watched them over the years, I became more conflicted about the role that caregivers played in our collective family life. On the one hand, I felt deeply grateful to them personally, for quite literally enabling us to be healthy and happy and connected to each other. On the other, I could not avoid the social and political context that set up these dynamics – insidious issues of race and class that created worlds of pain and unfairness. I felt increasingly guilty about it all, especially as I started wondering if I would repeat this very dynamic if I was going to have children of my own.

Ana Maria Arévalo Gosen

Venezuelan

Días Eternos

Caracas, Venezuela; March 2018

This image is part of my long-term project *Días Eternos* (Eternal Days) about the living conditions faced by women in preventive detention centres and prisons in Latin America. I took this image in 2018, inside the cell of a detention centre in La Yaguara, Venezuela. These institutions in Venezuela reflect the hell these women live through. As a result of procedural delays, these claustrophobic and dark centres frequently become overcrowded. The lack of space does not allow for separation of the women by crime or age. Twenty-two women share the space in this photograph, all of them in perpetual inactivity. They do not have permission to go outside of the cell. They spend their time writing letters or making drawings for their children, reading the Bible, sharing cigarettes or ironing their hair. To survive, they depend on members of their families, as they are the ones who must provide their own food and water. They work together so that no one dies of hunger. They share everything: mattresses, clothes, the intimacy of their love stories, the tears shed for their children.

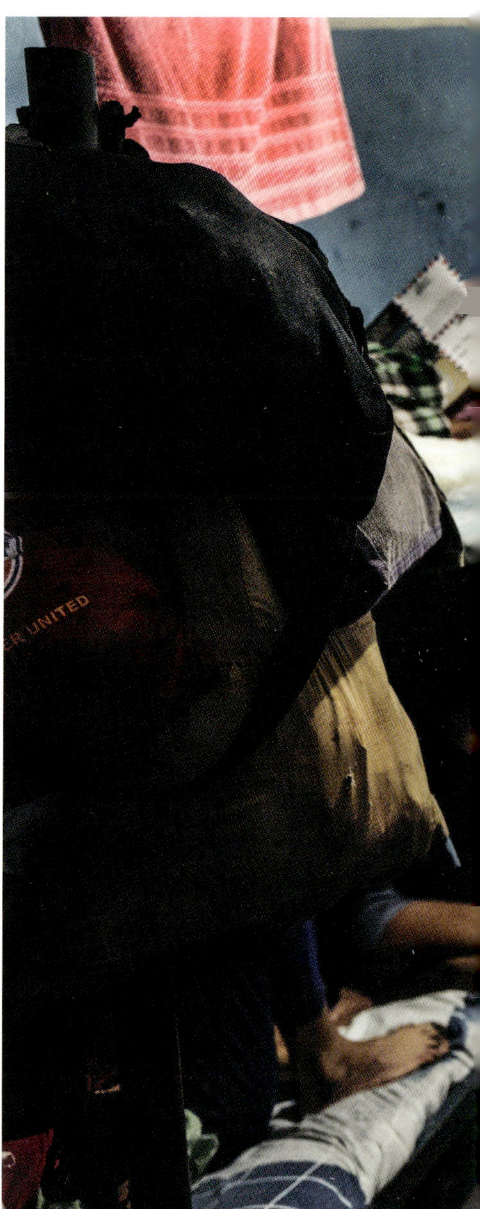

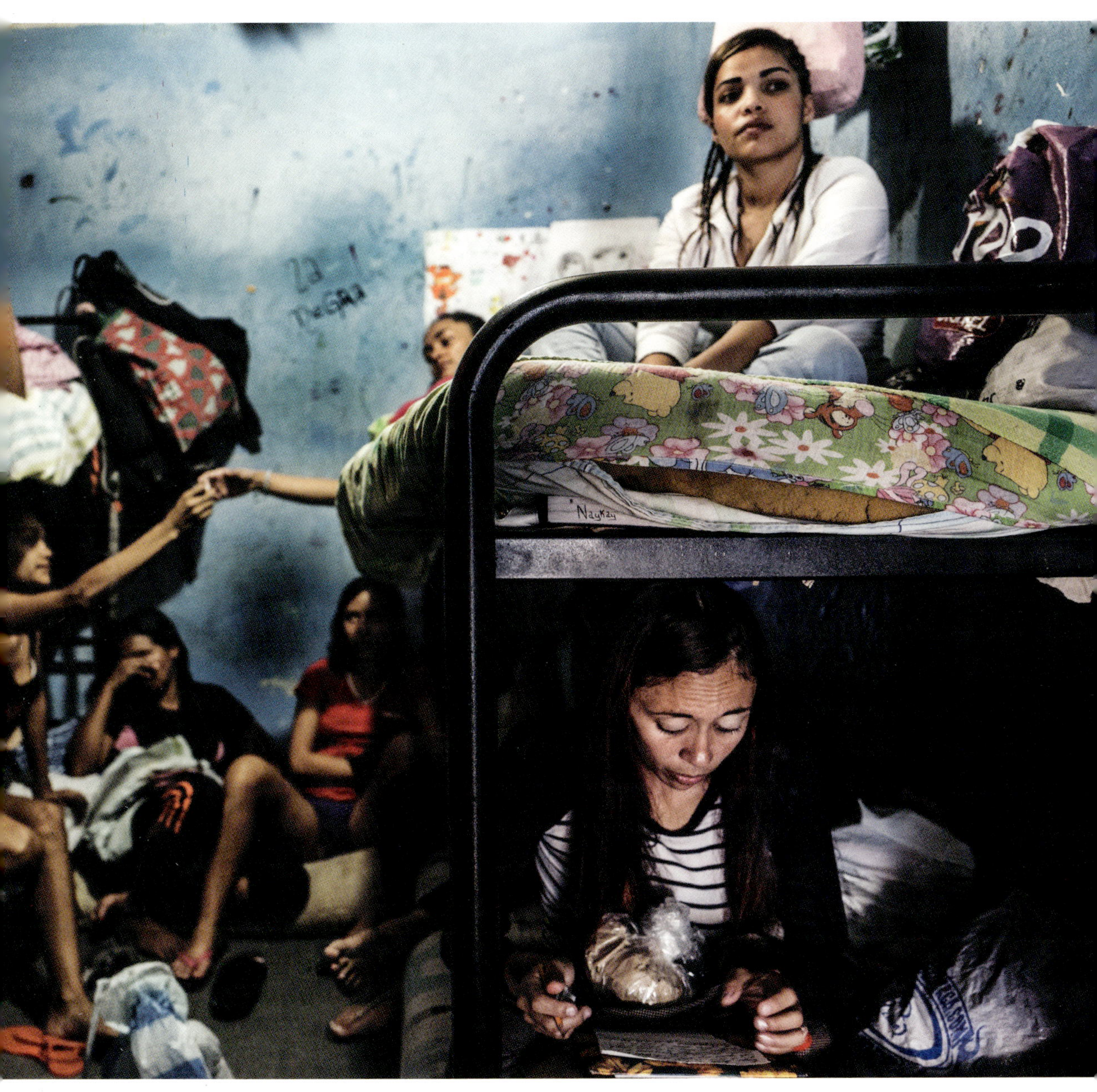

Sara Aliaga Ticona

Bolivian

Cholita tenías que ser

La Paz, Bolivia; 2019

This photograph is part of my series *Cholita tenías que ser* (You had to be cholita), where I explore the essence of the chola Andean woman who has turned her clothing into a symbol of resistance. The braids, the hat, the blanket and the skirt seem to be pieces that not only reveal an identity, but also form a unit of strength. In making this photograph I remember that I was comforted by the confidence and security with which a cholita looks at herself in the mirror. I could understand the insecurities created when we look in a mirror and do not find what society expects. But while these women are not alien to these types of social pressures, they fight to be themselves anyway, and find in their clothes resilient support from which they reinforce their identity. This project was born from a turning point in my life, where I questioned my own identity as an Andean woman, which led me on a search to feel part of something and see myself reflected in someone. I turned to my family album where I met my great-grandmother, Sara, who was chola. I have some memories of her and others I have met throughout my life, which is why I identify with them, although I do not dress like them. There is something in their way of being, in their strength, in their resistance, that identifies me.

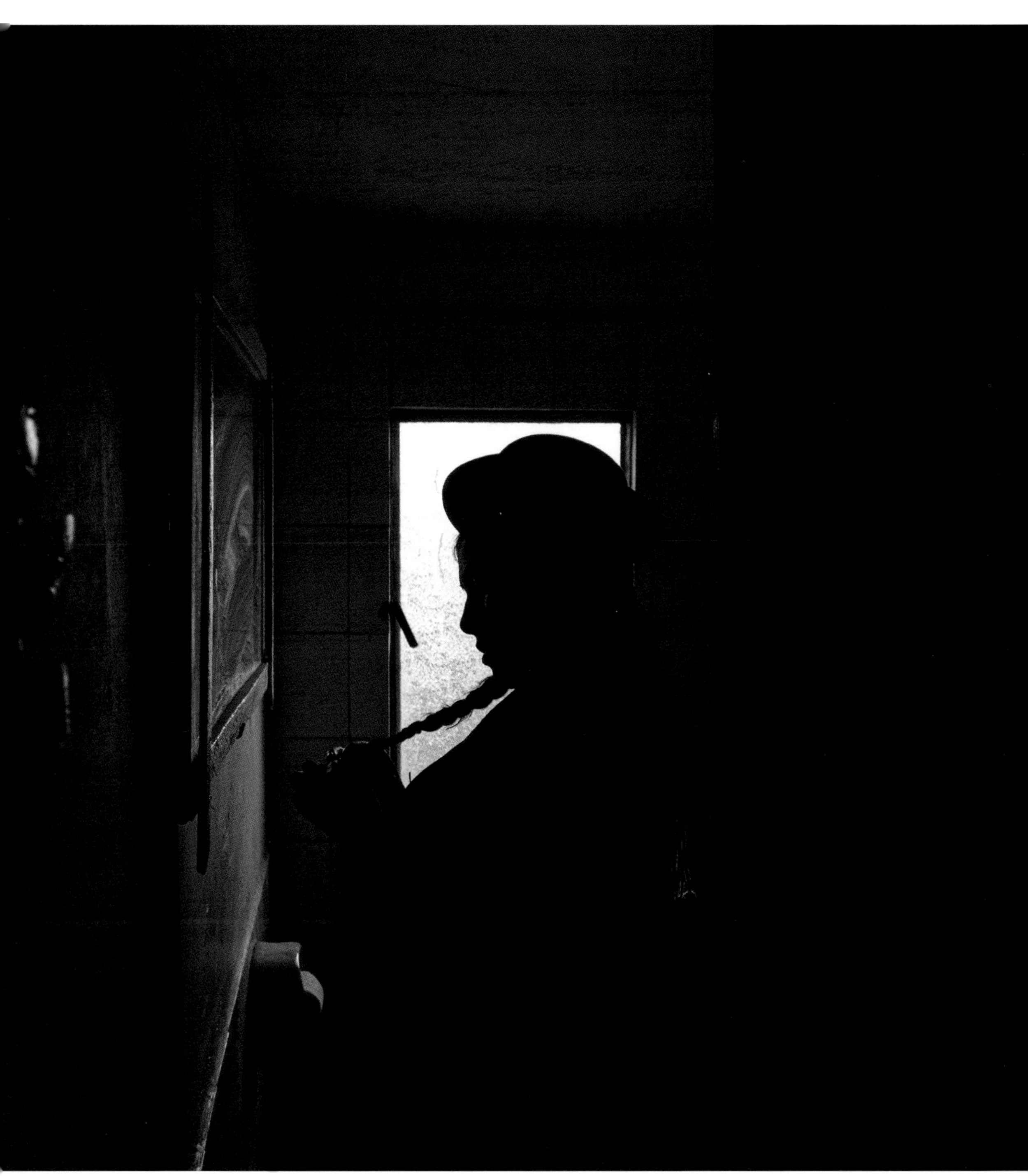

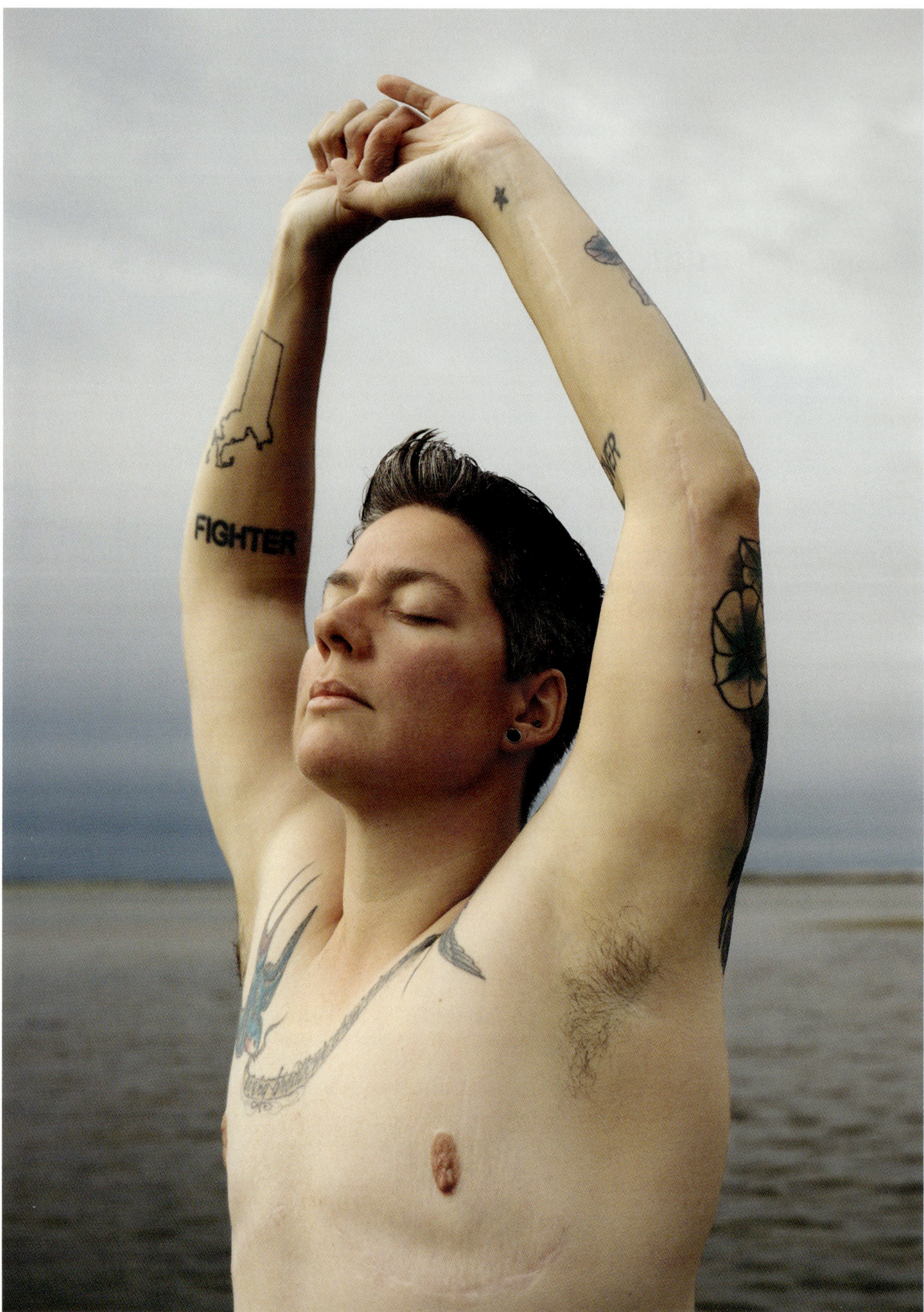
FIGHTER

◀

Jess T. Dugan

American

Self-portrait (reaching)

Provincetown, Massachusetts, USA; 2021

Self-portrait (reaching) is part of my long-term project Every Breath We Drew, an intimate and highly personal meditation on identity, desire and the search for meaningful connections with others. This series includes self-portraits, portraits of individuals and couples and still-life images. Self-portraiture has always been a significant part of my practice and, over the years, I have found that sharing my own story openly and honestly allows for others to share theirs with me. While this work is rooted in, and heavily informed by, queerness, it is not simply illustrative, depicting people from one particular group. Rather, it is expansive and complex, investigating themes of desire and personhood in a fluid, multi-faceted, deeply personal way. The identity of the subjects varies; my gaze as a photographer, however, is always informed by my own queerness and my experience of actively defining my identity, often in opposition to societal expectations. Every Breath We Drew also functions as a conceptual self-portrait, as my choice of subjects – and the moment we create together – is an essential element, reflective of my personal subjectivities and desires.

▶▶

Danielle Villasana

American

Abre Camino

San Pedro Sula, Honduras; 2019

For a decade, I have been photographing both the threats facing transgender women throughout Latin America and their resilience despite deeply rooted phobias. I have been dedicated long term to this issue because the situation for women in this region is dire: 80 per cent of trans homicides occur here and most trans women do not live past 35 years old. While they are heavily marginalized and discriminated against across Latin America, in Central America they are further threatened by the region's endemic violence from gangs, clients, police and even family members. In the most recent chapter of this work, *Abre Camino* (*Open Road*), I have documented not only the push factors compelling trans women to flee Central America, but also their journeys north towards the United States and the challenges they face on reaching the country they perceive as a safe haven. By following women long term, such as Alexa Smith, who is pictured here in the centre with friends in San Pedro Sula, Honduras, I strive to paint a more truthful, humanistic portrait of this community that is often narrowly portrayed by the media. By showing the larger context of these women's lives, I hope to educate people on how transphobia and discrimination have far-reaching, harmful consequences.

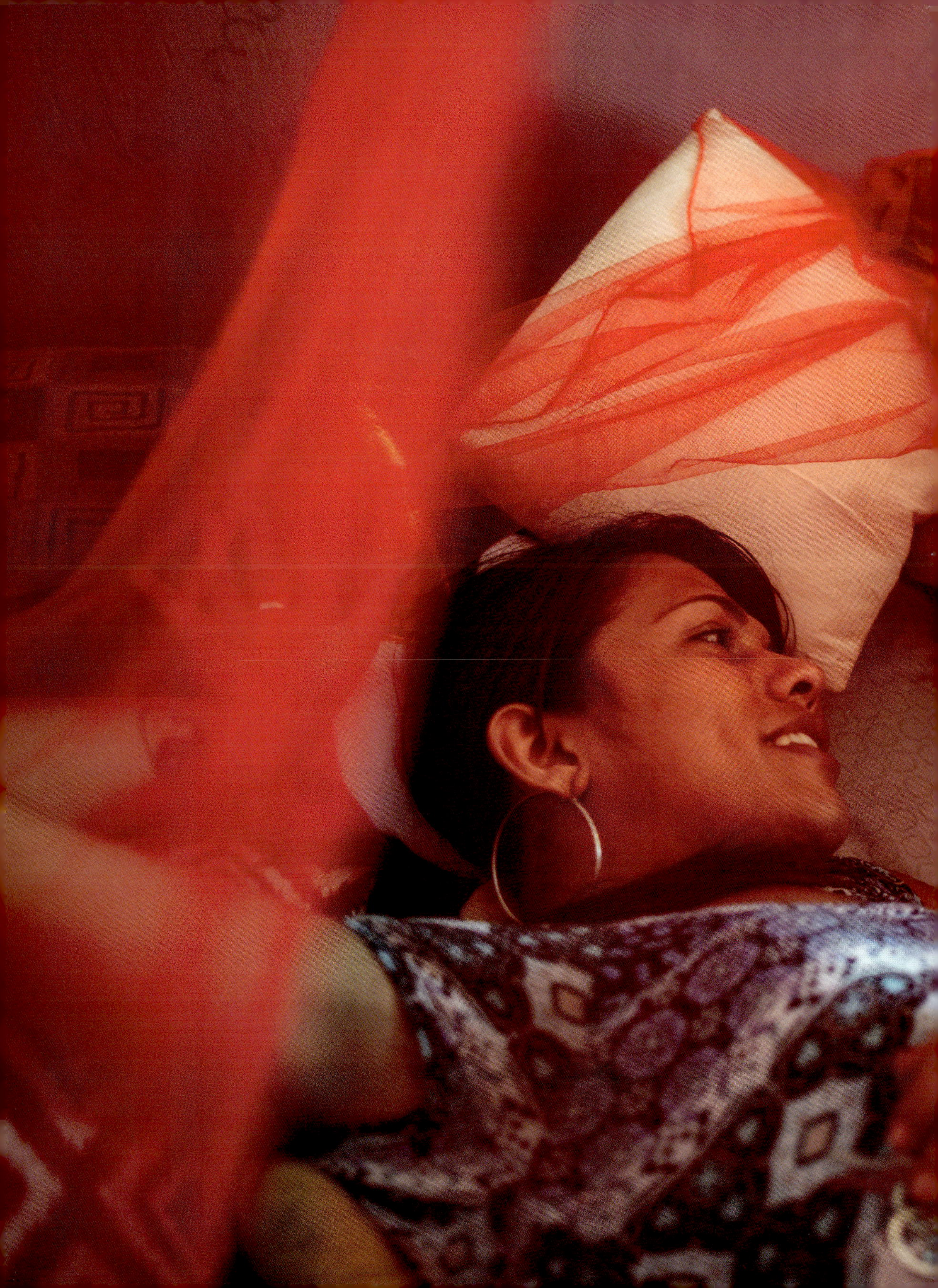

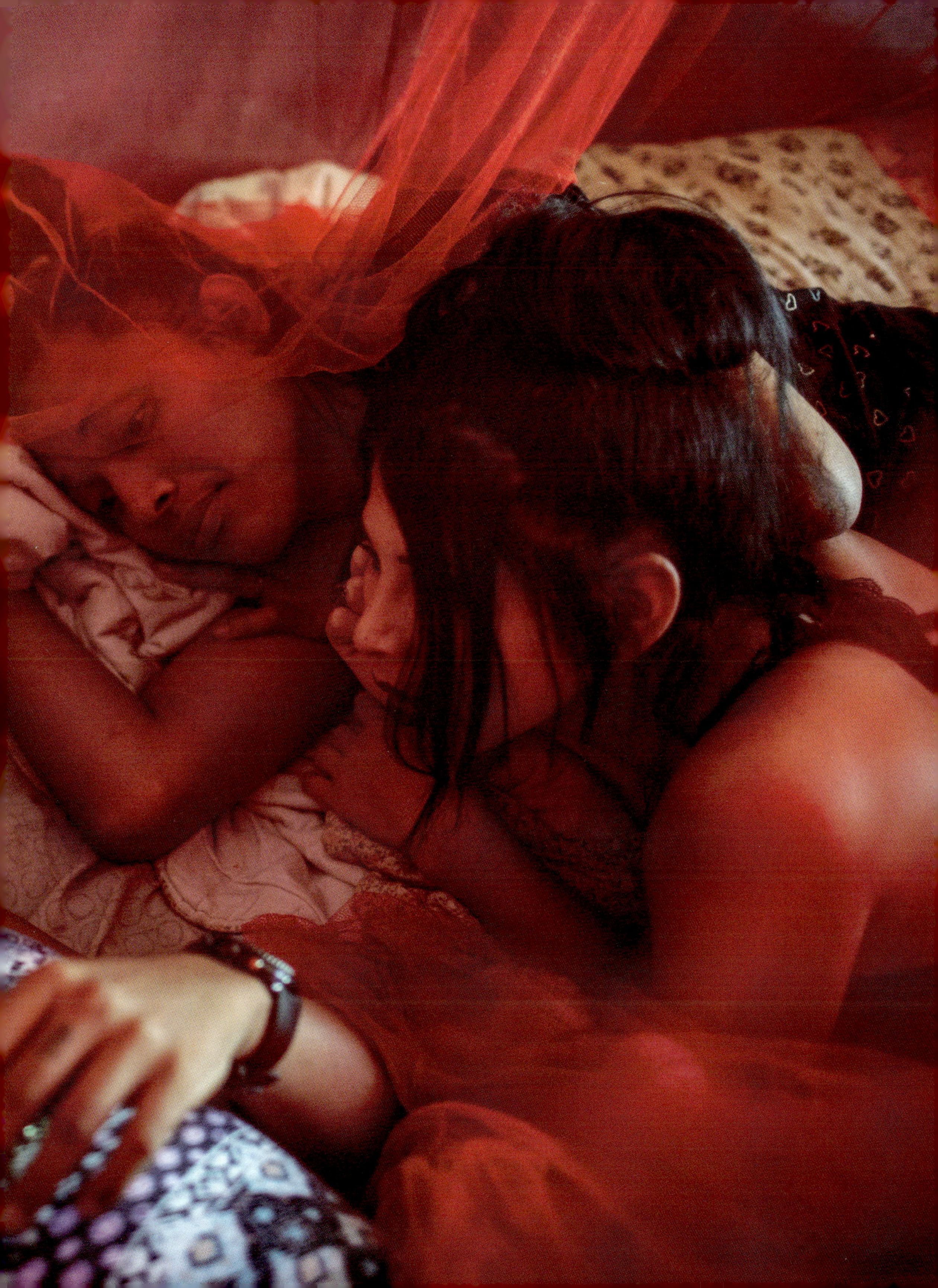

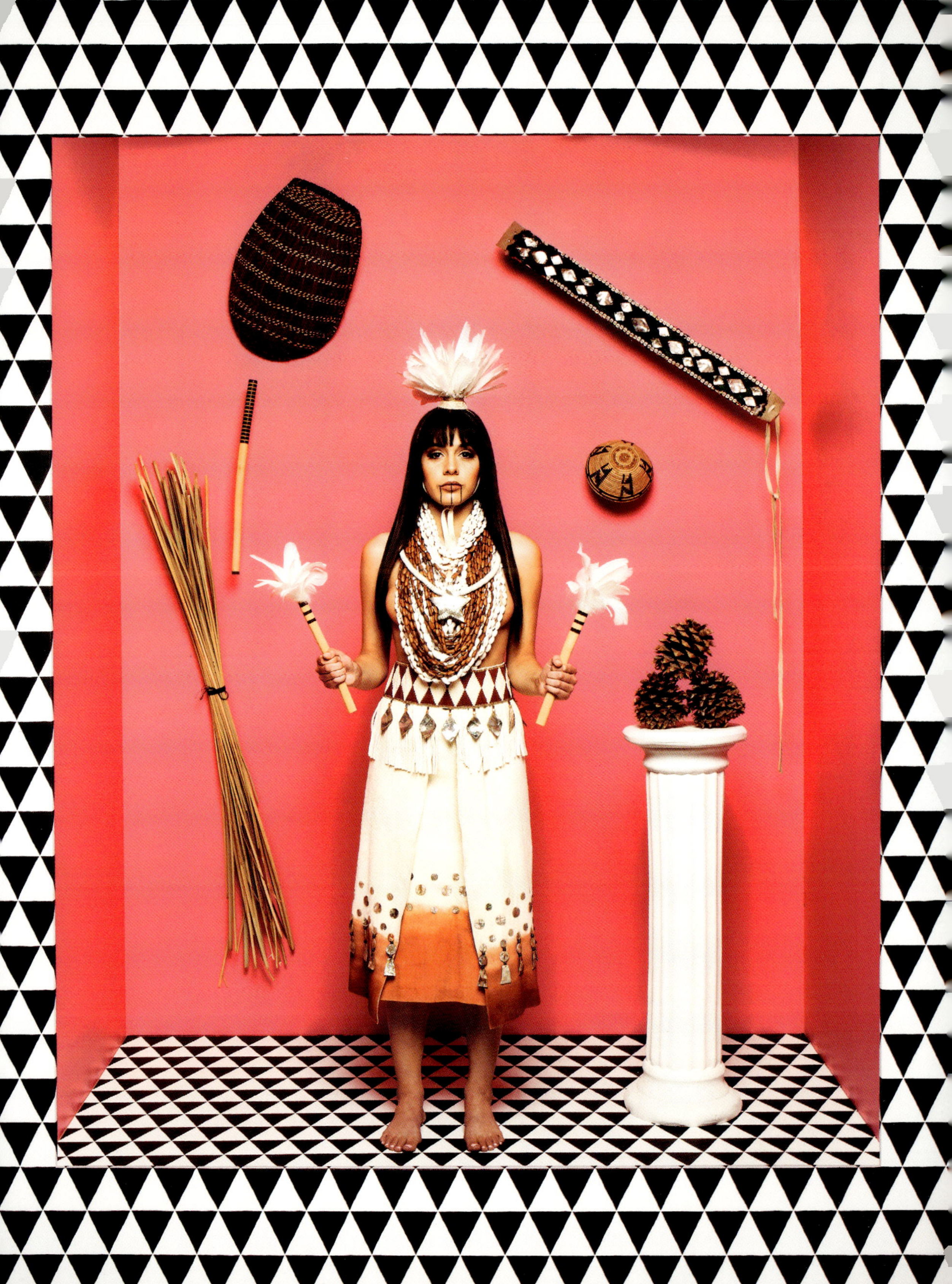

◀

Cara Romero

American Chemehuevi

Naomi

Santa Fe, New Mexico, USA; 2018

Naomi is part of my series First American Girls, an intergenerational and collaborative effort to show Native American women from multiple tribes in ways that highlight their modernity and diversity. The series aims to elevate accurate depictions of Native American women in regalia, highlighting cultural transmission and the details of high craft traditional arts of each region. The project combats the stereotypical and monolithic depictions of Native women and girls that we so often see in dolls, Halloween costumes and other racist, demoralizing products that dehumanize young Native women and lead to epidemics like the crisis of Missing and Murdered Indigenous Women. I want my daughter to have a different experience with 'seeing' herself and her likeness in a good way. Together we built a life-sized doll box and created the graphic design with vernacular from Naomi's tribe (Northern Chumash). By visually elevating the regalia, the viewer has the ability to see the incredible artistry and detail her mother, Leah Mata Fragua, put into these objects. She has a winnowing basket, clapper sticks, basket hat, mallard pelt and clamshell dance belt, and pinecones on the pedestal that represent the centre of their cultural universe. In this image, we see intergenerational love, resistance and resilience in this First American Girl.

▶▶

Laurence Philomène

Canadian

Paint me like one of your pre-raphaelite boy-girls

Montreal, Canada; February 2019

This image was shot as part of Puberty – a long-form, self-portrait project that looks at the intimate and vital process of self-care and becoming oneself as a nonbinary person. Since January 2019, I have been documenting the changes testosterone generates in my body and moods through daily photographs. The resulting images are simultaneously staged and candid, created by setting up a tripod in my home and surroundings as I go about my routines. Set in highly saturated domestic spaces, these photographs look at intimate details of transition that are seldom represented and often kept private. Looking at HRT as a process without a fixed end goal, Puberty challenges viewers to consider identity beyond binaries. Having dedicated my practice to documenting nonbinary lives since I began photographing as a teenager, Puberty allows me to dig deeper into what it means to have autonomy over our stories as marginalized individuals. I work with the hope of providing representation for, and solidarity with, future generations of queer and trans individuals as they navigate both personal joys, and institutional hardship and erasure. This is a love letter to my community.

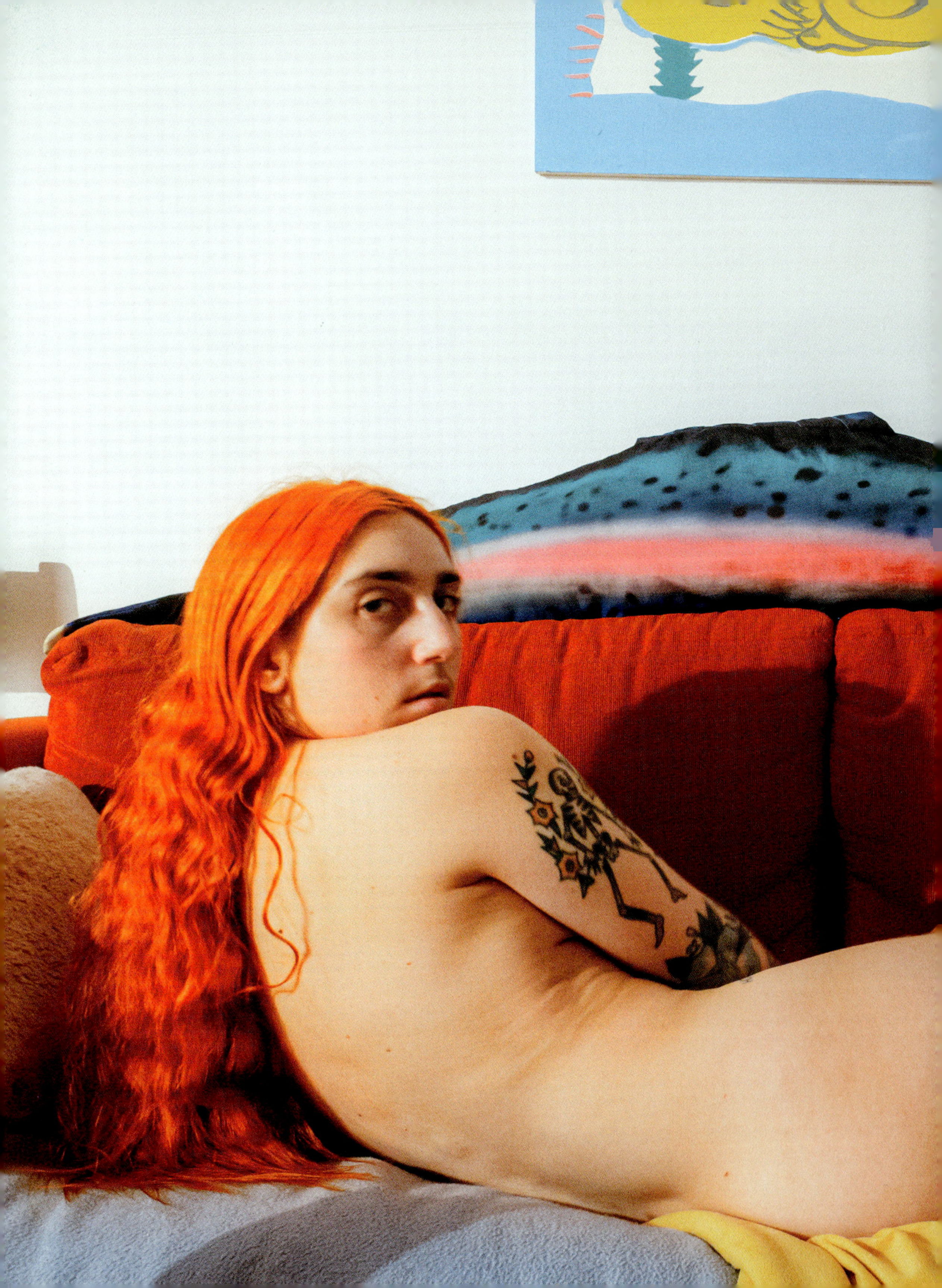

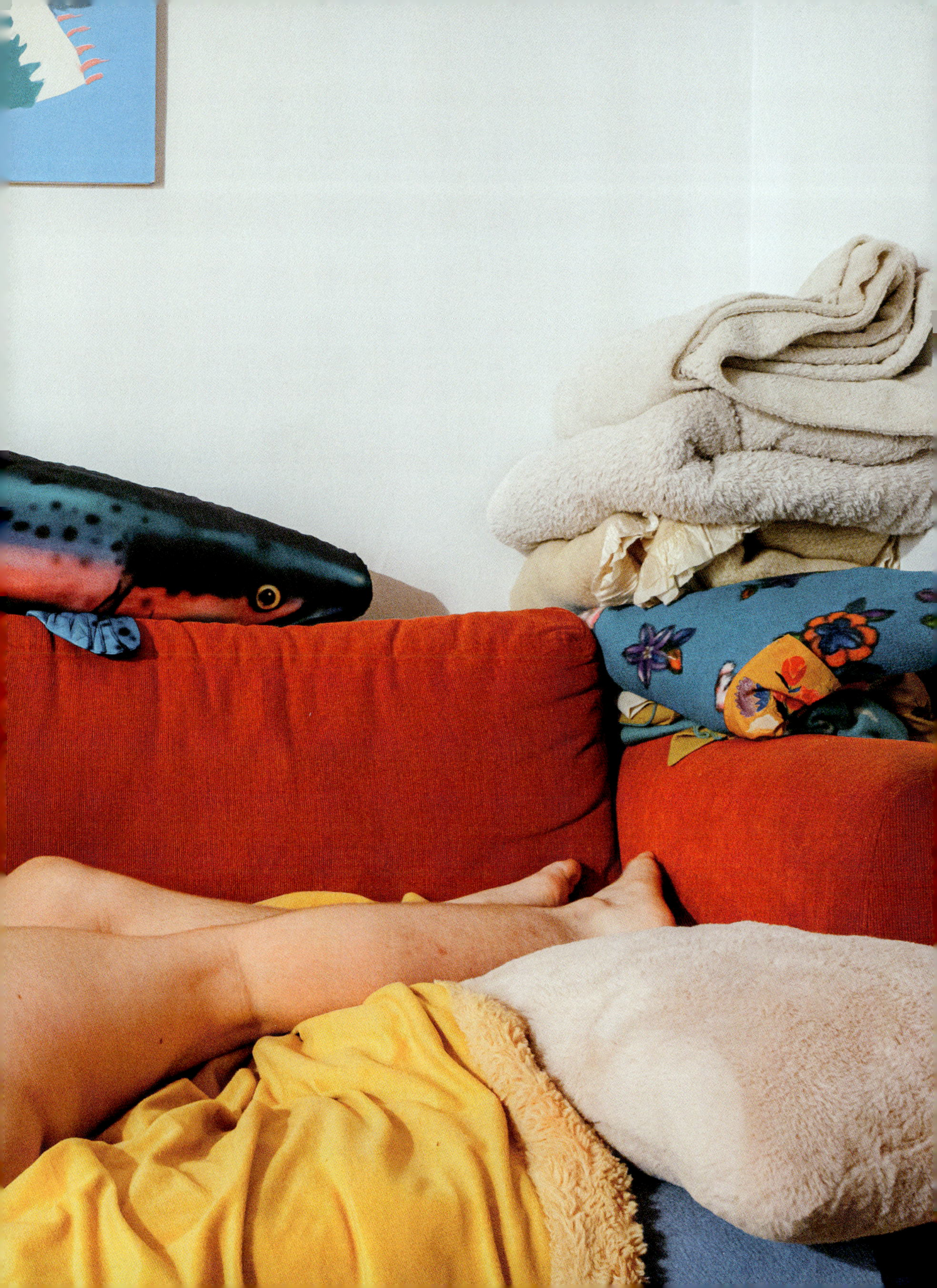

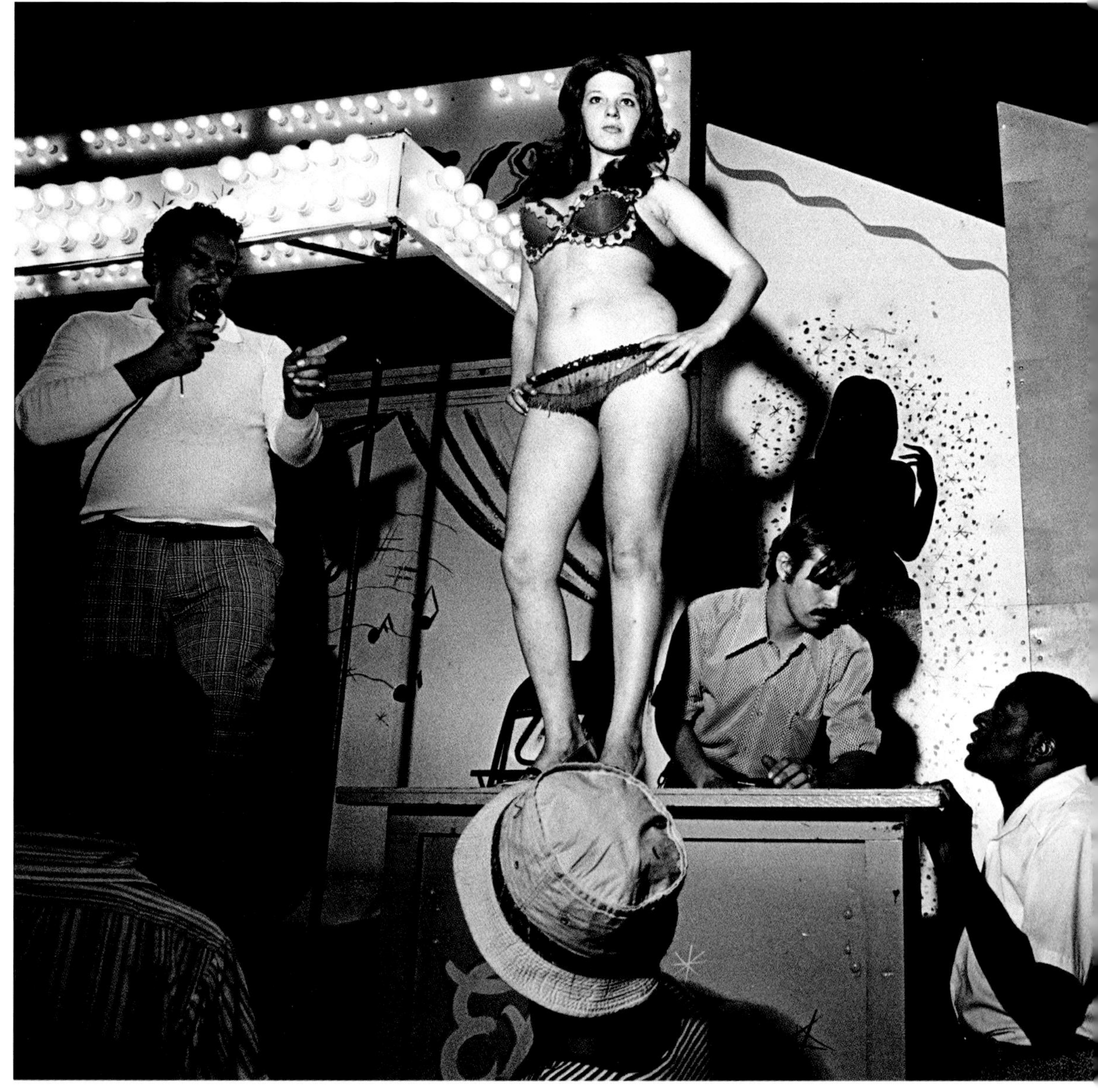

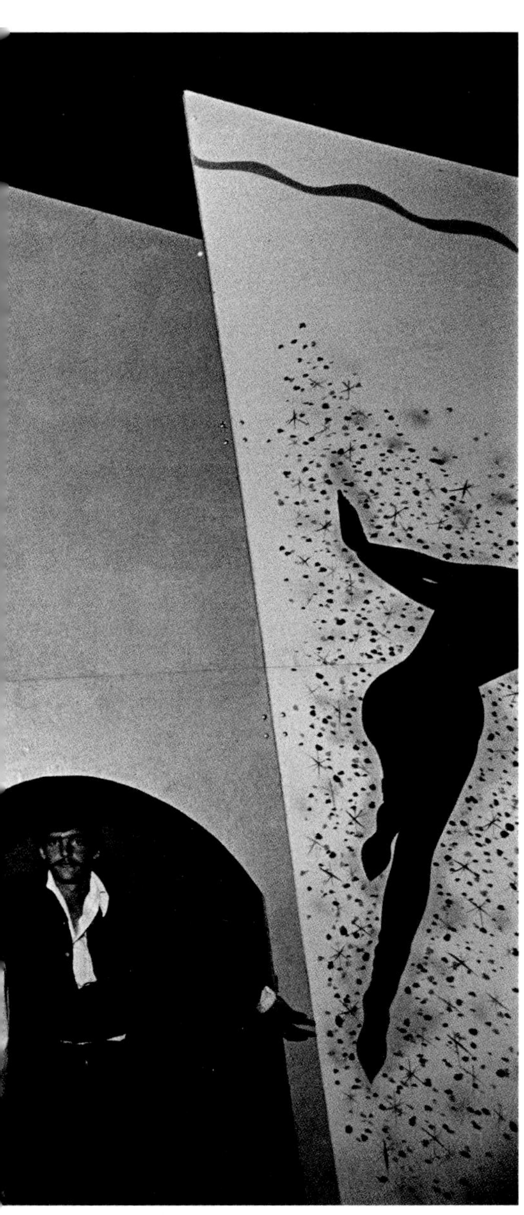

Susan Meiselas

American

Lena on the Bally

Essex Junction, Vermont, USA; 1973

Between the games and rides at the state fair in Essex Junction, Vermont in 1973, I saw a number of men surrounding a woman on a stage, which seemed more like an auction block. Soon after, I met her. Lena, the woman who was looking out past the audience, had a sense of power expressed in her body and her gaze. The man with a microphone talked about her, the man below sold tickets, the manager leaned in and another man controlled the doorway. Together they tried to make sure that women like myself did not enter the tent, which was 'For men and men only, no ladies, no babies'. Being excluded propelled me forward. I wanted to know how she perceived herself being seen. Over the next three summers, I followed the girl shows each weekend, travelling from town to town, bringing back the pictures I was making of them. I was both looking and listening. From the beginning, I wanted their perceptions in words to wrap around my photographs, which is how my project on Carnival Strippers launched and evolved.

Annie Flanagan

American

Untitled

Williston, North Dakota, USA; 2014

Maria's eye fracture is disguised by make-up as she prepares to board a train home. Less than a month prior, she moved hundreds of miles to Williston, North Dakota, seeking work during the oil boom. We met in 2014, while I was working on a project about people experiencing intimate partner violence and sexual assault, photographing with them as they sought safety and support throughout eastern Montana and western North Dakota. This project was hard and, frankly, I had no idea what I was getting myself into. I learned lessons during those years – the importance of being well rested and level headed, of safety, of clearly discussing consent. In the last months of that project, Charlotte and Shirley, two women I met through local shelters and had photographed with for years and months respectively, died. They were both found dead, in the cold, alone. And there is still uncertainty around each of their deaths. It took me years to realize that I stopped working on this project because of the pain and confusion surrounding this grief. I still think about them often, reflecting on how we prioritize who we pay attention to, systematically neglect and all those people who die fighting.

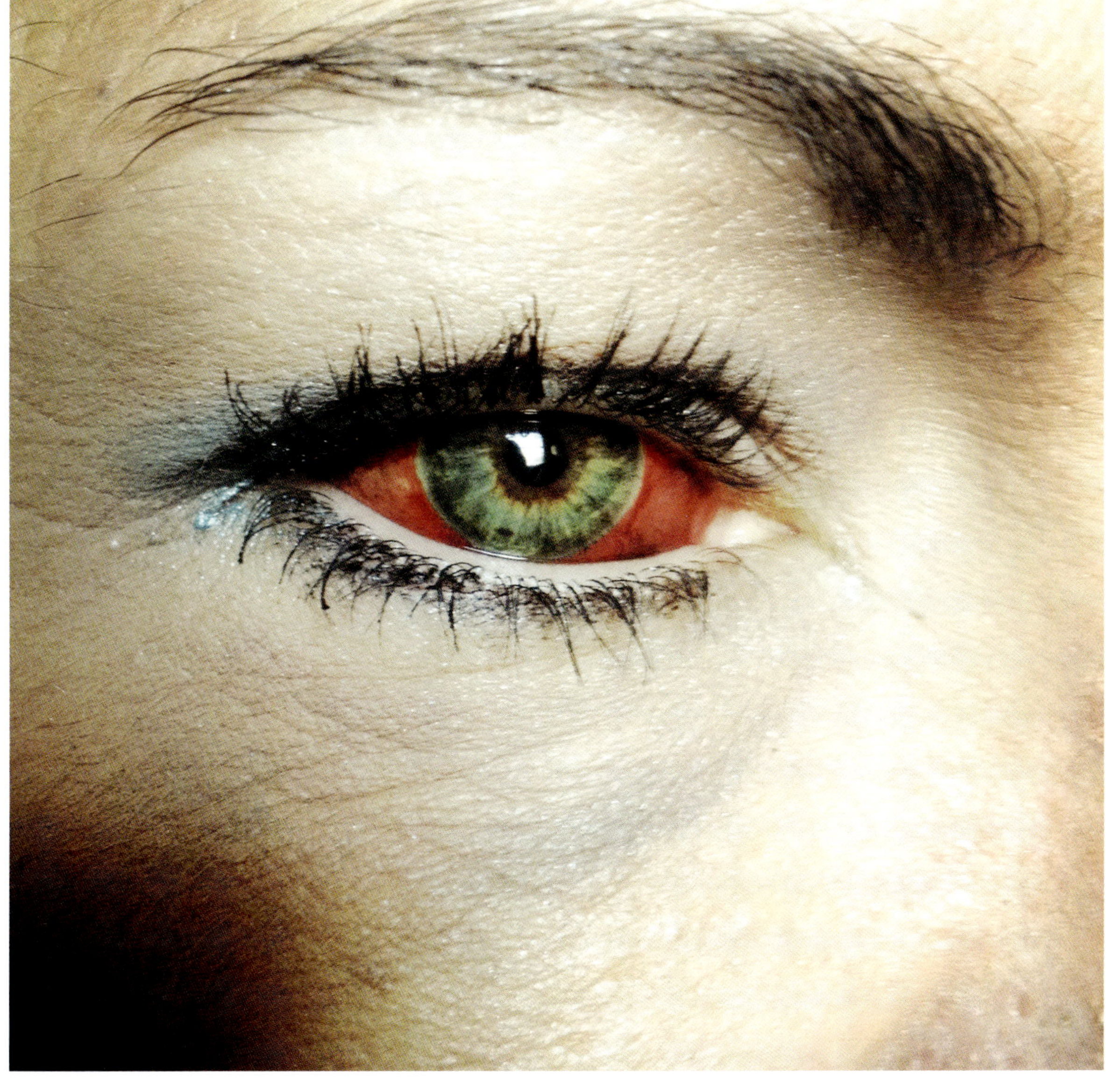

Lynn Johnson

American

A Face Between

Cleveland, Ohio, USA; 2017

Katie Stubblefield got the call almost three years to the day since she arrived at the Cleveland Clinic to repair the damage done when she attempted to take her own life with her brother's shotgun. The surgery took over 30 hours. Throughout, there were images of Katie and her altered face, on a board above the medical teams. Sixteen hours into a transplant operation, surgeons finished the intricate task of removing the face from an organ donor. Awed by the sight and by the gravity of their work, the team fell suddenly silent as staff members documented the face in between its two lives. The surgeons would spend 15 more hours attaching the face. Katie has had several faces, according to her mother, and now she has another – a completely new identity. Soon after, the medical team entrusted Katie to the ICU team, her family had their first look at her new identity. They seemed both stunned and grateful. There would be a long road of healing ahead. Photographing in surgery was familiar to me, but there is very little in this profession or, for that matter, in life, that prepares one to document such a suspended moment.

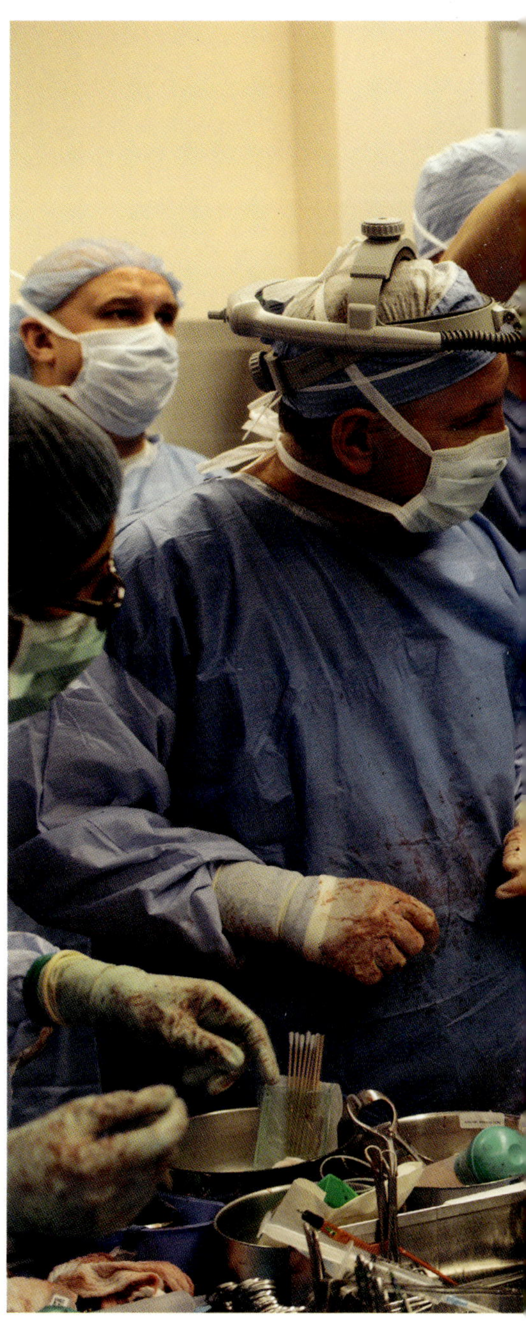

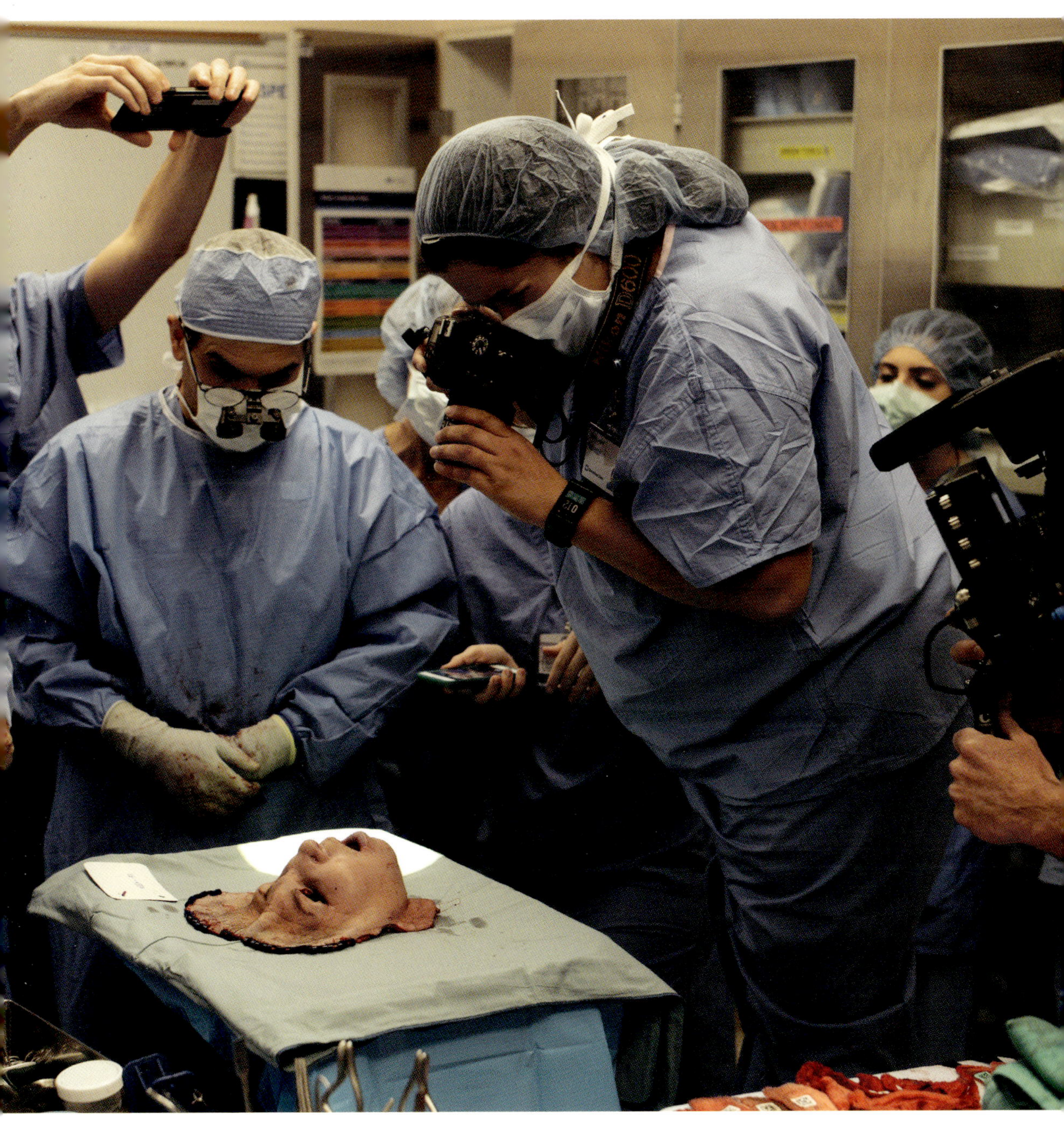

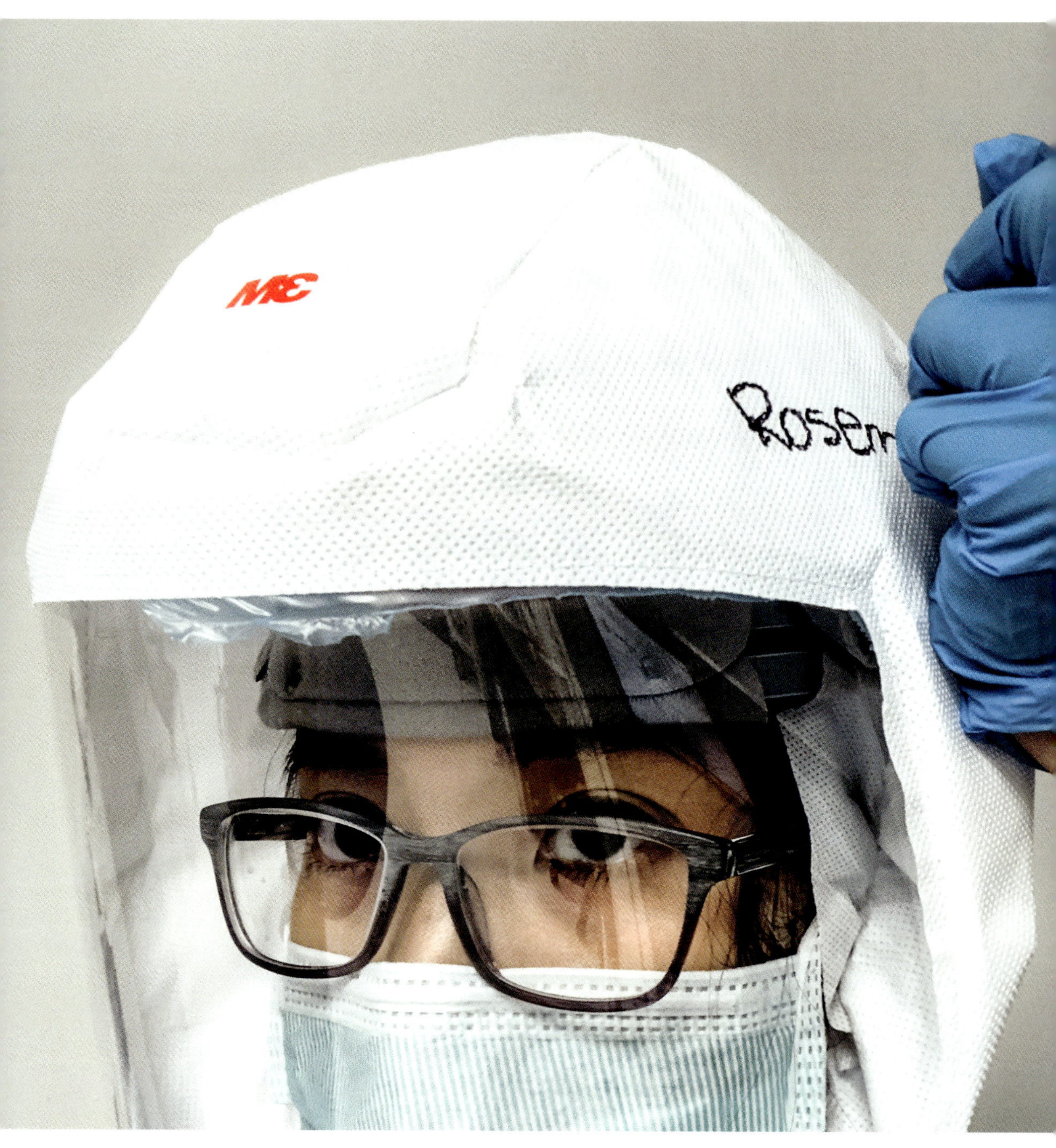
Rosen

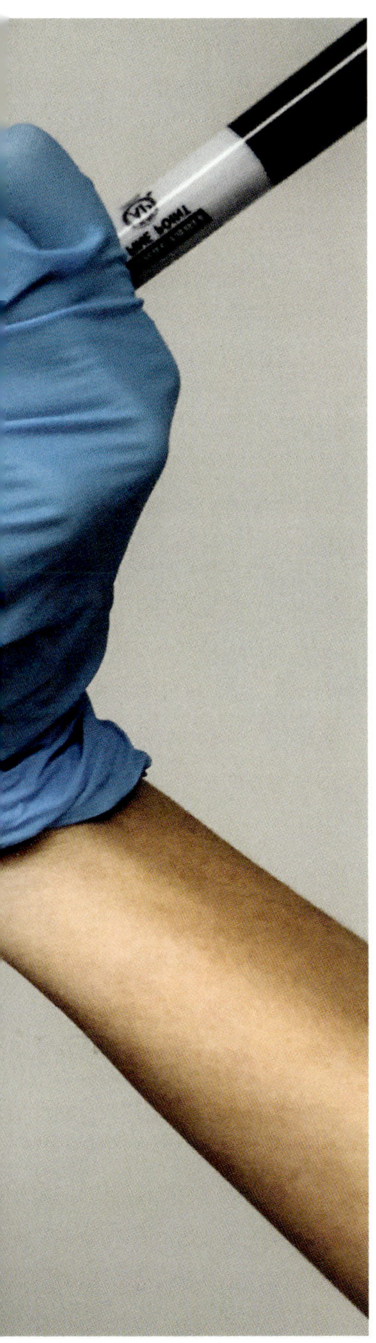

Rosem Morton

American Filipina

Donning and Doffing

Baltimore, Maryland, USA; 2020

About a week after the confirmation of a COVID-19 patient in Maryland, my unit rushed out a flurry of new policies and procedures. As a collective unease grew in the hospital, I realized I was uniquely positioned to chronicle behind the scenes as we prepared for the worst. Now, a year later, I can truly unpack, remember and feel. I am most drawn to this image of me writing on my PAPR (powered-air purifying respirator) hood. The hood hooks up to a battery-operated respirator that was shared among the hospital staff. This very same hood lived in my locker for the past year. With the limited availability of personal protective equipment, I had to wipe and reuse this once-disposable hood for the duration of the pandemic. The only difference is my name, rewritten many times over, has faded with all the wiping and reuse it has endured over the year. It reminds me of what we continue to endure as the pandemic wears on. On the day this photo was taken, 24 March 2020, there were 349 confirmed cases of COVID-19 in Maryland and four deaths.

Arin Yoon

Korean American

John's hearing aid

Fort Leavenworth, Kansas, USA; April 18, 2021

My long-term project To Be At War explores the social impacts of war on the military community. To understand my new role as a military spouse living on a remote military base, I began taking pictures to make sense of this life. I do not recall at what point I realized John had poor hearing. Service members are at a greater risk of hearing loss than their civilian counterparts due to repeated exposure to high-intensity noise such as small arms fire and explosions from training exercises and deployments. It is something I became accustomed to and now, my children too. John was shot in 2007 during the 'surge' in Iraq. It was not until recently that the children were old enough to notice the scar on his right shoulder. 'Will Daddy get shot by a sniper again?' my youngest asked. I began thinking about the trauma that we inherit through John's experiences with war. I wanted to make a photograph of John's hearing aid, which, for me, symbolized this secondary trauma. When our son, Teo, drew close to his ear, his face close enough for John to feel the warmth of his breath, I knew this was the photograph that I was trying to make.

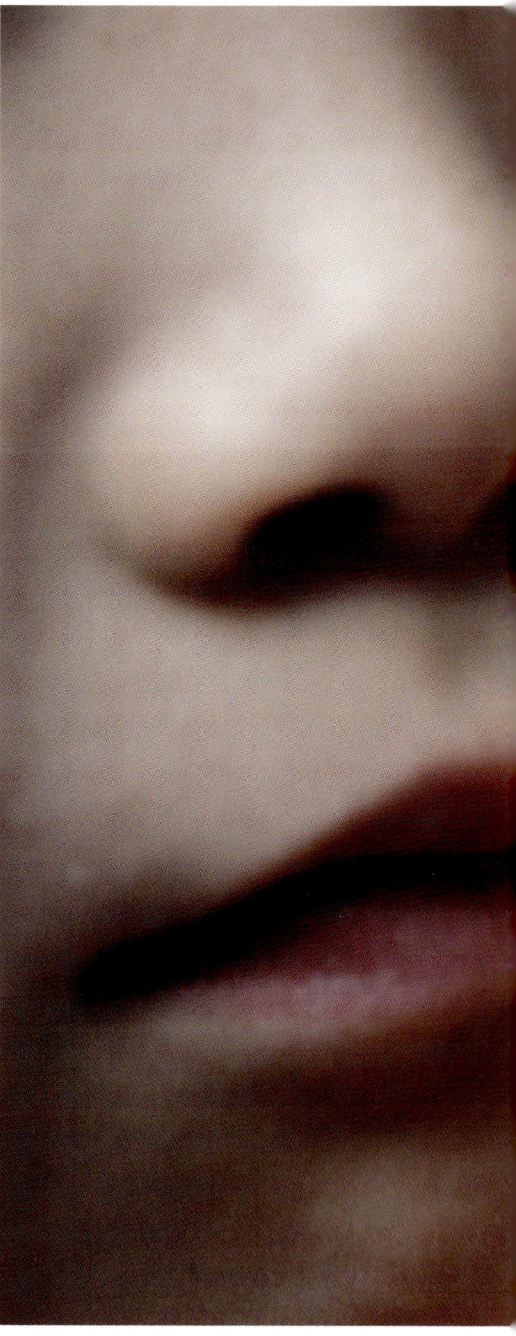

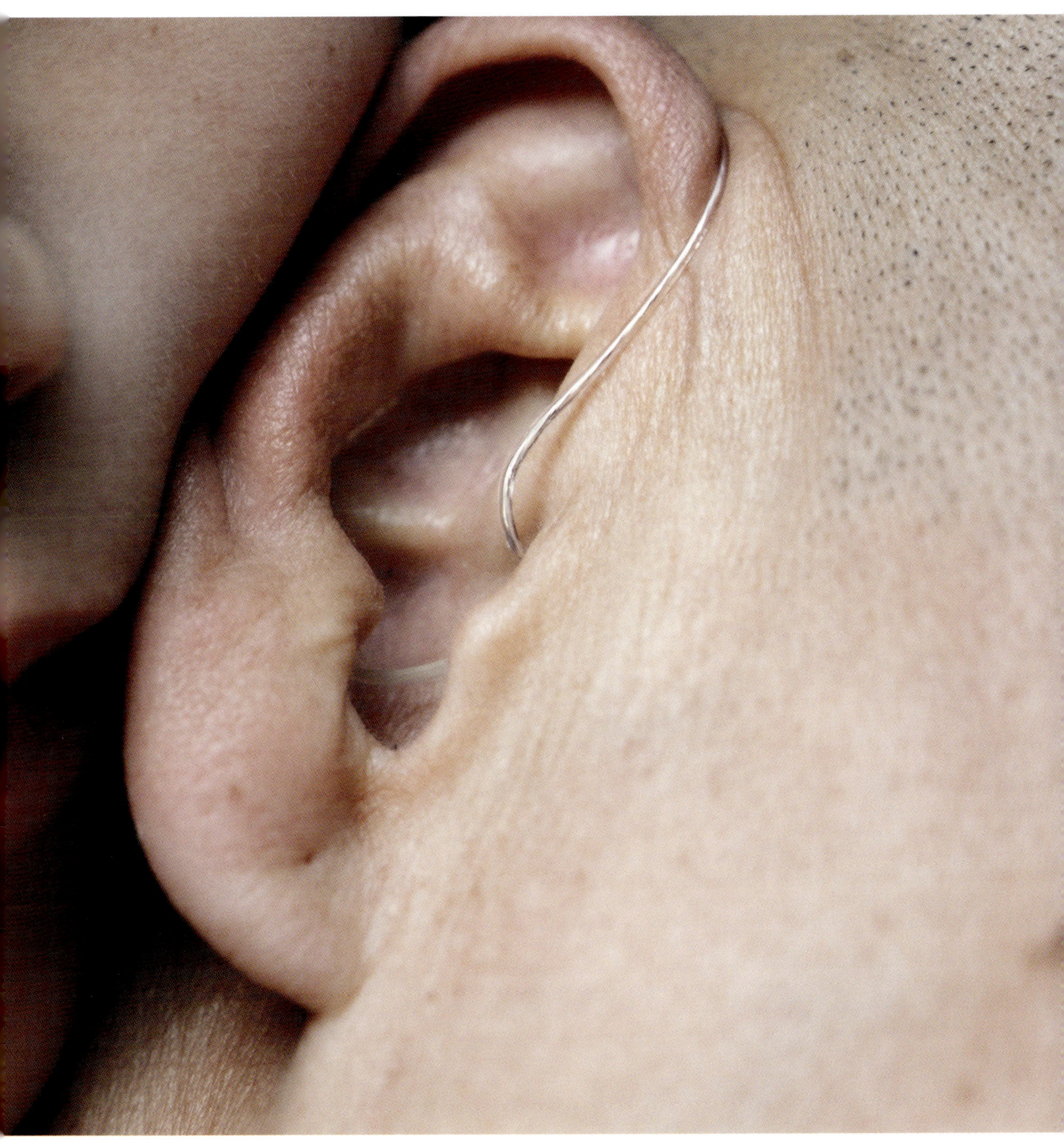

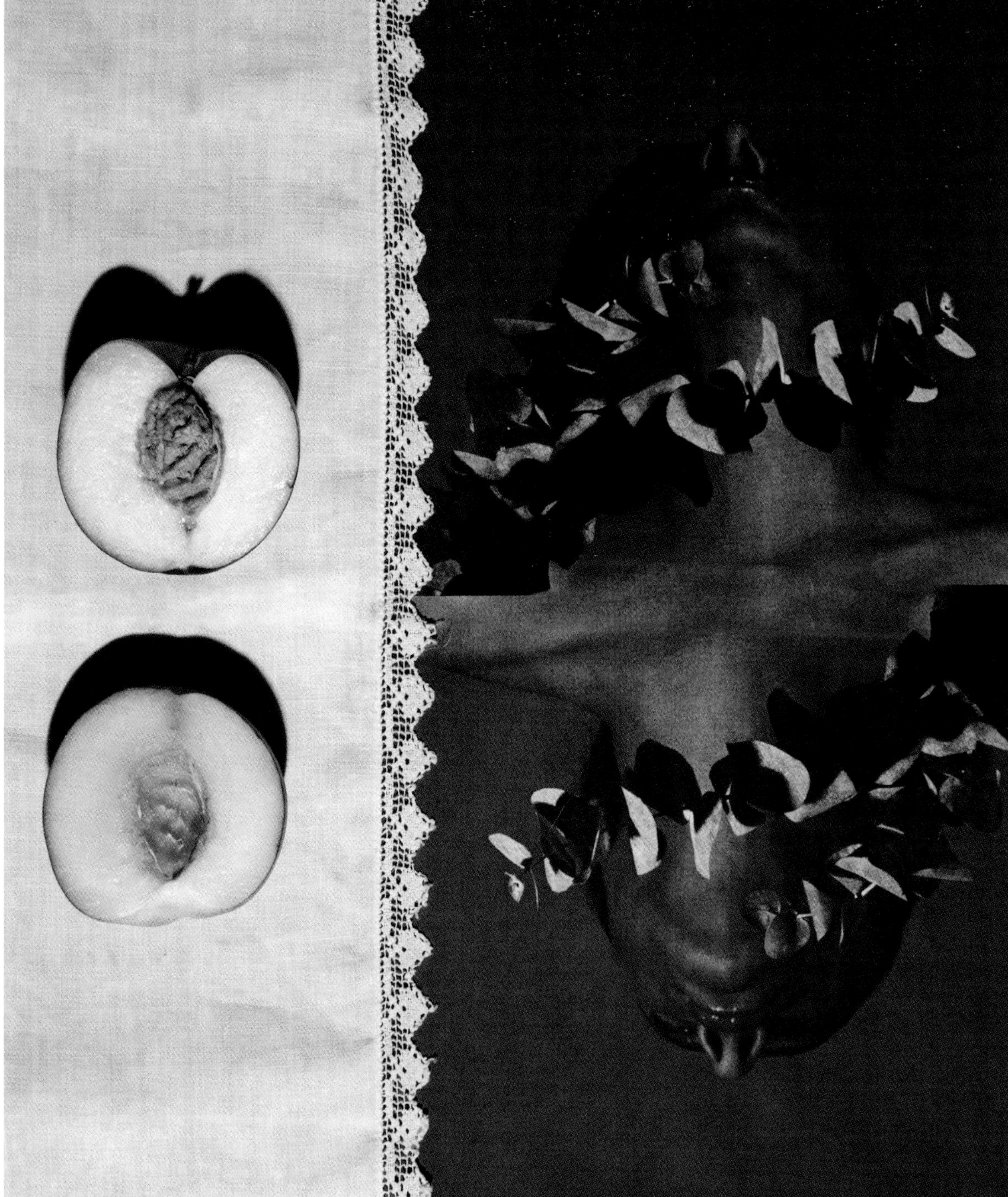

Maha Alasaker

Kuwaiti

Self Still Life

Woodstock, New York, USA; 2019

Identity can never be universally defined. Yet artists have long investigated identity beyond cultural or geographic classifications, which we often easily accept as stand-ins for identity in a larger sense. When we ask ourselves and others for a definition of self, we often turn to questions like 'Where are you from?', which result in more questions that bring us no closer to a true accounting of identity. A still-life is an artistic genre that depicts inanimate commonplace objects, both natural and man-made, my photo series Self Still Life explores the transient aspect of human life meant as a memento mori. Displayed as a cluster, the images act as a sequence of mirrors whose details represent a reflection on identity and the depiction of the self. My black-and-white self-portraits often manifest through collage. Objects, fruits, lace or powder are incorporated with overlapping human silhouettes or body parts, whether it be an eye, lips or a hand. The accumulation of inanimate objects along with the human figures works as a collection that reminds us of the surrounding world that makes us who we are. In this sense, photography and the digital represent both the medium and the object to analyse.

Rozette Rago

American

Sisters

Los Angeles, California, USA; 2019

Sisters is an image from my long-term series recreating stills from my favourite movies growing up. The project started as an experiment in what these movies would look like if they were re-cast with Asian folks and how that representation could have impacted me as a teenager. I grew up in the Philippines, in a small town outside of Manila, and I spent a lot of my free time at home downloading and watching movies that were not available in local cinemas or video stores. I imagined myself in worlds depicted by Sofia Coppola, Spike Jonze and Richard Linklater (this image recreates a still from Coppola's *The Virgin Suicides*). What would it be like if I had the same freedom as these characters? In Diablo Cody's *Juno*, I wanted to be like the whip-smart character Juno and not the Asian protester Su-Chin, who spoke in imperfect English. In a way, my career is built upon that desire to reclaim the ways in which people who look like me are depicted. When I photographed the cast and director of *Crazy Rich Asians* in 2018, it suddenly felt like the tide was turning. Being able to be a part of that moment made me proud to do this work as an Asian American.

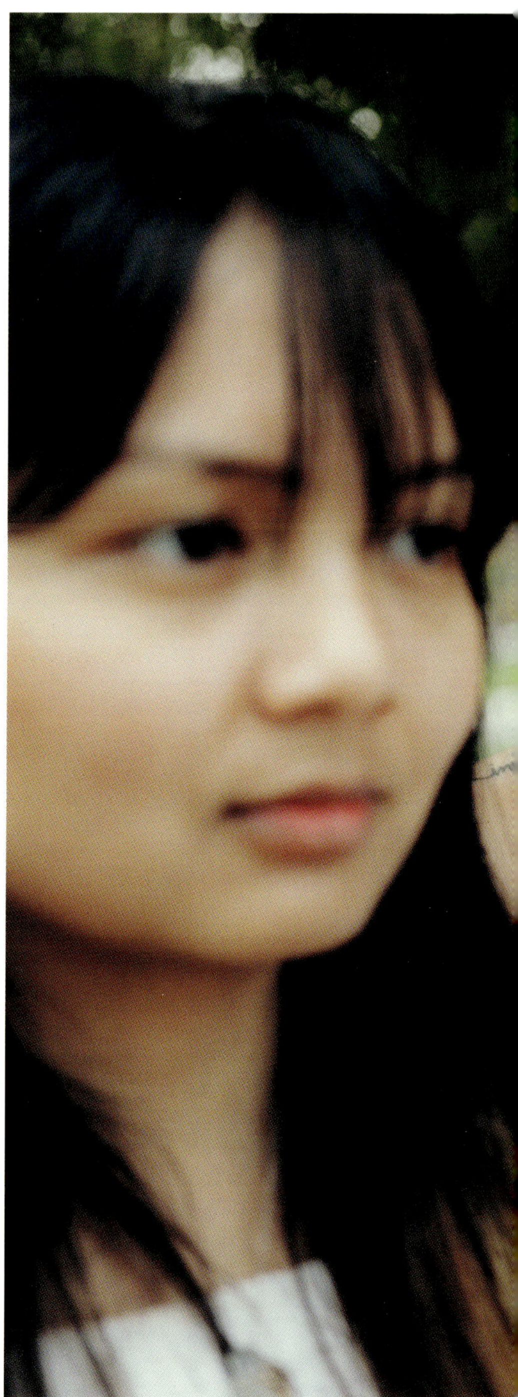

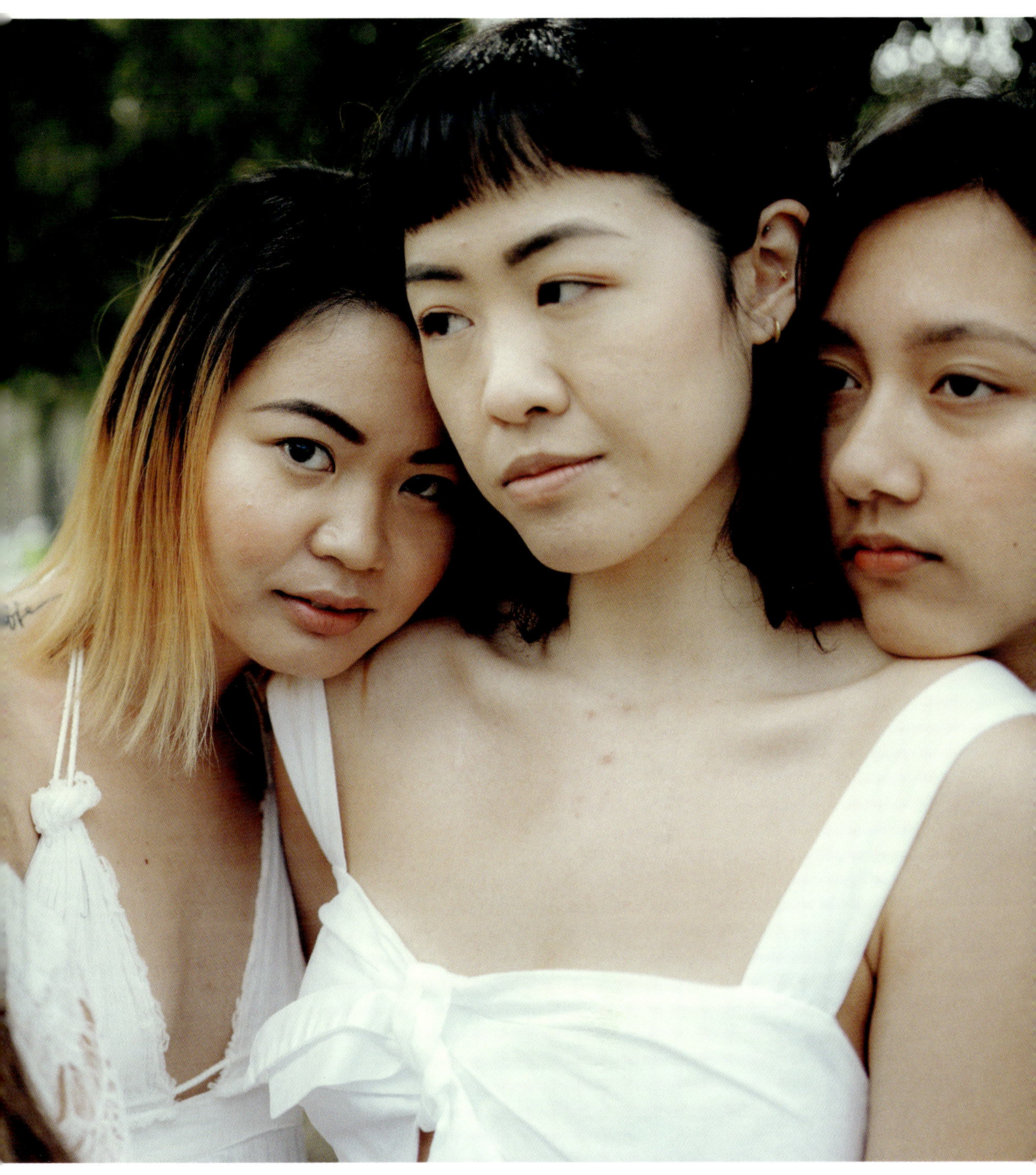

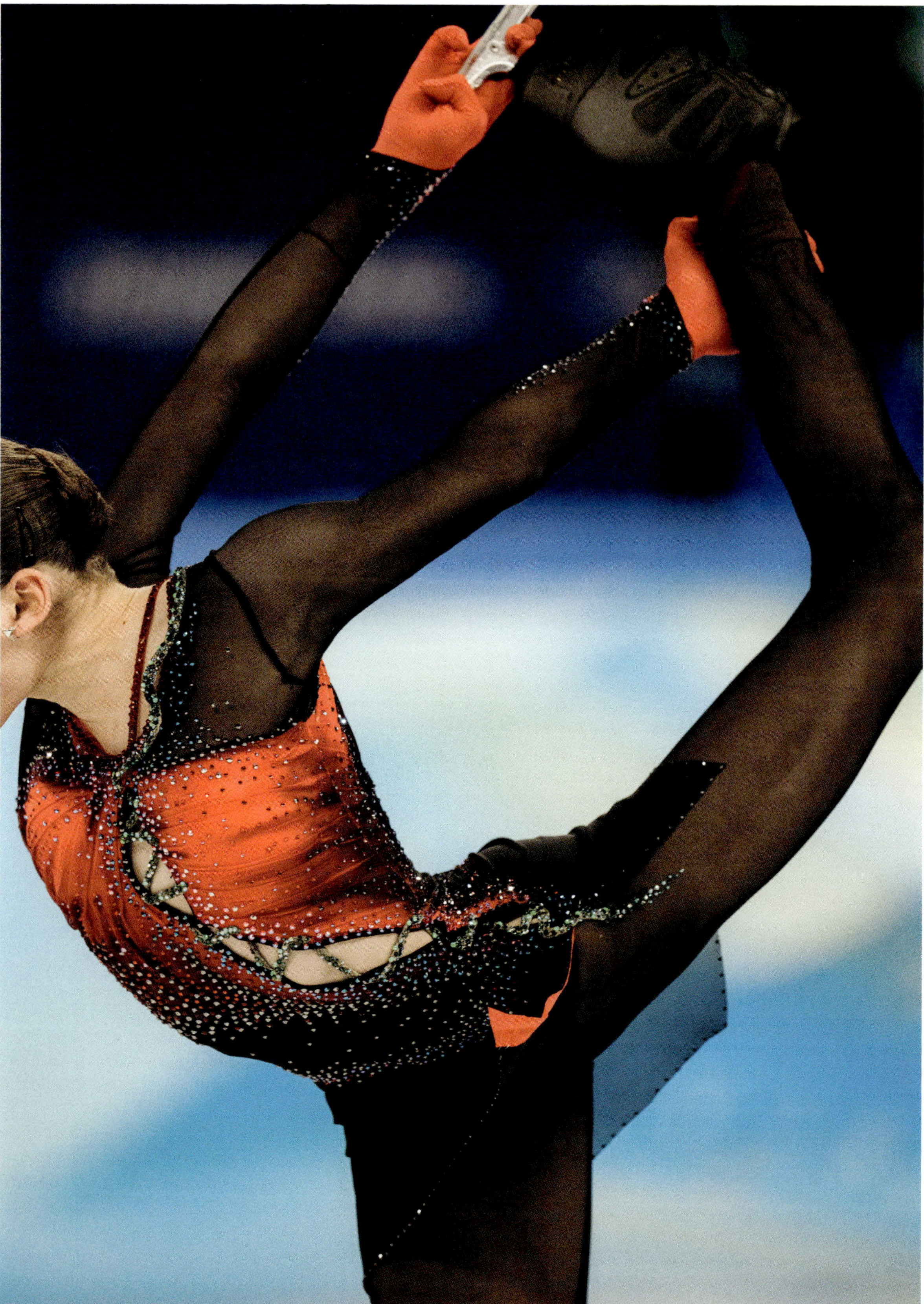

◀

Gabriela Bhaskar

American

Kamila Valieva, 15, Team ROC

Capital Indoor Stadium, Beijing, China; 2022

Kamila Valieva, competing for Team Russian Olympic Committee in the team figure-skating event, lands a quad jump during this women's free skate and becomes the first woman to do so in a Winter Olympics. I was photographing in Beijing for *The New York Times*, and spent a long time thinking about how best to capture these athletes, many of whom were still girls, as they performed immensely challenging jumps and spins while wearing dainty costumes. I was trying to find details that could speak to their strength, athleticism and grace. A few days later, Valieva would be at the centre of a doping scandal. The 15-year-old tested positive for the banned heart medication trimetazidine in a test from December 2021 that was released only after the Olympics had started. Valieva was expected to medal in the individual events. After a long saga of hearings about a ban on her competing, she was allowed to compete, but she could not win a medal nor could anyone else who medalled with her until the details of her case, and the adults around her, were investigated. Valieva fell multiple times in her final event and left the ice in tears. The young athlete placed fourth and her case was still pending at the close of the Olympics.

▶▶

Oksana Parafeniuk

Ukrainian

Untitled

Korosten, Zhytomyr region, Ukraine; 2017

This photo was taken as part of my project GOALBALL: Field of Vision, which focuses on the lives of young goalball players from the Zhytomyr region of Ukraine. I was inspired to start this project after I learned that the Ukrainian Paralympic team took an impressive third place in the Rio Paralympic Games in 2016, despite the challenges faced by the community of 2.7 million people with disabilities in Ukraine. Before this project I did not know anything about the sport of goalball, which was originally created for visually impaired and blind people after World War II, to aid the rehabilitation of blind veterans. But meeting Svitlana Moroz and Serhii Khodakivskyi, the trainers who have dedicated years of their lives to creating the next generation of professional goalball players, inspired me to create this project. This photo was taken during one of my first visits, when I was still exploring the rules of goalball. In the photo, Oleksandr stands in the position ready to accept the ball and wears eyeshades. All the athletes play in full darkness, while the members of the opposing team listen for the sound of the incoming ball and attempt to block it with their bodies.

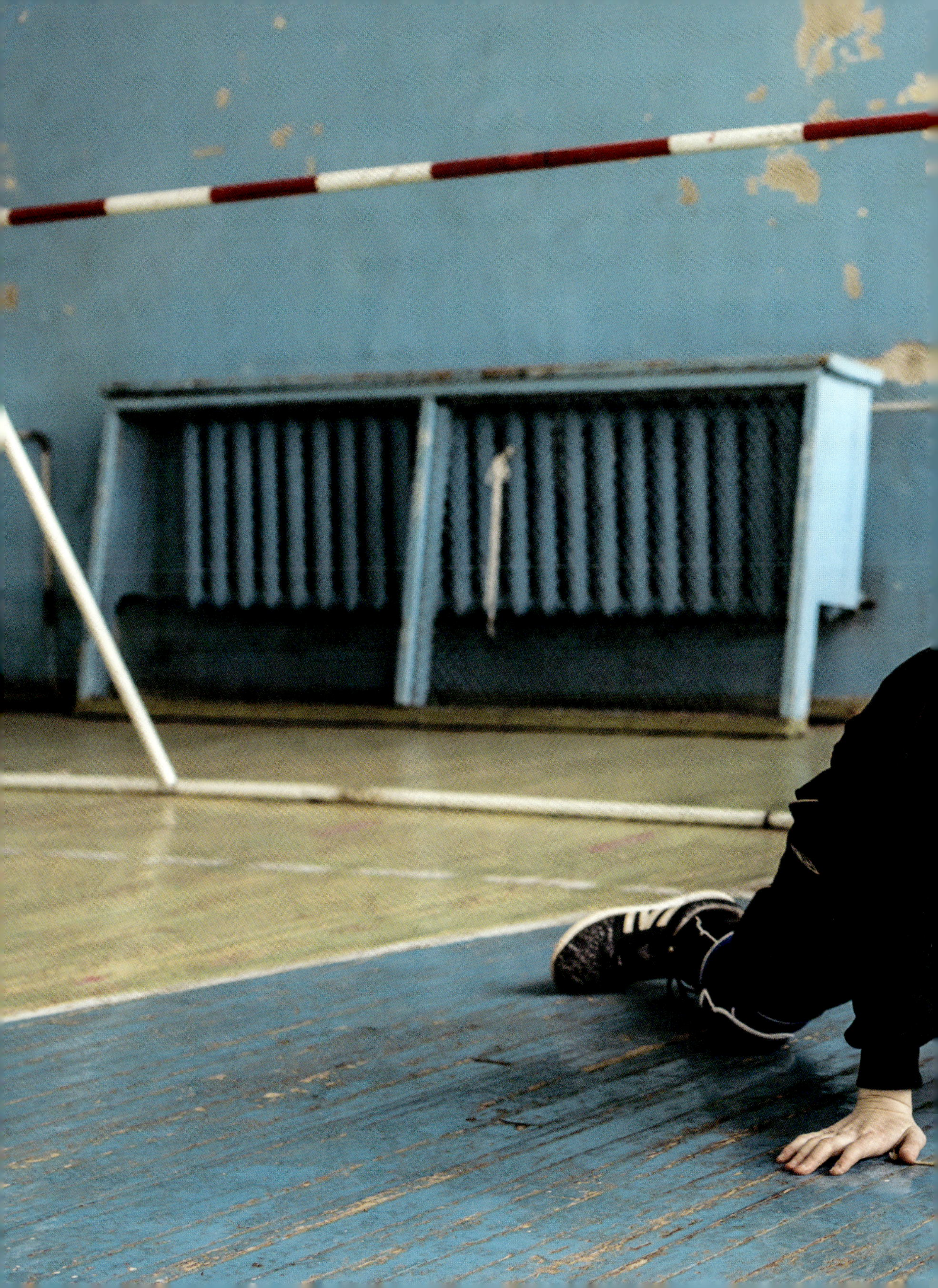

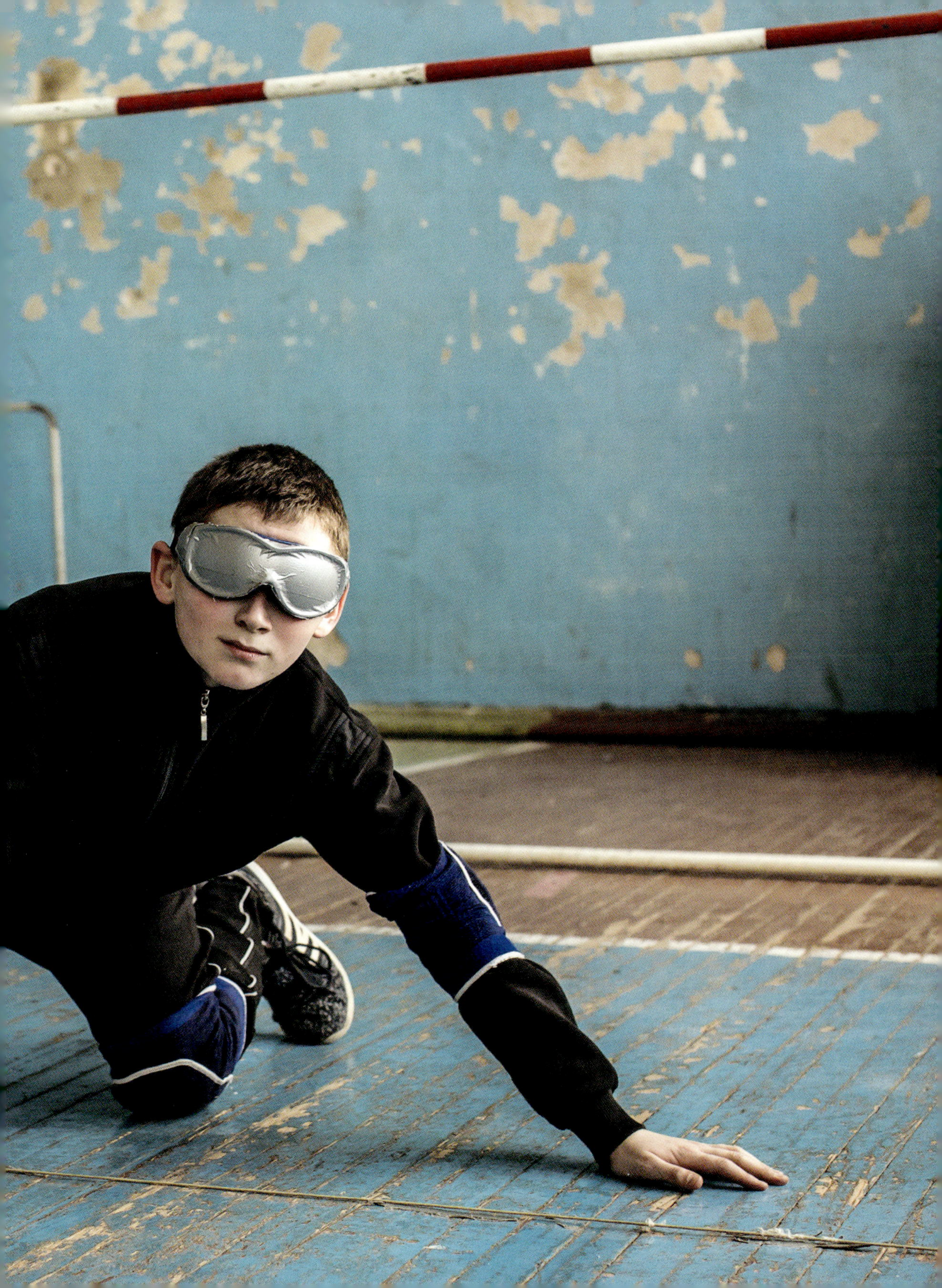

Haley Morris-Cafiero

American

Anonymity Isn't for Everyone

New York City, New York, USA; 2010

Anonymity Isn't for Everyone became the first image of my series Wait Watchers and was created serendipitously while I was producing a self-portrait for a different project. When I reviewed the film, I noticed that, even though we were in New York's Times Square and surrounded by videos, lights and sounds, a person standing behind appeared to be sneering at me. It was the catalyst for a social experiment where I documented the gaze of strangers who pass by me while I perform mundane tasks in public all over the world. Even though I do not know what the strangers are looking at or reacting to, the images depict the experience of a body that is considered 'grotesque' by Western beauty standards, that is transgressing a space where it is not wanted (the public space). The project went viral, and I received tens of thousands of messages, was the subject of blogs and posts criticizing how I look. Twenty-five of the bullies were identified and used as the source material for my series The Bully Pulpit. A series created in collaboration with 25 people who contacted me with stories of how Wait Watchers inspired them to change their lives was released in 2022.

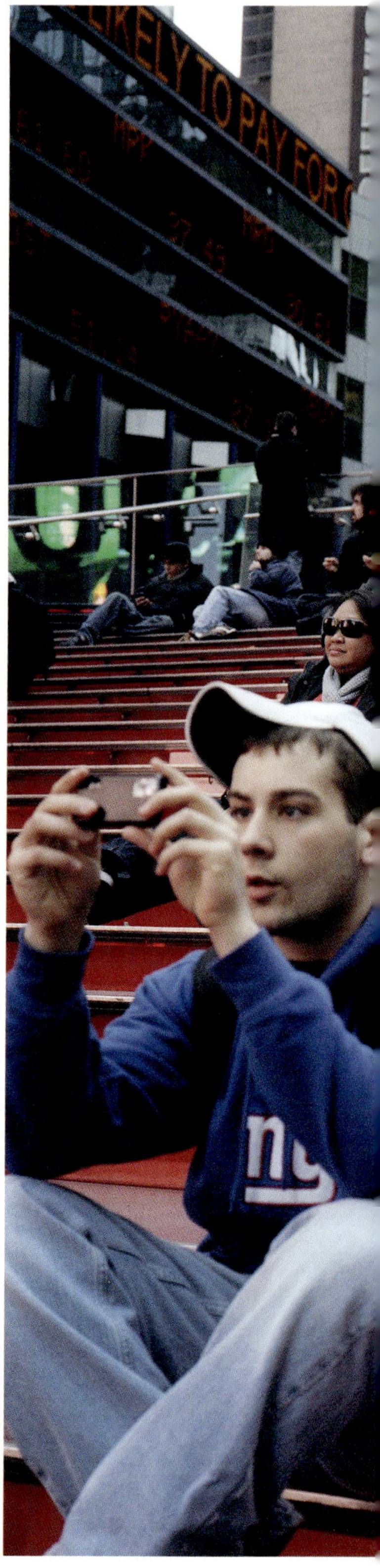

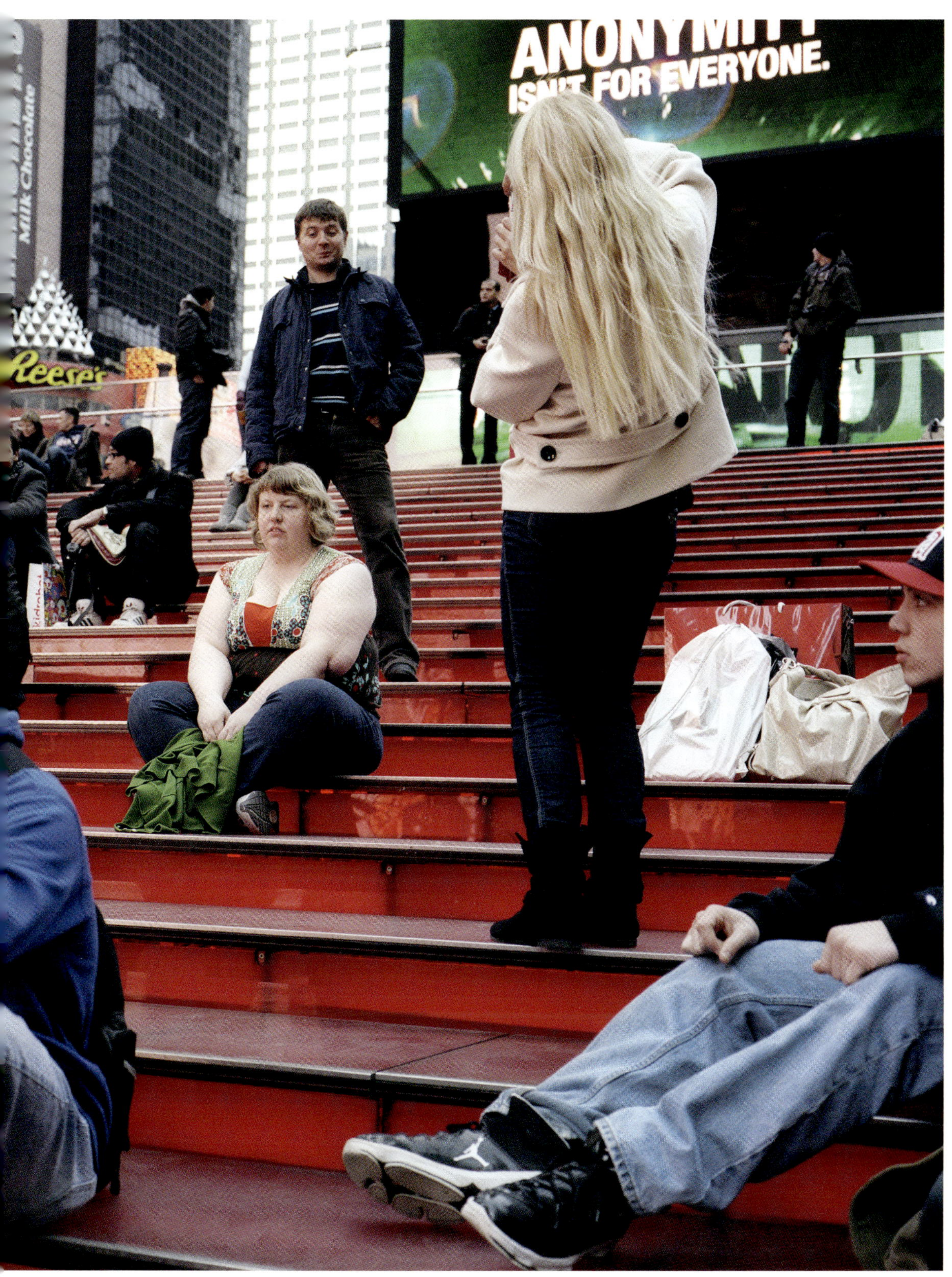
FOR EVERYONE.
Milk Chocolate
Reese's

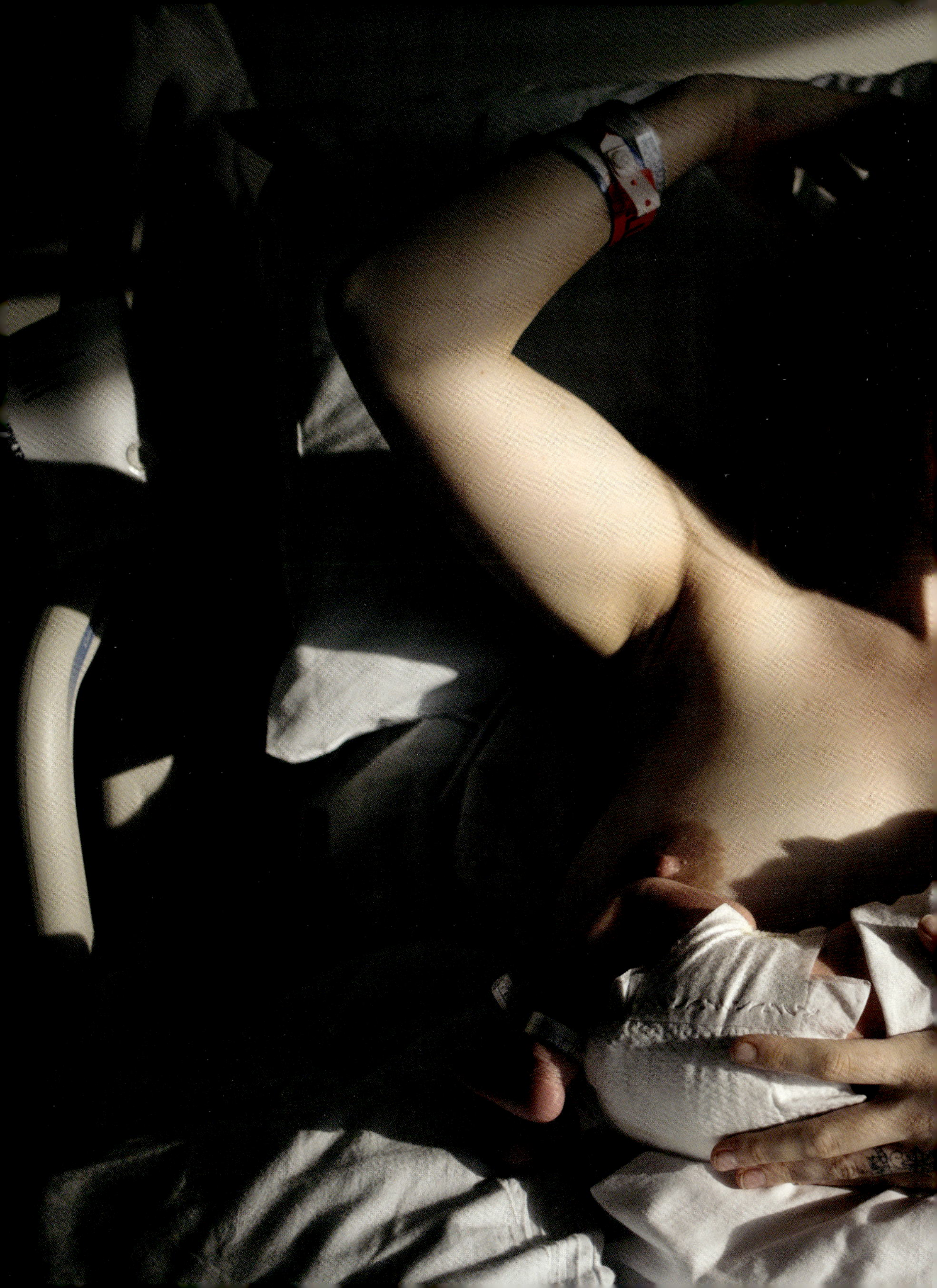

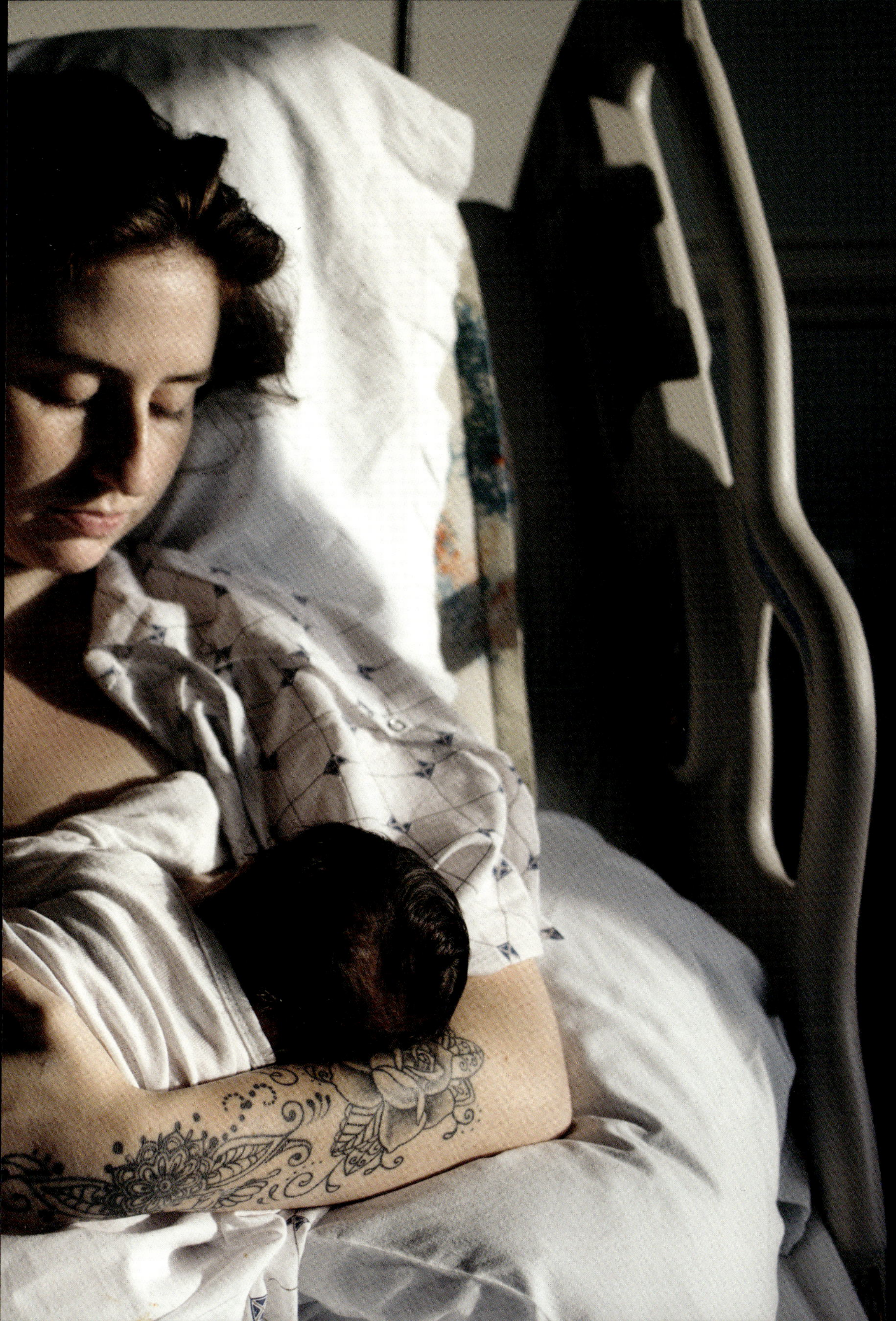

◄◄

Alicia Vera

Mexican American

Eden and Aiden

Fairhope, Alabama, USA; 2018

Eden and I met and became friends in 2010, while I was working on a project about strippers in San Francisco. When I began photographing her, she was 18 and had just started dancing at the Roaring 20s strip club after years of fantasizing about the idea. Though I initially began photographing her as she worked in various facets of the sex industry, the close relationship that evolved between us led to my presence and documentation of many major events in Eden's life. I was there when she moved after leaving an abusive relationship, I witnessed her graduate from yoga teacher training on her 25th birthday and I was invited to photograph the birth of her first child. The night after I arrived in Fairhope, Alabama, where this image was taken, Eden woke up in a pool of blood, days before her due date. Her partner calmly rushed us to the hospital, where we learned that a placental abruption had occurred, and that Eden would be having an emergency C-section. The epidural failed during the surgery and both Eden and her new son, Aiden, experienced a traumatic birth. This is a photo of them recovering together.

►

Charmaine Poh

Singaporean

Ele and Lee

Singapore; 2018

Ele and Lee is part of my project, How They Love (2017–2019), which explores the complexities of performing queer feminine identity in Singapore. Brought into a studio and given an array of wedding props and costumes to choose from, the participants interact with matrimonial tropes and constructed gender roles, resulting in images that align with their vision of self-representation. Projected onto the backdrop are their parents' wedding portraits, a visual reminder of the heteronormative histories that have shaped many LGBTQ people's lives, and a juxtaposition to the possibilities they are in the midst of creating. Through the use of the set, as well as the use of dramaturgy in the direction of their portraits, participants confront the way they perform their gendered identities in the everyday. In creating new imagery of queerness that echoes Jose Esteban Muñoz's idea of queer futurity, the series is an attempt to make visible and validate narratives that have long been relegated to the margins. The process of engagement is in itself a form of world-making and resistance-forming, blurring the lines between performance and the everyday.

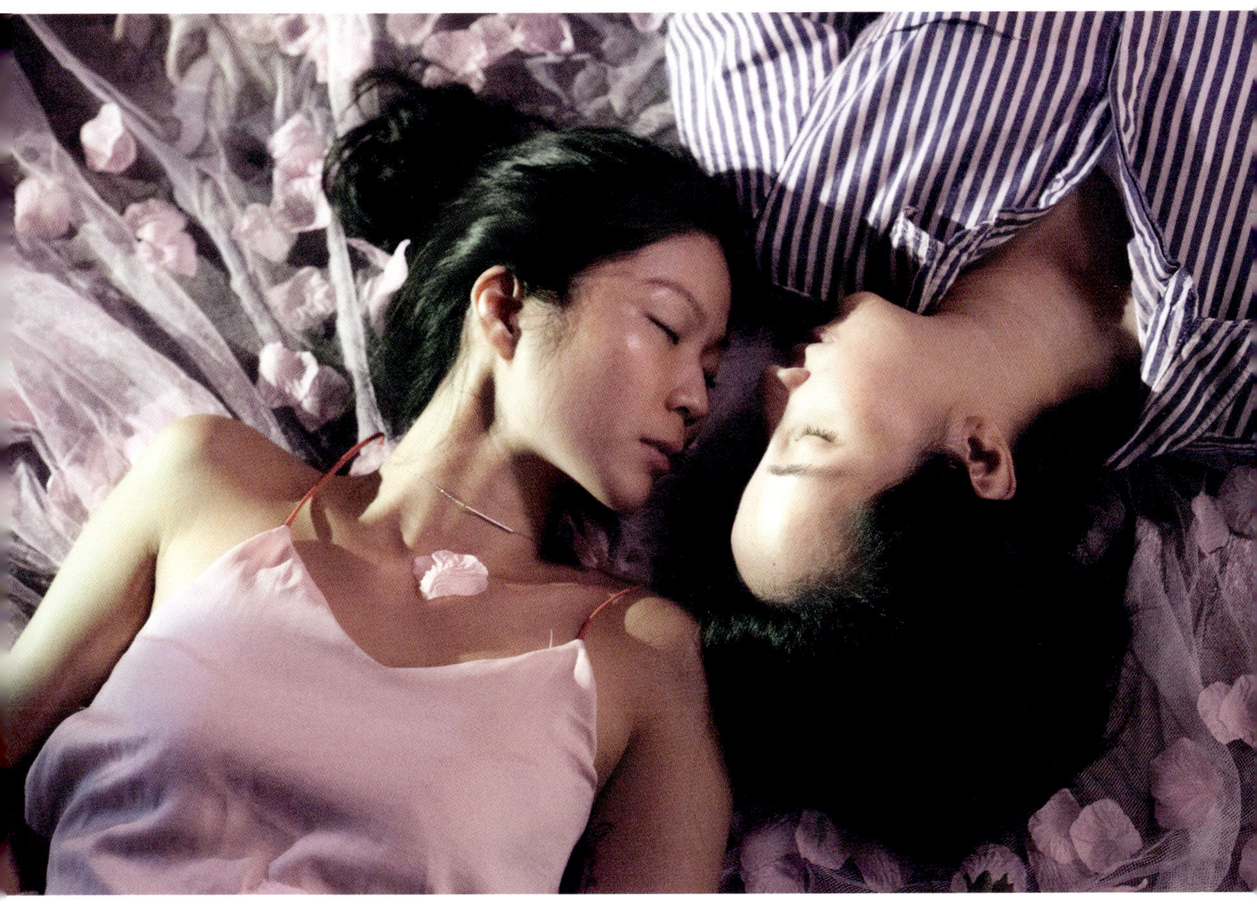

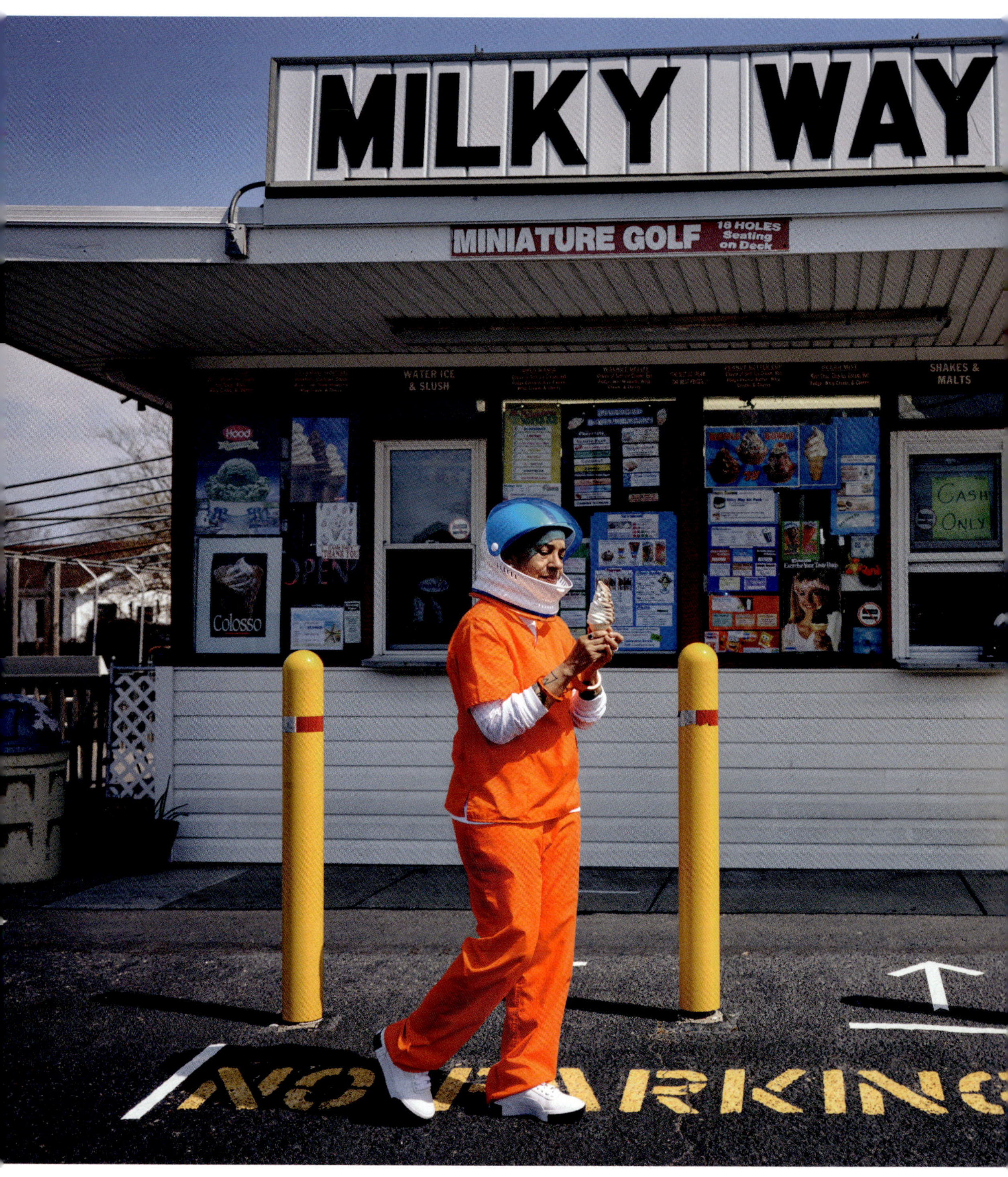
MILKY WAY
MINIATURE GOLF
18 HOLES Seating on Deck
WATER ICE & SLUSH
SHAKES & MALTS
Hood
Colosso
OPEN
THANK YOU
CASH ONLY
NO PARKING

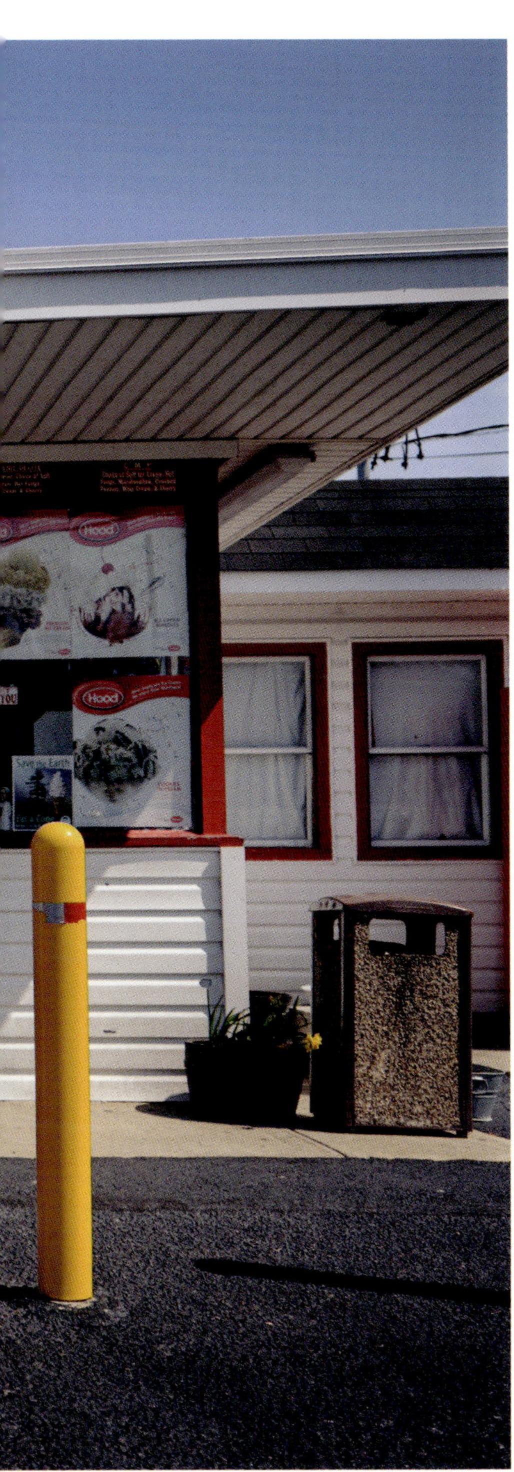

Lola Flash

African American

Milky Way

Villas, New Jersey, USA; 2021

This image is part of a self-portrait series entitled syzygy, the vision, which examines far-reaching facets of intersectional disadvantage that manifest through an enduring history of unsettling cultural conflicts and legacies. *Milky Way* is one of the more gleeful photographs in this body of work. It reminds me of my love-filled childhood and family visits to our local ice-cream haunt. Here, I become 'syzygy', the gender-fluid avatar on a journey to freedom. syzygy is pictured holding a chocolate and vanilla ice-cream cone, getting ready to devour it. Using the framework of Afrofuturism as an interdisciplinary cultural aesthetic that draws upon Black culture and its intersection with technoculture and science fiction, syzygy, the vision symbolizes the universal alter ego. They tell a narrative specific to Brown and Black bodies about existential identities shaped by conflicting societal norms about 'being' and 'otherness' within a technological and global orbit. This series reflects my hope for a divine future where we can soar far away from hashtag chatter into a narrative of substantive pure joy and value.

Photographs give us the ability to access the many ways in which we, as humans, forge relationships to places. The ability of a photograph to freeze time feels especially poignant when thinking about the inevitable effects of climate change and how the continued transformation of our planet will remove many from their homes, destroying links between humans and their places. But while these images at times show us the power of nature and our inability to control it, we also see how places as small as an apartment or as vast as the ocean become sites of refuge, exposing the deep ties between us and our homes, countries and planet. These photographers use their images to both commemorate and mourn the ways in which we shape our planet and it shapes us.

02

Place

Camille Seaman

American Shinnecock Montaukett

Supercell in Minnesota, Near Browerville, MN 20 June 2014

Minnesota, USA; 2014

We do not often chase in Minnesota, not because there are no storms or tornadoes there, but because of the trees. Trees mean you cannot always see what is coming. This trip we took the chance. I know that many people view these types of images as frightening. I see them as wondrous and awesome in the true sense of the word. Our planet is so extraordinary. To witness beauty and true power is my honour and privilege. I hope that my work inspires viewers to nurture their own relationship with our only home. It was Jacques Cousteau who said, 'You will not love something you do not know, and you will not save something you do not love'. My aim as a photographer is to help introduce our planet to the viewer. To create greater empathy and compassion where perhaps there was no relationship before. To show something they may never have seen, or if they have to show it in a way that helps to trigger that spark of curiosity. If my image is a spark that ignites a fire in them to be more engaged, more aware, more appreciative, or even more in awe of the magnificence that is our only home, then I think my task is a noble and worthy pursuit.

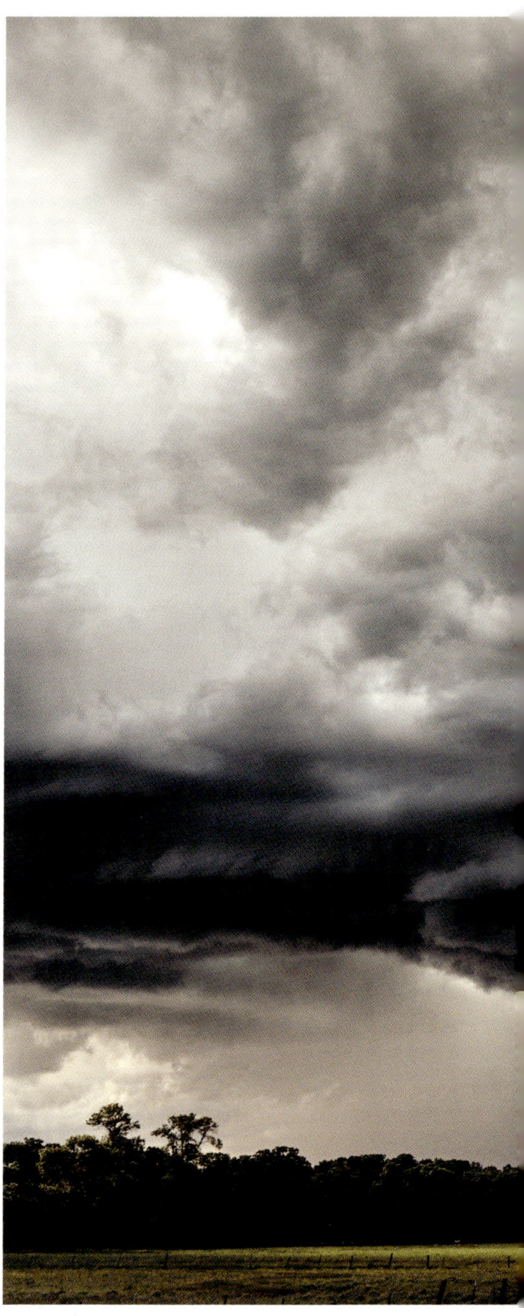

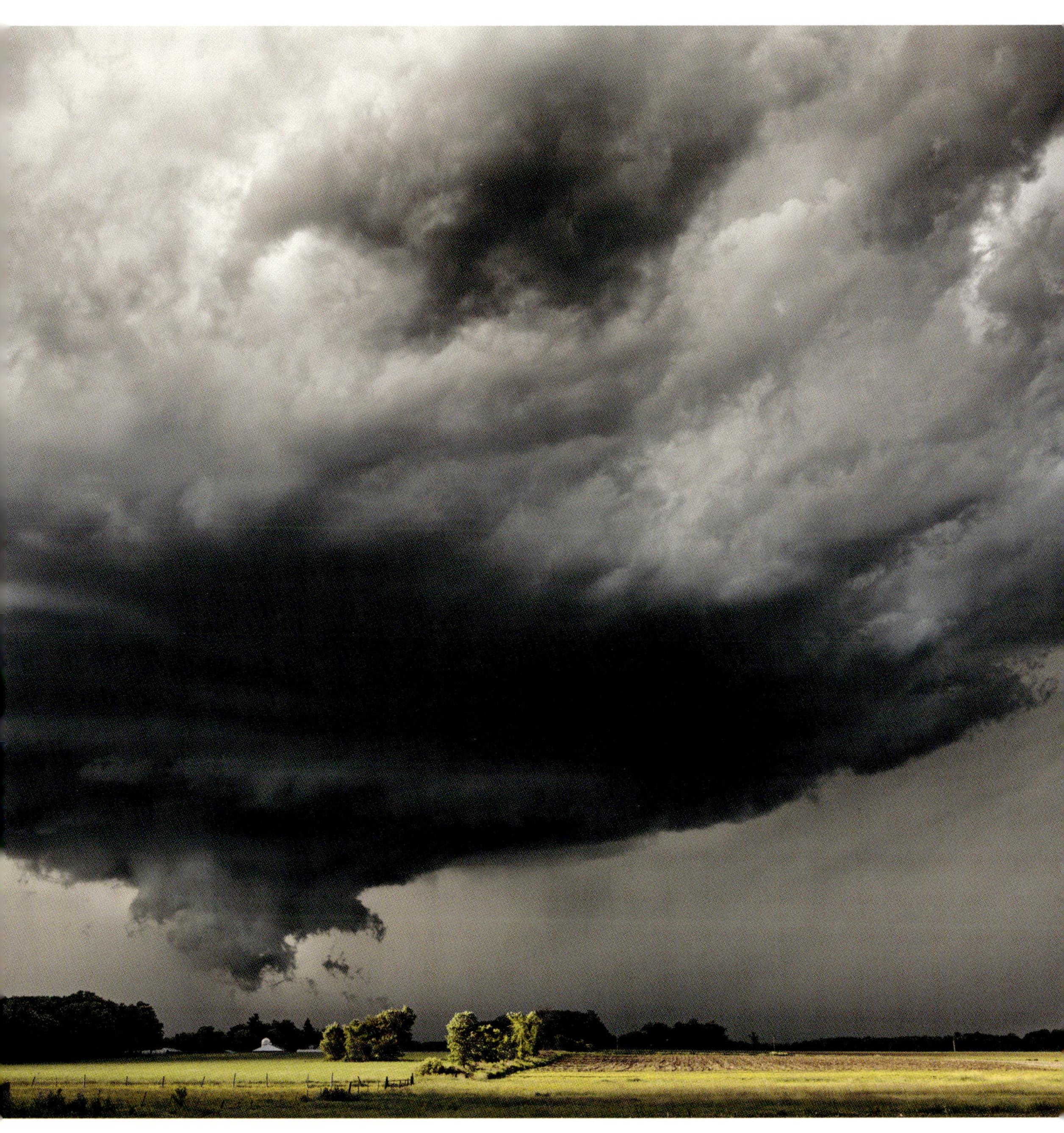

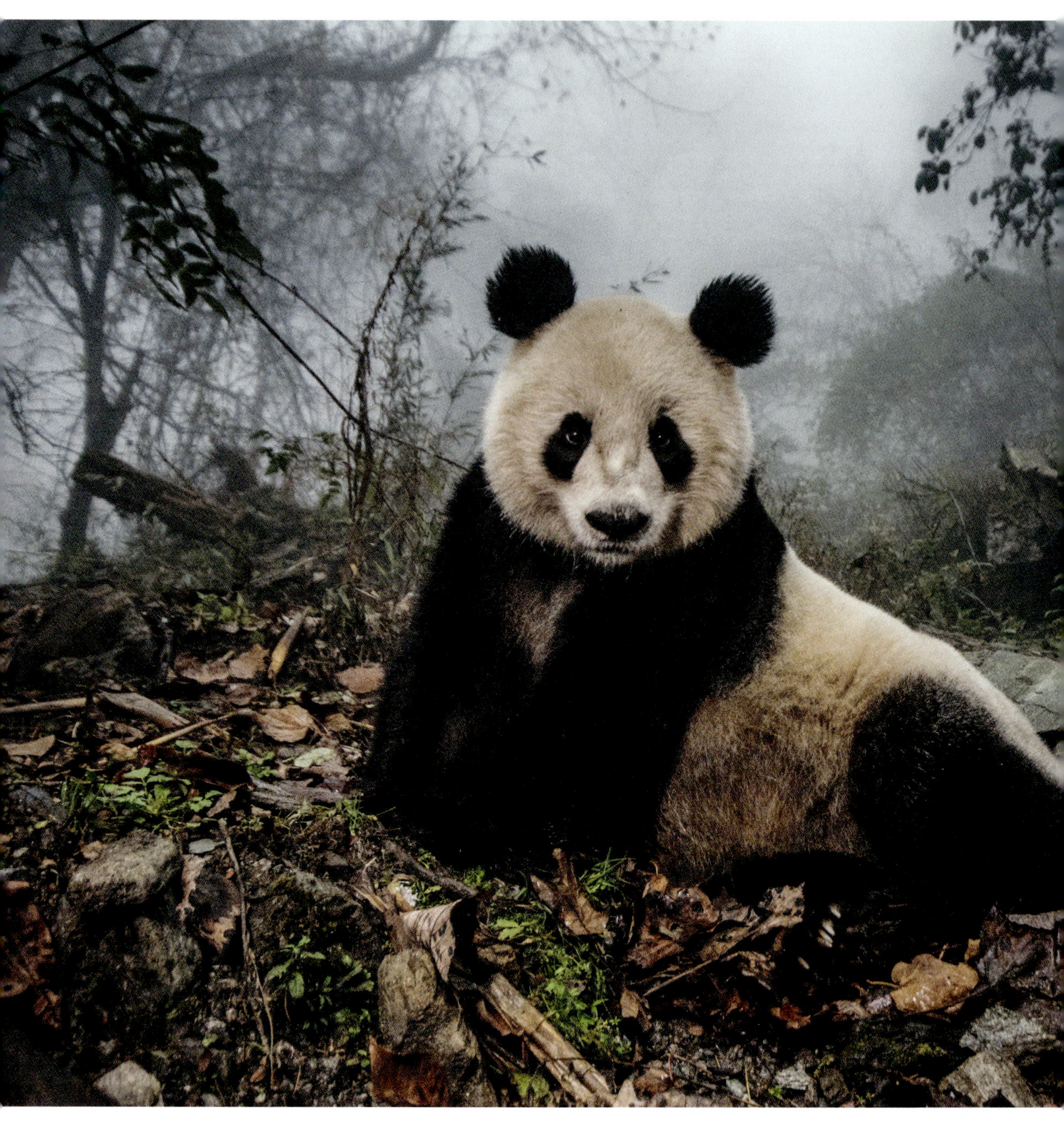

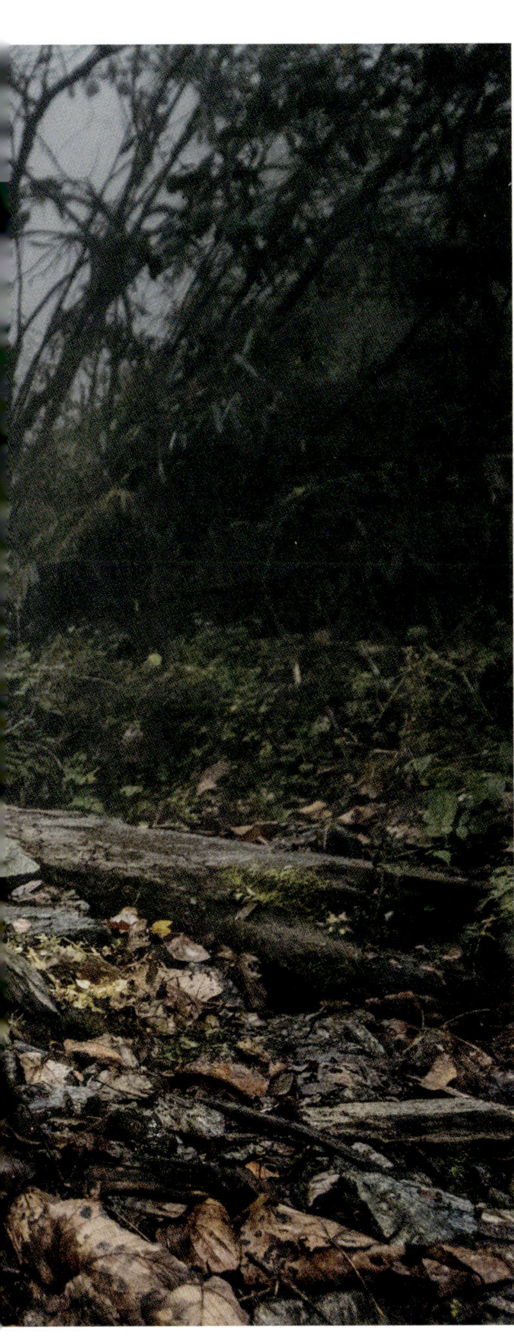

Ami Vitale

American

Yeye in the Mist

Wolong, Sichuan Province, China; 2016

I began my journey into the world of pandas as a photographer documenting captive pandas being released into the wild. I had a front row seat as a panda named Hope was released, and as she trundled off into the forest, she took with her the aspirations for her entire species. I spent the next three years investigating the world of pandas. The Chinese treat these million-dollar bears with kid gloves and do not allow access easily. In order to get close, I had to dress up as a panda. It's harder to rock a panda suit than you may imagine, especially when you look like a bank robber and particularly when it's scented with panda urine. Pandas go by smell, not sight, so it was a stinky endeavour, but one I'd happily do again if asked. Today, there are fewer than 2,000 giant pandas in the wild. Over 30 years, researchers have been working on breeding and releasing pandas, augmenting existing populations and protecting their habitat. The slow and steady incline in the population of giant pandas is a testament to the perseverance and efforts of scientists and conservationists. China may be on its way to successfully saving its famous ambassador and in the process of putting the wild back into an icon.

Paula Bronstein

American

Birds in Flight

Mazar-e-Sharif, Afghanistan; 2009

I spent more than 20 years documenting Afghanistan in the aftermath of the American invasion. During that time, I travelled around Afghanistan, recording how Afghans conducted their lives against the backdrop of a never-ending violent war and a brutal Taliban insurgency. As a woman photojournalist working in a conservative Muslim country, I have often been daunted by the strength and endurance of women from Afghanistan. I felt it was important to focus on an intimate look at the plight of Afghan women and their daily struggles, as I was naturally drawn to women's issues and the problems they face in a male-dominated society. In this everyday scene, white pigeons take off as Afghans come to feed the birds at the Blue Mosque in Mazar-e Sharif, Afghanistan. It became part of my first book, *Afghanistan: Between Hope and Fear*, which was published in 2016. I continued to cover Afghanistan, returning in 2021 when President Biden announced the withdrawal of the US military, and staying close to six months to cover the historical end of the 'forever war'. The country continues to find itself balanced between opposing forces and I find myself continually drawn back.

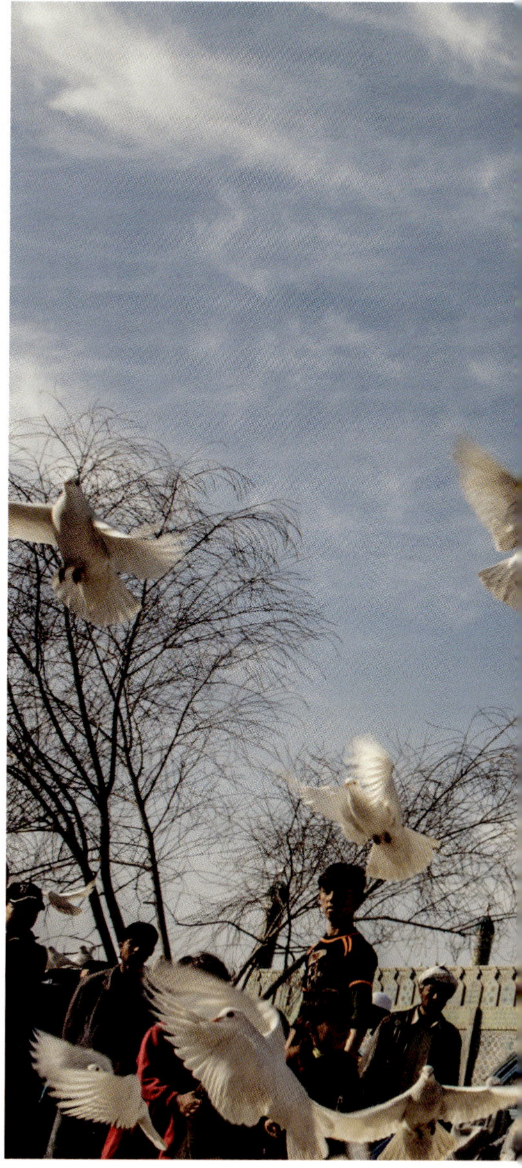

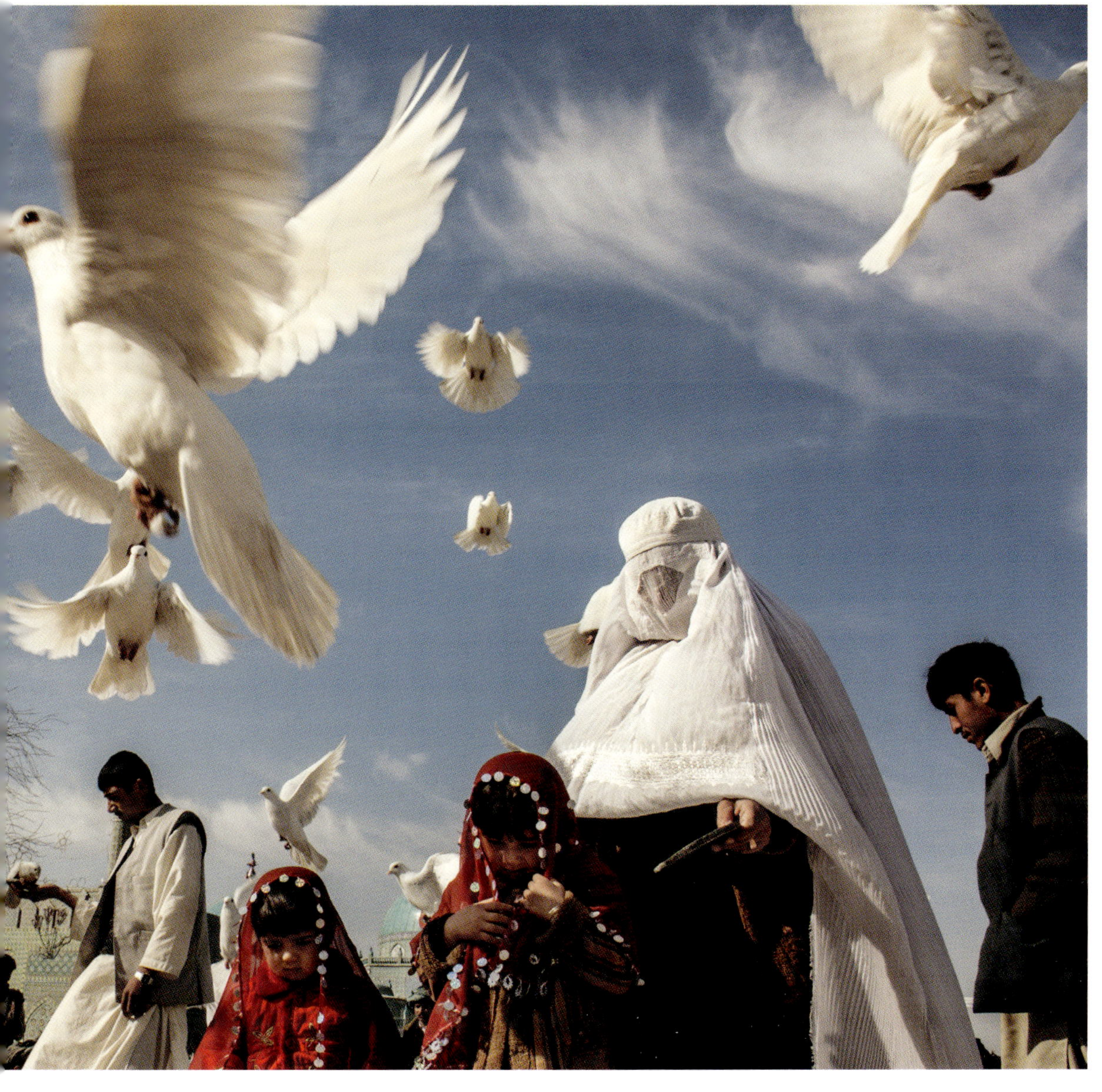

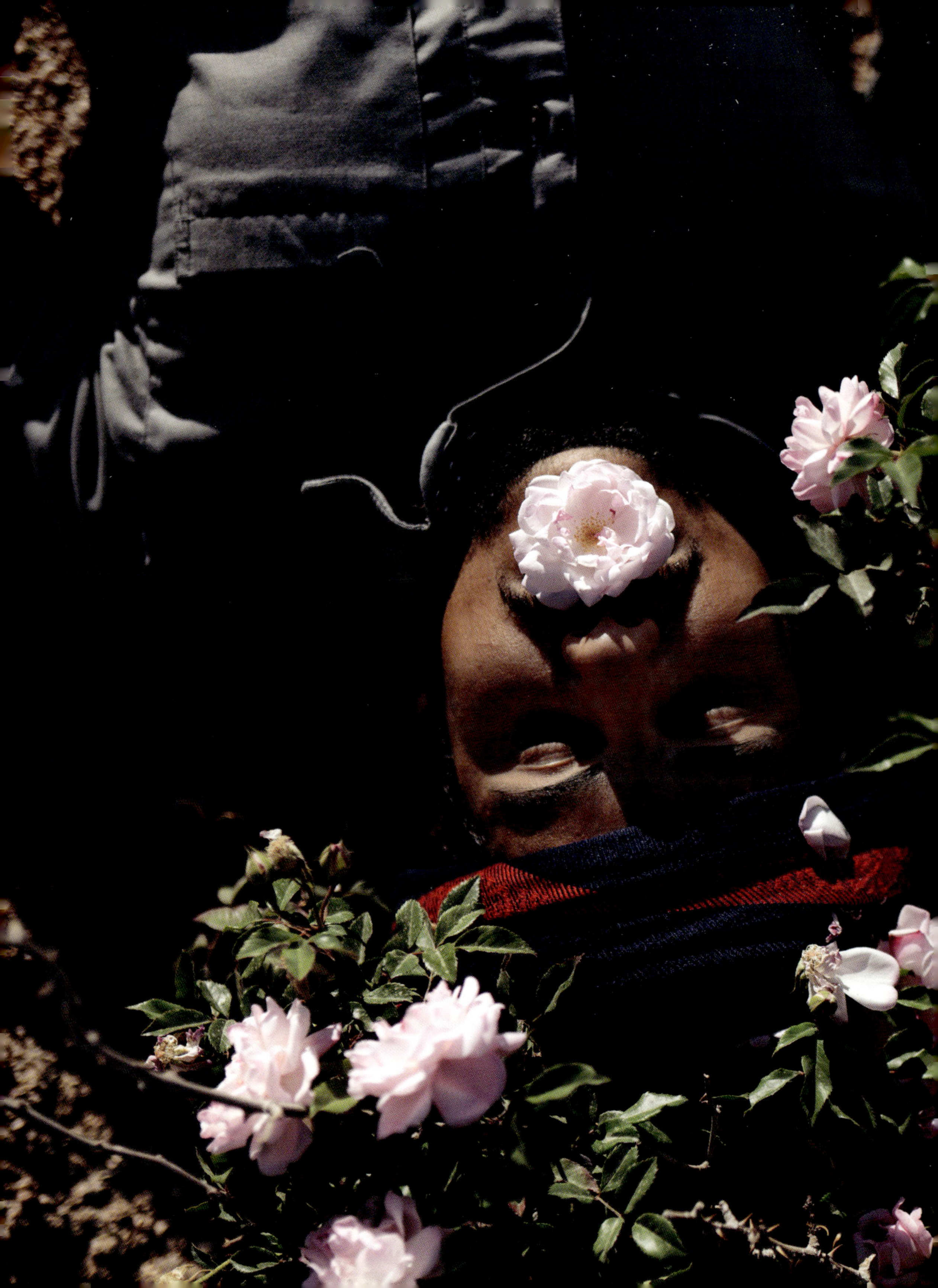

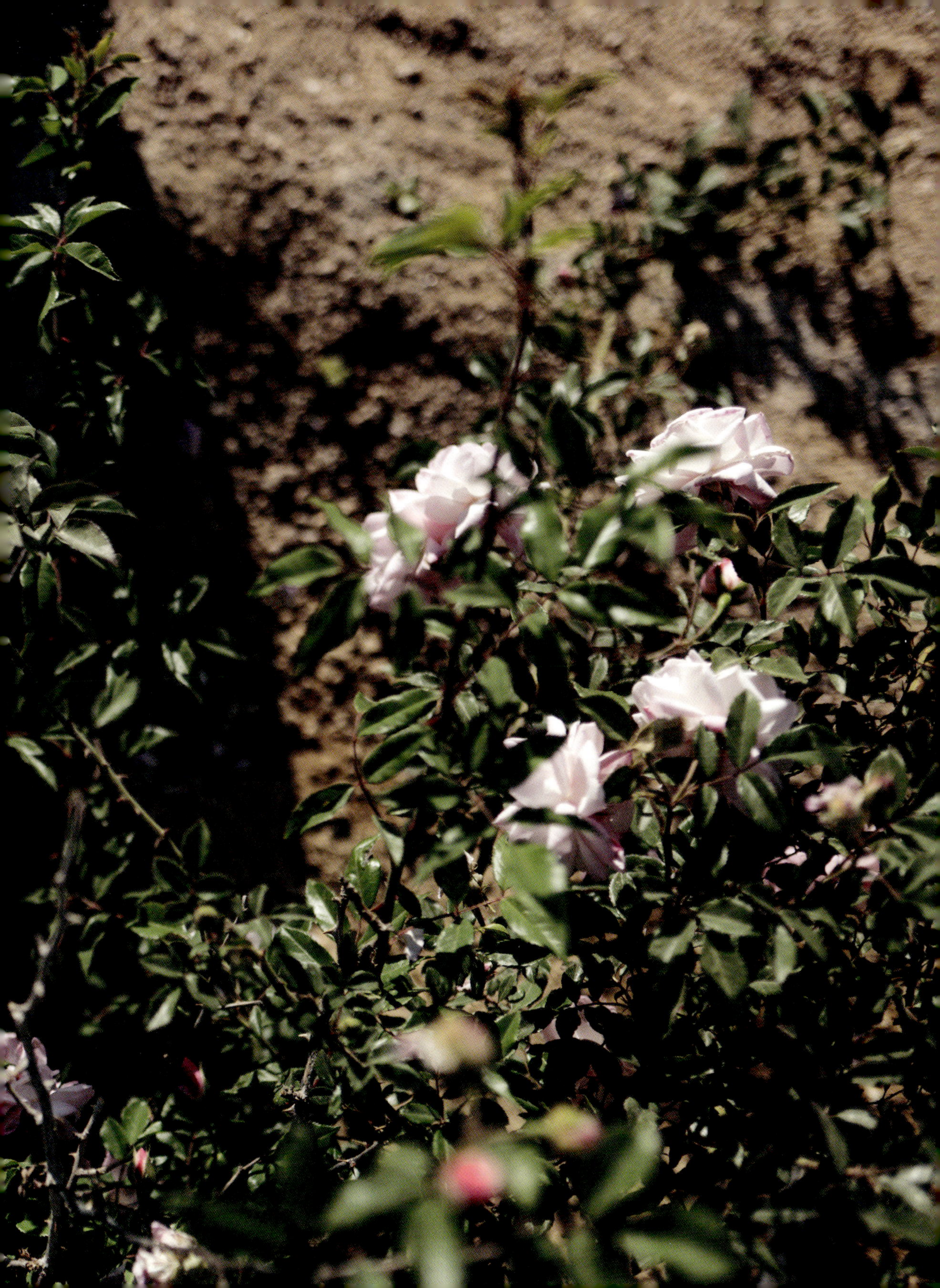

◂◂

Rehab Eldalil

Egyptian

Moussa Algebaly in his Garden

St Catherine protectorate, South Sinai, Egypt; 2020

This photograph of Moussa holding the flower of the tea plant used to reduce period and labour pain is part of my long-term project The Longing Of The Stranger Whose Path Has Been Broken, where I explore the notion of belonging and the interconnectedness of people and land. This allows me to reconnect to my own estranged Bedouin ancestry. Like many Indigenous communities around the world, Bedouins of Sinai are commonly misrepresented in the media, portrayed as isolated from, and a threat to, modern society. But through it all, they remain the keepers of the land, protecting it from harm as it provides them with blessings in return. This interconnectedness, forged over the centuries, accounts for the community's resilience in the face of challenges. After years of drought, a major flood occurred in mid-March 2020, providing an agricultural opportunity for the Bedouin community amid the economic impacts caused by the pandemic. For the community whose main source of income is tourism, the flood is a miracle in disguise. The land has given back to its keepers in a time of crisis. It is this interconnectedness that survived in my blood and drew me back to this land to find my roots and way home.

▸

Nyimas Laula

Indonesian

Aurel

Rote Island, East Nusa Tenggara, Indonesia; 2021

The last time I was travelling – just for the sake of travelling – was probably in 2016, when I spent almost a month in the Banda Islands, Indonesia. I consider myself to be a hermit by nature, unbothered by stillness and a boring routine. For a long time, travel was just a state of transit in my mind before working. The pandemic has changed the way we travel, it grounded me, and most people, in the four walls of the space I love to call home. At the end of 2021, I decided to visit Rote Island – the southernmost point of Asia. On one of the evenings I spent staring at the vast Indian Ocean as the sun set to the horizon, I met Aurel, who shared a calm and tender moment with her dog as she bathed in the water. This photograph hits differently – it somehow feels warm, softer and more tender compared to other photographs I have made. As a working photojournalist, I usually gravitate towards newsworthy images, created in a fast-paced environment around issues I care about. This photograph inspires me to rethink how I work, to slow down and to look into slower, quiet moments that I often overlook, and to explore beyond my usual approach.

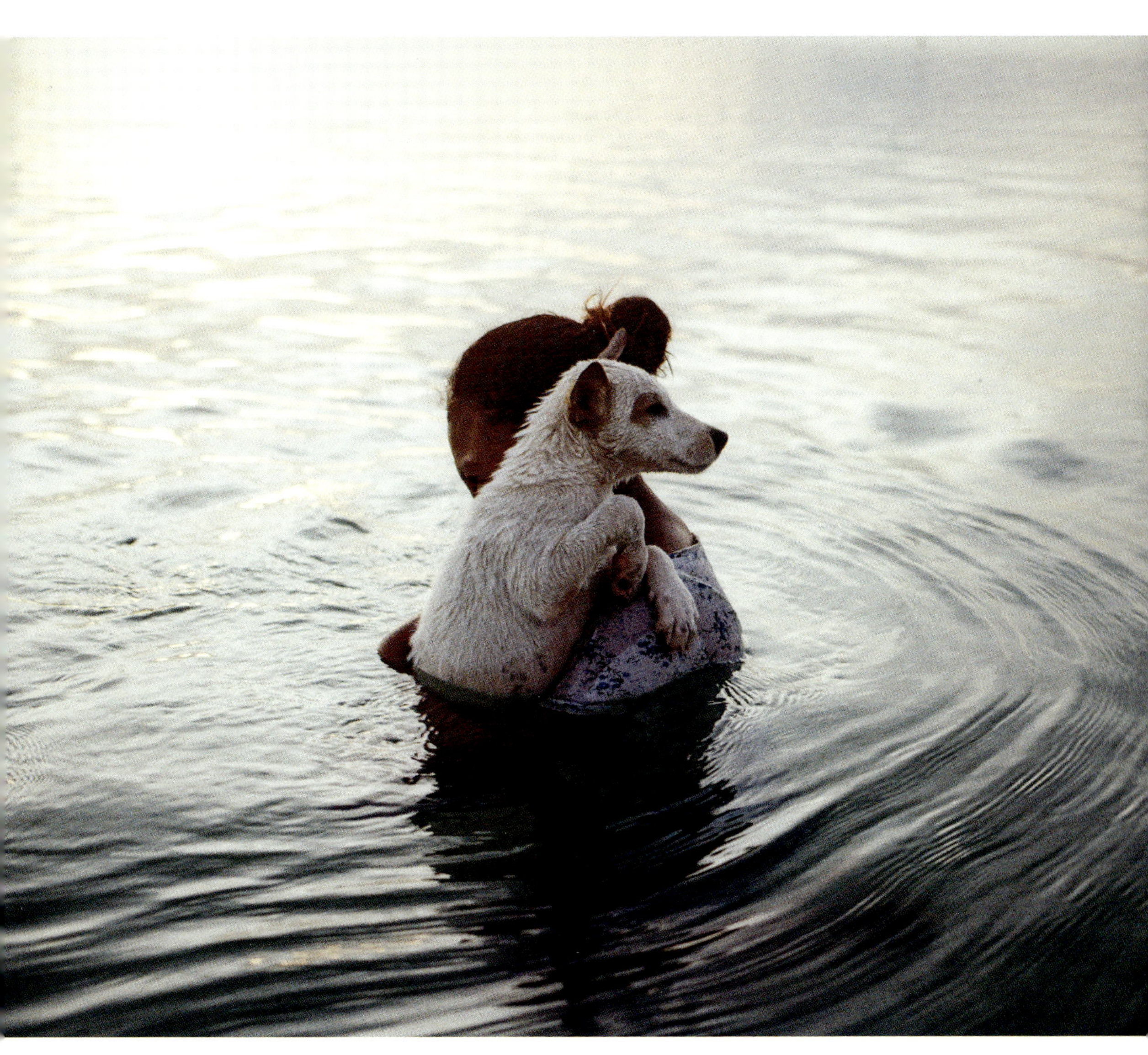

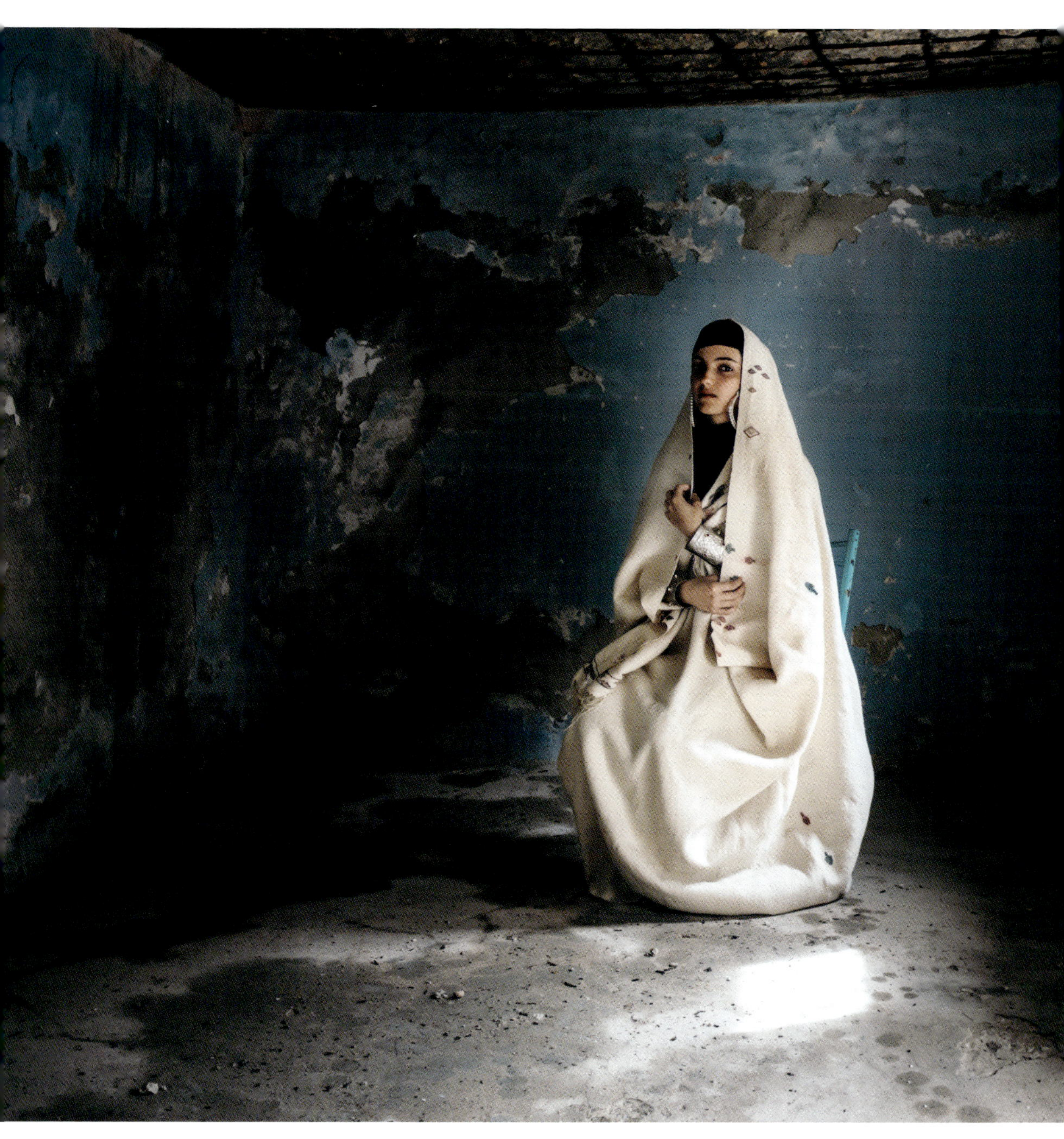

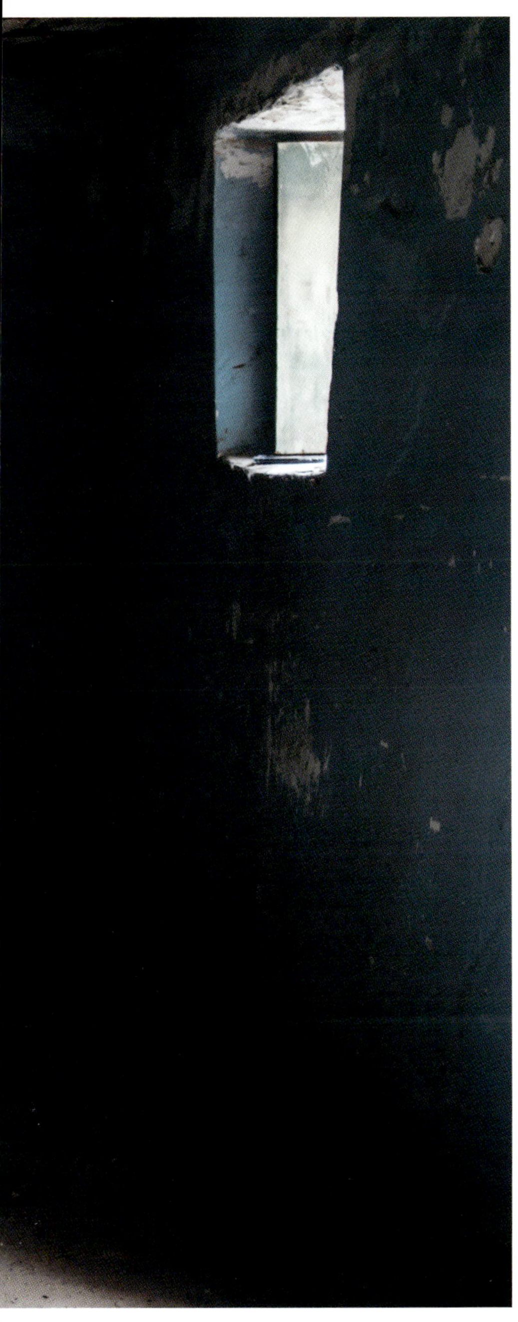

Nada Harib

Libyan

from Women of Libya
Yefren, Libya; 2018

Before I started to explore my country through my camera, Libya was hidden beneath layers of mystery. When I looked at the work of photographers telling stories from different countries, I realized that I had rarely come across Libyan photographers capturing Libyan stories in the same way. I longed to hear our voices talking about our lives. After the revolution, Libyans, including myself, began to recognize the value of our culture and traditions and are now trying their best to revive them. In 2018 I started my ongoing project Women of Libya to explore my Amazigh roots and revive the cultural heritage of my hometown in the Nefussa Mountains. This photograph of my cousin Mira is a part of that project, which interweaves various stories expressing women's courage, their traditions, the social challenges that they face and their relationship to their environments. This project is as much about them, as it is about myself. Mira wears our grandmother's *tlaba*, a traditional wool garment, to reflect our family's roots. Focusing on the lives of women in this way is challenging, but being a Libyan woman has allowed me to present a different perspective and vision of Libya to the world.

Maddie McGarvey

American

Mary and the Wind

Carnegie, Oklahoma, USA; 2019

In May of 2019, I embarked on a solo road trip from Oklahoma, through Texas and into New Mexico. As a photojournalist, I document social issues with a special focus on photographing rural America with dignity. I love meeting interesting people in places that are not often covered and learning something new every single day. On this trip, the Kiowa tribe graciously invited me to photograph a powwow while I was in Carnegie, Oklahoma. At the powwow, I noticed a woman with the most beautiful silver hair. Her name was Mary Wade, and she ended up being the kindest woman who told me many stories about her life and the traditions of the tribe. I am a naturally shy person and sometimes have to build up the courage to ask to take someone's photograph. But over the years as a photographer, I have learned that the moments I push myself out of my comfort zone lead to meeting the most amazing people who are happy to have a new friend and share a part of their story. The days on the open road with no real destination, stopping whenever anything catches my eye, and encountering incredible people make me grateful to live life with a camera in hand.

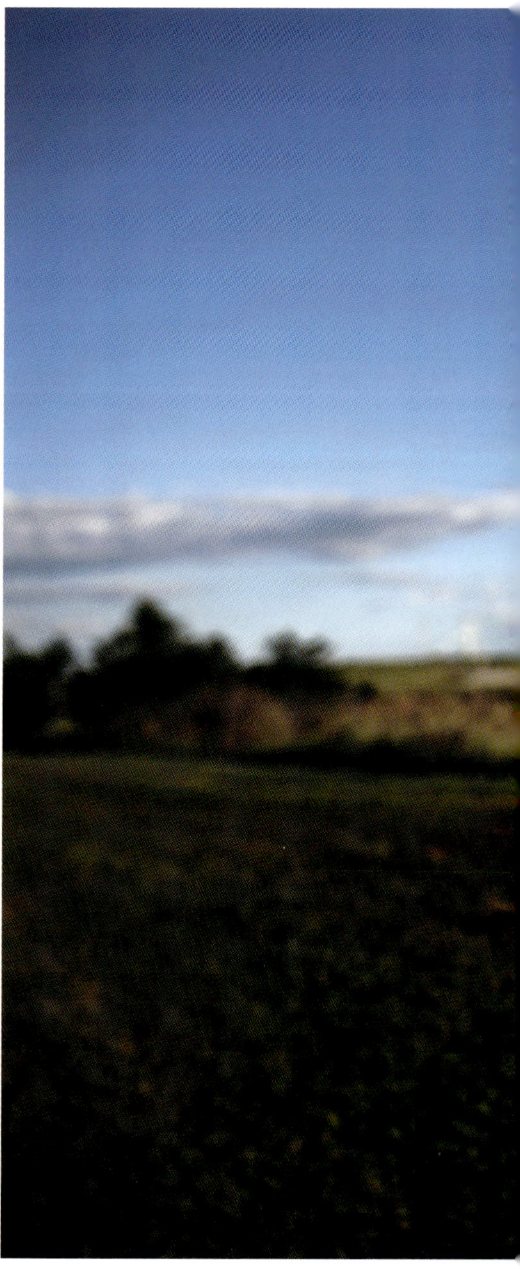

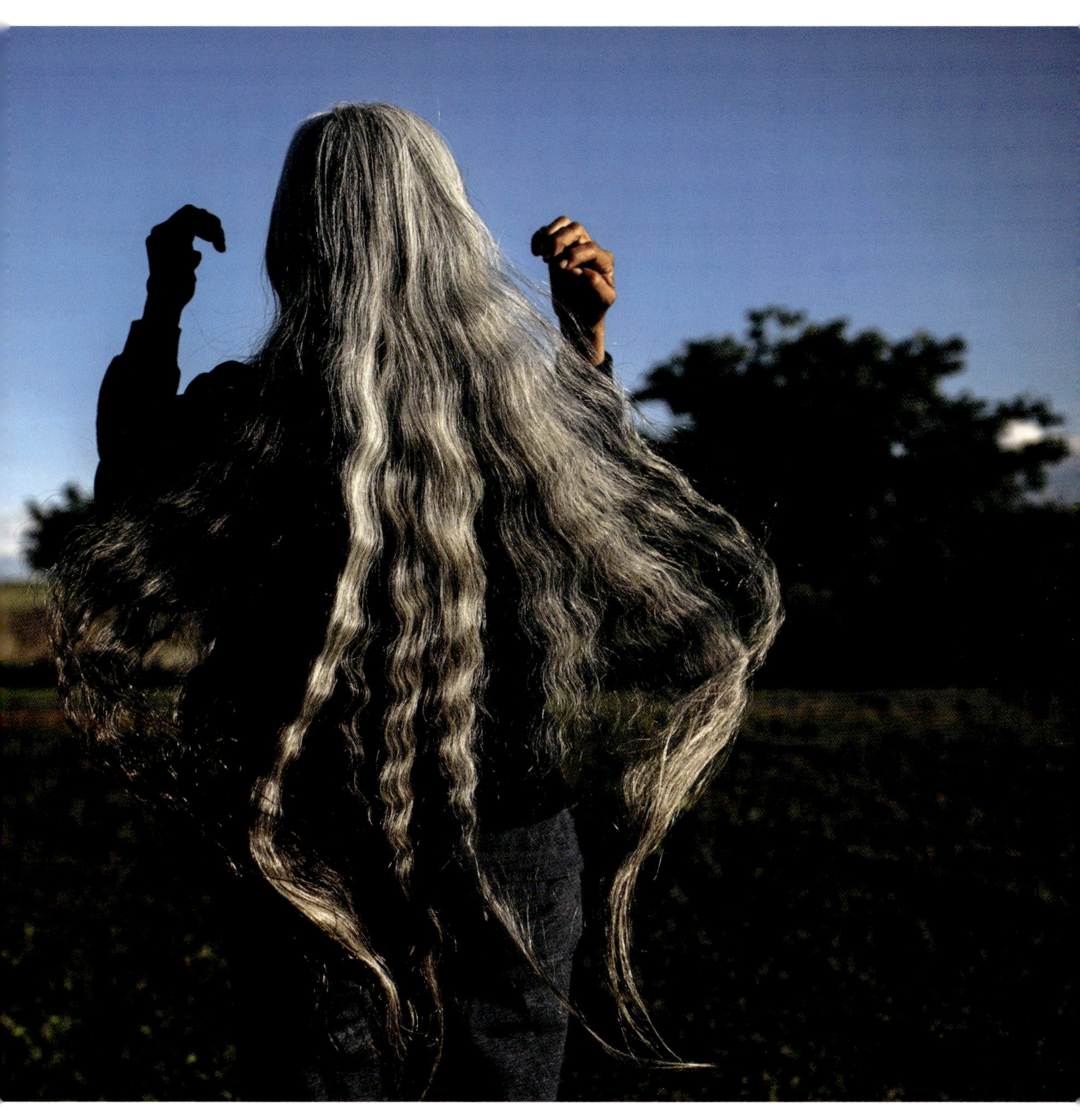

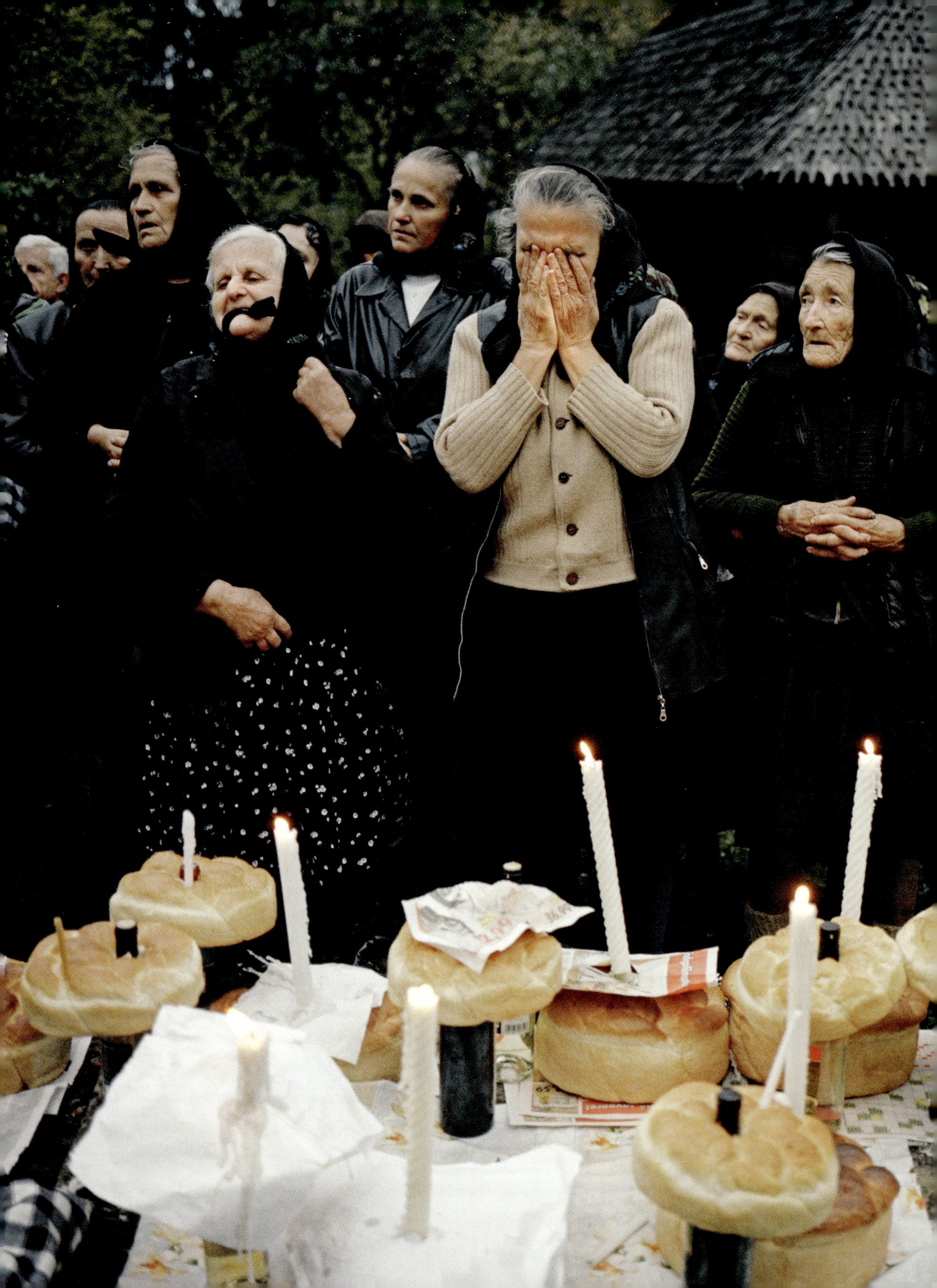

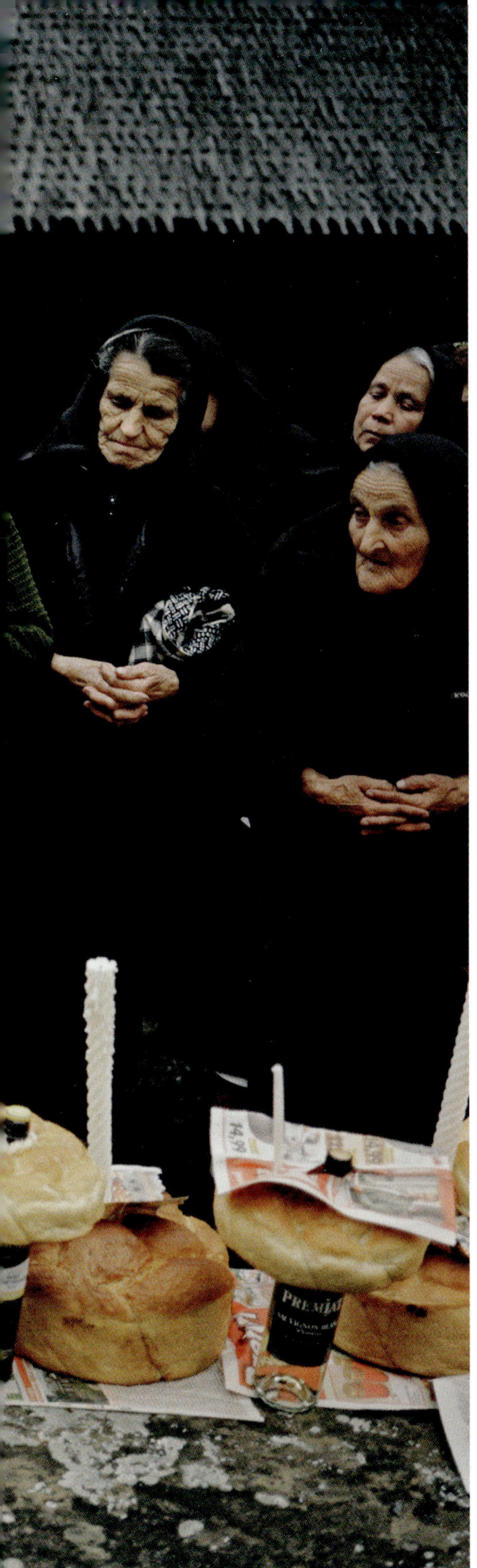

Rena Effendi

Azerbaijani

Day of the dead celebration

Maramures, Romania; 2012

In Maramures, Romania, an isolated region in the northern Carpathian mountains, I documented agrarian communities and their culture of haymaking. They are often called the last peasants of Europe – for centuries, these small villages in Transylvania have maintained hay meadows, raised cattle and operated self-sustainable farms. The agrarian fairy tale that is extinct in western Europe still exists here. But today, this world is on the brink of extinction, as local small-scale farmers cannot compete with European imports or industrialized farming methods and youths leave the countryside for cities. As horses are traded in for tractors and wooden houses and gates are disassembled and sold off for furniture parts, this pastoral dream is vanishing. In the Budesti village of Maramures, I witnessed the day of the dead celebration. Bread and wine were brought to the priest from each family along with a piece of paper naming deceased family members attached to a candle. The priest then collected the papers and sang the names of the dead family members in a prayer, commemorating them. The bread was later collected and distributed among the village poor.

Mary Kang

South Korean American

Bliss

Thimphu, Bhutan; 2015

I stumbled upon this scene of Bhutanese students enjoying leisure activities in a yard after their school hours in Thimphu, Bhutan, in 2015. As a South Korean American who immigrated to the United States when I was 11 years old and did not get to revisit my motherland as much as I wished, this scene made me feel very connected and nostalgic. Seventy per cent of Korea is covered with mountains and seeing children playing outside in the Himalayas reminded me of my childhood in South Korea. Our shared Asian culture of hospitality gave me a certain degree of belonging and made me feel welcome. I found myself connecting strongly to the area as someone who is familiar with a similar set of cultural traditions. I asked if I could join in their games, and they welcomed me in. There was an atmosphere of joy and a clear connection to nature those afternoons playing in the mountains. I took these pictures as a record of these blissful memories, which were created after my own childhood memories resurfaced and made me long for something more tangible.

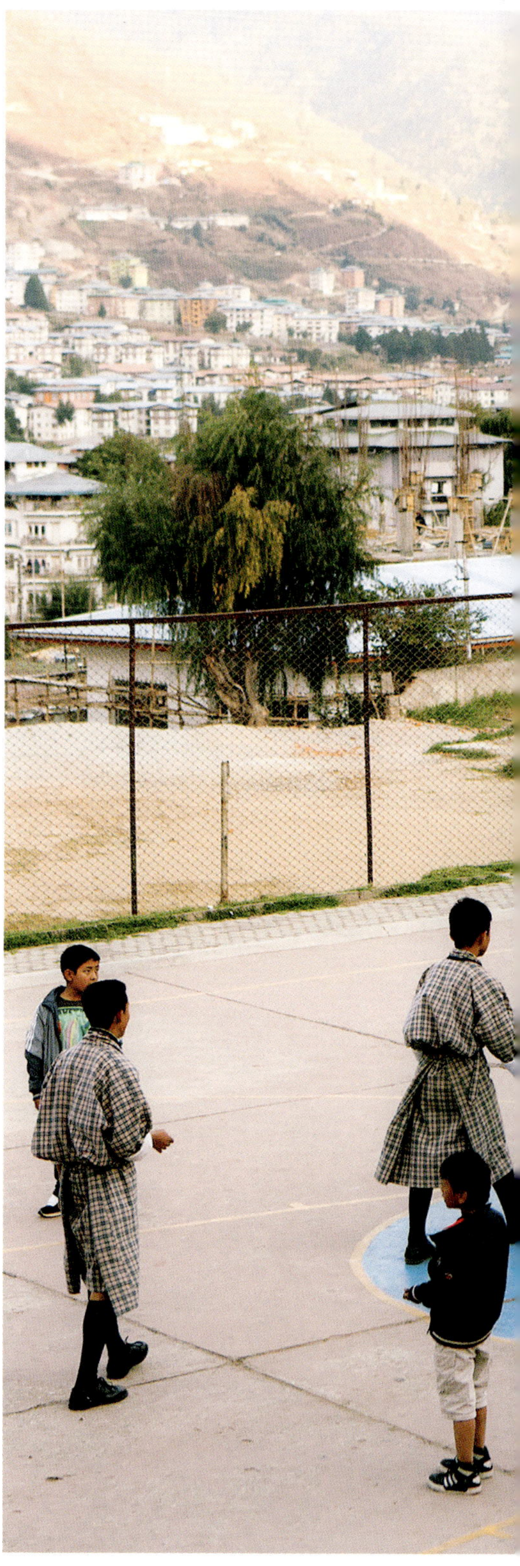

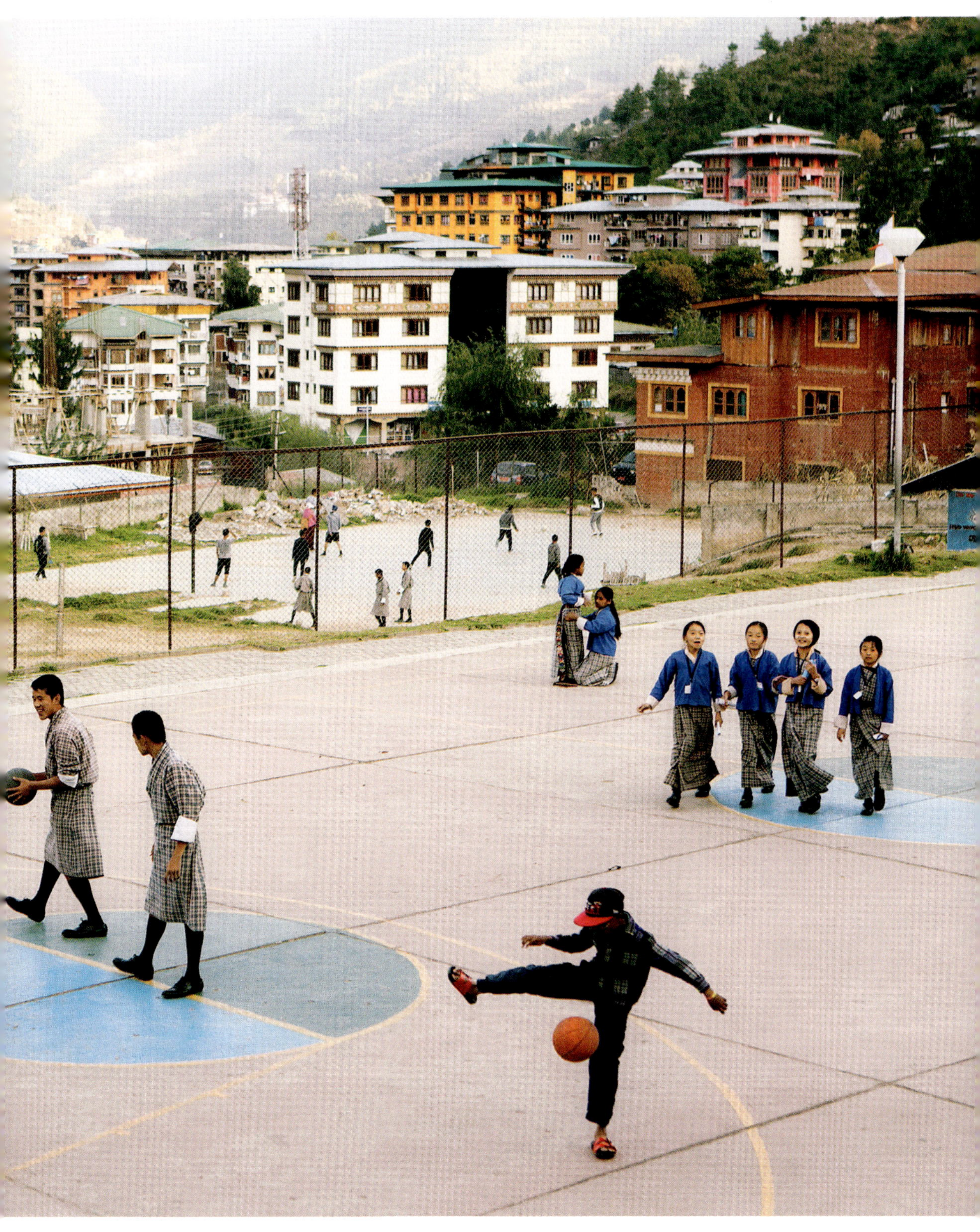

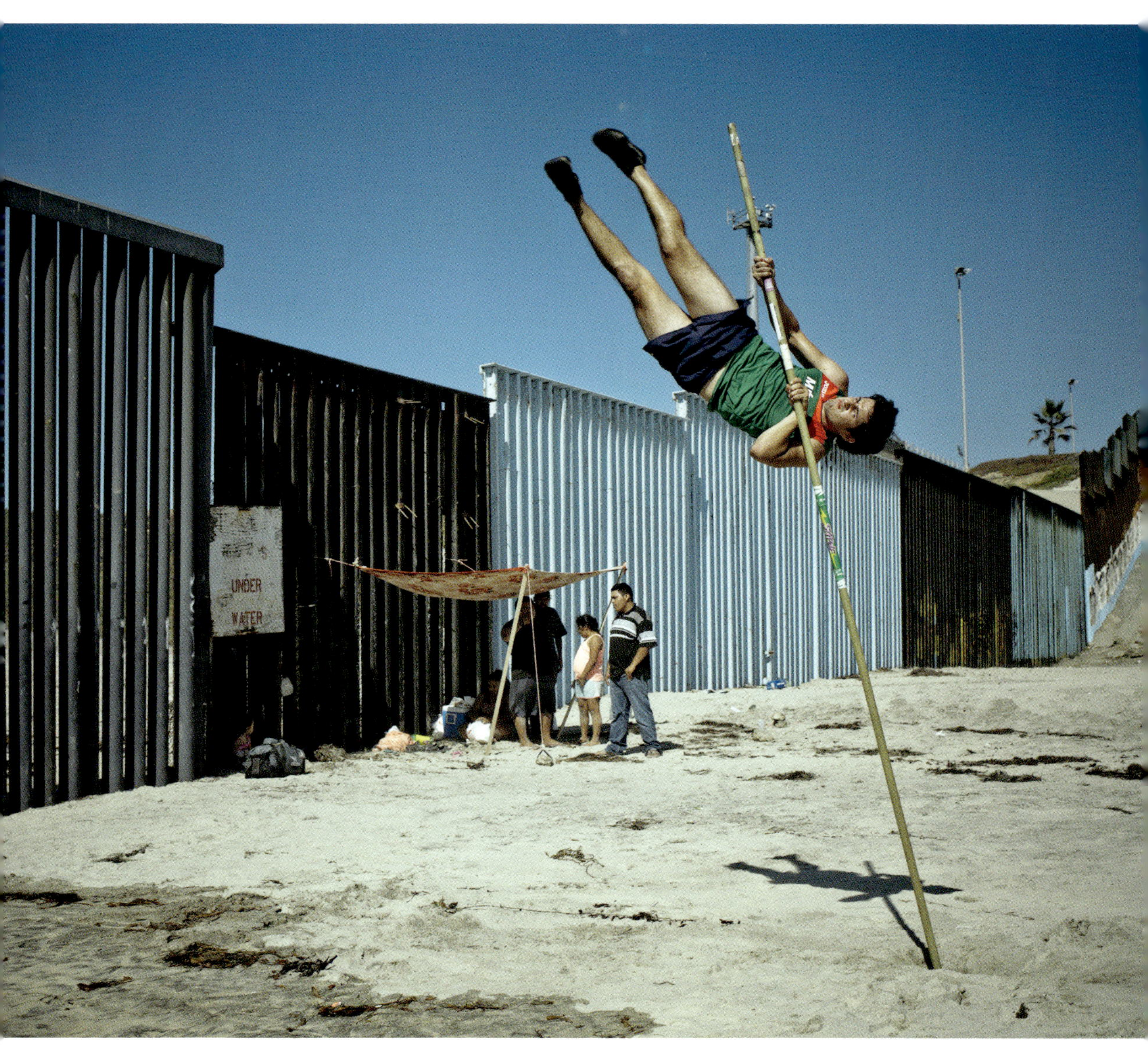
UNDER
WATER

◀

Cristina de Middel

Spanish

El último beso

Tijuana, Mexico; 2018

This image is part of the series Journey to the Center that presents the migrants of the Central American route as heroes rather than victims or runaways. I started the project in 2015 after finding Felicity, a roadside attraction town along the Mexico–California border that claims to be the official centre of the world and formed a link with Jules Verne's adventure novel. After 10 years as a photojournalist, I realized that the strategy of raising awareness by escalating drama only makes it more difficult for our audience to engage and feel connected to the news. I have since approached many classical documentary stories from a personal angle and with complete narrative freedom. With such an over-reported topic as migration, I decided to cultivate admiration instead of pity in viewers, and for this image, I contacted the athletic club of Tijuana and asked them to have jumpers train by the border fence. For me, this image shows the absurdity of borders when removed from their symbolic power, how brave migrants need to be to cross the border and also how different the understanding of migration would be if we shifted the way we present it to the world.

▶▶

Tanya Habjouqa

Jordanian American

Women in Gaza

Gaza City Beach, Gaza; 2009

During the 2009 Gaza War, I remember watching in horror, the devastation wrought by two-tonne bombs on the civilian population that had already endured layers of trauma from decades of Israeli occupation. It was triggering, especially as four years earlier, I had documented the 2006 Lebanon War. Yet the majority of Lebanese people had the ability to flee . . . via ships, land borders, the mountains, quieter corners of the country. But Palestinians could not escape. Just a few months after, media focus on Gaza circled almost exclusively around women's rights under Hamas, without any reference to how the devastation also affected women's lives. Unable to gain a press card, I found my way from the Israel-controlled border with an NGO. I decided to explore Gaza exclusively through women. Within just a few weeks, I started to feel a circling depression. I found myself retreating along the same sea highway. It was there that I found Palestinian families pausing, often in silence. I found this family – in perfect communion with the sea and each other – and felt a sense of healing from the testimonies I was gathering. I took the picture and was beckoned to join them.

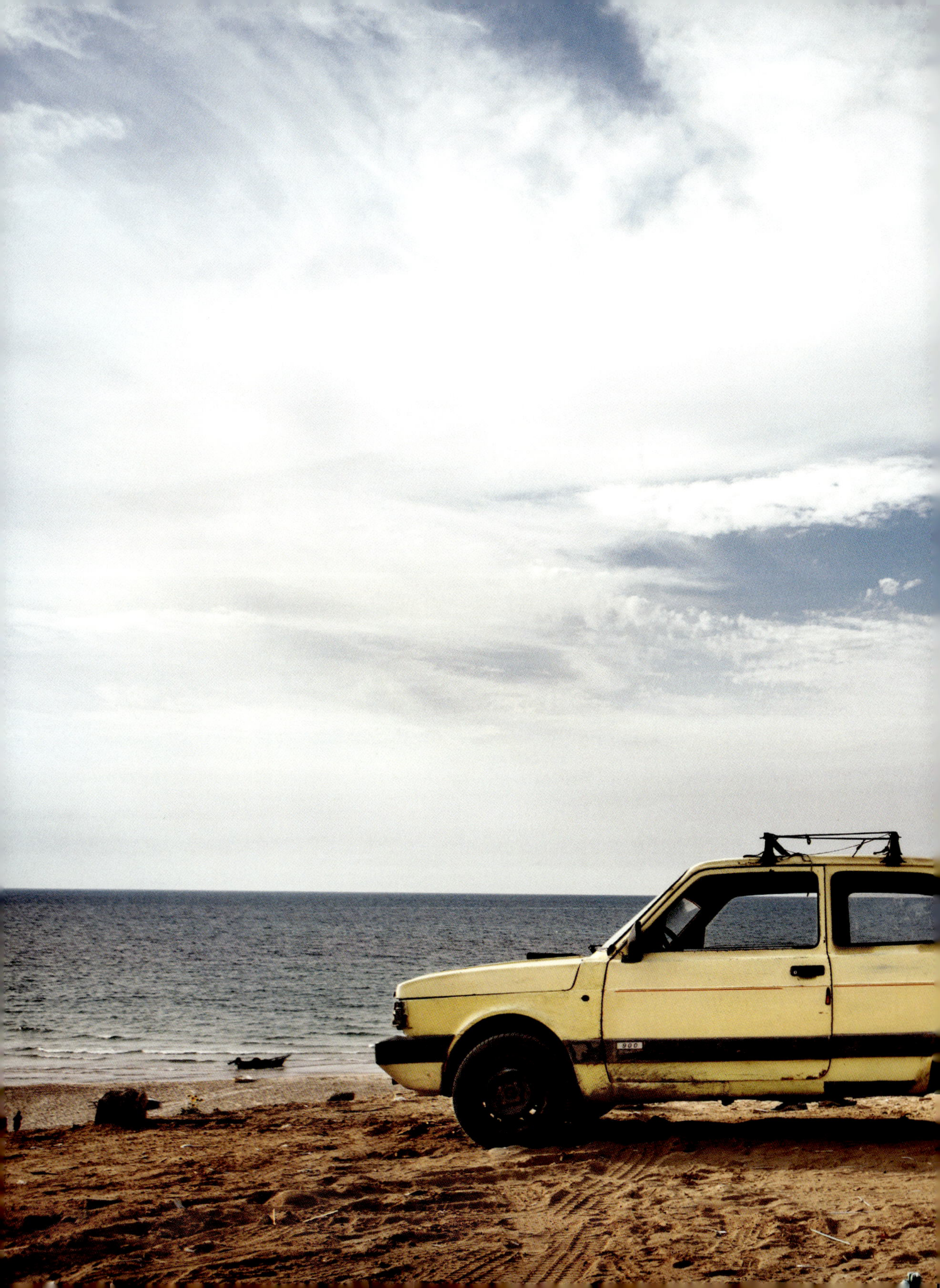
900

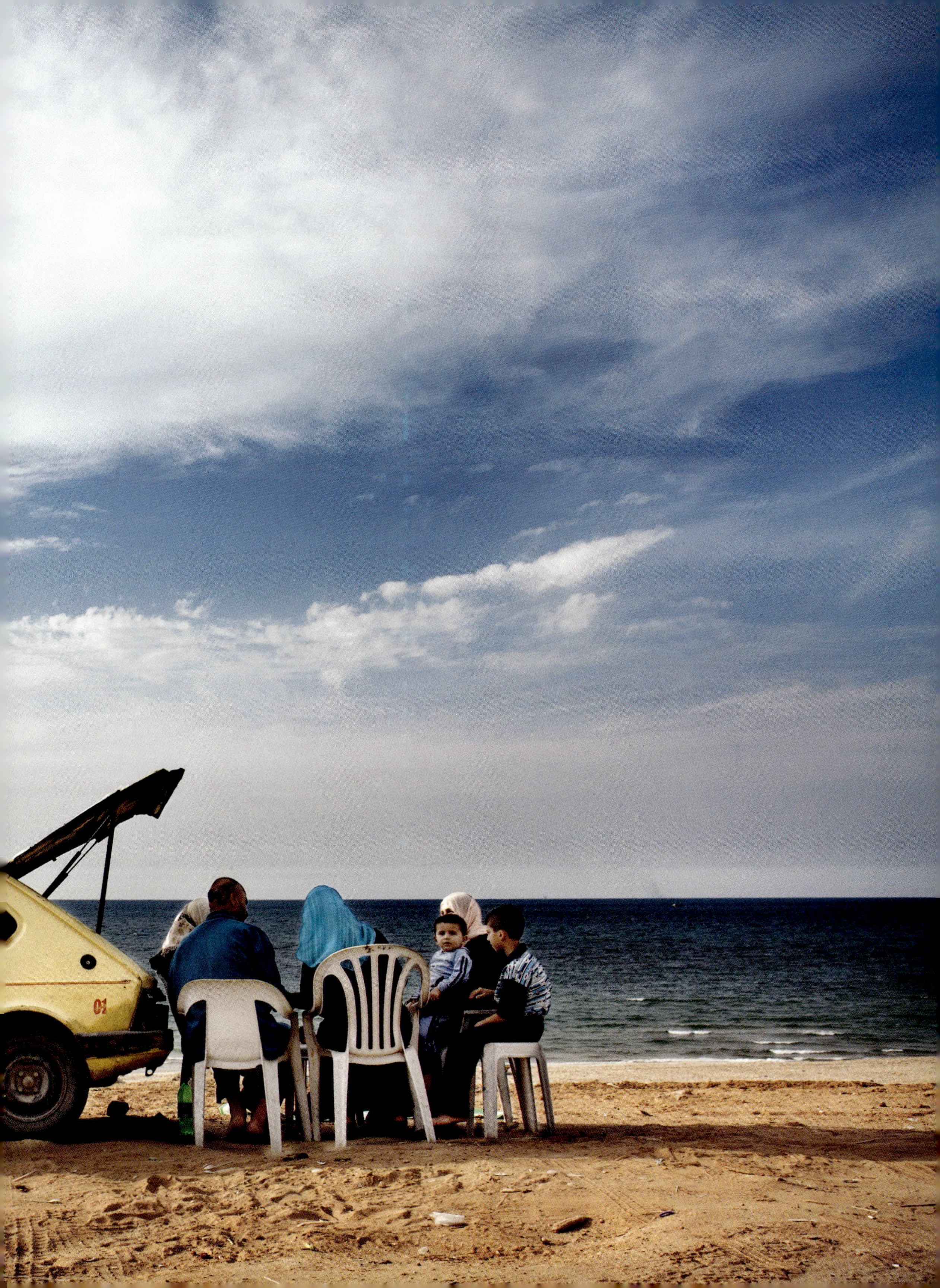

Irina Unruh

German

Shy Girl

Kyrgyzstan; 2019

My *Shy Girl* photograph from January 2019 is one of my dearest pictures from my long-term project, Unfolding Kyrgyzstan – Where the Poplars Grow, about my reencounter and my relationship with my native country. I was born in today's Kyrgyzstan when it was part of the Soviet Union and immigrated to Germany in 1988 as a nine-year-old girl. Since 2008, I have regularly visited Kyrgyzstan, now an independent and democratic country in central Asia. Meeting the shy girl was an adorable coincidence. I was driving down the long road on the north shore of Lake Issyk Kul with two friends in the car when I saw this bus in the distance. My friends laughed at me for wanting to stop immediately and run and take a picture of this 'old and broken' bus. But for me, it was a beautiful encounter with the past and reminded me of my childhood in Kyrgyzstan. When I reached the bus, I noticed it was without wheels and that children used it as a playground. While one shy girl decided to be photographed, several other children played hide and seek. They are hiding in the bus, having fun and laughing.

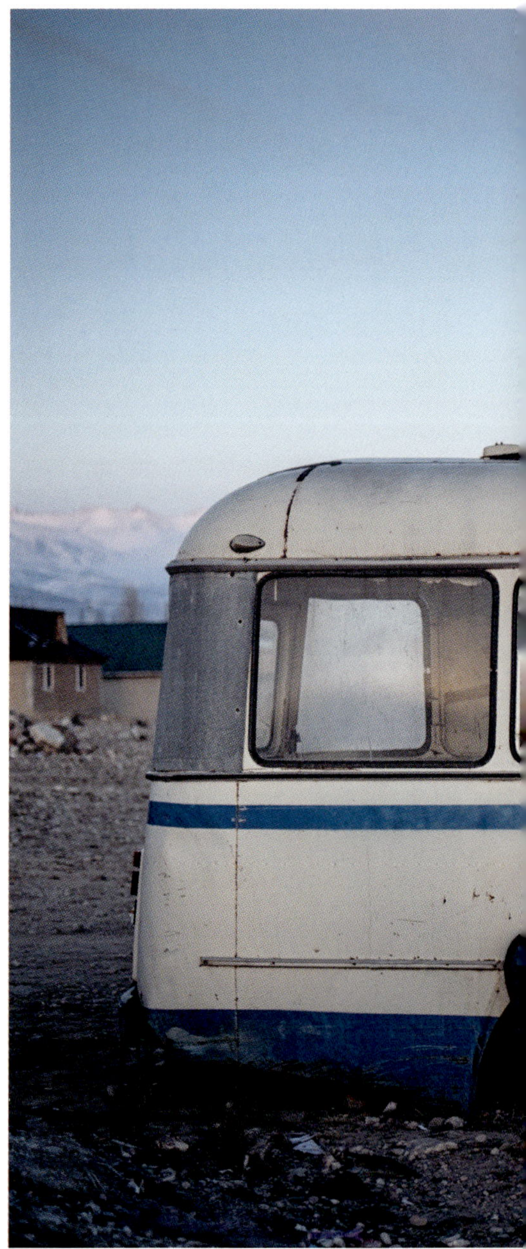

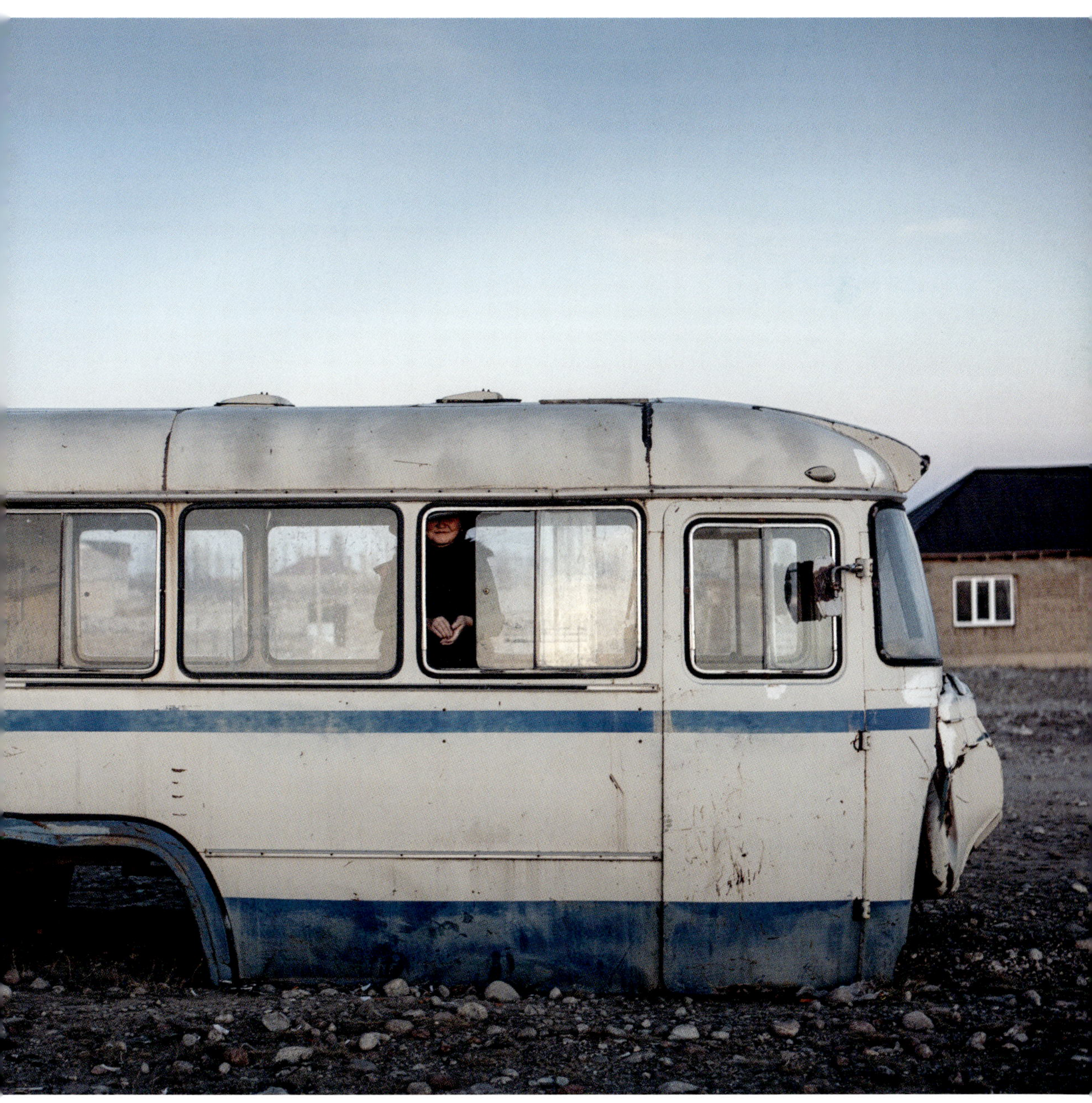

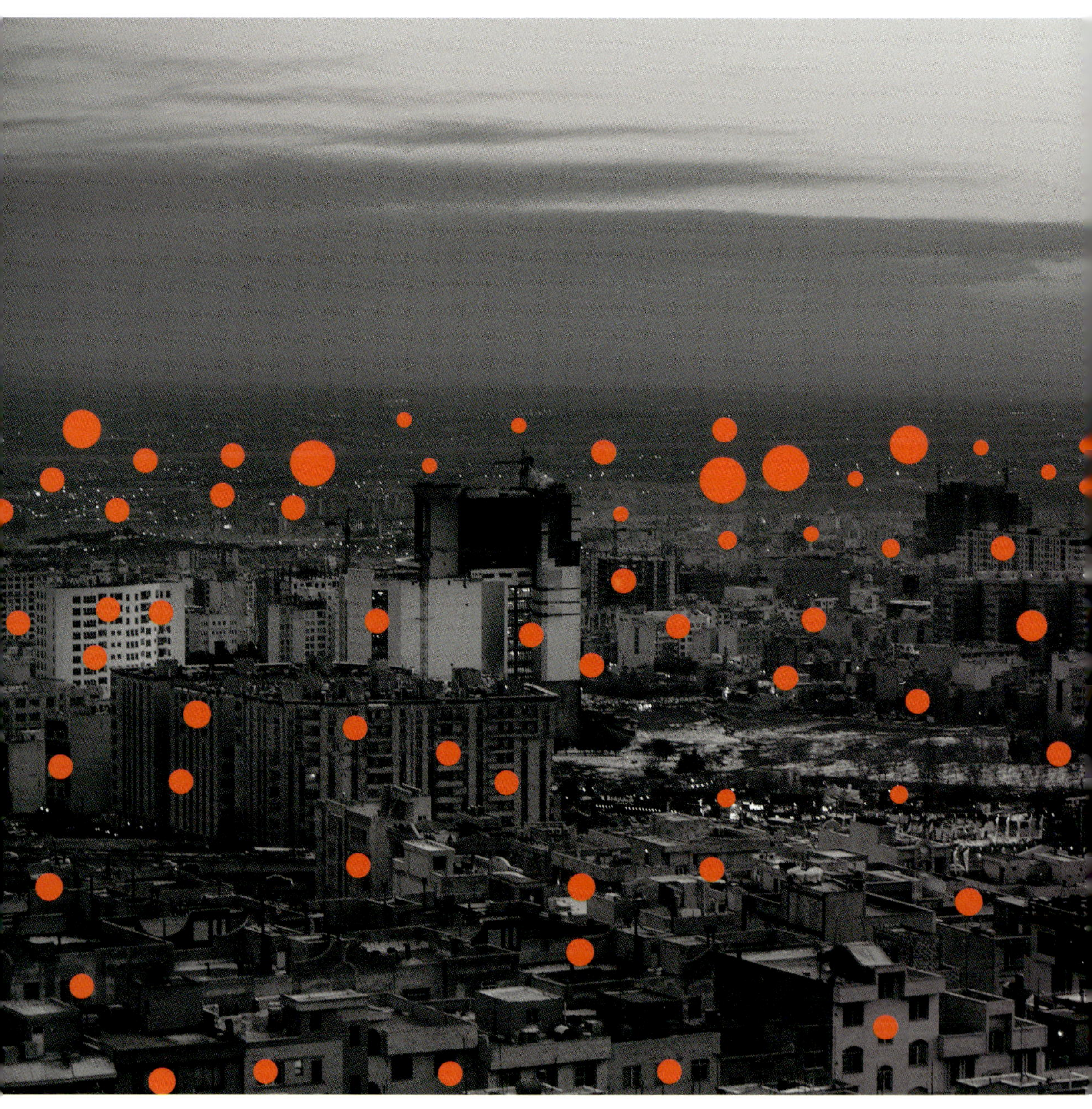

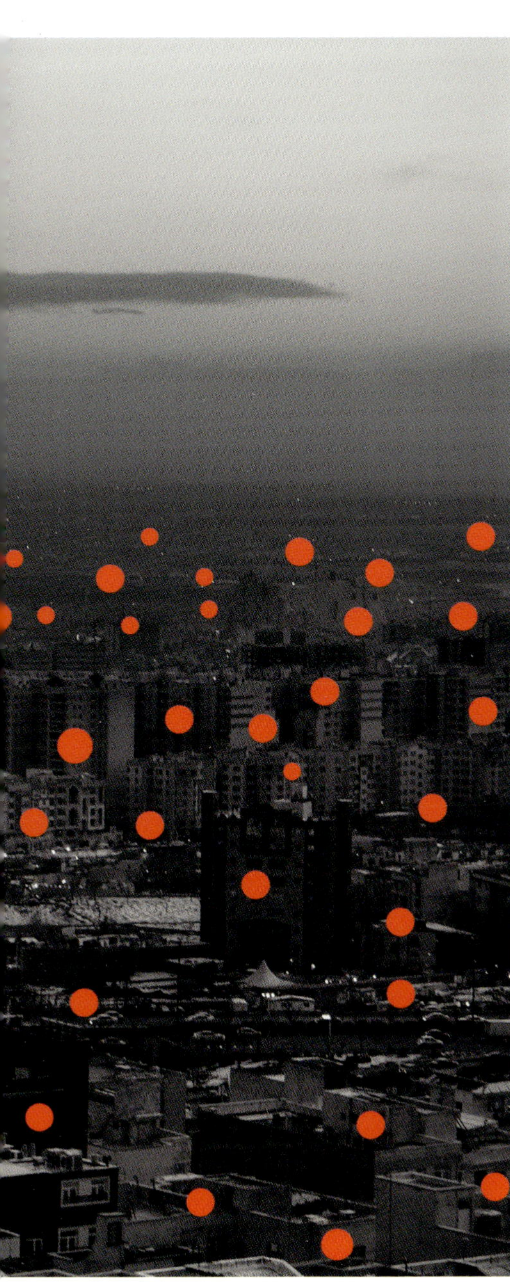

Mojgan Ghanbari

Iranian

Tehran's view in March 2020

Tehran, Iran; 2020

I captured this photo of the Tehran skyline in February 2020. It was an ordinary moment on a regular day and I did not know this was going to be my last time in a public place before the COVID-19 pandemic. For the next 40 days I went into a self-quarantine, facing the fear of the unknown, loss, death and sickness. I noticed that, more than being just a storyteller, I was the subject of this significant narrative. That realization inspired me to start a photography project somewhat like a diary. Outside my home, Iran's death toll was rising every minute. The reality of life in my hometown, Tehran, was changing and its coverage in the media did not represent my feelings. In my attempt to link the past to this new reality, I stared at my photographs from life before the lockdowns. Everywhere seemed to be a dangerous contagious spot now and apartments were filled with families who were grieving for the loss of their loved ones. Something compelled me to change my Tehran skyline photograph to black and white and add the red dots as an expression of how the pandemic was affecting people in this place. In March 2020 alone, 2,575 people died in Iran.

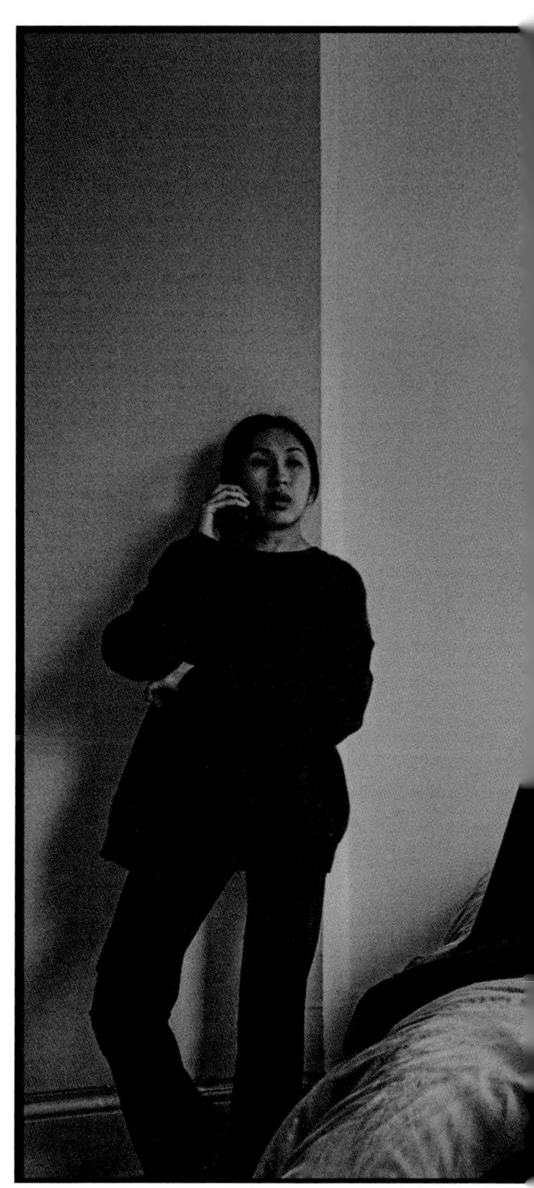

Haruka Sakaguchi

Japanese

Quarantine Diary: March 25, 2020

Brooklyn, New York, USA; 2020

This is an image from a photo diary that I kept during the first month of lockdown in New York City, from the official shelter-in-place order that spanned 20 March to 20 April 2020. I have a history of depression and live alone, so I feared that isolation would exacerbate past mental health issues. I gave myself an assignment to make one photo every day to restore some semblance of routine and normalcy during the early days of the pandemic. The diary entry for this image reads: 'Woke up to news that my Chinese friend got jumped on the subway last night. He was on his way back from the hospital, caring for his brother who was recently admitted for a non-COVID-related illness. He is okay physically, but his partner fears that it may have triggered his PTSD. I spent the rest of the day trying to stay busy and productive, so my mind doesn't wander off to dark places. I'm scared to go outside.' When starting out in my career as a documentary photographer, I strove for journalistic objectivity – since the pandemic, however, I have become more open to non-traditional approaches to storytelling, like turning the camera on myself.

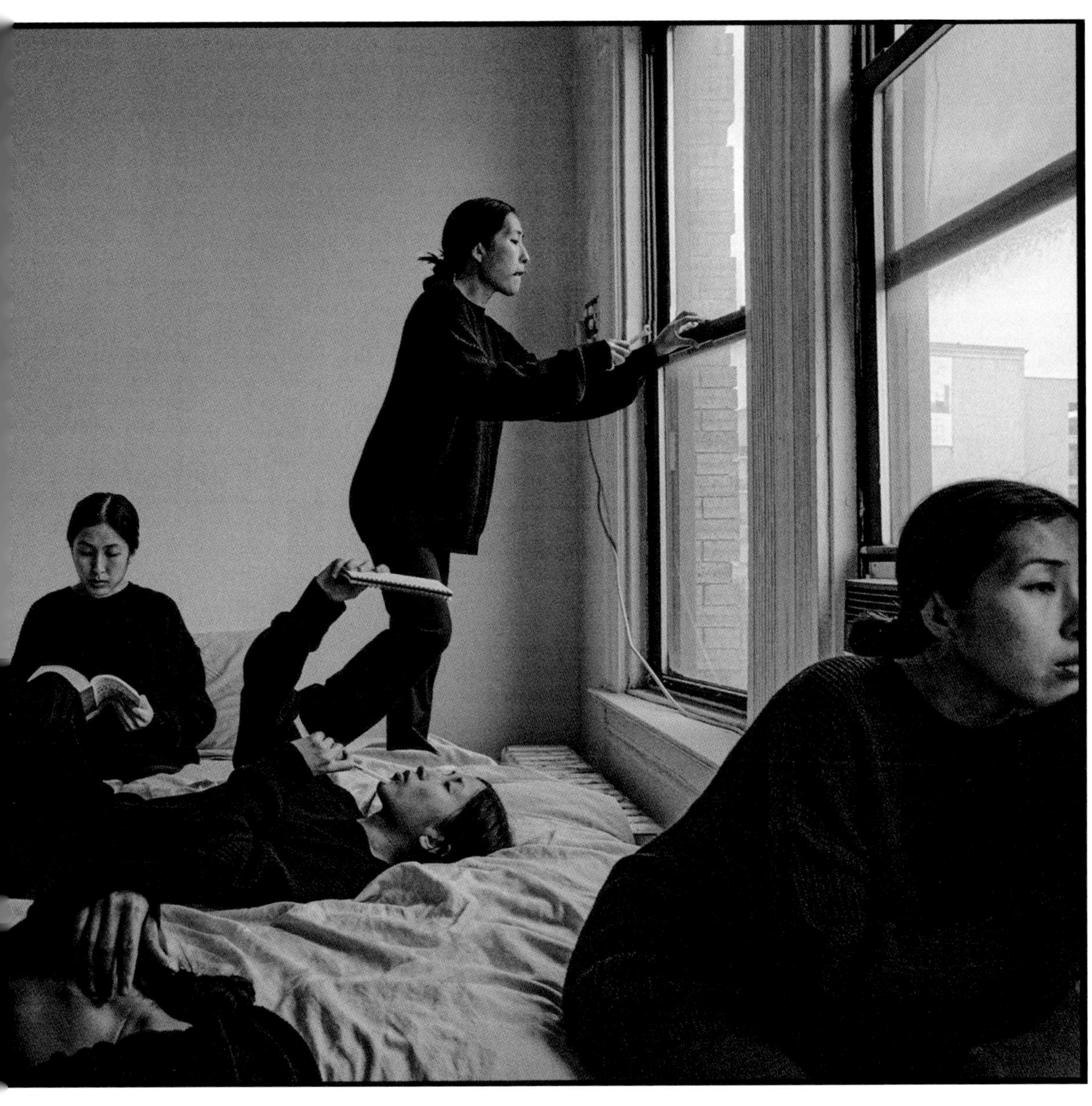

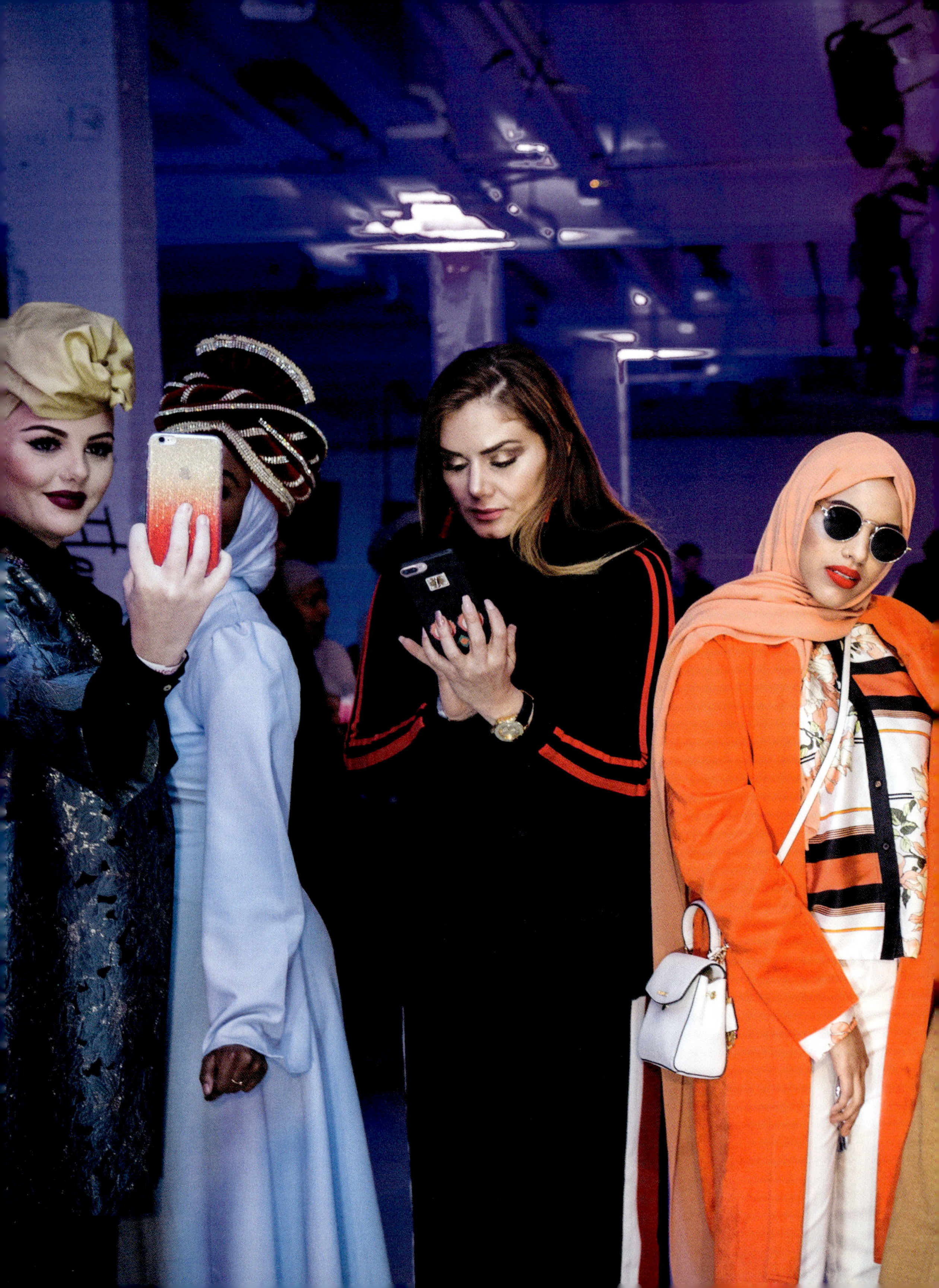

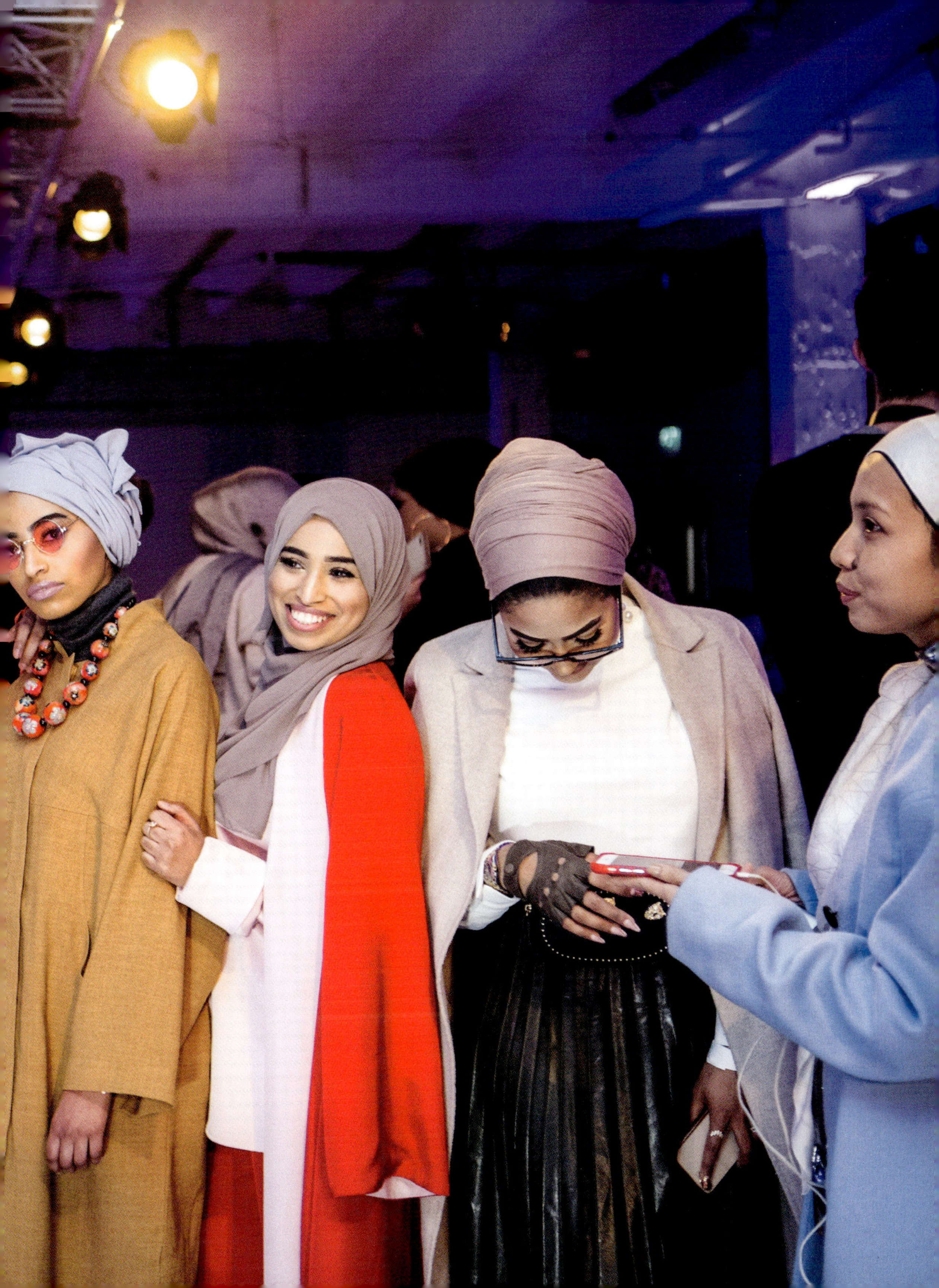

◂◂

Natalie Naccache

British Lebanese

Modestly

London, UK; 2018

In this photograph, attendees pose before a fashion show at the London Modest Fashion Week. Modest fashion has exploded in recent years and become a major trend in the fashion industry, reflected in the popularity of Somali-American model Halima Aden, who graced the cover of *Vogue* magazine in a headscarf in 2018, and is frequently seen on international Fashion Week catwalks. In my work, I often challenge preconceived ideas of the Middle East in modern-day society, so I travelled to London, Qatar, Dubai and Kuwait to investigate this fashion trend disrupting the fashion economy. The term 'modest fashion' refers to wearing less skin-revealing clothing, loose clothing and covering of the body according to one's own comfort and religious beliefs. Luxury fashion houses such as Dolce & Gabbana now sell *abayas* (a simple, loose over-garment, essentially a robe-like dress) and the fashion houses DKNY, Michael Kors and Zara launched Ramadan collections. Big brands can no longer ignore the strong spending power from Gulf countries, and now have catered towards modest fashion in the region and the Western world. Through social media, Muslim women have shared fashion trends, make-up styles and ways to style a headscarf, creating a large online community and providing evidence that fashion and religion can mix.

▸

Olivia Locher

American

In Alabama it's illegal to have an ice cream cone in your back pocket at all times

New York, New York, USA; 2013

In 2012, I was photographing a friend for my thesis and out of nowhere he said, 'In Alabama, it's illegal to have an ice cream cone in your back pocket'. That ridiculous fact haunted me for over a year. The next year, I was visiting my family in Pennsylvania, when the impulse struck to go out and turn this idea into a photo. I knew I'd never be able to get a perfect ice cream cone back to my studio, so instead I brought a makeshift studio to the local ice cream stand. My friend Jackie became the model. We unloaded our car with a large purple canvas that I painted to serve as a backdrop and off we went to get a cone. We found our way to a wooded area behind the stand. Jackie put the ice cream in her pocket, and we waited for it to start melting. Creating this image taught me that you can always make photographs even under unusually strange conditions; you just must go with the flow and trust the idea. That photograph was the birth of my project, I Fought the Law, where I created a visual representation of one weird law from each American state.

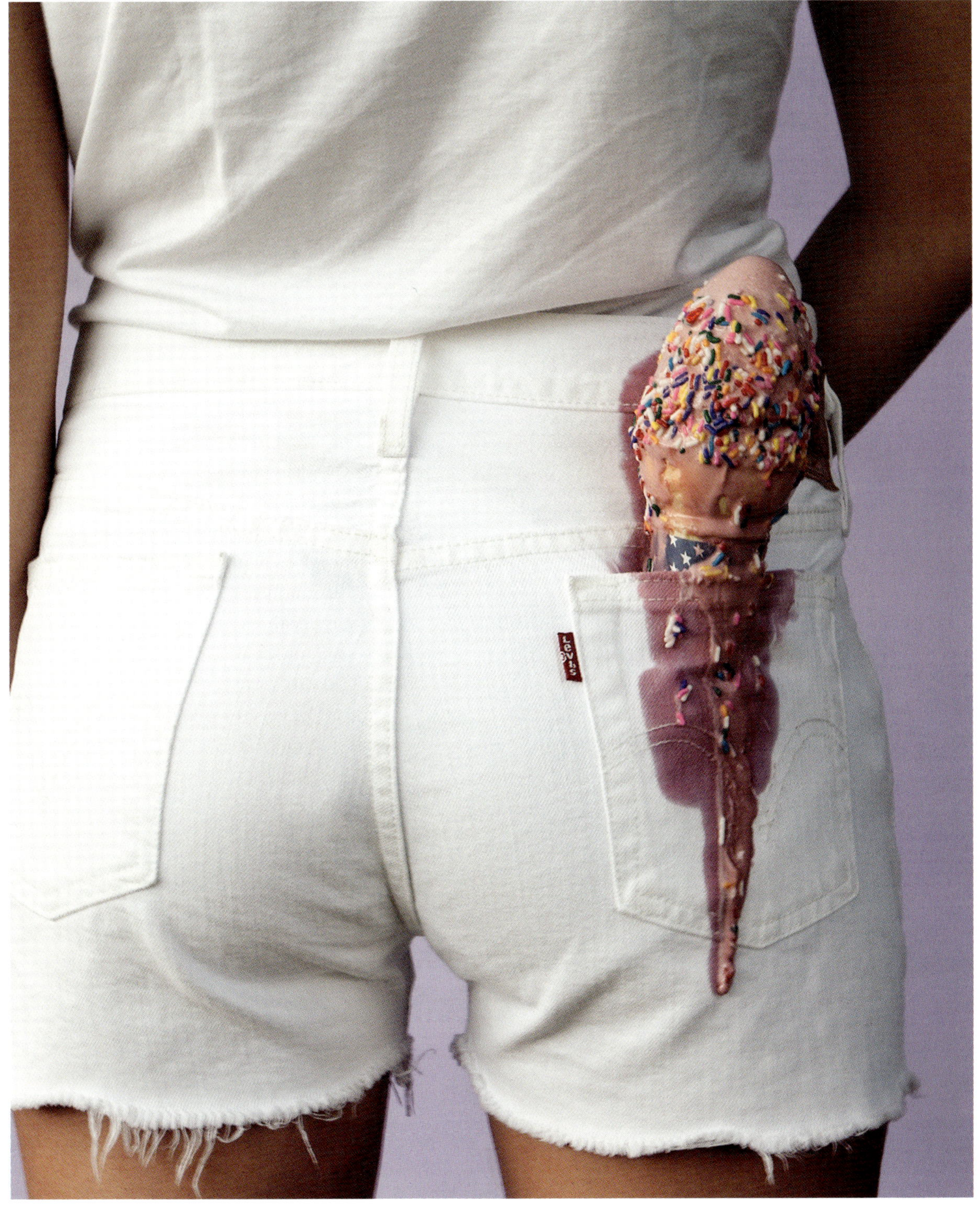
Levi's

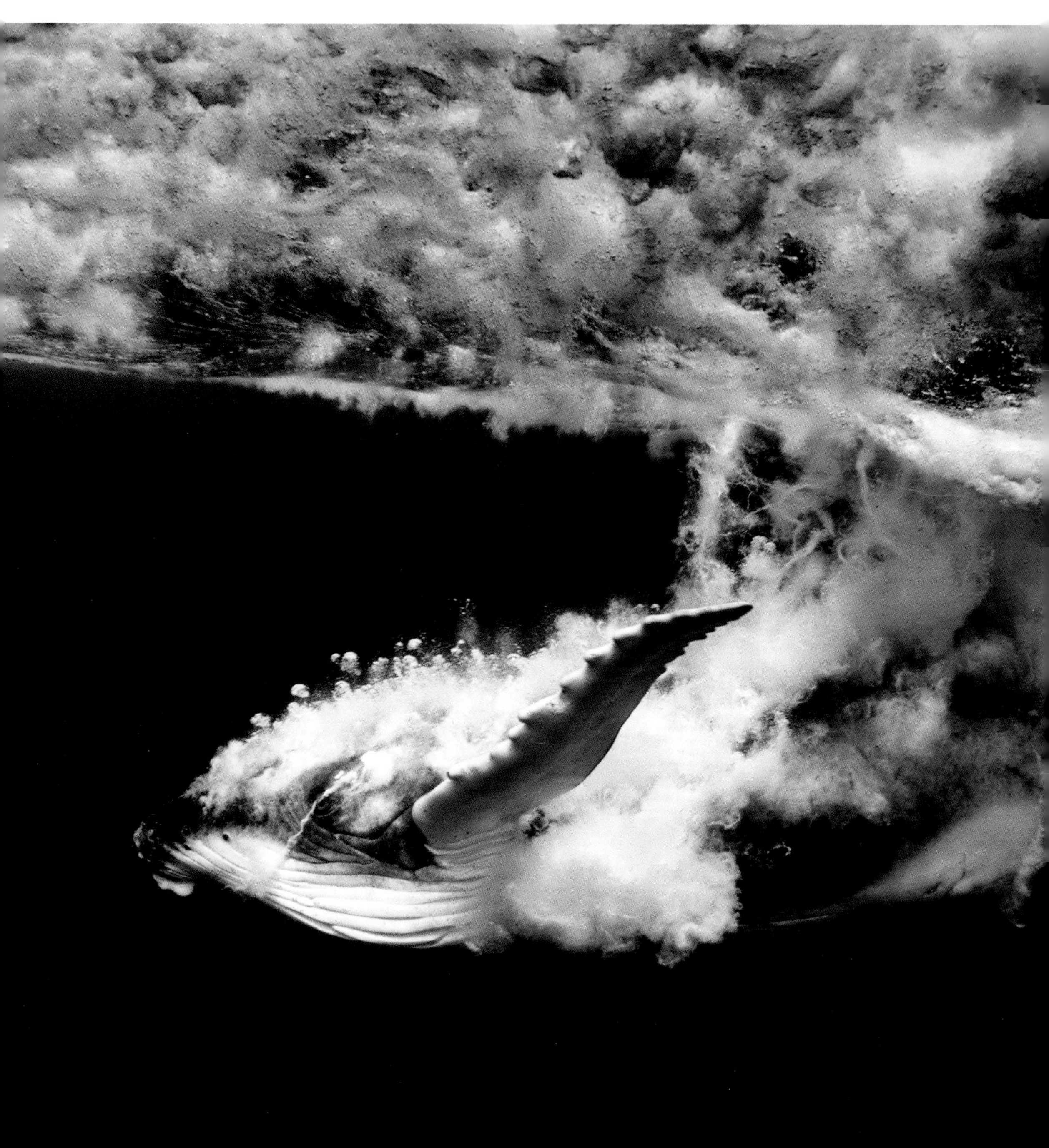

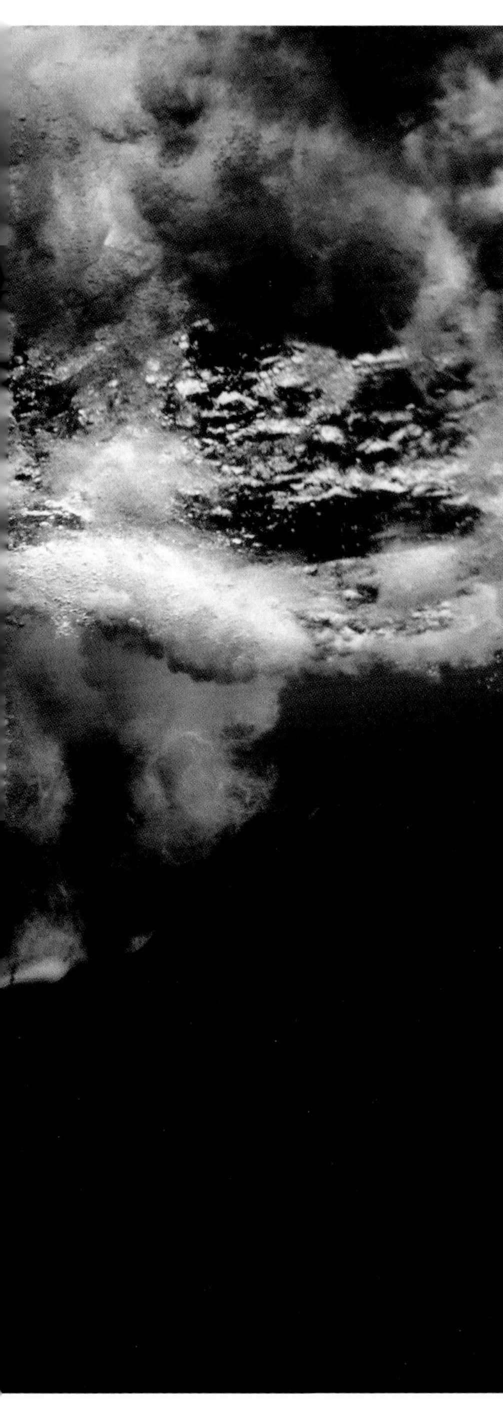

Michaela Skovranova

Australian Slovakian

Submergence

Vava'u, Kingdom of Tonga; 2014

Every year, thousands of humpback whales migrate from the nutrient-rich waters of Antarctica to the warm waters of Tonga to breed and give birth. Young calves are often seen breaching and displaying similar behaviours to their mums – they play and imitate them while they learn how to navigate the ocean. For the first year of a calf's life, the mother will always be nearby as they prepare and support them throughout their migration. The annual migration of humpback whales is one of the largest and longest animal movements in the world. The calves are believed to consume up to 150 litres (40 gallons) of their mother's milk per day, allowing them to gain weight at the rate of about 45 kilograms (100 pounds) per day in preparation for a long journey south. This juvenile humpback whale was photographed post-breach just metres away from us. The landing created a small forceful wave. I was lucky to press the shutter moments before the whale disappeared in a haze of bubbles. This was my very first time documenting humpback whales. I have never had an experience like it since, and likely never will. It was truly a special moment to share with these gentle giants.

Nicola Muirhead

Bermudian

The Waves

The River Thames, London, UK; 2020

This is an image from my series Unseen, a collection of Polaroids taken in London during the COVID-19 pandemic. Like most photographers, I sought to document my days in isolation. However, I felt a huge disconnect from the images I was capturing. None of them conveyed the urgency of the present moment and the seriousness of this time in history – nor the collective fear and anxiety felt across the globe. I started experimenting with our frontline of defence, the disinfectants and household cleaners meant to keep us safe from the virus, and applied them directly to the Polaroids. This process created dream-like and often dystopian manifestations of the world around us, uncovering what I felt looked like the 'face' of the coronavirus in the unassuming moments of daily life. The series then grew into a visual exploration of the psychological landscape of the pandemic, as I ventured out into the city of London, and eventually to various parts of the United Kingdom. This ritual offered a moment to pause and reflect, recognizing the resilience of the human spirit in the midst of this invisible threat and how simple moments once taken for granted, are now all the more meaningful and sacred.

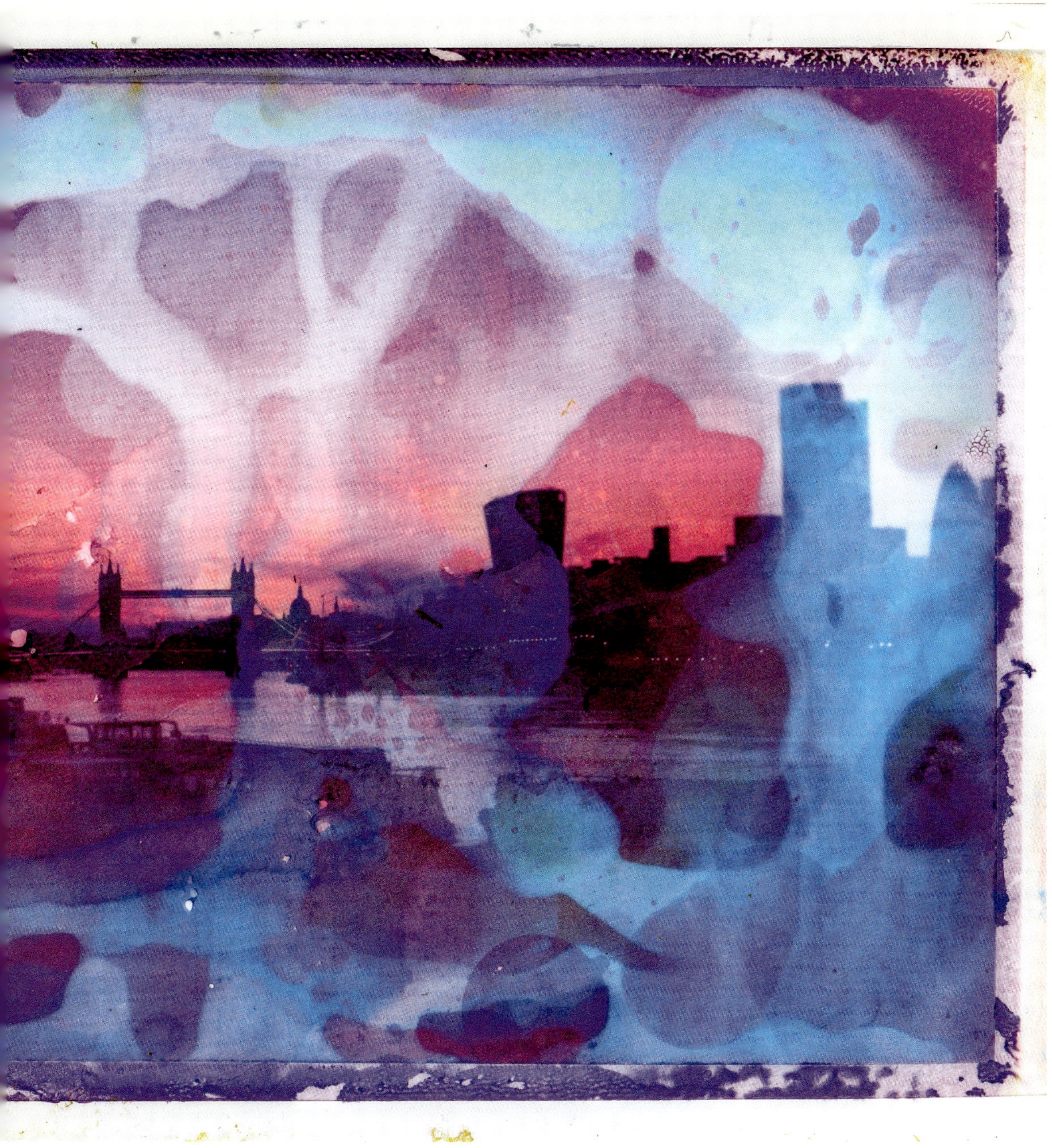

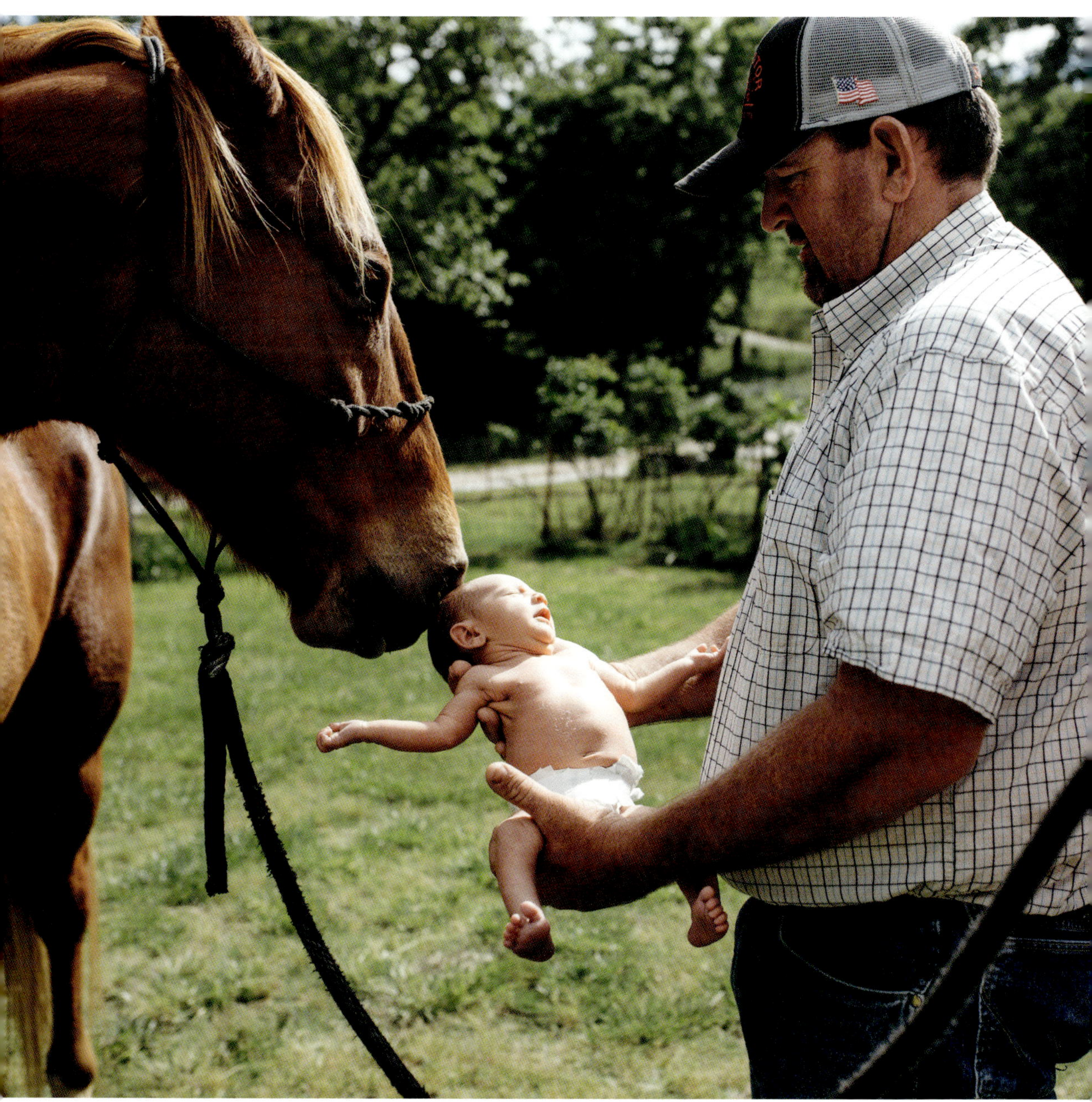

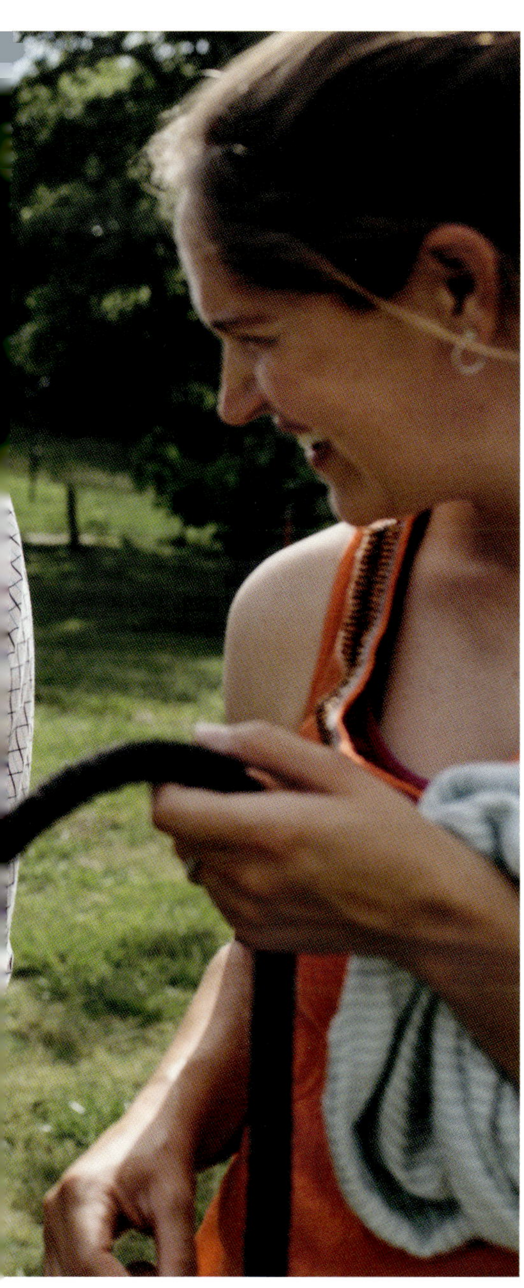

Terra Fondriest

American

The Introduction

Harrison, Arkansas, USA; 2017

This image was part of a turning point in my photography, as the reaction to this photo opened my eyes to the larger audience that was interested in seeing images of everyday life in rural America from the perspective of someone living it. I was visiting my good friend Rachel to meet her newborn son Kal and snap some baby pictures. Rachel and I go back; having bonded over our love of horses, we met pre-kids, pre-marriage and rode horses most of those days (the 'glory days' as we jokingly call them). She ended up marrying a local cattle rancher and horses are part of their everyday life. So, when we were walking around their farm, it felt natural to include the horses. This moment was not any sort of unique idea, it unfolded in front of me and I clicked the shutter. And while I did not think much of it at first, it received strong reactions when I shared it more widely. This got me thinking how moments from our everyday lives that seem pretty mundane might be interesting to outsiders. This became the early stages of my decade-long project Ozark Life, documenting life as I see it here in this rural portion of the United States from the perspective of a mother and community member.

Sarah Pabst

German Argentinian

The Jump

Weddell Sea, Antarctica; 2020

Adélie penguins jump from an iceberg in the Weddell Sea. I took this photograph while working on an assignment on climate change and the Southern Ocean. This was the first time I had been away from my daughter for several weeks after becoming a mother. Besides the magic of the moment, the sound of the ice, the cold and these funny, yet graceful little creatures, I felt deeply related to that mid-flight penguin. It was somehow me throwing myself into this life, accepting who I am, my job, my passion. The Adélie penguin population is in decline, as are all others depending solely on krill, the foundation of the food chain. Penguins give important insight into what is happening on a global level. Seeing climate change so directly changed me deeply. I started to focus even more on environmental issues in my personal work. Three days after I took this photo, on 7 February 2020, a record high temperature of 18.3°C (64.9°F) was logged on the continent of Antarctica. Directly after our return, the pandemic arrived in Argentina, and we found ourselves in strict quarantine.

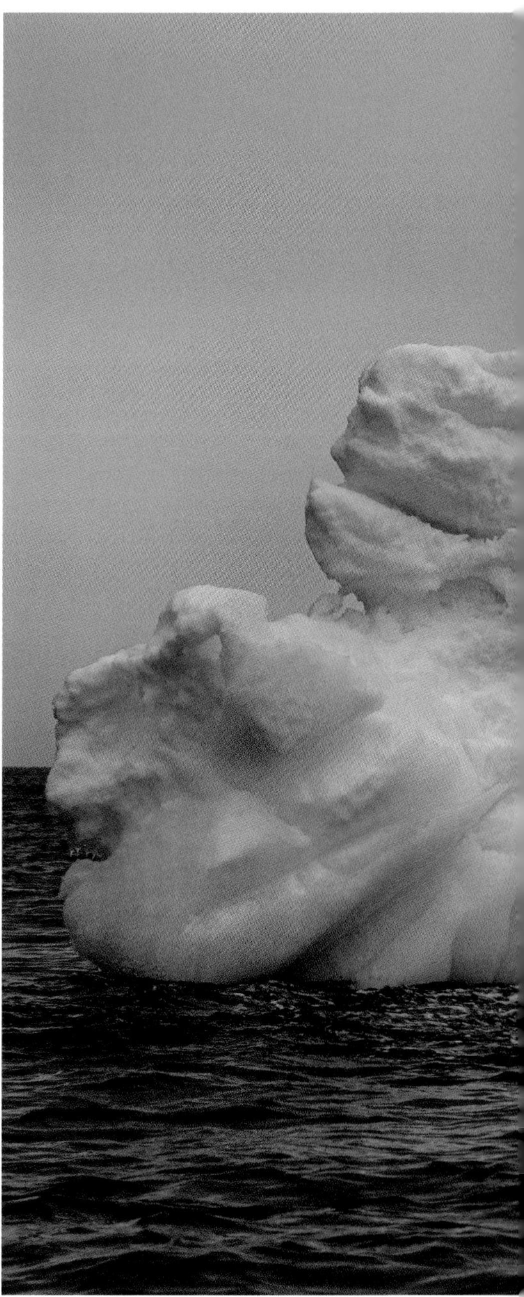

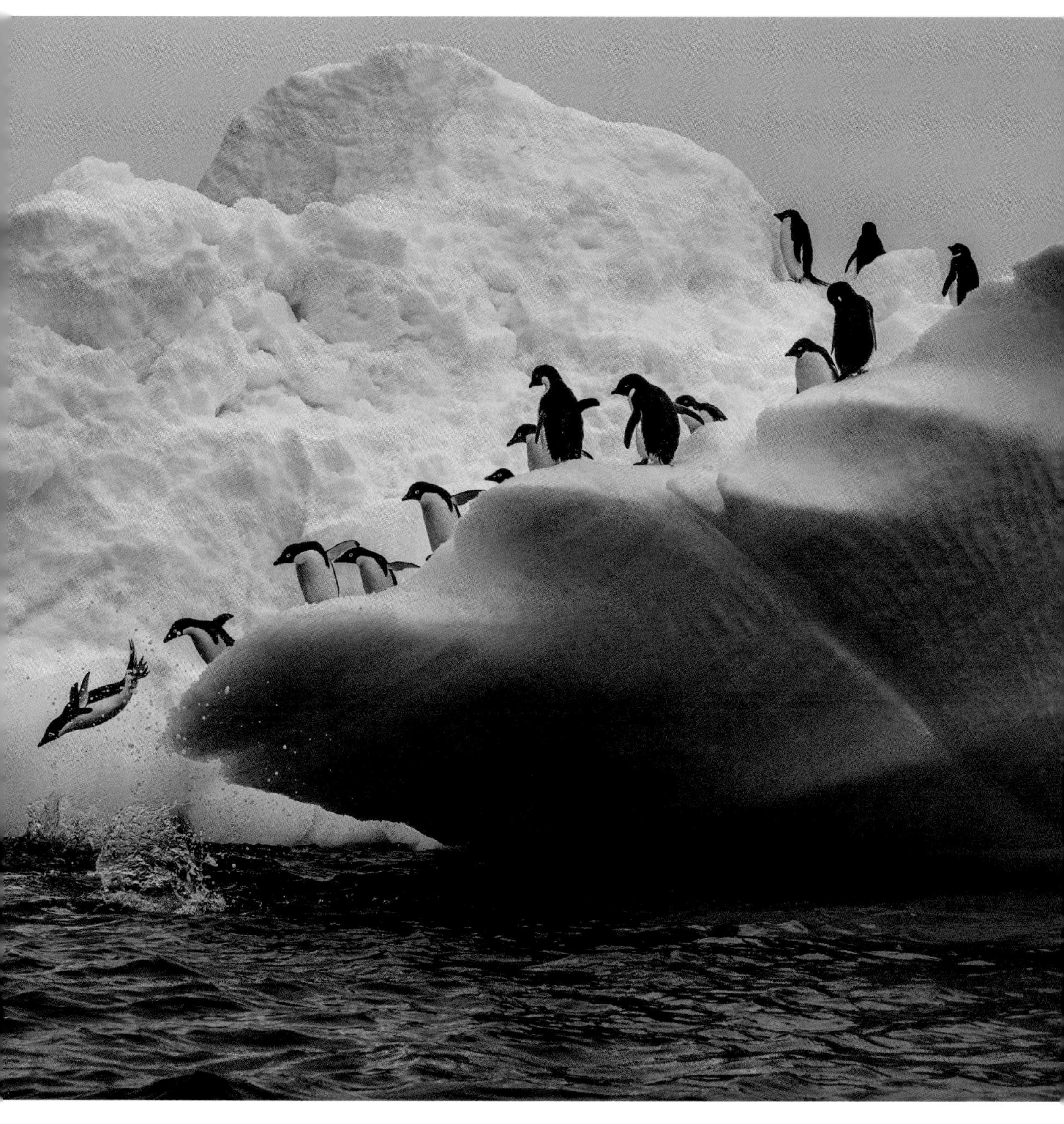

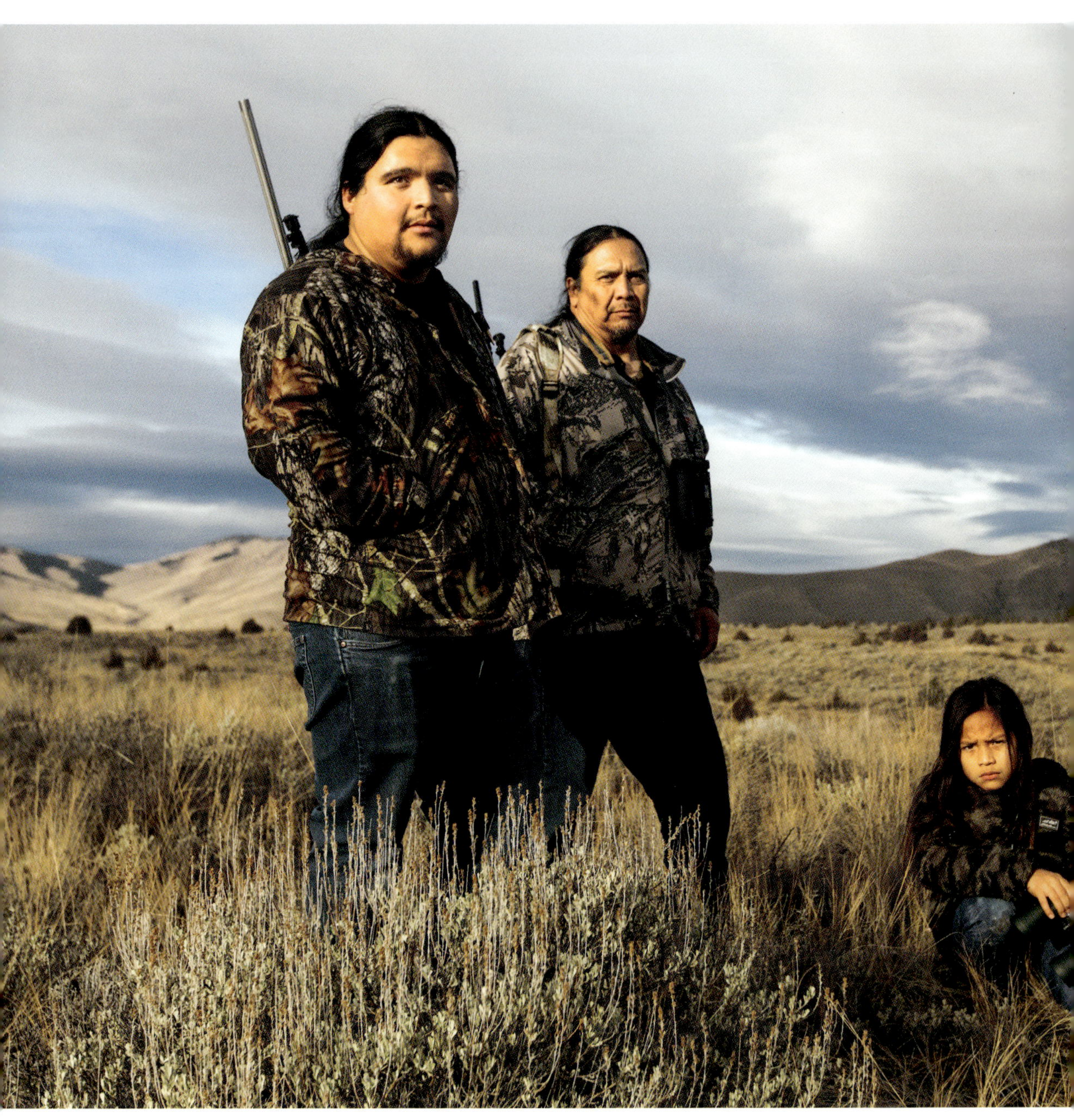

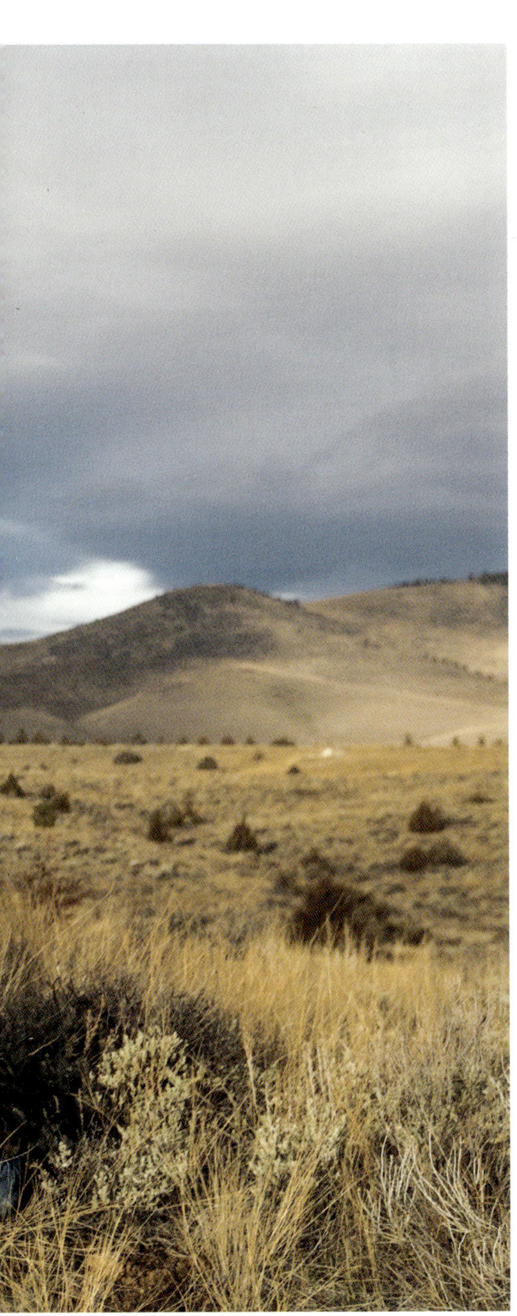

Tailyr Irvine

American

Thanksgiving Hunt

Flathead Reservation, Montana, USA; 2021

We began the day at sunrise near the bottom of a mountain on our reservation. My father and myself on one side of the hill and my brother and nephew on the other. We hiked up and around hills through miles of brush along a river until we met in the middle. As we walked, my dad told me about the memories certain trees, mountains and saddles held from similar trips with his father. We talked about the relatives we lost this year visiting our dreams. We did not talk at all for long stretches. My brother shared his own stories of the land with my nephew. This photo of my father, brother and nephew represents generations of memories and stories. It represents the depth and history of hunting in our family and shows how the quiet moments, like the moment in the image, are the foundation of our traditions. Photographing my family is my way of shifting the narrative from the damaging, stereotypical portrayals of Native Americans produced by outsiders for centuries to a narrative that is honest and represents pieces of my life and my family's lives as Salish and Kootenai people.

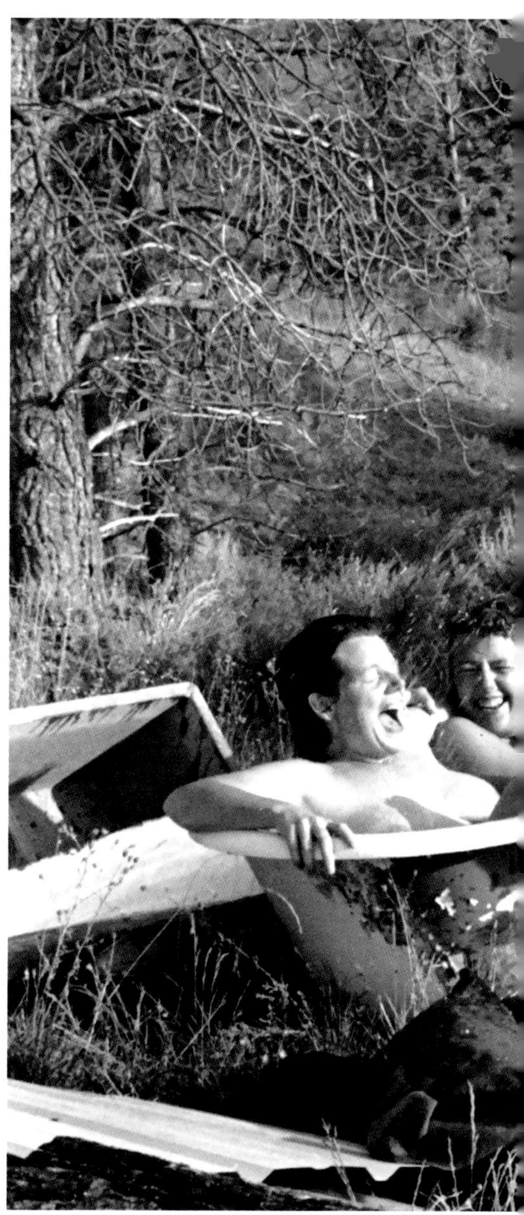

JEB (Joan E. Biren)

American

Three in a Tub

Bitterroot Valley, Montana, USA; 1987

I made this image as I was photographing for my second book, *Making A Way: Lesbians Out Front*, originally published in 1987. I wanted my book to include as many aspects of the lesbian community in the United States as possible. I went to places that people might not have expected to find thriving communities, like the Bitterroot Valley in Montana. Many women there built their own homes with the help of their friends. Those pictured here had just finished backfilling a ditch that ran a power line. They took a sauna and cooled off outside after they were done shovelling. Whenever I am on women's land where lesbians feel safe, I experience and witness a rare sense of freedom. I wanted to embrace this sense of freedom with my photographs. The women here are unselfconscious about being naked and their delight is unmistakable. Although other images from the Bitterroot Valley community were included in *Making A Way*, I did not have space for this one. *Making A Way* is being reissued by Anthology Editions because, in the United States and around the world, the rights of LGBTQ+ people are under renewed attack. We need positive representations of how to build community and fight back.

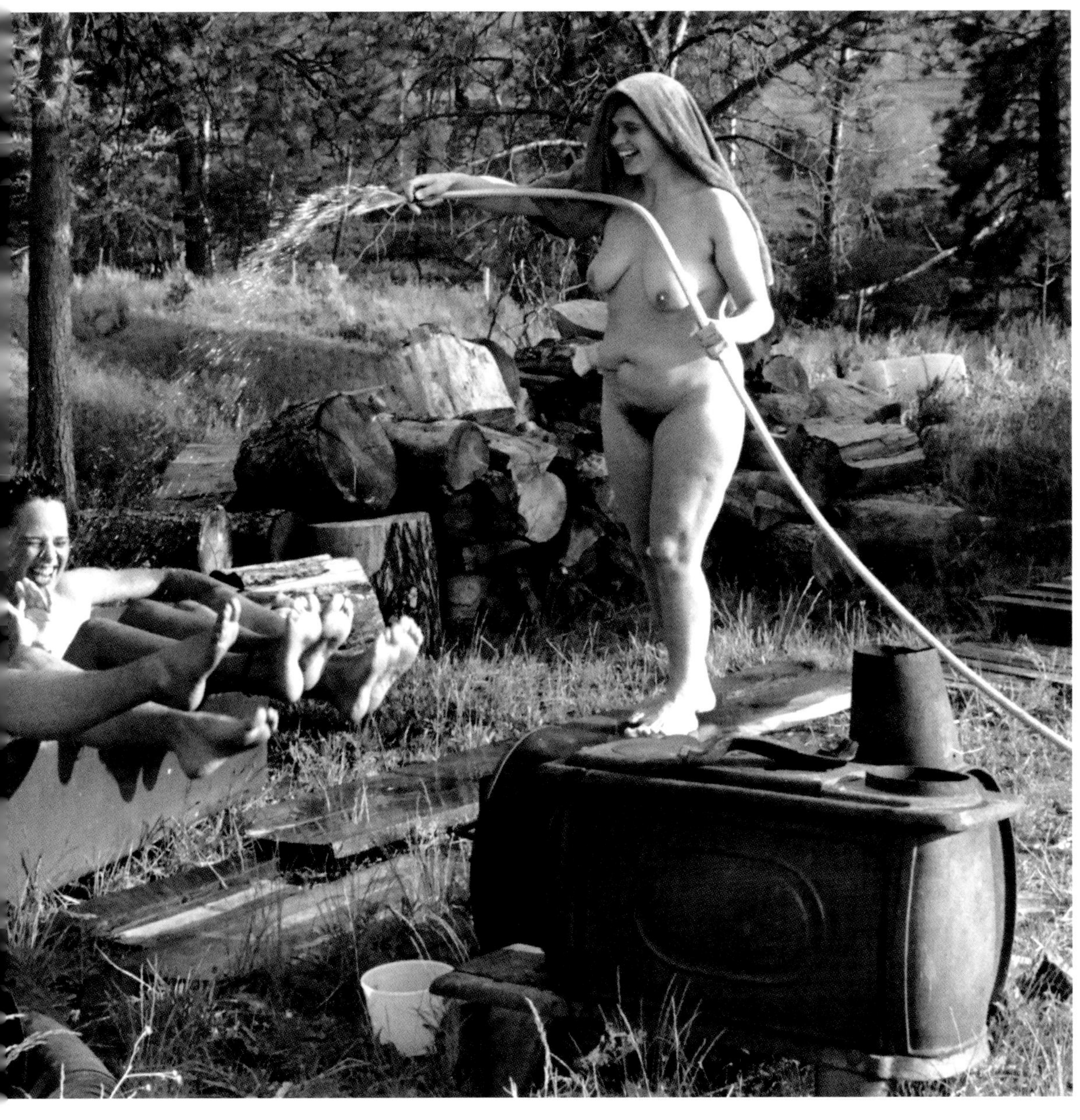

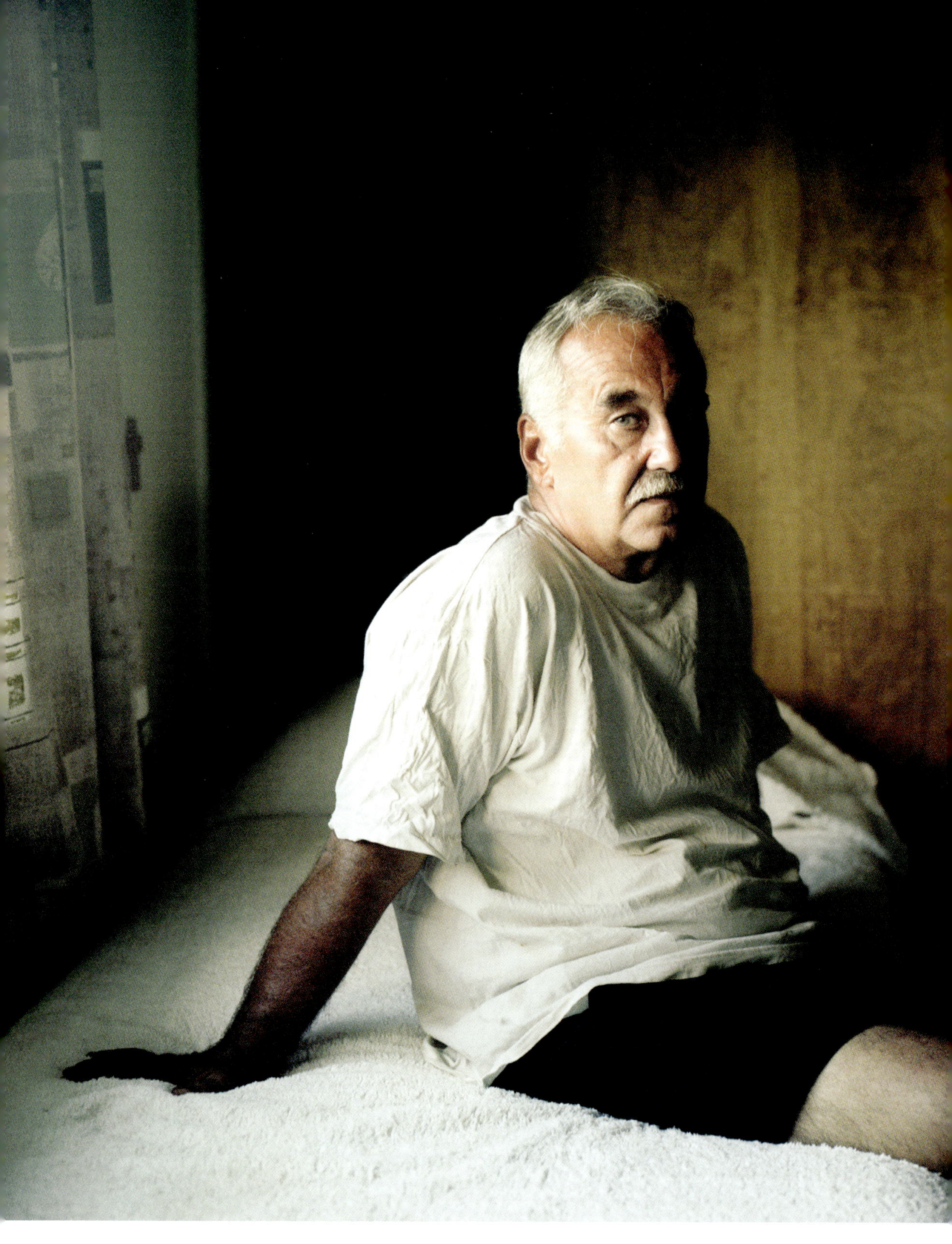

Rhiannon Adam

Irish British

Kevin Young, Up Tibi

Adamstown, Pitcairn Island; 2015

This portrait of Kevin Young was made as part of Big Fence/ Pitcairn Island, a project consisting of portraits, landscapes, interior shots, Polaroids, archive material and my own first-person narratives detailing the harrowing experiences of making the work as a lone female with no way to leave, creating an exploration of the psychological landscape of the island. Pitcairn, Britain's last Pacific Overseas Territory, is an enigmatic place, a volcanic blip halfway between Chile and New Zealand, measuring just 2 miles by 1 mile (3.2 × 1.6 kilometres) and accessible only by sea. It is now home to fewer than 40, most of whom are descendants of the Bounty mutiny – Kevin is an eighth-generation descendent. Pitcairn is well known as the archetypal paradise – an Anglo-Tahitian idyll, with multiple Hollywood adaptations reinforcing the fiction. But recently, a darker side to island life was revealed, when eight Pitcairn men (half of the adult male population), were convicted of sexual crimes against young girls in 2004 and 2007. As a result, islanders were suspicious of outsiders, journalists in particular. Sitters appear alone, photographed behind closed doors, out of sight of their fellow islanders. With each subject I had just one opportunity – many taking months of persuasion.

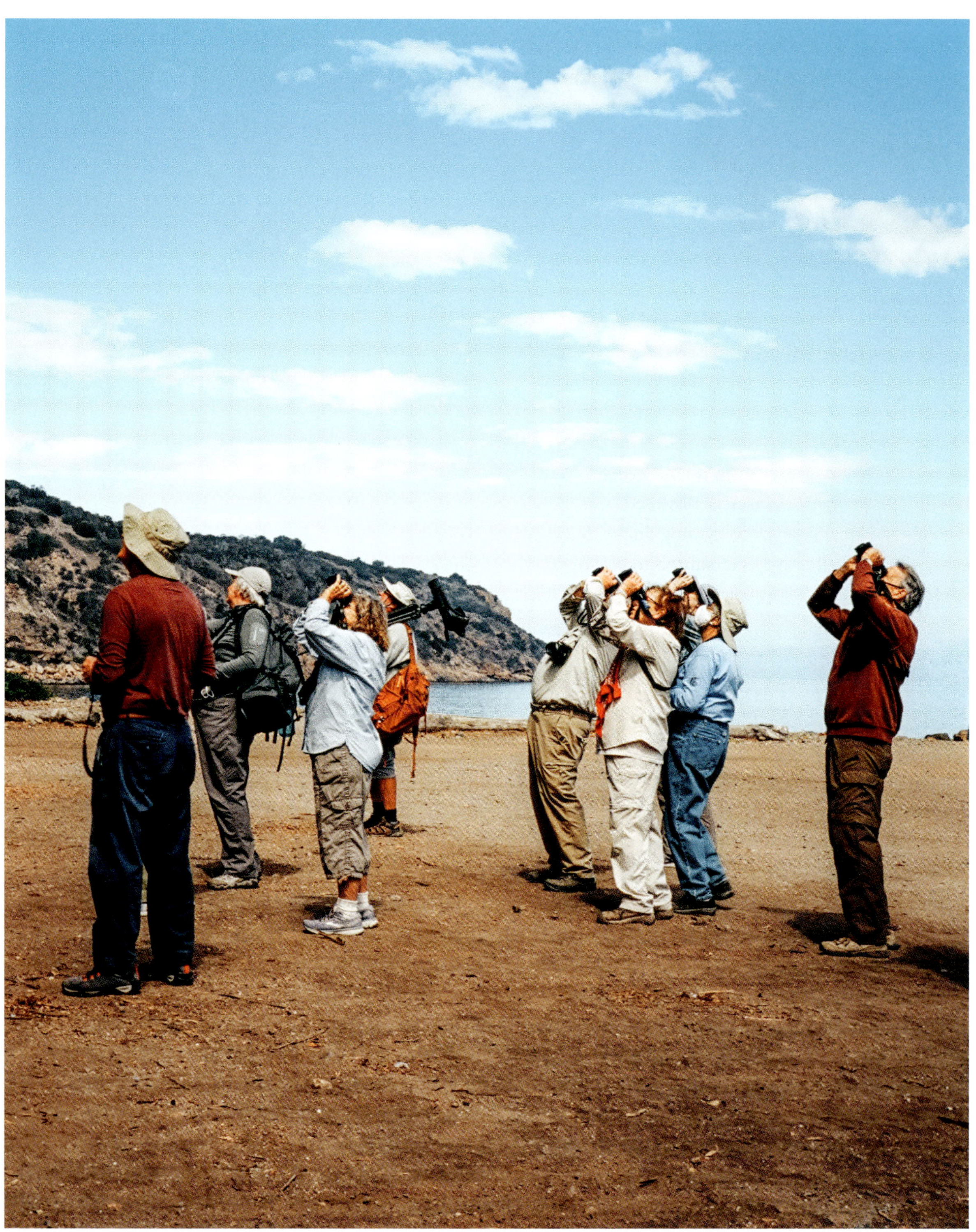

◄

Clara Mokri

American

Birdwatchers

Channel Islands National Park, California, USA; 2021

I first became interested in photography when I was in high school, when my grandfather was diagnosed with Alzheimer's. The idea that you could live your entire life and one day just forget it all terrified me. I became obsessed with the idea of documenting everything and everyone in the hopes that if I ever started to lose my own memory one day, my relentless documentation over the course of my life would help me remember. As I have gotten older, this obsession has turned into a passion for visual storytelling and a career of giving others a platform on which to share their own stories. In my free time, though, I still feel compelled to photograph all of the elements of my own life. I am particularly drawn to the subtle, mundane and oftentimes forgetful moments. I snapped this photo in passing while backpacking through Santa Cruz Island in Channel Islands National Park in fall, when we passed a group of day-trippers who had just arrived on the island to birdwatch. It was a quick, fleeting moment, but I remember being drawn to the idea that people have different ways of experiencing the same world.

►►

Hannah Reyes Morales

Filipina

Butanding

Tan-awan, Philippines; 2021

A fisherman feeds whale sharks in Tan-awan at dawn. His community of some 2,000 people built what became the largest non-captive whale shark tourism interaction in the world, drawing millions of tourists over the last decade, all eager to swim with the endangered species. Fishermen from the town lure the whale sharks by feeding them shrimp, guaranteeing a wildlife encounter for tourists, who have over the last 10 years brought money, jobs and industry to Tan-awan. Because of the whale sharks, there is now a high school in town. I met fisherfolk who were able finally to build homes and send their kids to finish their education. But there is a well-founded controversy around the impact of feeding whale sharks. Conservationists warn that feeding alters the natural behaviour of this endangered species. When the pandemic halted tourism, the town continued to feed the whale sharks at a financial loss, afraid that if they fail to return, the town may fall back into poverty. For me, this illustrates the complexities of conservation, and how intertwined it is with other human issues such as tradition, livelihood and education. How do we find a balance between communities grappling for survival with the needs of species in the natural world?

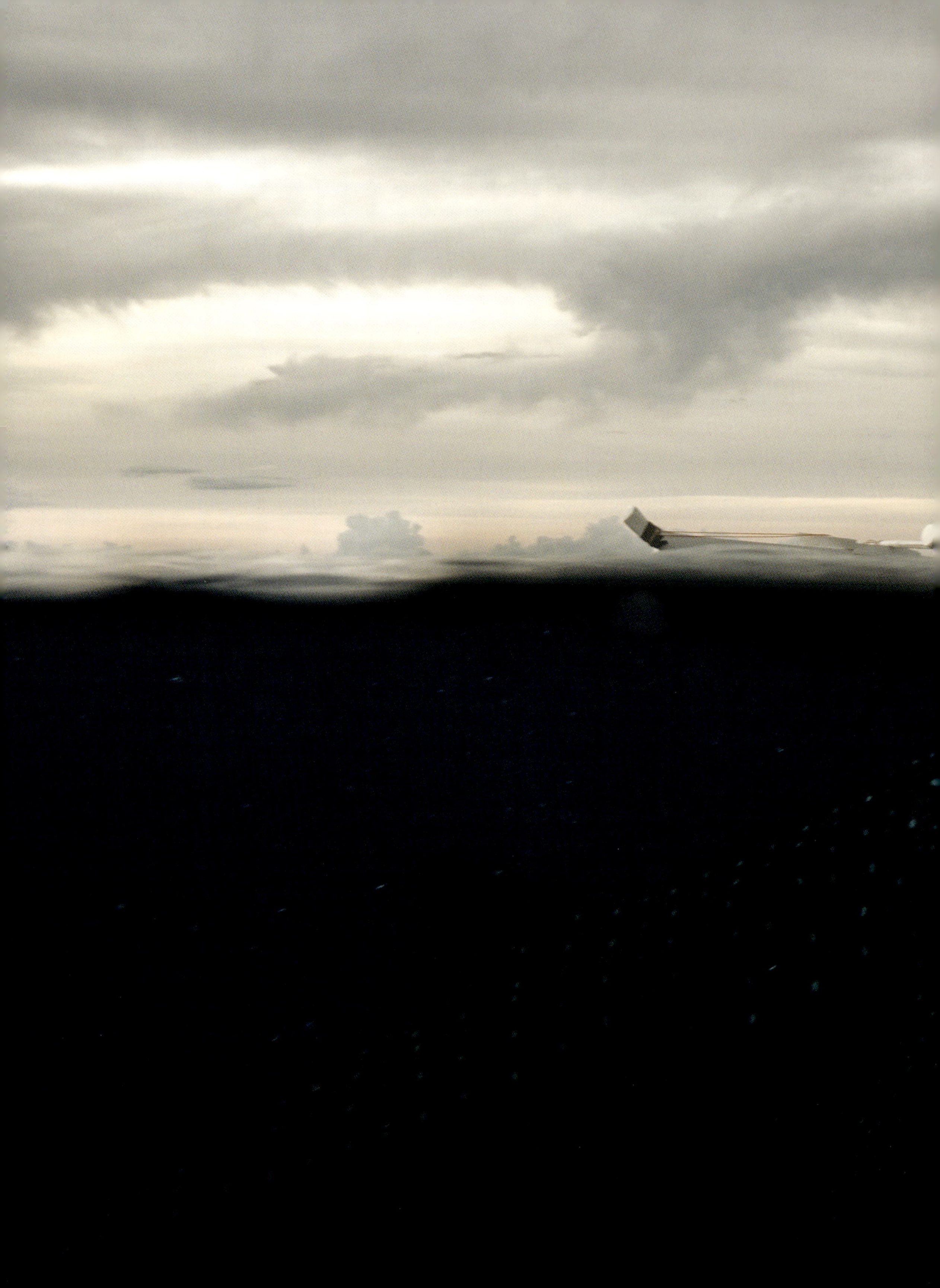

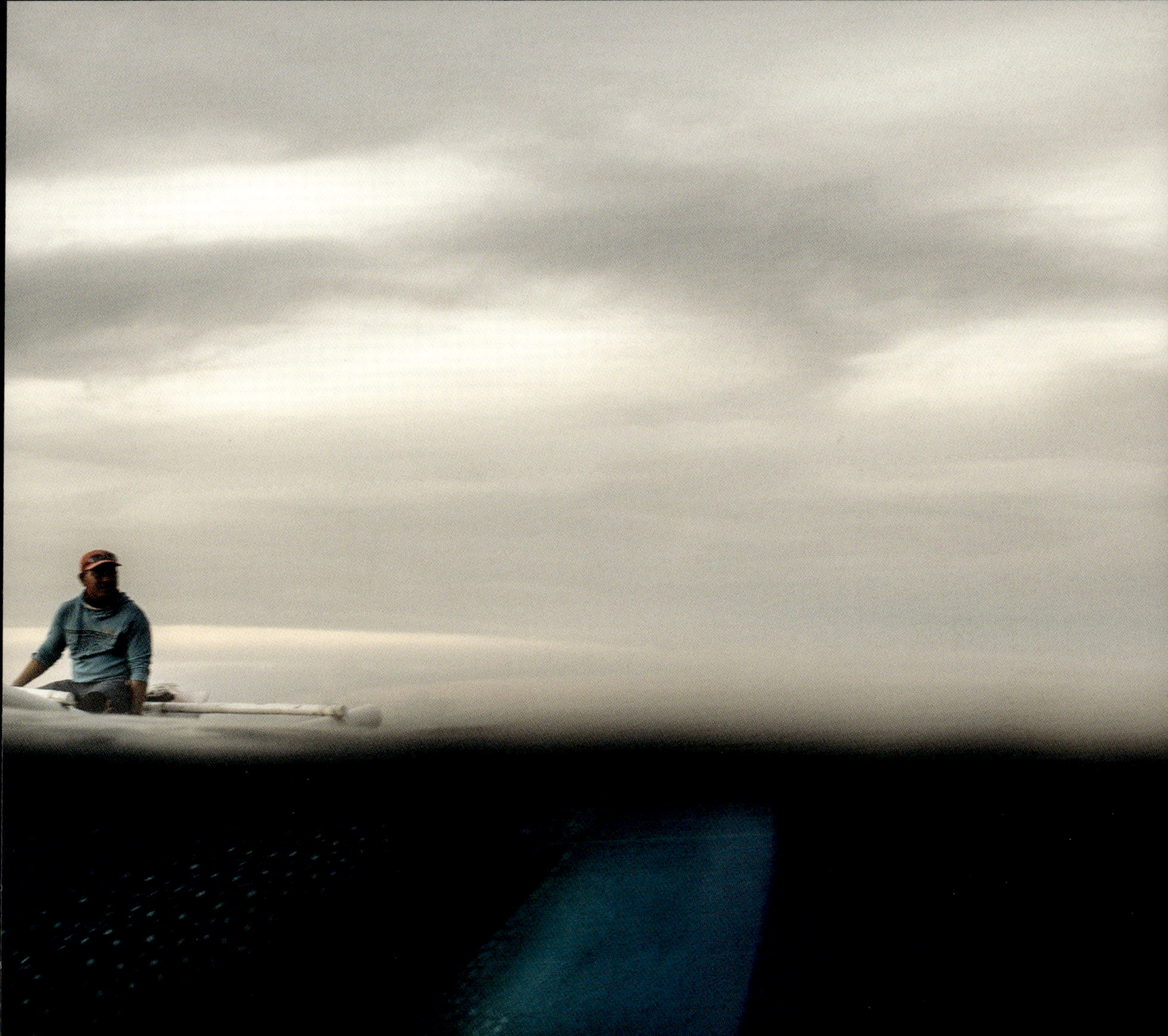

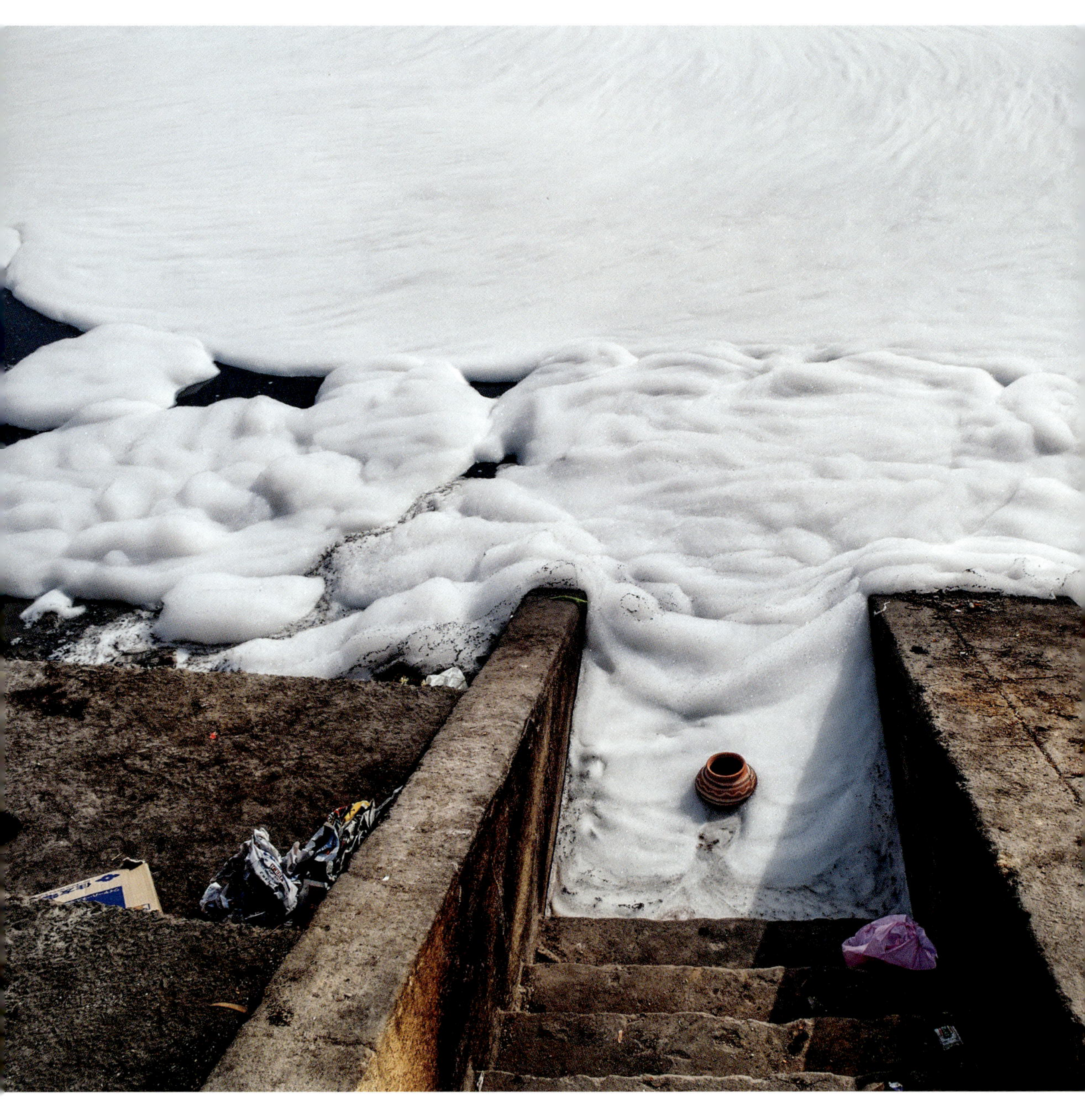

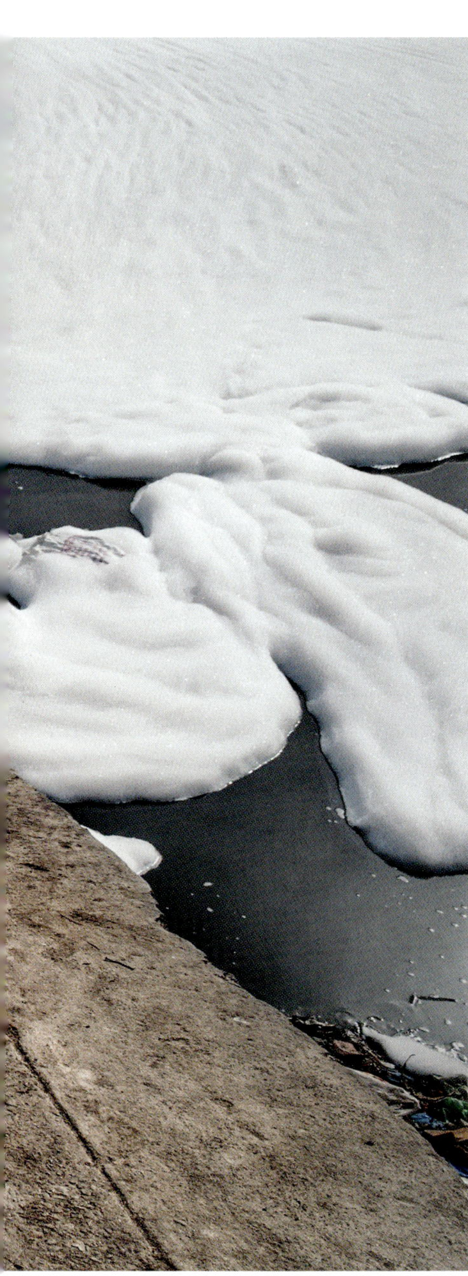

Saumya Khandelwal

Indian

The Womb of Yamuna

New Delhi, India; 2013

An earthen pot lies in the frothing Yamuna River in Delhi, India. The Yamuna is a dead river. While most of its waters are diverted to other areas before it reaches Delhi, discarded sewage and industrial waste clog what remains, making it unfit for any form of life. Thus, the polluted water, after passing through a barrage, crashes back into the river again, creating a white foam. My visits to the river became regular when I started looking at the condition of water bodies across the whole of India. This image is part of my larger body of work titled, Water, the Dying Lifeline, where I look at the life around bodies of water, and how much human civilization depends on them, and at the critical shortage of a once-abundant resource. It fascinated me that the same river that was at the centre of India's many religious beliefs could lie ignored. The Yamuna, which has been the source of life over decades and centuries, dies a silent death, and the womb no longer nurtures any form of life.

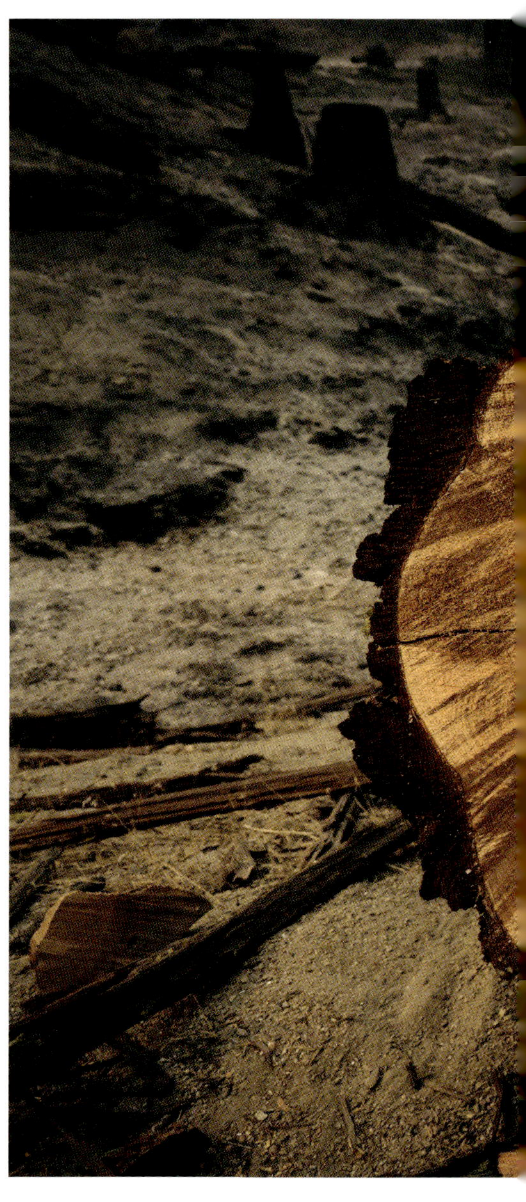

Tracy Barbutes

American

Smoldering

Sequoia National Forest, California, USA; 2021

I spent the day exploring the Sequoia National Forest, traditionally Western Mono/Monache and Tübatulabal lands, in areas along the Great Western Divide Highway and in and around the Trail of 100 Giants. I felt compelled to find and document giant sequoias that had survived multiple lightning-caused wildfires: the KNP Complex Fire burning to the north in Sequoia and Kings Canyon National Parks and this one, the Windy Fire, burning in Sequoia National Forest. I needed to bear witness to survival after having already documented so much devastation during the 2021 fire season. I should have carried a chainsaw and was fortunate that I could work my way around the burning logs and downed trees choking the roadways. I walked through powdery grey soil while breathing putrid, suffocating smoke and avoiding fire-weakened and damaged trees that crashed around me. I did a double take at this burning remnant, as ironically, it felt like the most 'alive' thing I had experienced thus far on the day's journey. In an instant, this downed tree, smouldering from the inside, became symbolic of a grieving, weeping planet, a Western landscape ravaged from drought and an inflamed nation fractured from deceptive narratives.

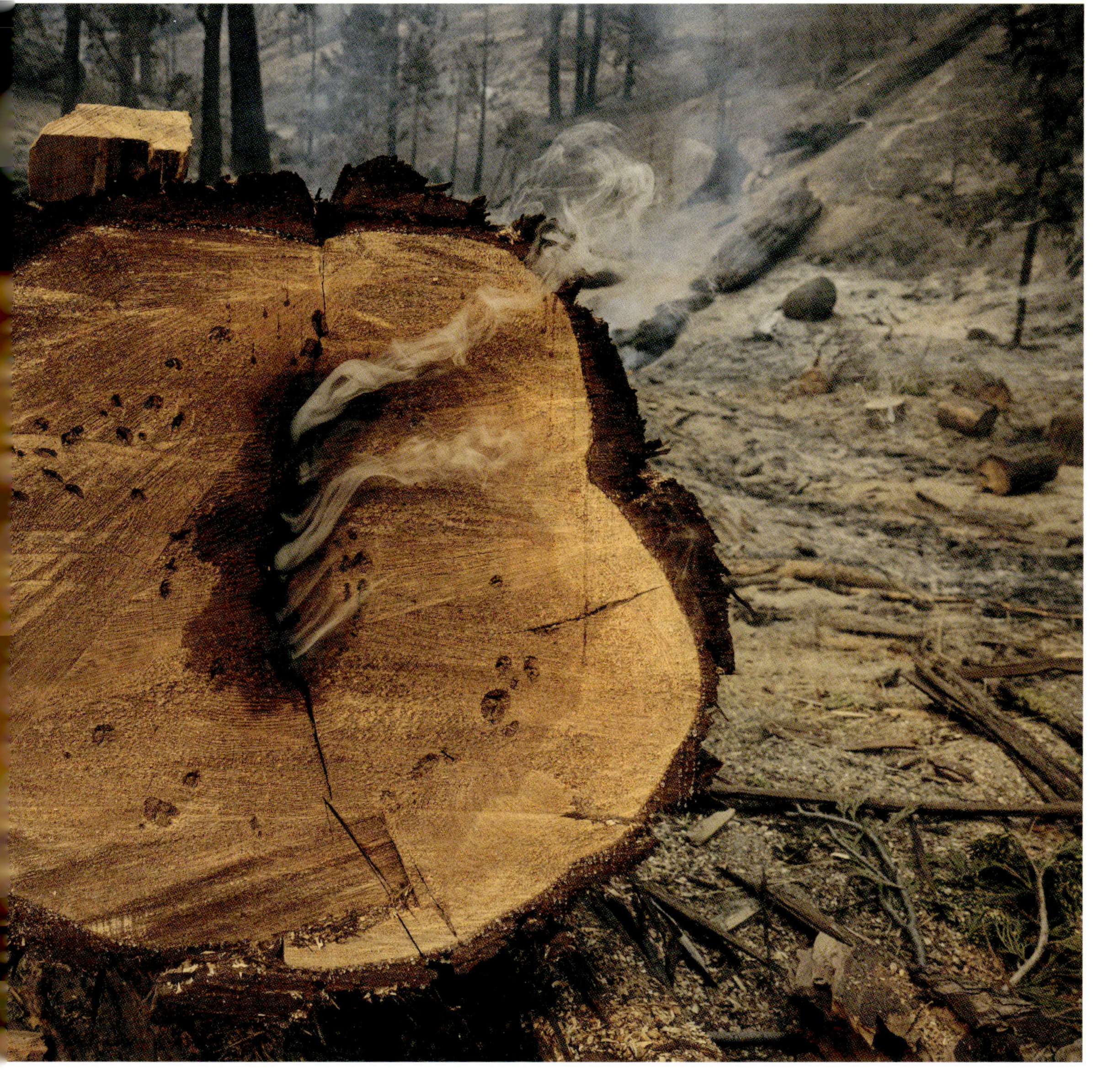

Some of the first journalistic applications of photography were in reporting on wars and conflicts; photographers were driven to depict their horrors to warn people of the toll on all of us. With time, conflict photography became driven by familiar tropes: you see one front-page news photograph and think you have seen it before. In subverting, or harnessing, tropes, these photographers invite us to look at moments on the periphery of conflicts, protests and violence. They are not shielding us from that violence but want to encourage us to see its effects with new eyes, to warn us of the stakes of becoming desensitized to the ways humans can destroy each other.

Conflict

03

Nina Berman

American

Fuck the KKK

New Jersey, USA; 1990

Early in my career as a photojournalist, I was interested in how white supremacists were organizing and the people who were showing up to stop them. My first pictures were made in the Southern US states of Louisiana, Tennessee and Georgia and documented neo-Nazis, KKK, skinheads and their Republican Party allies. When I heard a group of KKK and neo-confederates were going to assemble at a baseball field in Millville, New Jersey, I wanted to see what the community response would be. A sizable multi-racial crowd, many of them young people, confronted the Klan who were outnumbered and had to take cover behind the home plate fence. Some teenage boys went close to the fence and told the Klan what they thought of them. It was a glorious moment to witness. From that time forward, and throughout my career, I've been inspired by people who show up to protest and fight for democracy and equal rights. You can see parallels between that young man saying fuck you to the Klansmen and photographs of anti-fascist and Black Lives Matter protestors today.

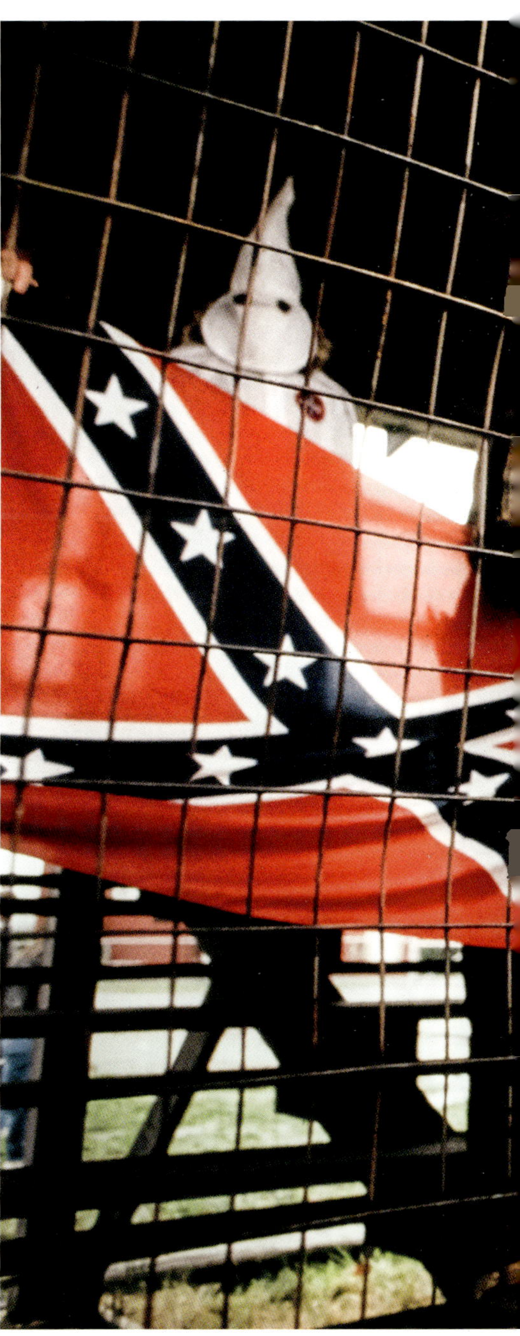

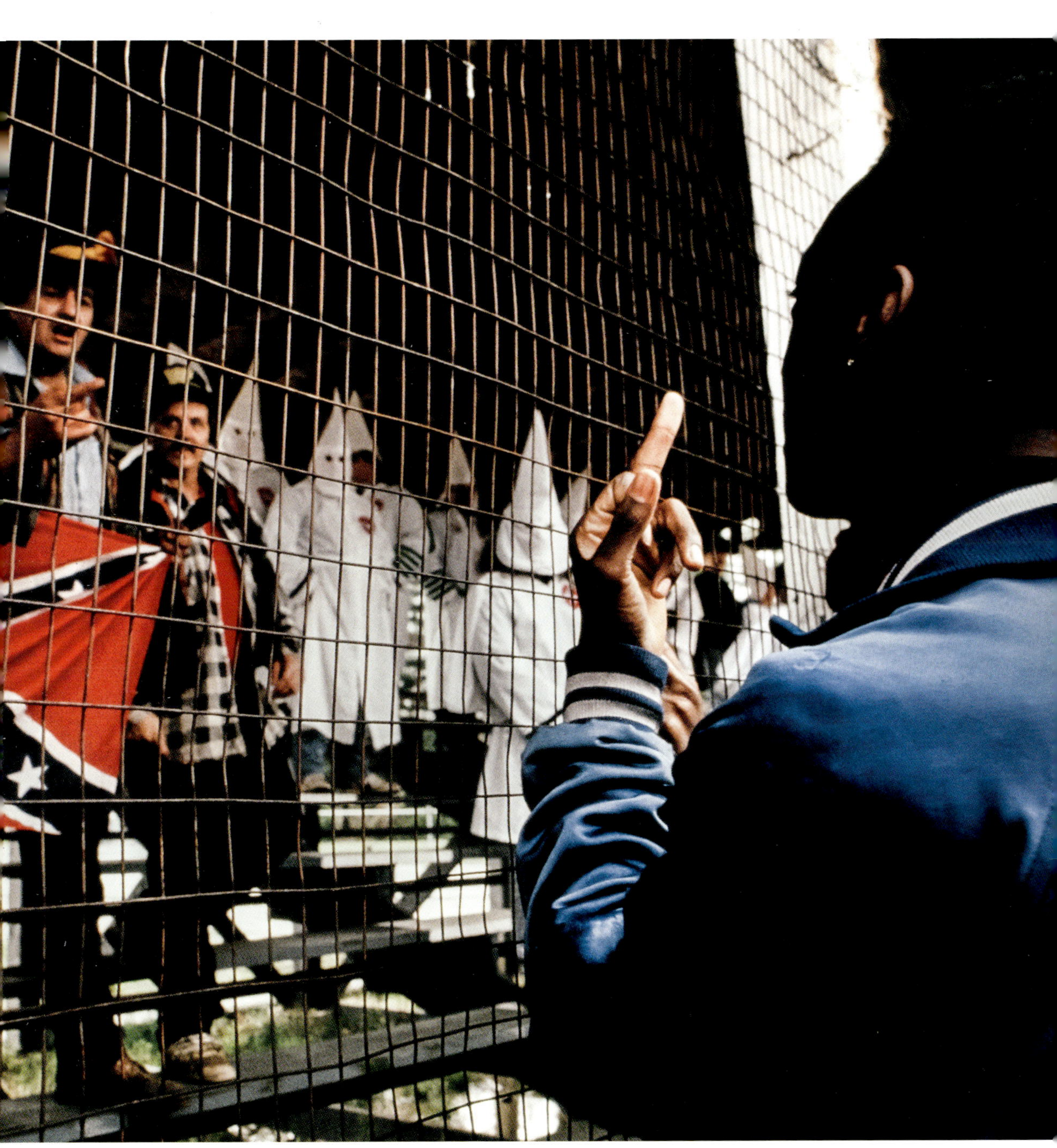

Patience Zalanga

Nigerian American

No Justice, No Peace

Minneapolis, Minnesota, USA; 2020

In November of 2014, I went to Missouri with a group of my friends to be in solidarity with the people of Ferguson. Months prior, former police officer Darren Wilson, a white man, killed 18-year-old Michael Brown, a Black youth. I had not considered the significance of choosing to document my time in Ferguson, which then led to continuing to document the protests taking place in my own city, Minneapolis. Six years later, the lessons I had learned over the years of witnessing the escalation that fomented the visceral response to George Floyd's murder came flooding back. When I took this image the day after former police officer Derek Chauvin murdered Floyd, I was reluctant to bring my camera to the protest. It had been my practice for six years, but the pain of once again seeing another Black man die at the hands of police, was devastating. So, with only my phone, I photographed. This photo is personal for me because it reflects the internal agony that had been submerged for so long, both personally and collectively. There are still few words to describe witnessing the monumental uprising in this city, and the emotion and psychological consequences of 25 May 2020.

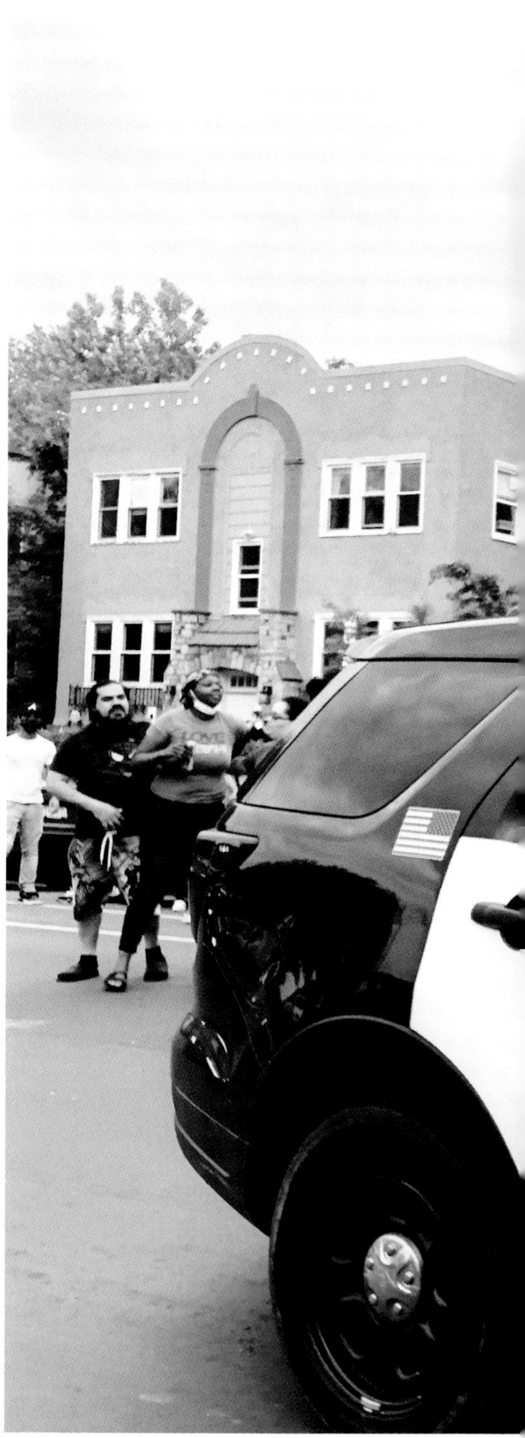

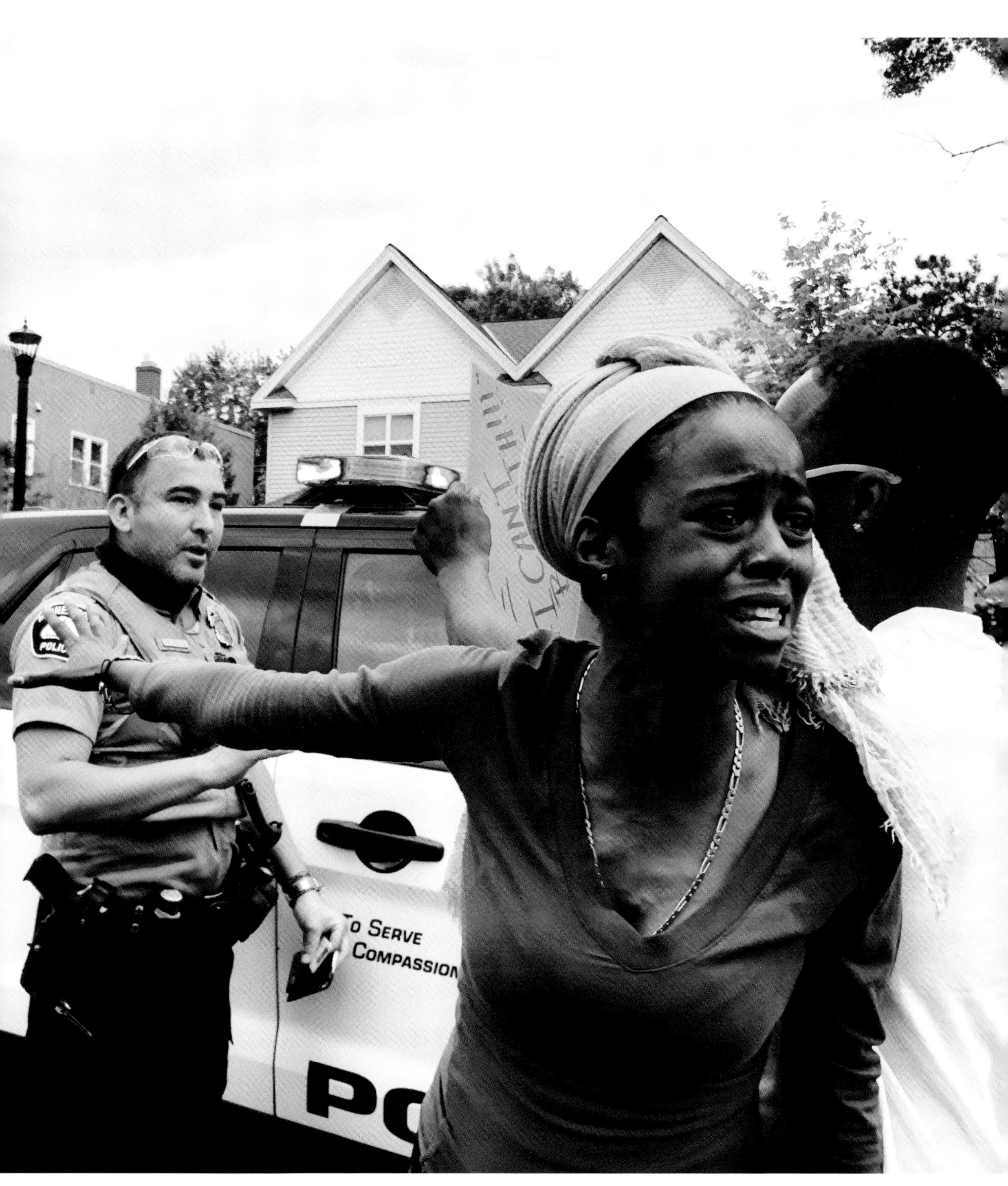
To Serve

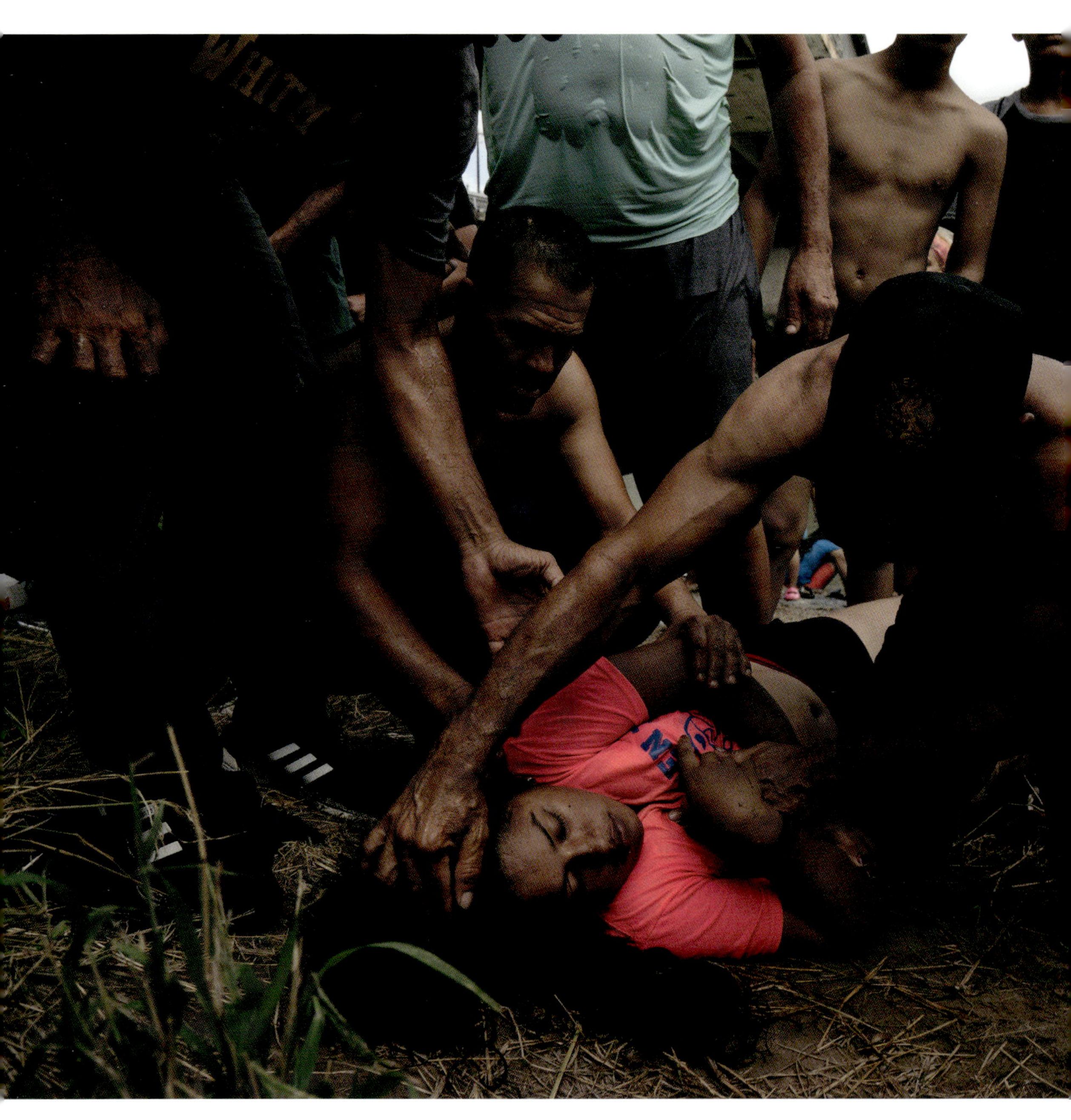

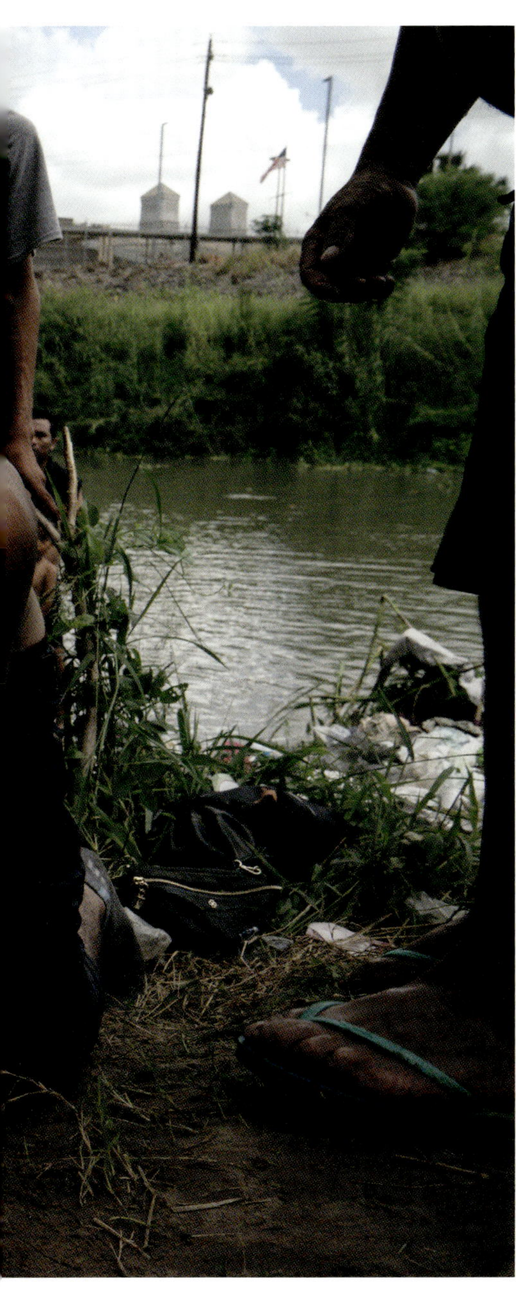

Verónica G. Cárdenas

Mexican and American

The Beginning of MPP

Matamoros, Tamaulipas, Mexico; 2019

In 2019, the Trump administration implemented the Migrant Protection Protocols (MPP), which sent asylum seekers back to Mexico while they waited for their cases to be heard. Many migrants bathed in the Rio Grande because there were no showers in the encampments, including Breni, seen here, who almost drowned while she and her father were waiting for their asylum case to be decided. Dozens of people drown every year in this river. Migrants living at this encampment in Matamoros, after being sent back under MPP, would say 'So close, but yet so far away'. As I was crossing the international bridge into Matamoros I heard the voices of migrants in the river, never thinking that a group of girls was drowning. I made my way to the river to find Breni being rescued, and I was afraid that she would die as she was not responsive. She was resuscitated in Mexico, but you can see the US flag is waving on the right. Months later, she would cross as an unaccompanied minor, and her father would join her at the beginning of 2021, when President Joe Biden allowed the asylum seekers that had been sent back under MPP to cross into the United States.

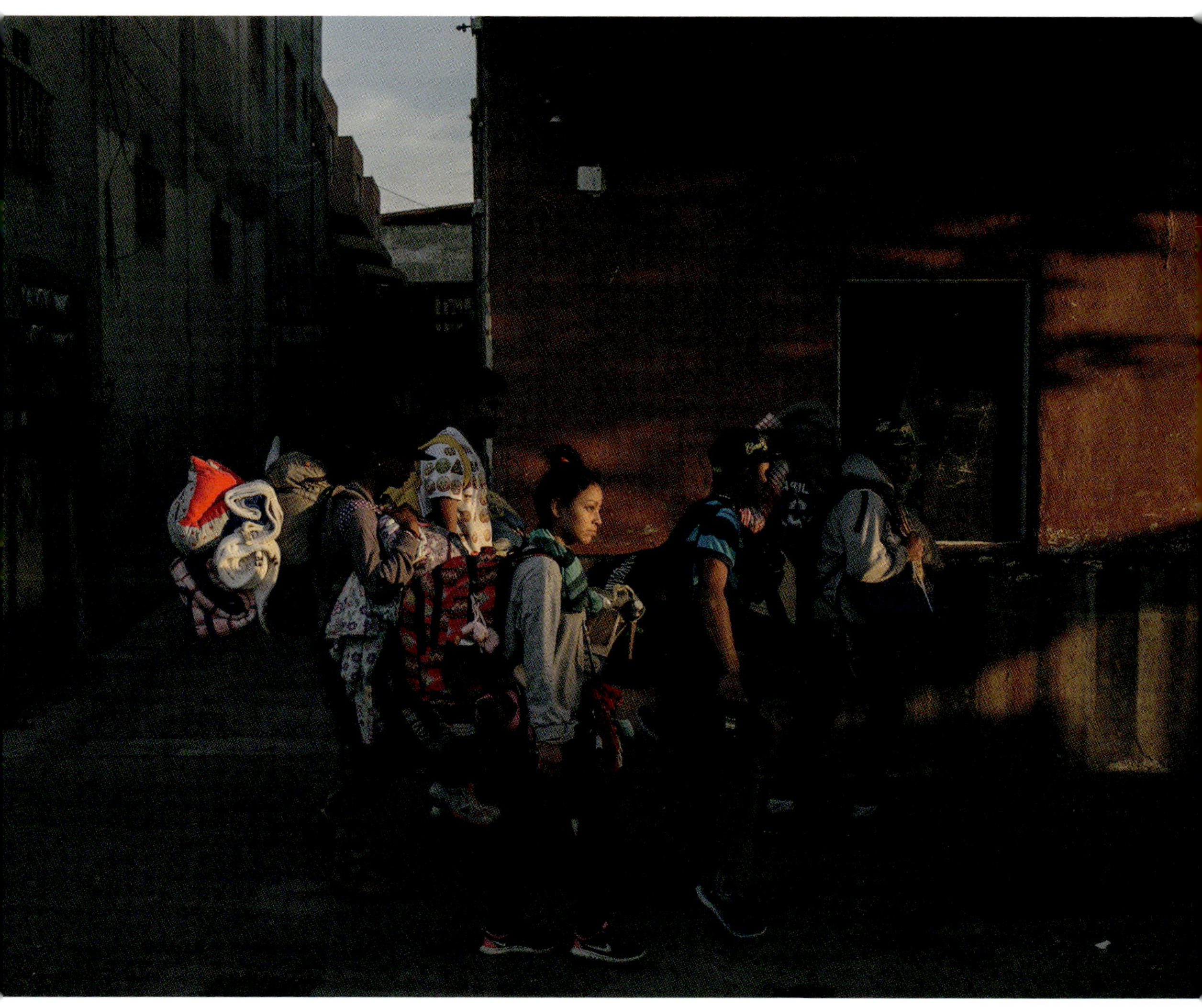

◀

Meghan Dhaliwal

American

Untitled

Tijuana, Baja California Norte, Mexico; 2018

I made this image in April 2018, while covering one of the migrant caravans that passed through Mexico that year. The group of nearly 1,000 people, mostly from Central America, had just arrived in Tijuana and began splintering as people looked for places to sleep for the night. This group of teens was walking through the late afternoon light towards a church that had offered up its pews. These caravans were receiving heightened attention from global news media after a series of inflammatory tweets from then-US President Donald Trump. It felt important in this moment, with so many eyes trained on this group of people, to make images that were both sensitive and explanatory. I was looking for moments to photograph that captured glimpses of the journeys these individuals had embarked upon, how long the road had been, how little they could carry with them. I also hoped that if I could capture moments among smaller groups of people, that the images could serve as a reminder that the caravans were groups of individuals with their own stories and not a single entity, 'the caravan'.

▶▶

Gabriella N. Báez

Puerto Rican

Ricky Renuncia Protests

San Juan, Puerto Rico; 2019

This image depicts one of the summer 2019 protests in Puerto Rico that resulted in the resignation of the island's governor, Ricardo Rosselló. The protests started after messages between high-ranking government officials, including Rosselló, were leaked, revealing sexist, homophobic and violent language. The messages showed obvious disregard for the lives lost after Hurricane María, which hit Puerto Rico in September 2017, completely altering the island's landscape and history. The principal causes of death in the aftermath were accidents, heart failure, diabetes and suicide. Many of these deaths could have been prevented if the government had organized a response and provided quicker access to electricity, water and essential services. While inconclusive, studies estimate the death toll from the hurricane was more than 4,500. Many of the protestors highlighted government corruption, misuse of emergency funds and the disappearance of resources like bottled water, canned food and electric generators. Others, like myself, had a personal reason to be there: Jorge G. Báez, my father, died by suicide in the aftermath of Hurricane María. Photographing and documenting this historic moment felt like my way of contributing to the struggle for justice on the island.

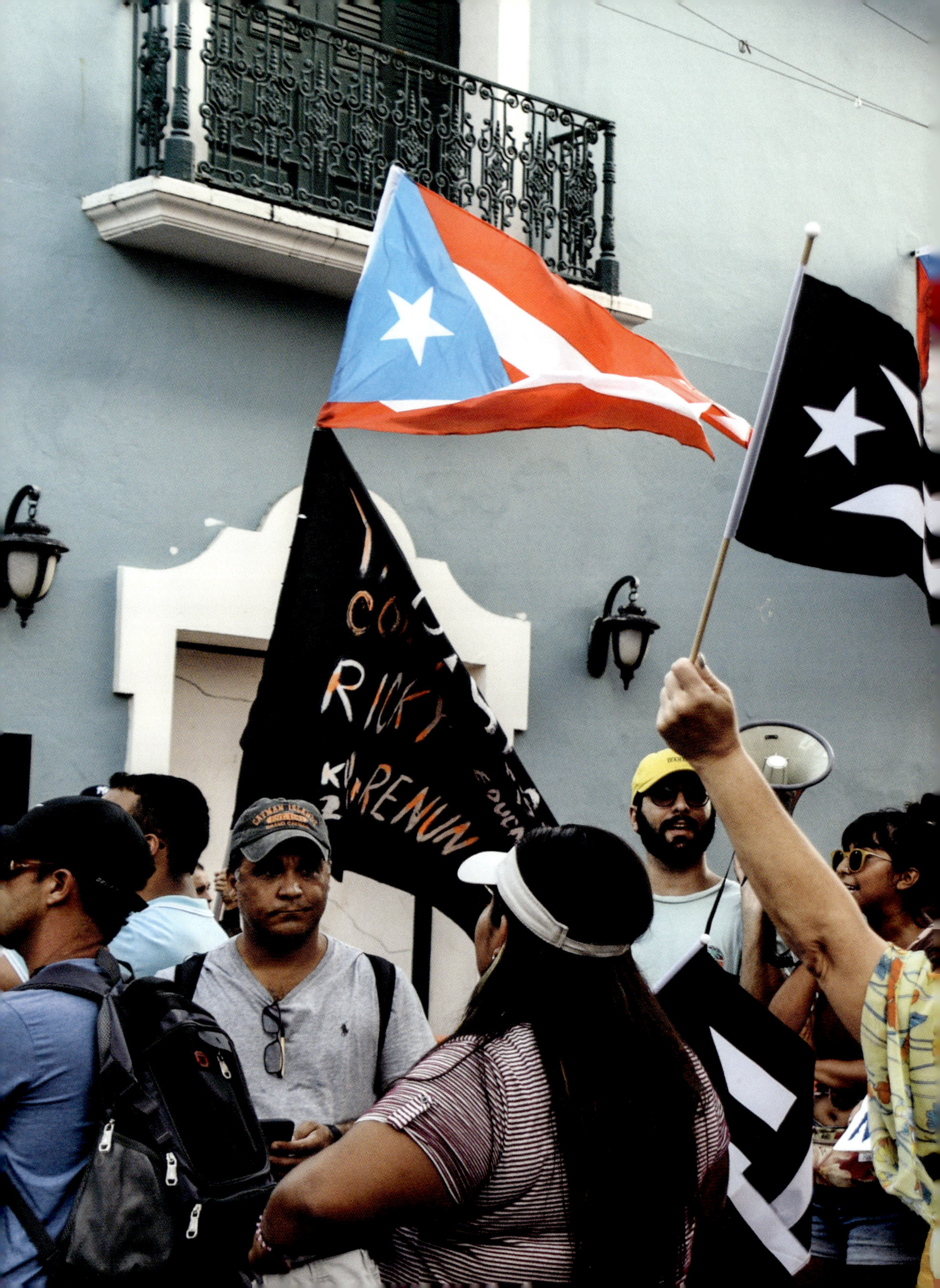
RICKY
CAYMAN ISLANDS

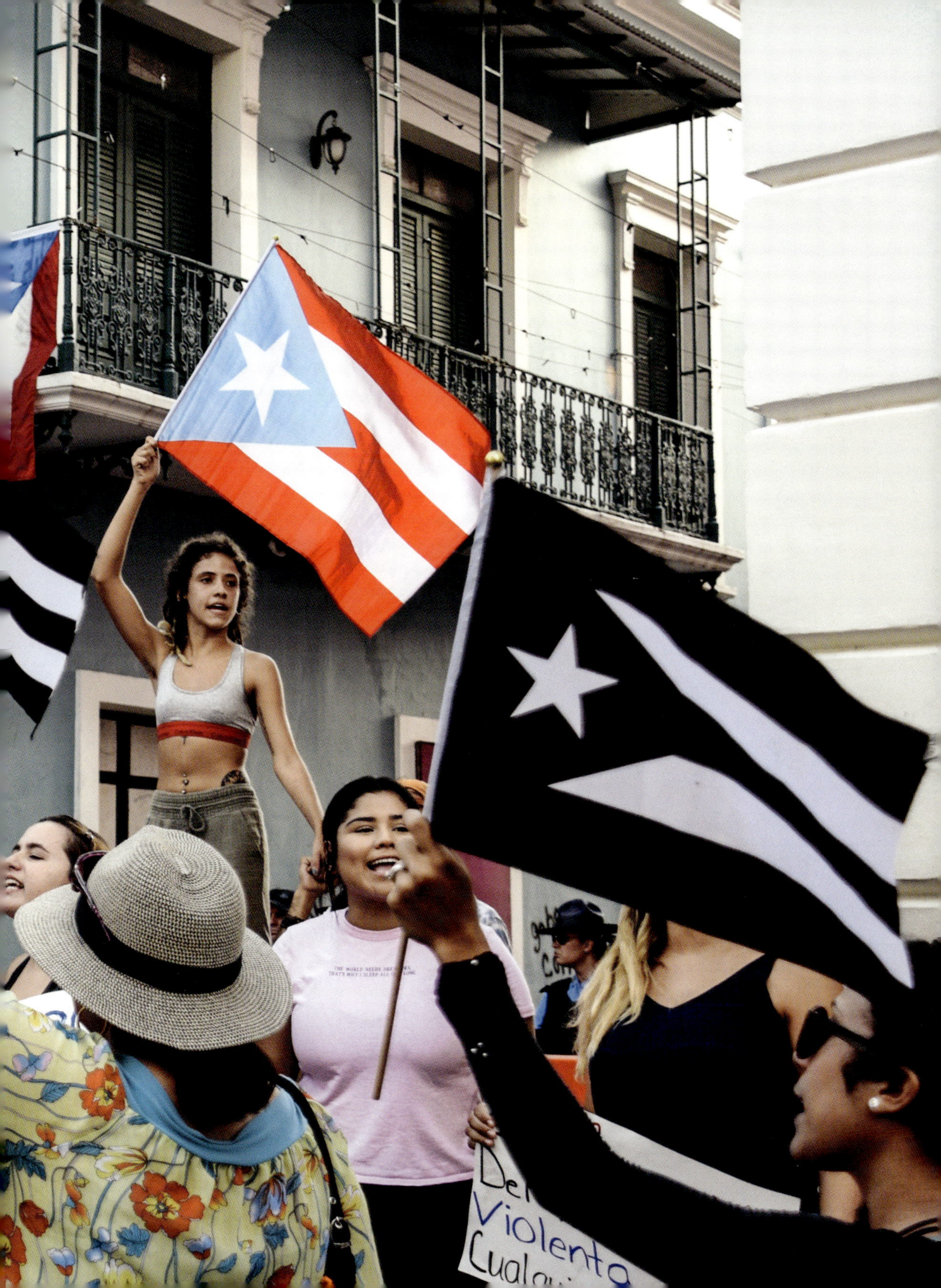
Violenta

Tara Pixley

Jamaican American

Liberation

Leimert Park, Los Angeles, California, USA; 2020

He guided the horse to slowly, powerfully, carefully step through the crowd as the Black Liberation flag billowed behind him. The scene enraptured everyone present – even the entirely Black police force assigned to the Leimert Park Juneteenth celebration. In light of the ongoing racial justice protests that gripped Los Angeles and the country that summer of 2020, the selection of Black cops to police the primarily Black celebratory crowd felt both intentional and infuriating. But the crowd ignored the police, focusing instead on the vision of a Black man atop a horse, waving a symbol that seemed to say 'a better world is possible'. I was on assignment documenting LA's largest Juneteenth gathering when I saw the horse through the crowd and rushed over to take in the scene with joy, feeling the awe I saw on the faces of the children who passed by, feeling the pride of the other Black folks who, like me, have so rarely seen Black people on horseback. It is moments like these that remind me of both the great privilege and responsibility it is to be a photojournalist – work I take very seriously as a Black queer woman who knows intimately the power of images to either wound or nourish.

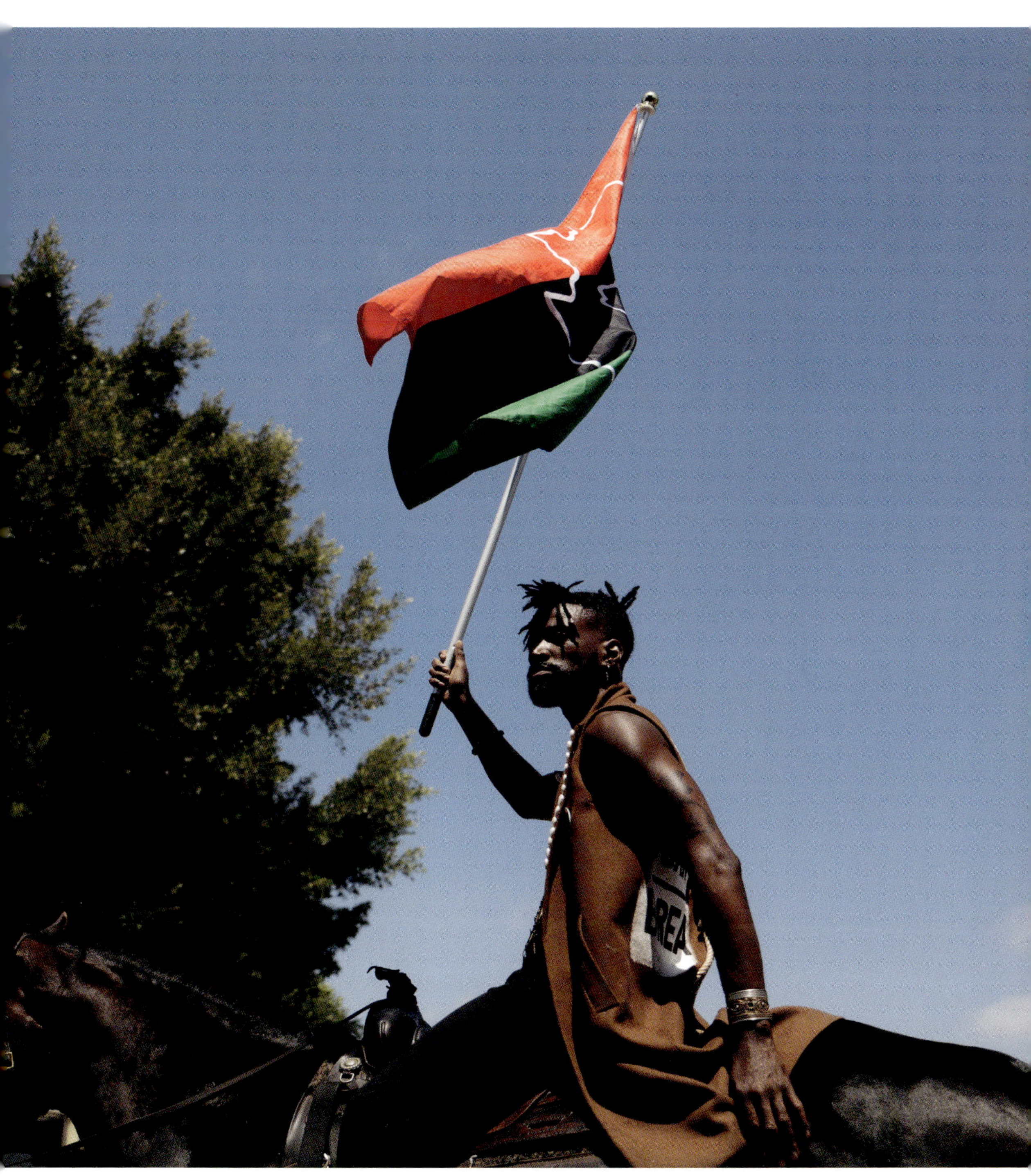

Adriana Zehbrauskas

Brazilian

Untitled

Phoenix, Arizona, USA; 2021

This image was taken on 6 January 2021, at the Arizona State Capitol in Phoenix. I had been covering the presidential campaign trail throughout 2020 and the subsequent 'Stop the Steal' protests in Arizona after Joe Biden won the election. Arizona's electoral votes were instrumental to Biden's win. Only two Democratic presidential nominees had won in the state in the past 72 years – Bill Clinton in 1996 and Harry Truman in 1948 – and there was a lot of tension in the air. I had grown somewhat accustomed to seeing protesters dressed in military attire and carrying large weapons, but it was the first time I had seen young women doing so. There was something about Aya, left, and Ashley, right, who came all the way from California to support Donald Trump, that drew my attention. Was it their defiant and fashionable pose as they held their guns? Aya's cigar and high heels? Ashley's leopard-print combat boots? I am not sure, but as that now historic day was ending and the light was turning blue, I knew that nothing would be the same.

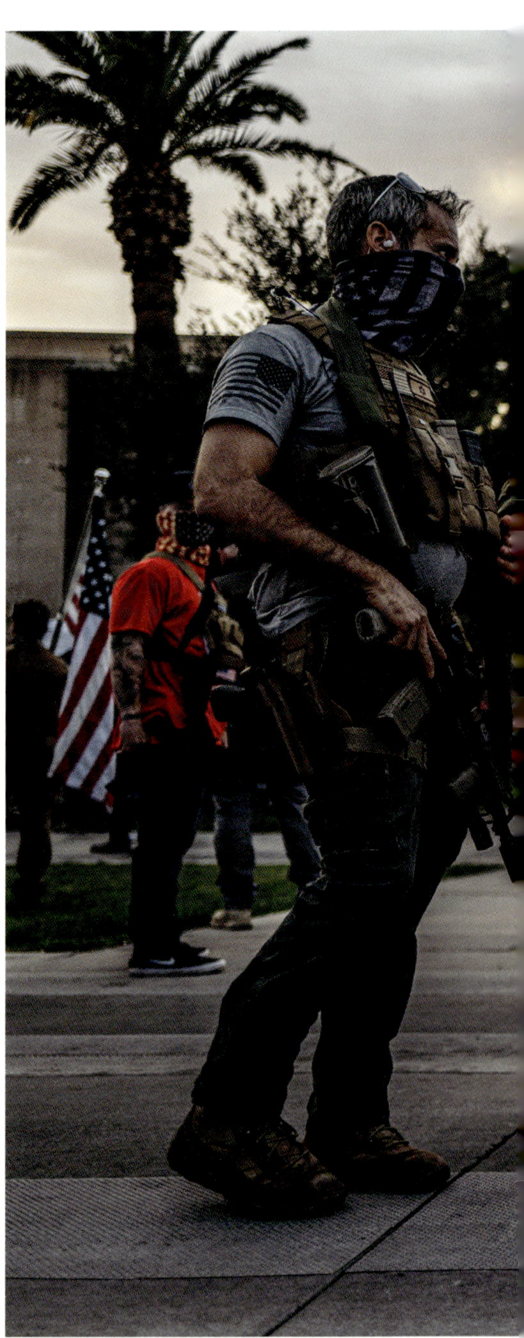

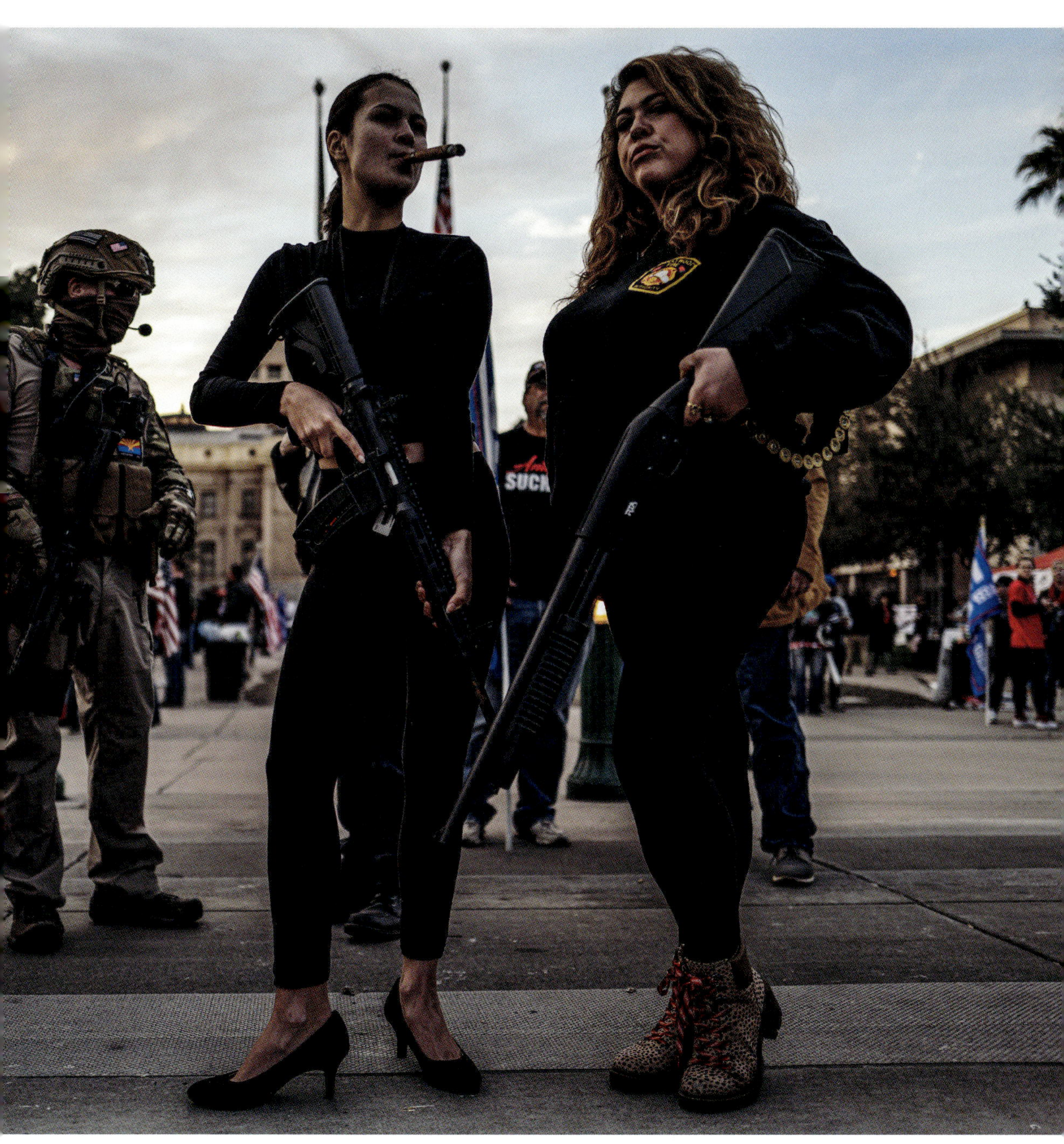

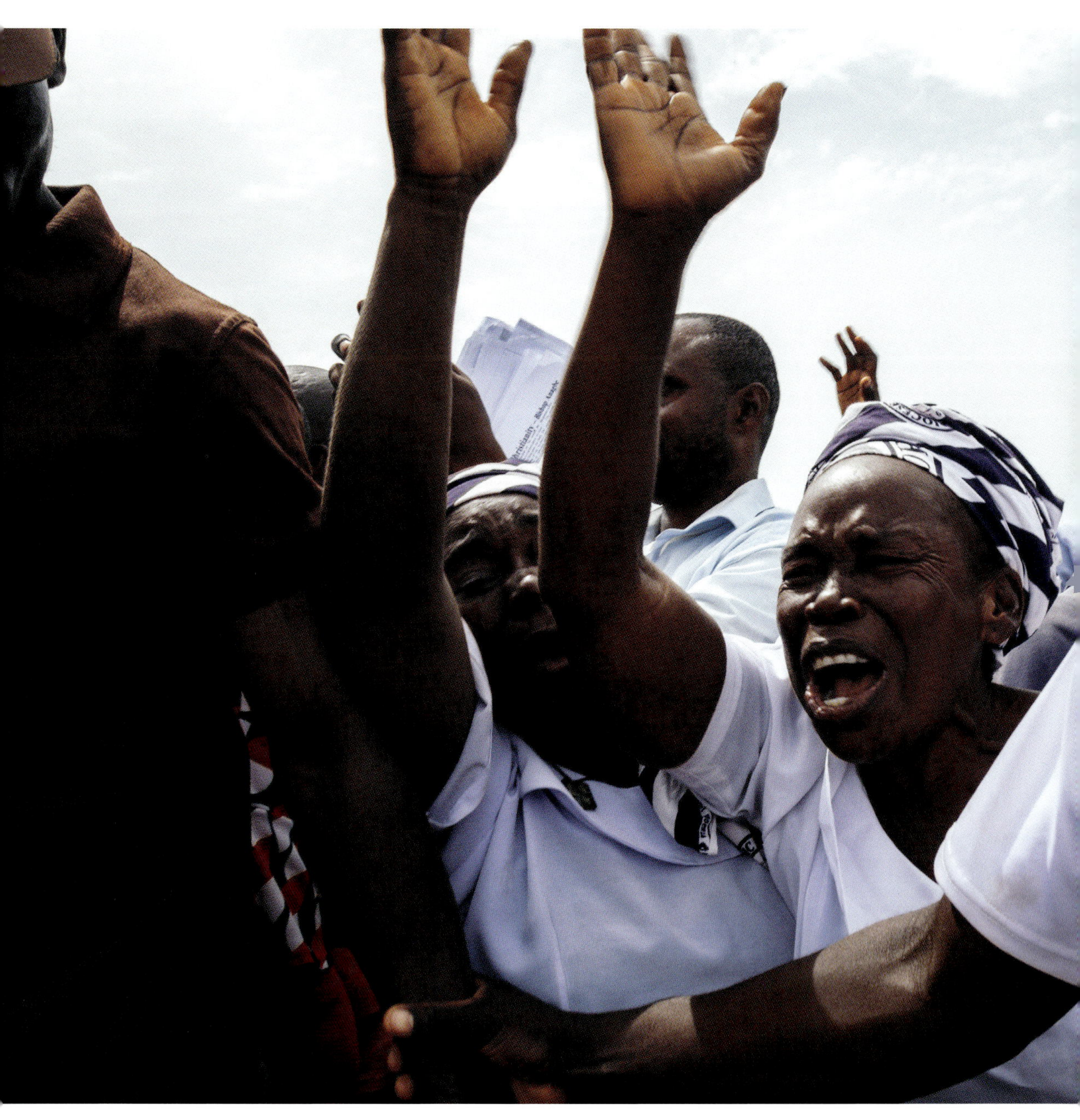

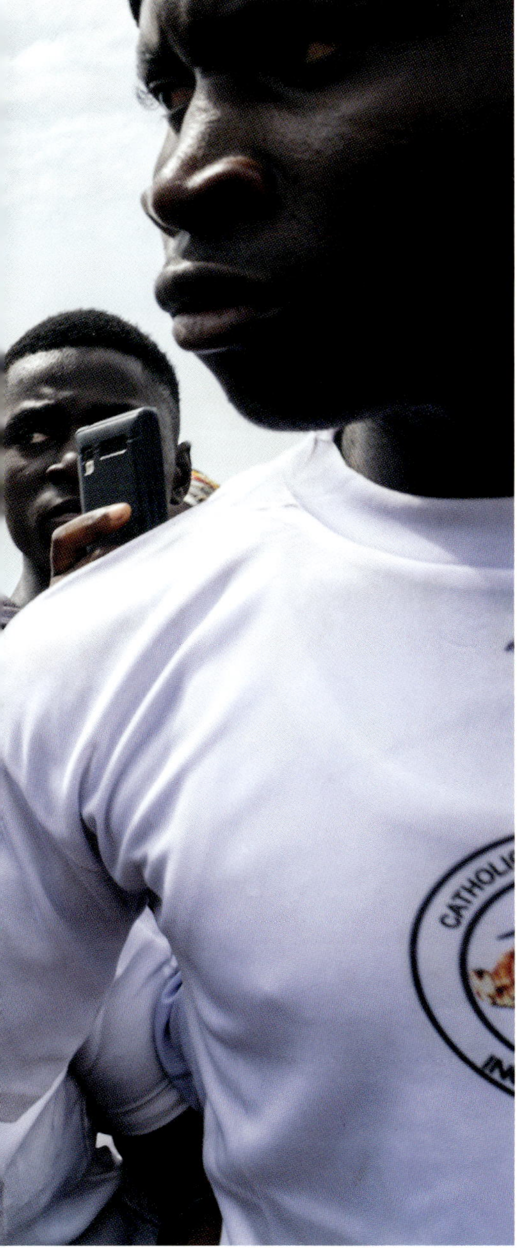

Etinosa Yvonne

Nigerian

Gone too soon!

Makurdi, Benue state, Nigeria; 2018

I took this image while on assignment for *The Wall Street Journal*. It was my first editorial assignment and I was asked to work on a story about the farmer–herder conflict in Nigeria. The two middle-aged women seen here are crying during a mass burial of people killed by herdsmen in the Aya Mbalom community in Benue state. The herdsmen allegedly killed 11 people during an early morning mass prayer. Prior to this incident, herdsmen had been ravaging communities in different parts of the state. Just before this assignment, I was working on a personal project called It's All In My Head, which explores the coping mechanisms of survivors of terrorism and extreme instances of conflict and cruelty. Covering this burial reinforced my need to continue that work. During this assignment, I saw people living in schools that had been converted to camps for internally displaced people. I remember when we got to the Internally Displaced Peoples camp, a crowd of more than a thousand drew close to us to see if we came with food or other supplies. This assignment reminded me of why I became a photographer, to bring to the fore underreported social issues.

Laurel Chor

Hong Konger

Anger

Yuen Long, Hong Kong; 2019

I took this photograph while covering the Hong Kong protests in 2019. It was early on, and no one was used to the escalating violence yet. The week before, a gang of masked assailants wearing white T-shirts had violently attacked commuters and protesters inside a subway station. The police did not show up for almost 40 minutes. The public, outraged at the apparent collusion between the police and gangs, took to the streets. I was at the rear end of the march when riot police began to advance in formation from behind. I started walking backwards, and through my viewfinder I watched as an elderly woman began to scream angrily at the police, asking them why they were doing this and why they were hurting young people. The police did not seem to know how to react, and simply ignored her, walking past her until she was swallowed by their ranks. I did not think too much about it until the following day, when I tweeted the photo and it went viral. It was overwhelming and humbling; I experienced first hand how, as photojournalists, our own work can be bigger than ourselves, and how powerful an image can be.

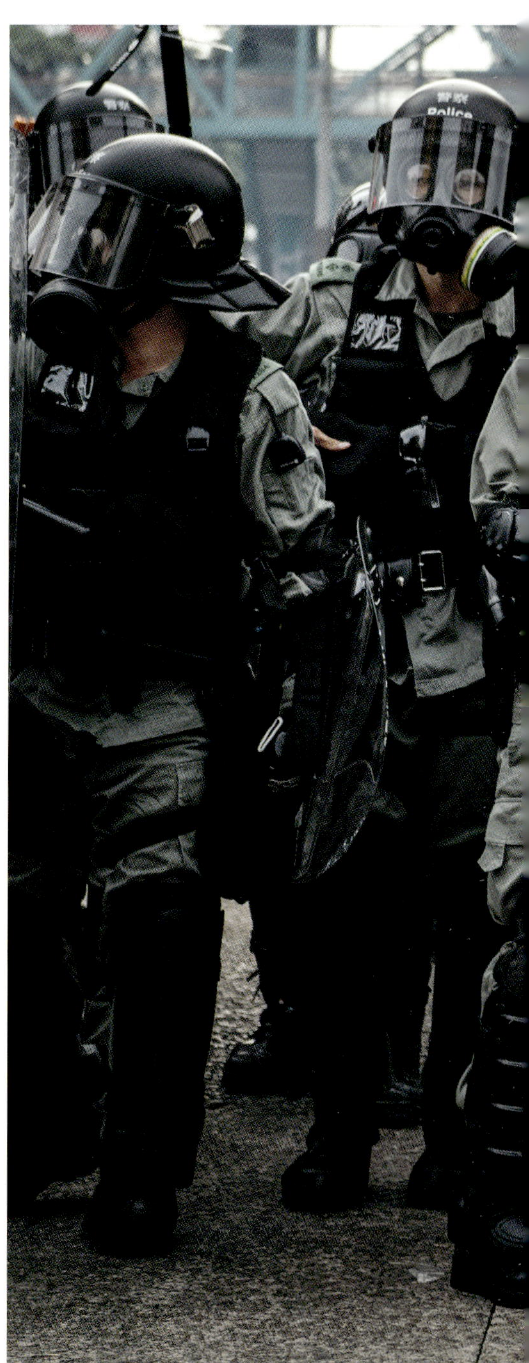

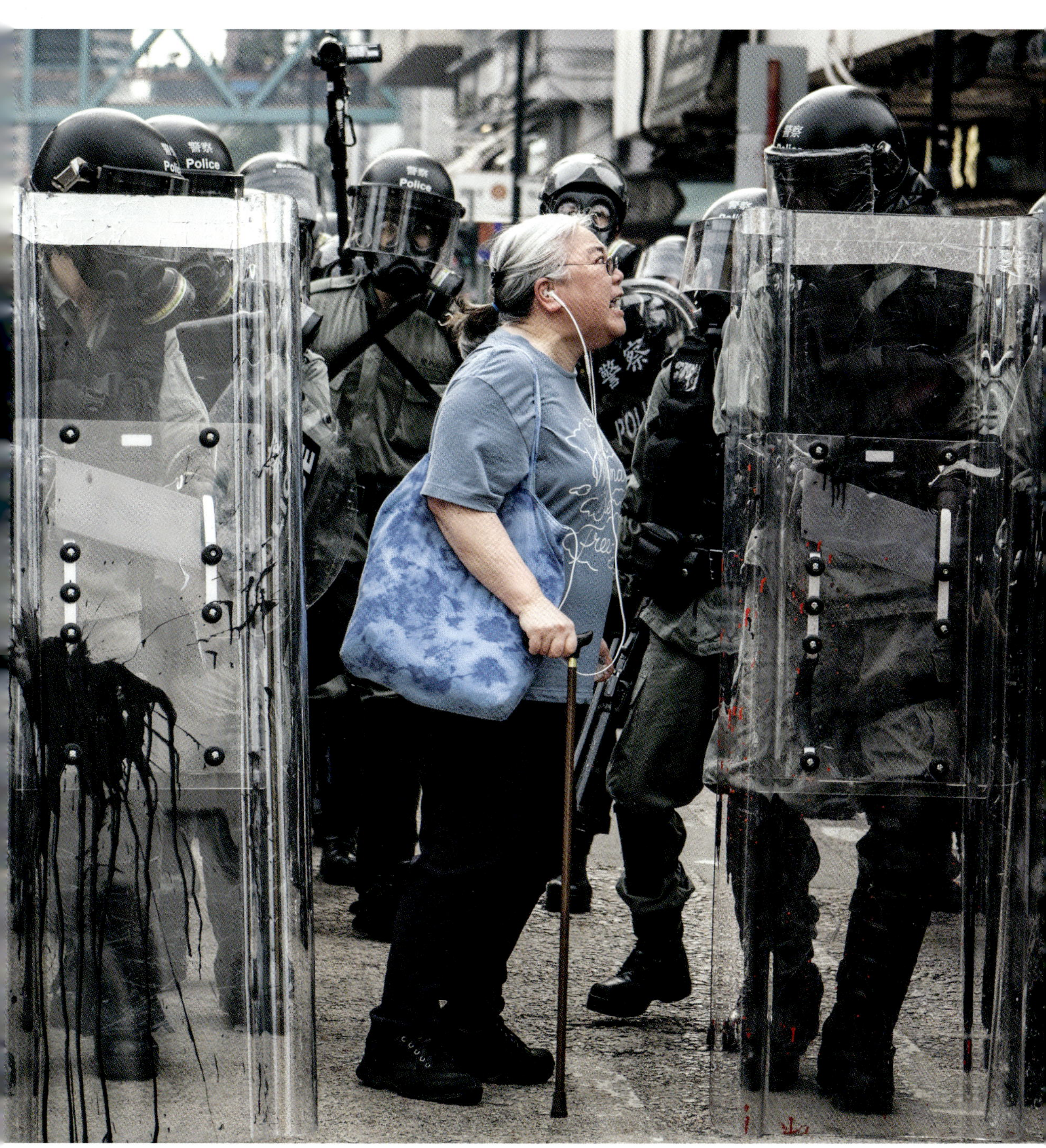
警察
Police
警察
Police
警察

Sumy Sadurni

Mexican Spanish

Stella Nyanzi's Roses

Kampala, Uganda; 2020

On 20 February 2020, Stella Nyanzi, one of Uganda's most famous activists and feminists, was finally released from a nine-month prison sentence that she had received for insulting the country's president on her Facebook page. I had been following Stella and her work for a few years by then because her form of crude, in-your-face activism – exemplified in *No Roses from my Mouth*, a book of poetry she wrote while in prison – really resonated with me. We knew she would give a press conference after court, but part of me feared it would be quiet. It was wonderful to be wrong, and to see this fearless woman put on a tiara and start screaming about the injustices that she and many opposition figures faced in Uganda. Her passion, her attitude and her voice had not been stolen from her during those months in jail. A few minutes in, the police started firing live ammunition onto the concrete pavement, into the air, really wherever their guns were pointing, in order to disperse her followers. All this to fail miserably at silencing a woman who speaks for thousands of others. I hope that by amplifying these voices, my work can one day achieve a fraction of what hers does.

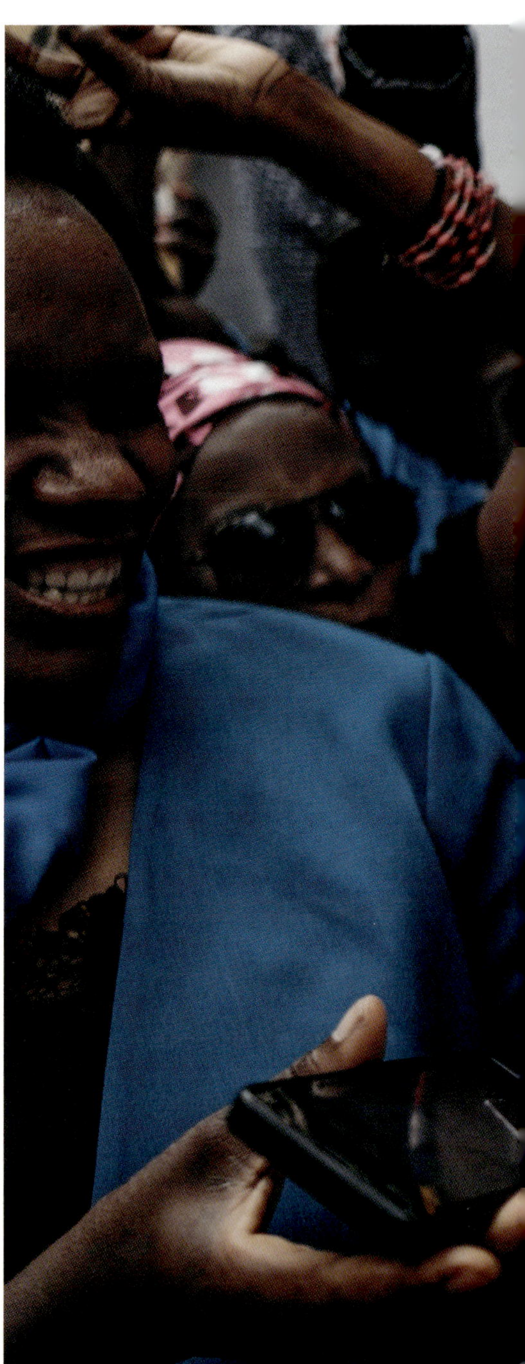

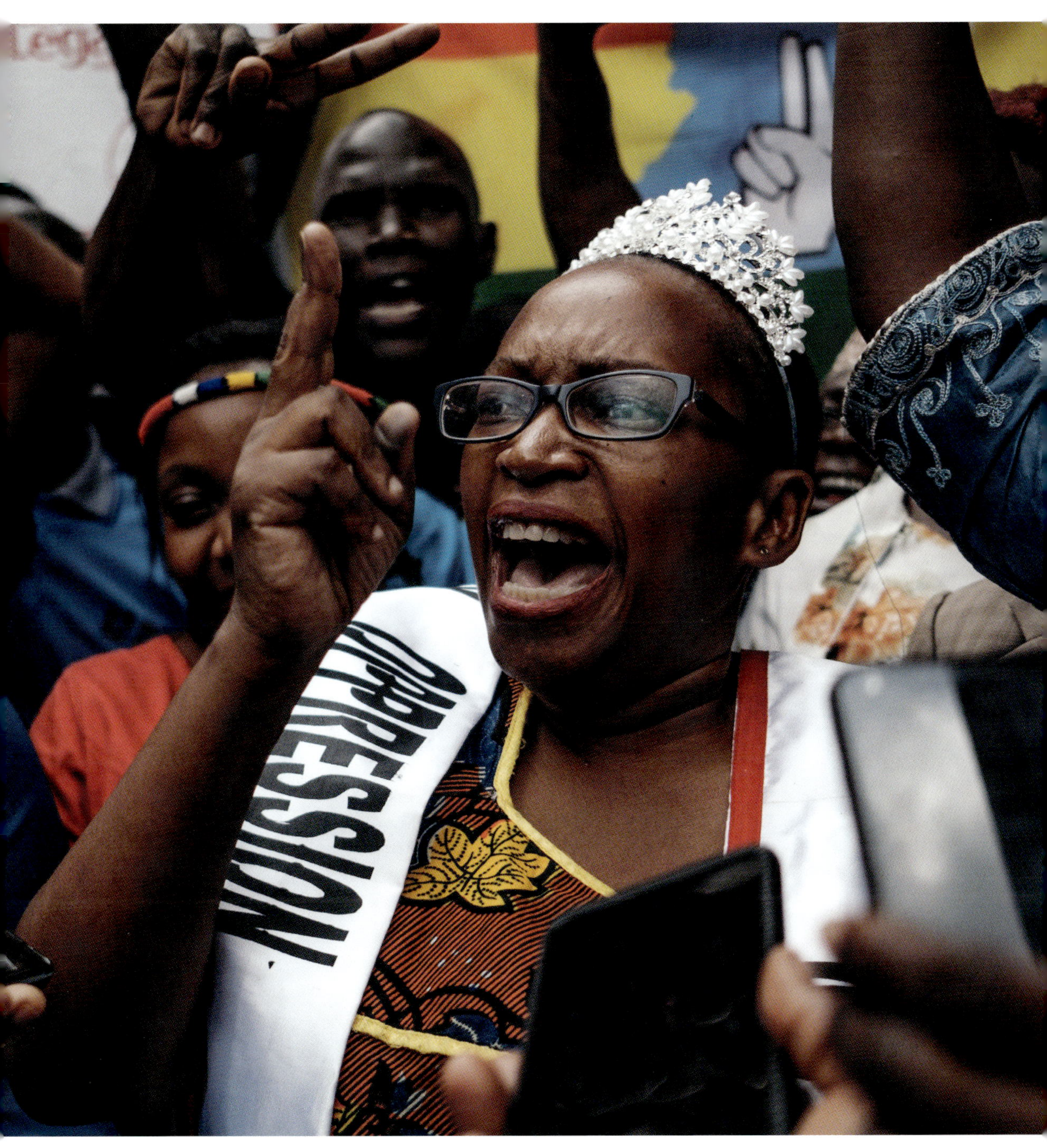

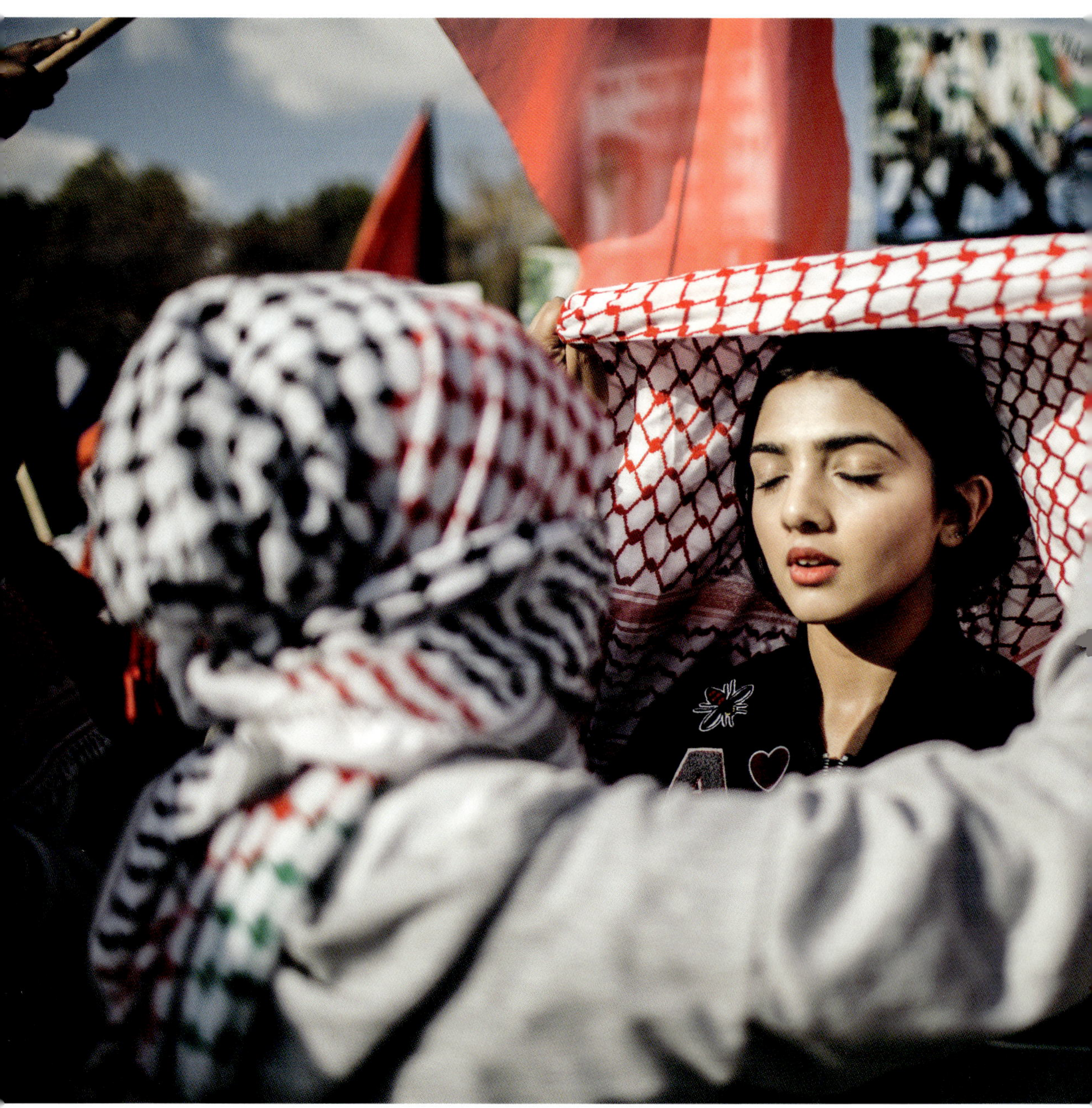

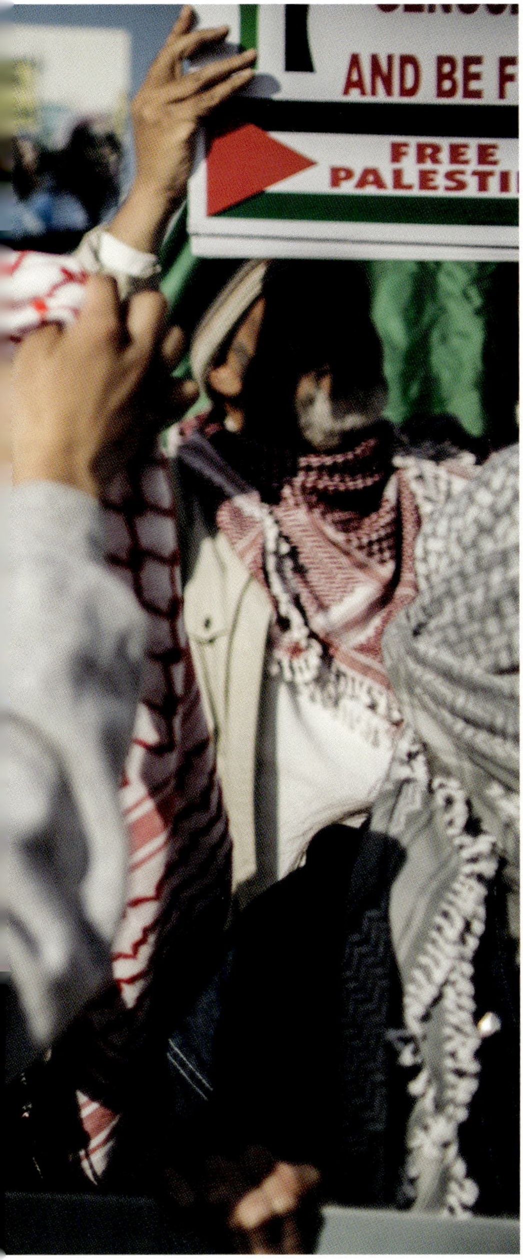

Gulshan Khan

South African

Keffiyeh

Johannesburg, South Africa; 2018

As a South African woman who grew up at the end of apartheid, knowing the face of oppression, of dispossession, understanding intimately generational struggle and, mostly, perseverance despite the odds, the Palestinian struggle is one that is very close to my heart. As photojournalists, we always create with the hope that our work can make some sort of impact, even if it is just to inspire someone to look again or think twice. To move people towards action, justice and healing, to build bridges and to foster a better world with our images is the ultimate goal, but I will take whatever small goodness that I can get. This image created so many full-circle and serendipitous moments. I had just given a talk about pictures and social justice in a little place called Roshnee in Johannesburg, at a community photo club. On the drive home I got the news that this image had made the list for *TIME* magazine's top 100 pictures of 2018. The girl in the image, Atiyya Dawood, comes from this very community in Roshnee, and on that day her image and this plea for justice would be seen all over the world.

Rania Matar

Lebanese American

Farah, Aabey, Lebanon, 2020

Aabey, Lebanon; 2020

As a Lebanese-born American woman and mother, my cross-cultural experiences inform my art. I have dedicated my work to exploring issues of personal and collective identity through photographs of female adolescence and womanhood, both in the United States, where I live, and the Middle East, where I am from. My work addresses the states of 'becoming' – the fraught beauty and the vulnerability of growing up – in the context of the visceral relationships to our physical environment and universal humanity. It is also about collaboration, experimentation, performance and empowerment. This image is part of my series SHE. In this work, I focus on young women in their 20s – the ages of my daughters. I portray the raw beauty of their age, their individuality, physicality, texture and mystery and I create a personal narrative with them. The process is collaborative and the women are active participants in the image-making process. Farah was part of the young generation who had been protesting in Lebanon, during the popular uprising of October 2019, demanding to get rid of the corrupt government. There were factions trying to undermine the protests and they burned Farah's car. We collaborated to portray the moment, immortalizing the car before it went to the dump. It was an act of resistance and it was important to tell her story.

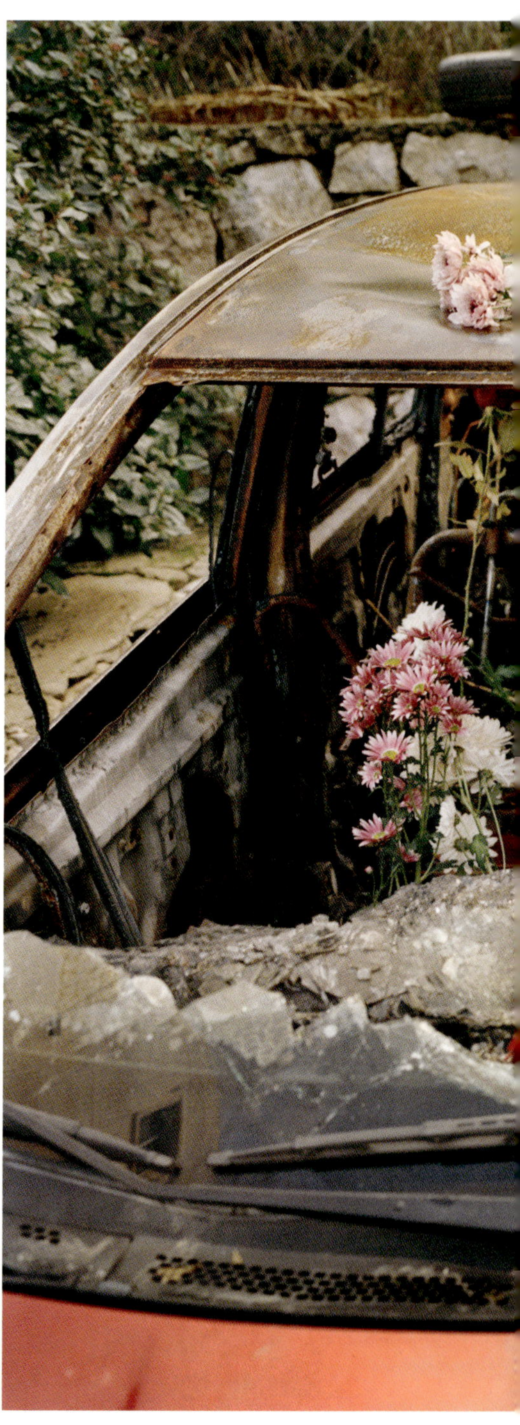

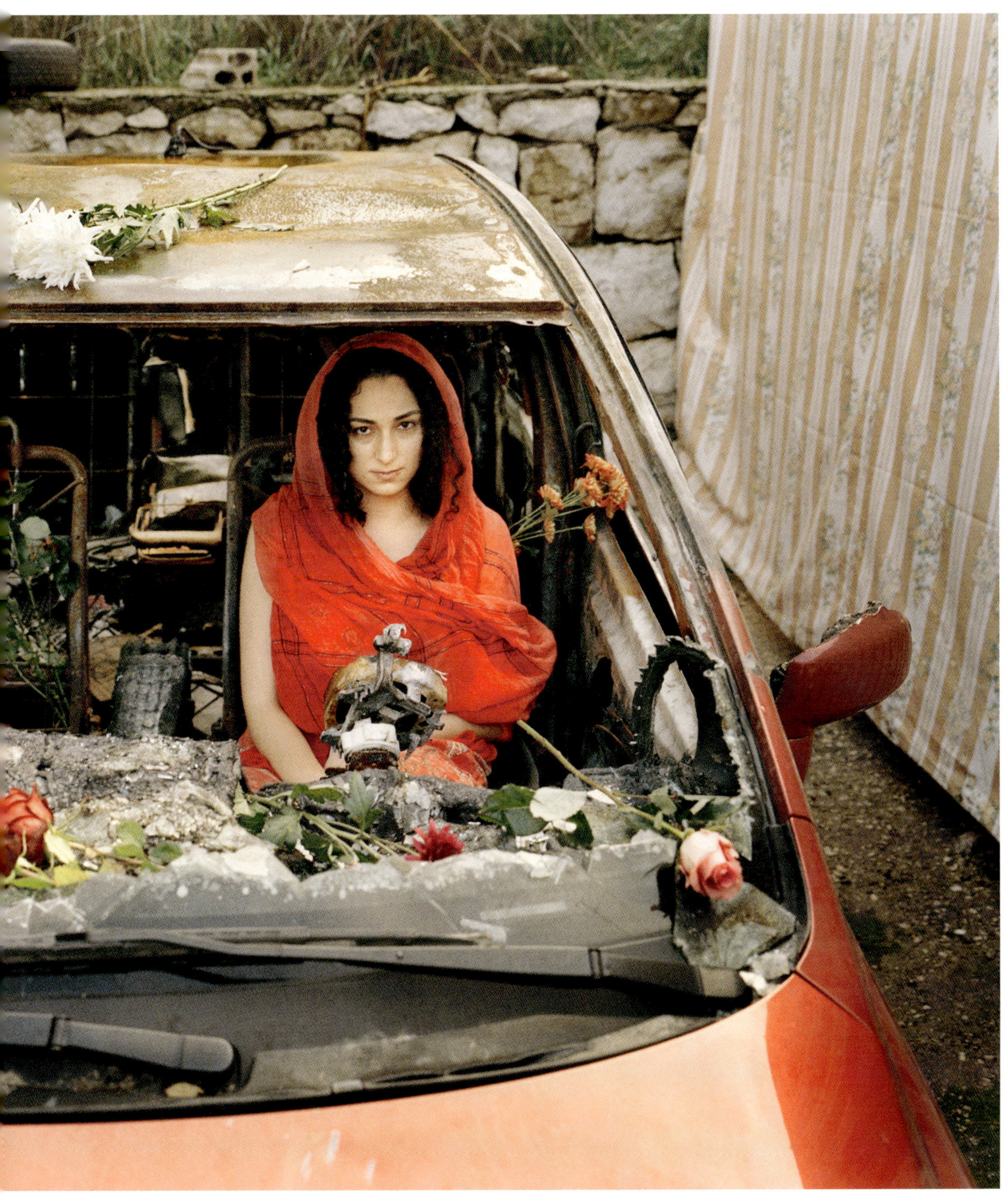

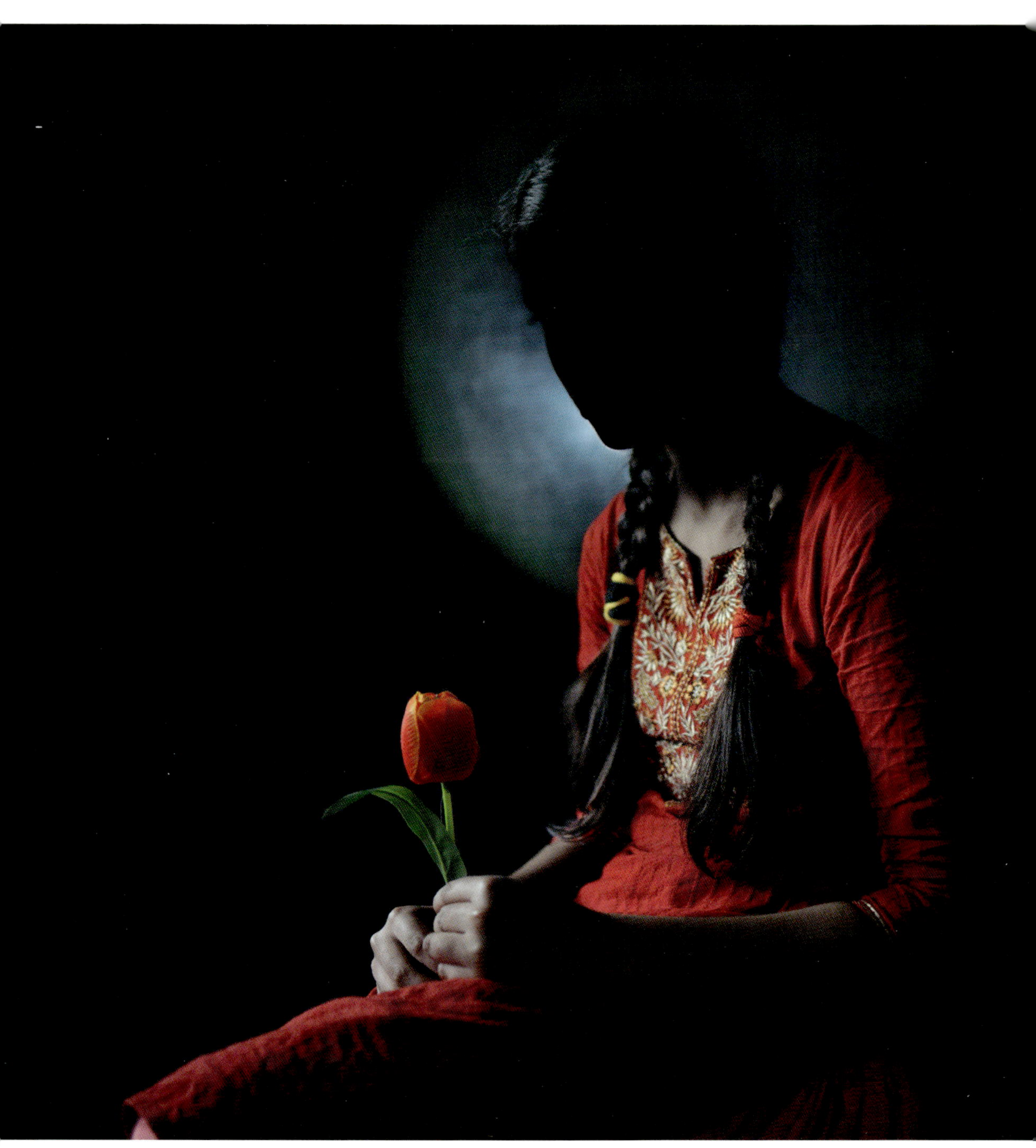

Smita Sharma

Indian

Portrait for A.

West Bengal, India; 2018

We Cry In Silence is my long-term project investigating cross-border sex trafficking between India and Bangladesh. Documenting the lives of trafficking survivors was challenging because of restrictive Indian laws that prohibit telling stories about underage sex crimes – partially to protect the children but also to protect the image of the state. I wanted to show the personality of the girls and share their stories even though I could not show their faces. To make anonymous portraits and yet make them look beautiful was like solving a visual puzzle. I made this portrait of A. at a shelter that cared for some 80 to 90 girls and women who were victims of abuse or who are still considered to be at risk. A. had eloped with a man several years prior. After she overheard him making plans to sell her to a brothel in Kolkata, she managed to escape. She was found at the railway station in Canning, West Bengal, India, by representatives of Childline, an organization that helps children in distress. She was then brought to this shelter where she was counselled by mental health experts. A few months later A. was reunited with her family.

Carol Guzy

American

War and Innocence

Kukes, Albania; 1999

They came by the thousands. Ragged and weary. Wailing women carrying children with distant stares. The elderly trying to hold back the tears. Some injured. Many terrified. Serb aggression was unleashed on ethnic Albanians with a vengeance as NATO bombs began to fall in the spring of 1999. It was called ethnic cleansing. I saw Agim Shala, only two years old, passed through the barbed-wire fence into the hands of his grandparents at a camp run by the United Arab Emirates in Kukes, Albania. The flood of humanity into neighbouring Albania and Macedonia was massive. Harried aid workers tried to keep up with the flow. Tent camps were set up as refugees waited in limbo for their uncertain future. But in the middle of so much chaos, I knew this was a joyful photo of members of the Shala family finding each other again, and learning that they had all made it to safety after fleeing Kosovo. This photo went on to win the Pulitzer Prize in 2000, one of four I've been honoured with in my career.

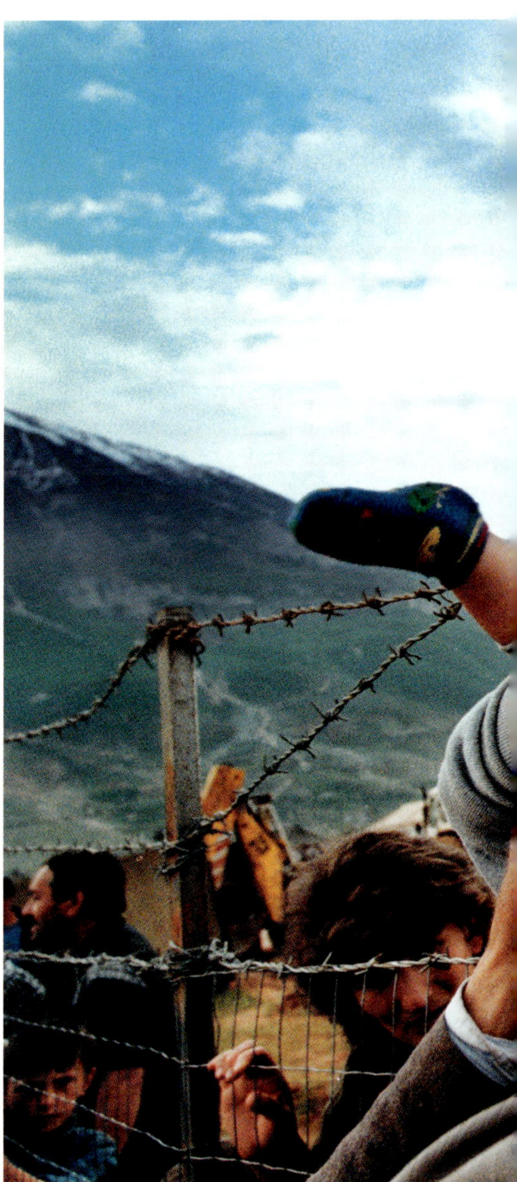

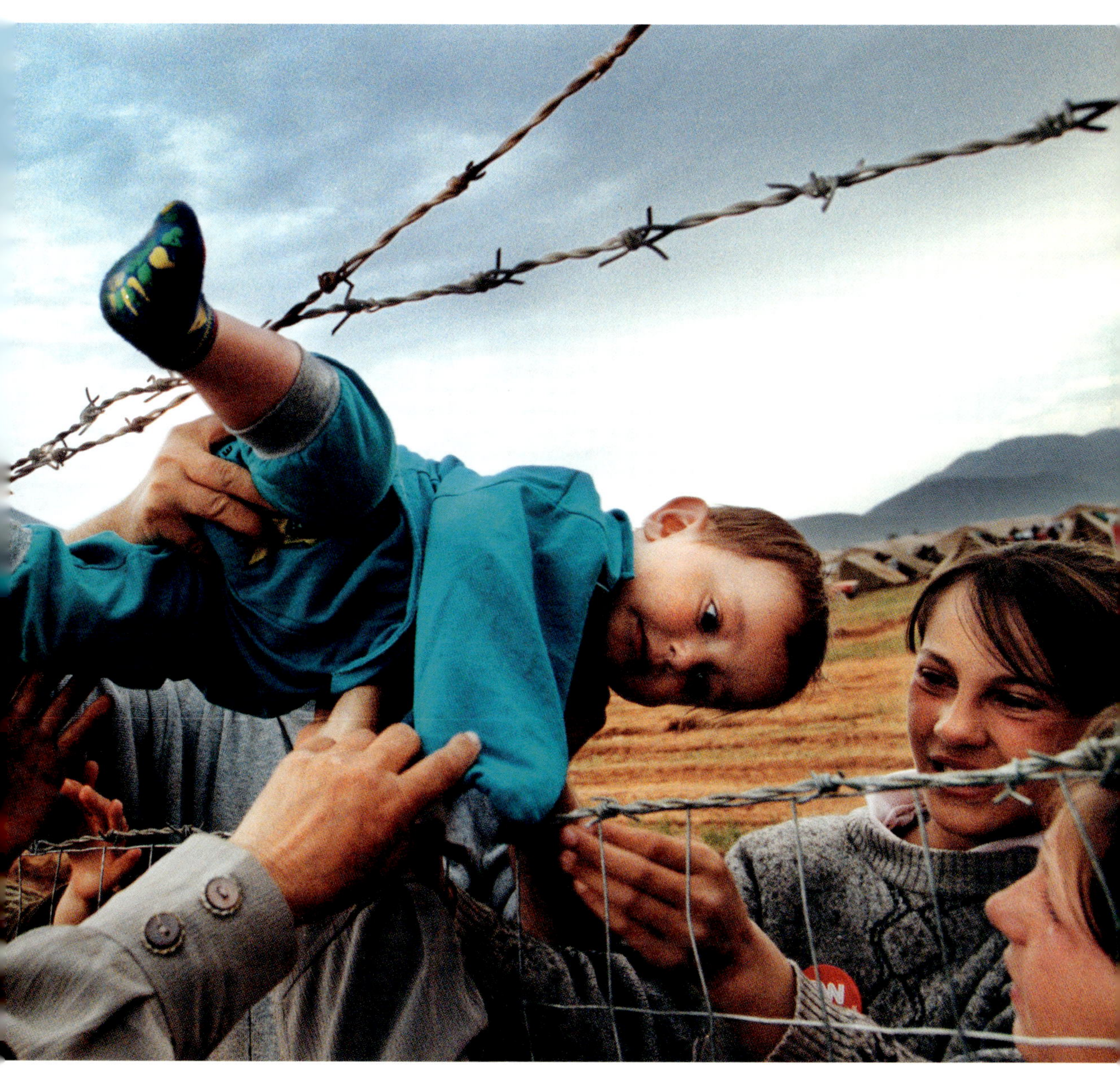

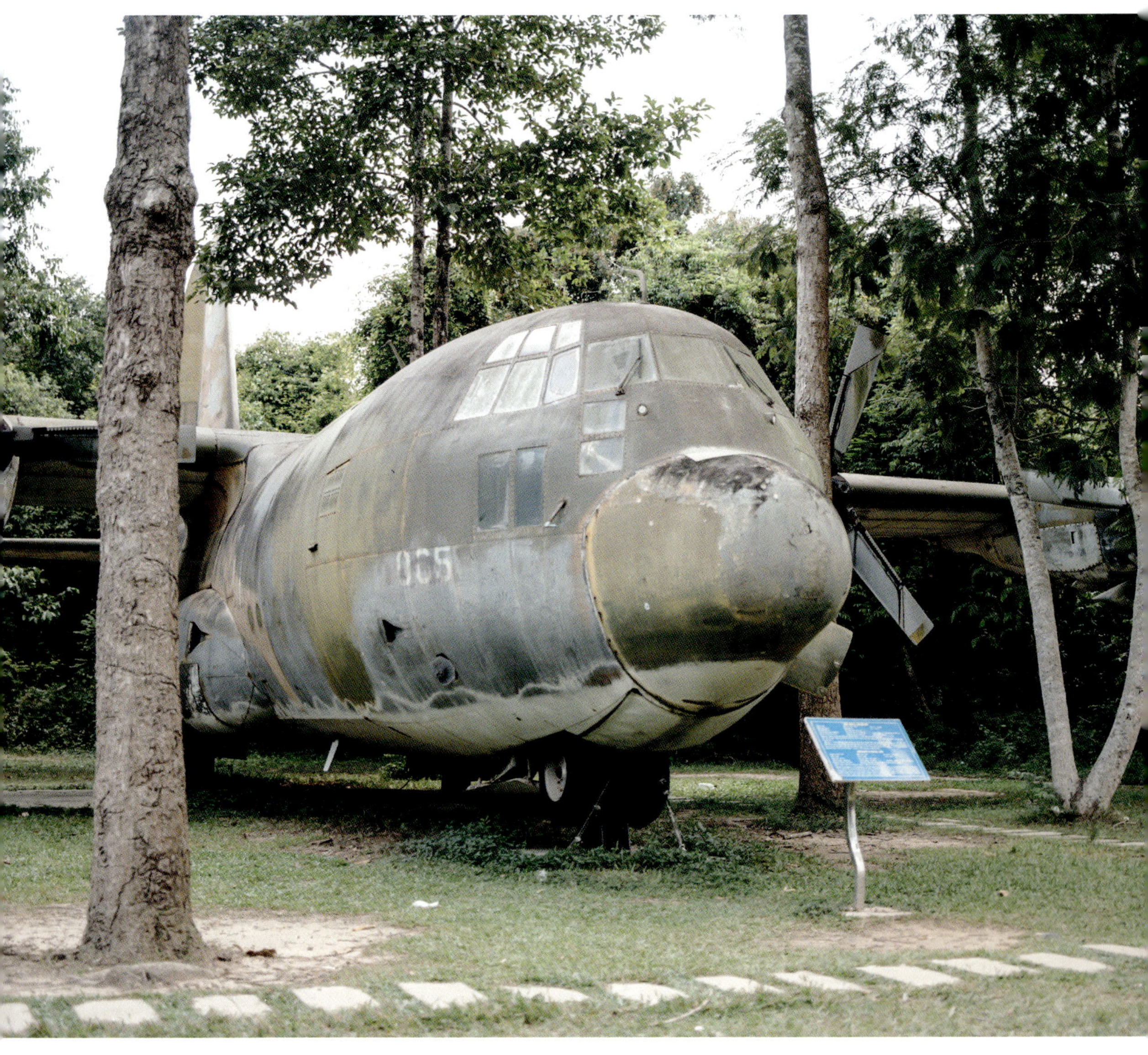

◀

Yen Duong

Vietnamese

War Plane

Cu Chi, Ho Chi Minh City, Vietnam; 2021

This image is part of my ongoing series Alternative Imaginaries, a conceptual project that explores the intricate interrelationship between collective memory, private history and political amnesia in modern-day Vietnam. Growing up in a post-war and post-truth era in a country still haunted by its past, and later on working as a photojournalist for various foreign media throughout Vietnam, I am always confronted with the polarization of information and conflicting versions of history. This ongoing work is a self-inquiry of the inherited and invented memories that inform my understanding of Vietnam's turbulent history and how it is connected to the present day. Intrigued by the concept of 'prosthetic memory', I documented the evidence of time in Vietnam's changing landscapes and juxtaposed images taken in both public and domestic settings with online found images of the American war in Vietnam from 1955 to 1975. It is an attempt to see the thin line between fact and fiction, to question our identity as a nation and to remember the things that might have been forgotten. Every gesture is a reminder of the past. Every image, a cancellation of history.

▶▶

Susannah Ireland

British

Chinook Takeoff

Char-e-Anjir, Helmand Province, Afghanistan; 2009

In August 2009, I was freelancing in London primarily for the *Independent* newspaper. I heard that there was a spare place alongside the newspapers' defence correspondent to embed with the British army in Helmand Province, Afghanistan. Naturally I jumped at the chance, as I was keen to document the military operations in the run-up to the forthcoming presidential elections that would be crucial in determining Afghanistan's future for years to come. In this image, British army troops shelter from the dust storm as their Chinook helicopter departs from Char-e-Anjir town in Helmand Province, Afghanistan, 12 August 2009. A local building in the area was taken over by the British armed forces Prince of Wales's Company as an outpost of the Welsh Guards regiment in Nad-e Ali. Helmand Province was a Taliban stronghold, a key centre of opium production and part of the wider ongoing International Security Assistance Force's operation to clear the region of insurgency control. I had to wear clear goggles in order to see directly into the dust storm without getting sand in my eyes, but it enabled me to find the small and important details in the image, such as the wedding ring on the soldier in the foreground.

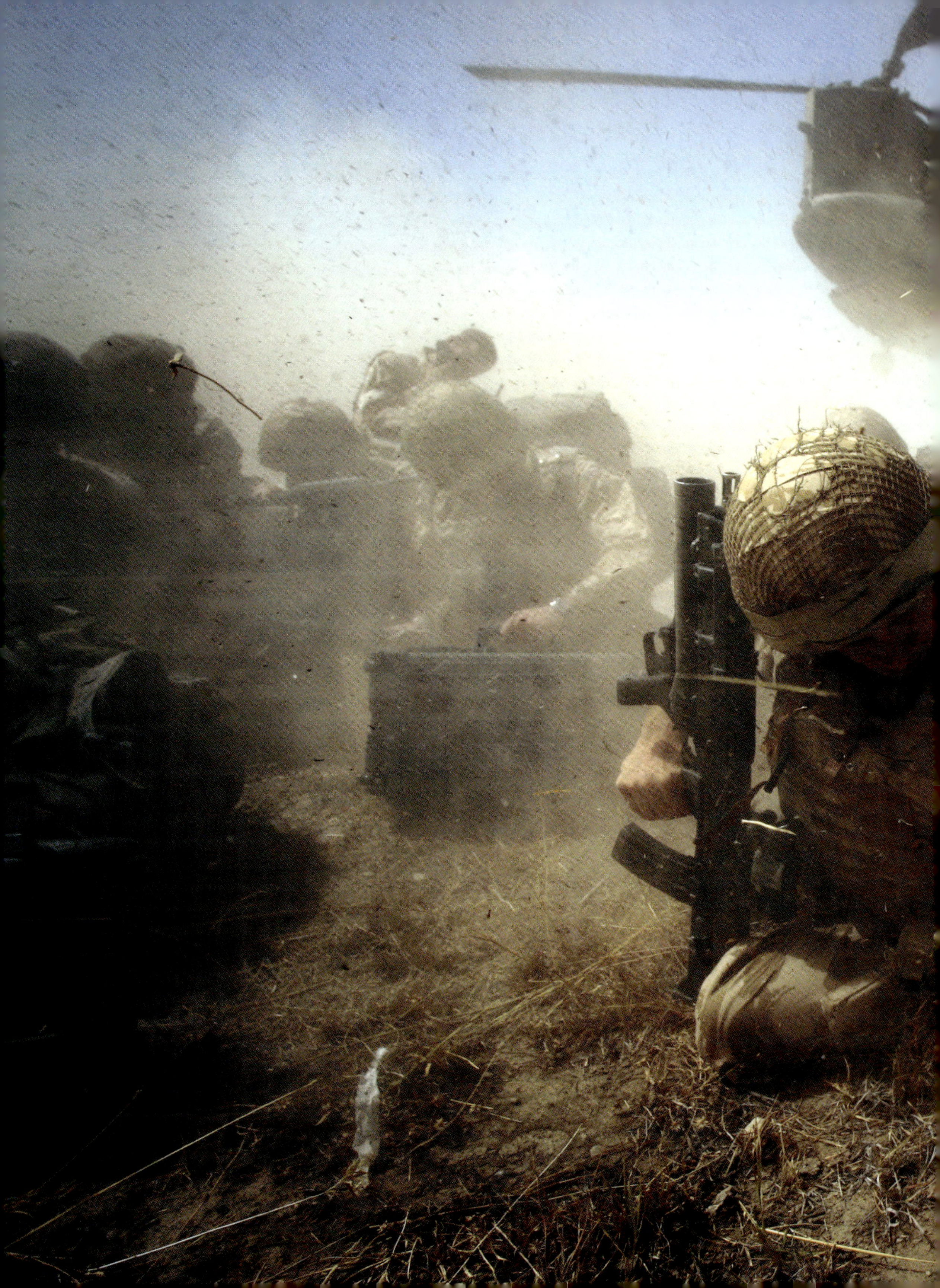

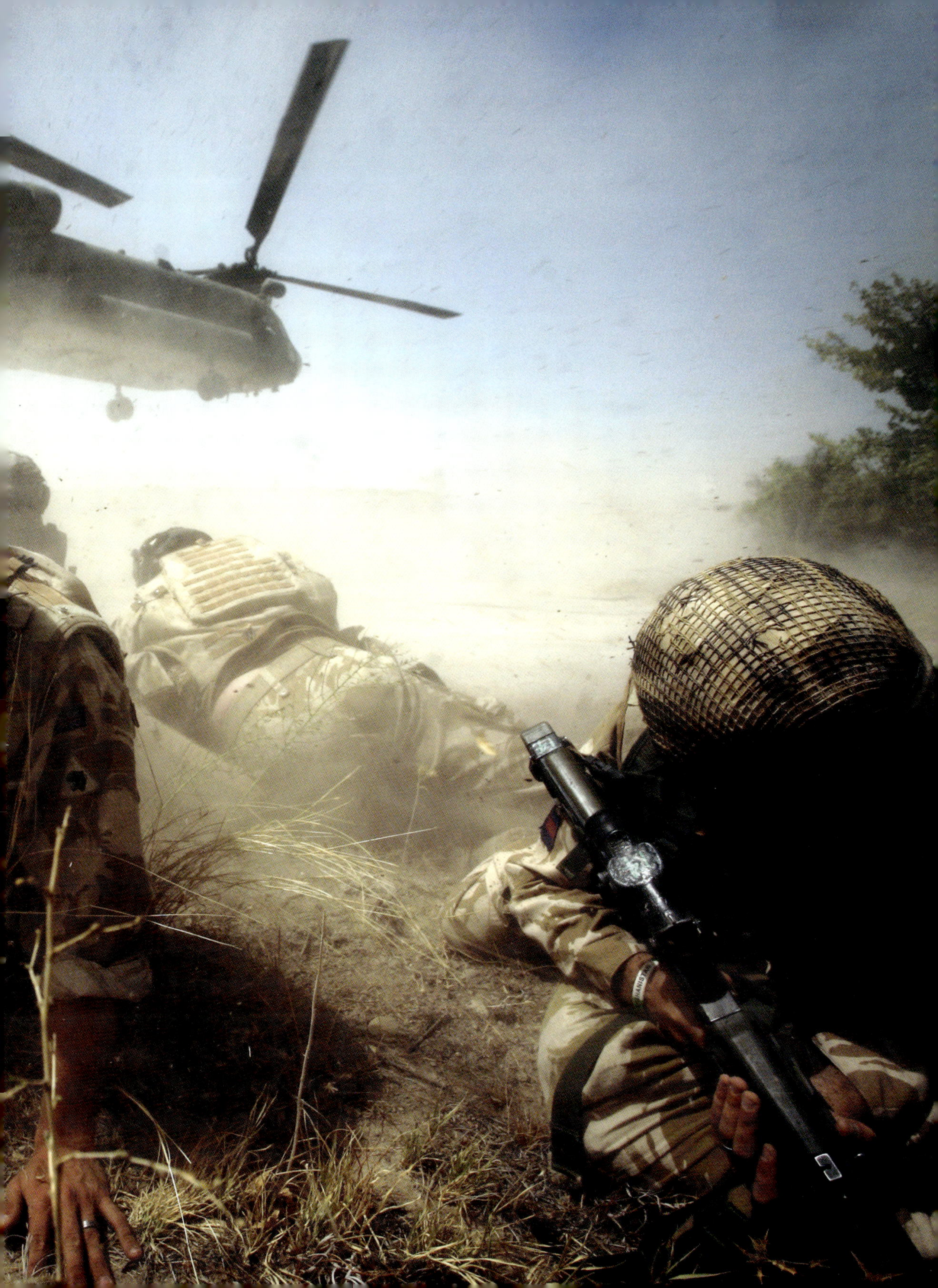

Sim Chi Yin

Singaporean

Helicopter, from One Day We'll Understand

Duxford, UK; 2020

For my series, Interventions, I photographed archival prints from the British Imperial War Museum on a lightbox, merging verso and recto of the prints into one plane. The captions, papers and different coloured wax pencil markings on the backs become visible. It is a sort of montage created by light, in-camera. These prints are the colonial visual record of the so-called 'Malayan Emergency' – a euphemistic term used by the British for the 1948–1960 war between anti-colonial insurgents and British and Commonwealth troops in the Malay Peninsula and Singapore. My paternal grandfather, a leftist journalist and educator, was imprisoned by the British at the start of the conflict and later deported to China where he was executed for his socialist beliefs. It is fruitless to try to use the master's tools to dismantle the master's house, but given the lack of a visual record on the side of the leftist guerrilla movement, I have had to use colonial imagery to visualize this war. The colonial archive mostly shows triumphant white bodies 'smashing' the local leftist insurgency, but I have reinterpreted and repurposed the images to try to narrate this war afresh. When viewed as a single photograph, the merged sides expose the layers of indexing that happen in the colonial archive, and question what and how we know of and remember this war – and others like it.

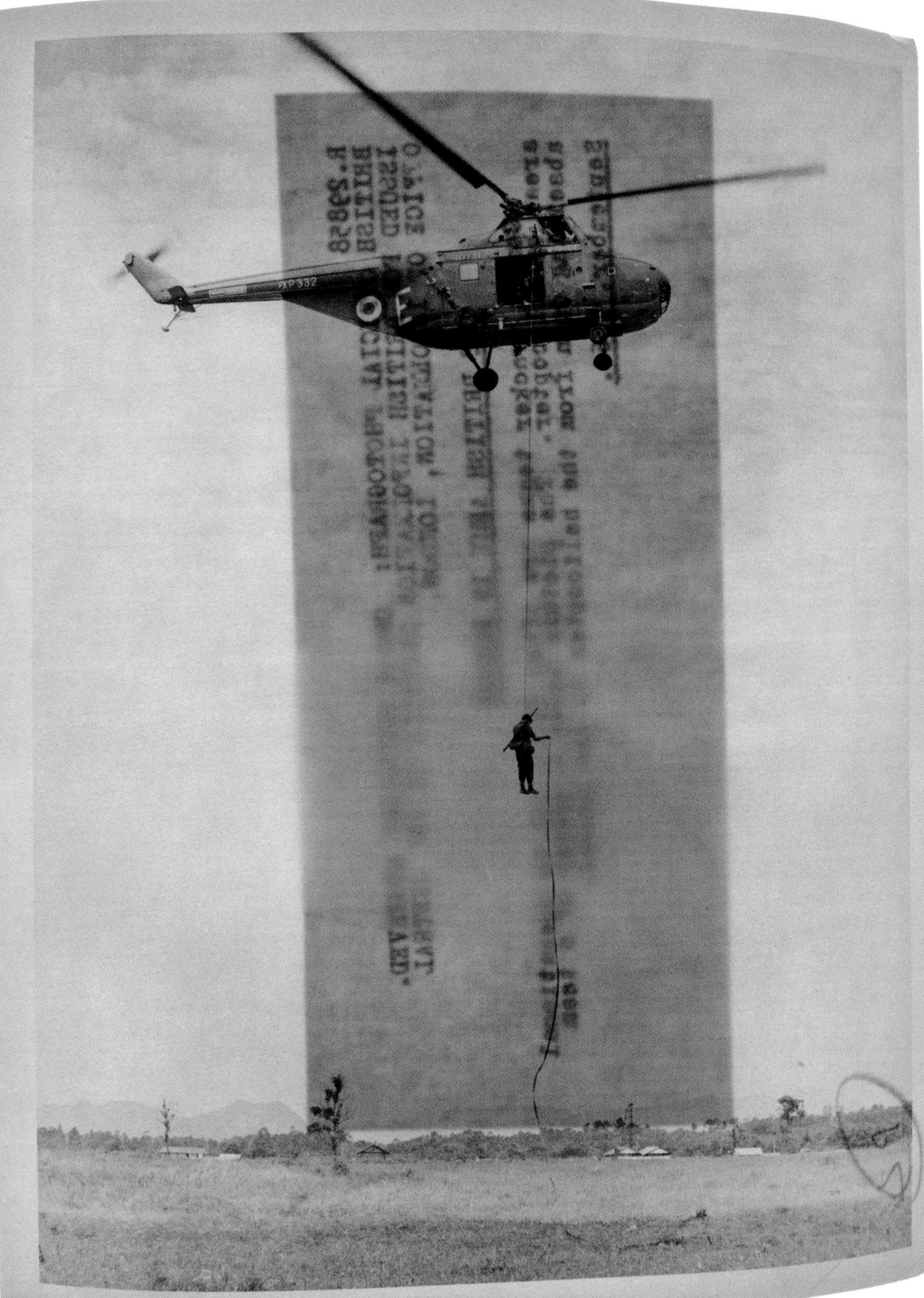
XP332

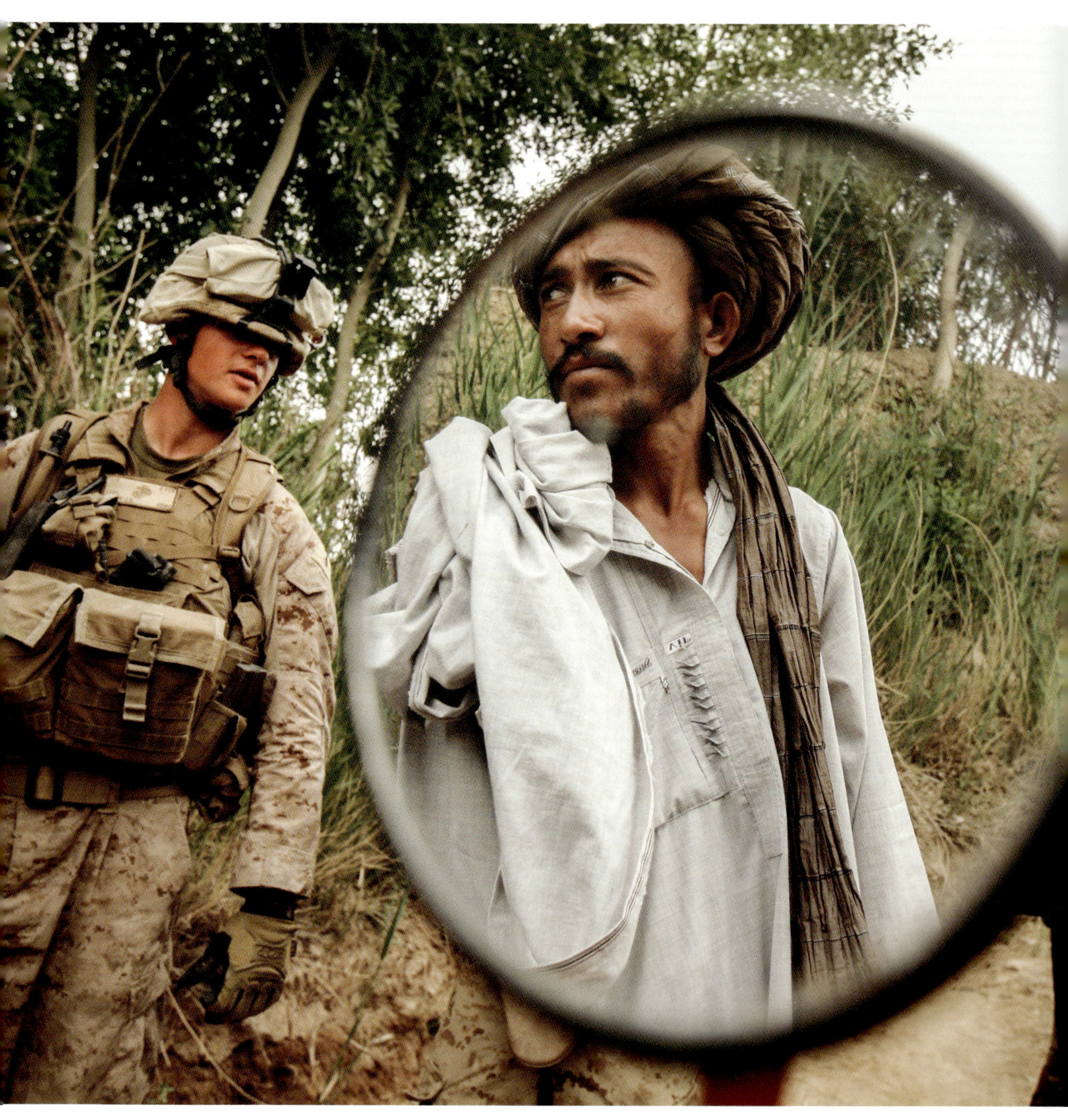

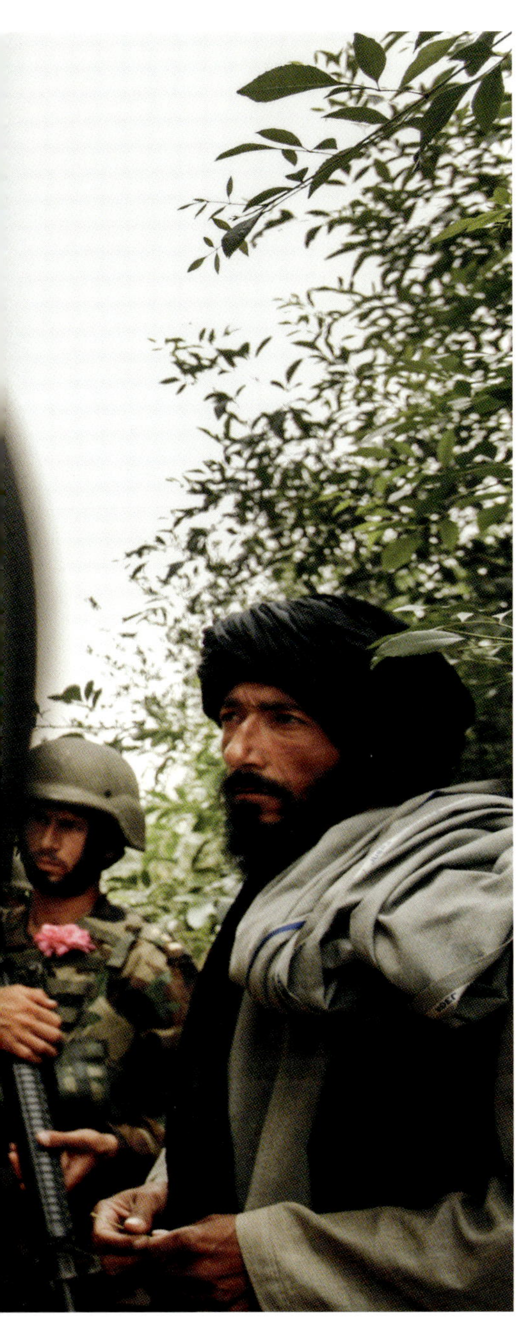

Asmaa Waguih

Egyptian

Why did you come here?

Afghanistan; 2010

An Afghani citizen is seen in the mirror of his motorcycle after being stopped and searched by US Marines while patrolling in the Karez-e Sayyidi area near Marjah district in Helmand province. I took this photo while I was on a patrol with some Afghani army members, one of many embeds I have done while working for Reuters to cover the conflict in Afghanistan. I have also covered different embeds as a freelance reporter in Iraq after the fall of Baghdad from 2003 to 2006. Many times during the embeds, US Army members would stop locals for a search to check if they are part of the insurgency. But I have also noticed that the insurgency is partly due to the presence of the foreign army. This photo shows the reaction of the local Afghans and represents the two sides of the conflict; the invaders and the drama of the Afghanis and how much each side belongs to two different worlds. Throughout my work as a journalist, I have always been interested in this theme, conflict and armed struggle. It takes different shapes and makes room for extremism and terrorism to flourish.

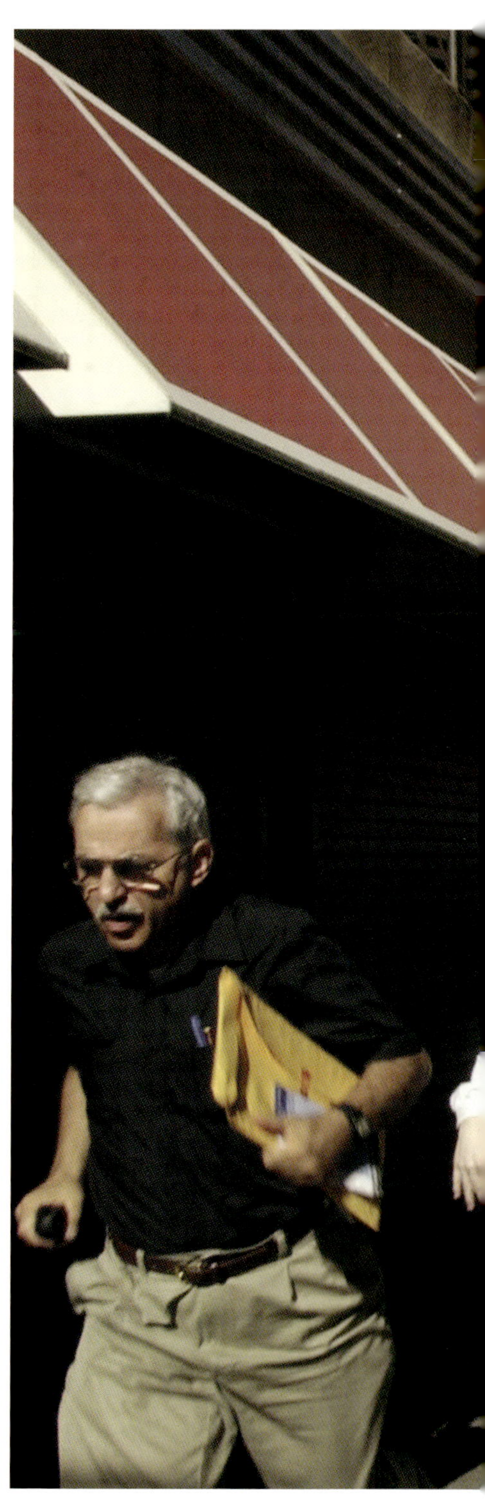

Suzanne Plunkett

British American

Men flee from the collapse of the World Trade Center in New York

New York City, New York, USA; 2001

I was just a few streets away when the first tower collapsed. I heard someone yell, 'It's coming down!' before the world I was in came crashing down. As the chaos thundered towards me, I managed to turn and capture this scene of oncoming panic. There were many photographs taken that day in New York that reflect the horror of the 9/11 attacks. That mine is among those regularly republished on anniversaries is, I think, down to the very human stories it tells. While it was easy to see the atrocities as assaults on America, my photo was a split-second glimpse into the fear and the terror of the people caught up in this moment. Twenty years on, I have met several of the men in the photograph and have heard their stories about that day and the tragedy and trauma that followed. Although this photo reflects a shared moment when we all stared into the abyss, it belongs to them and their families. Working as a staff photographer for the Associated Press in New York at the time of the attacks then led me to work extensively in Afghanistan and Indonesia. After that I settled in London, where I worked on staff for Reuters before becoming a freelancer.

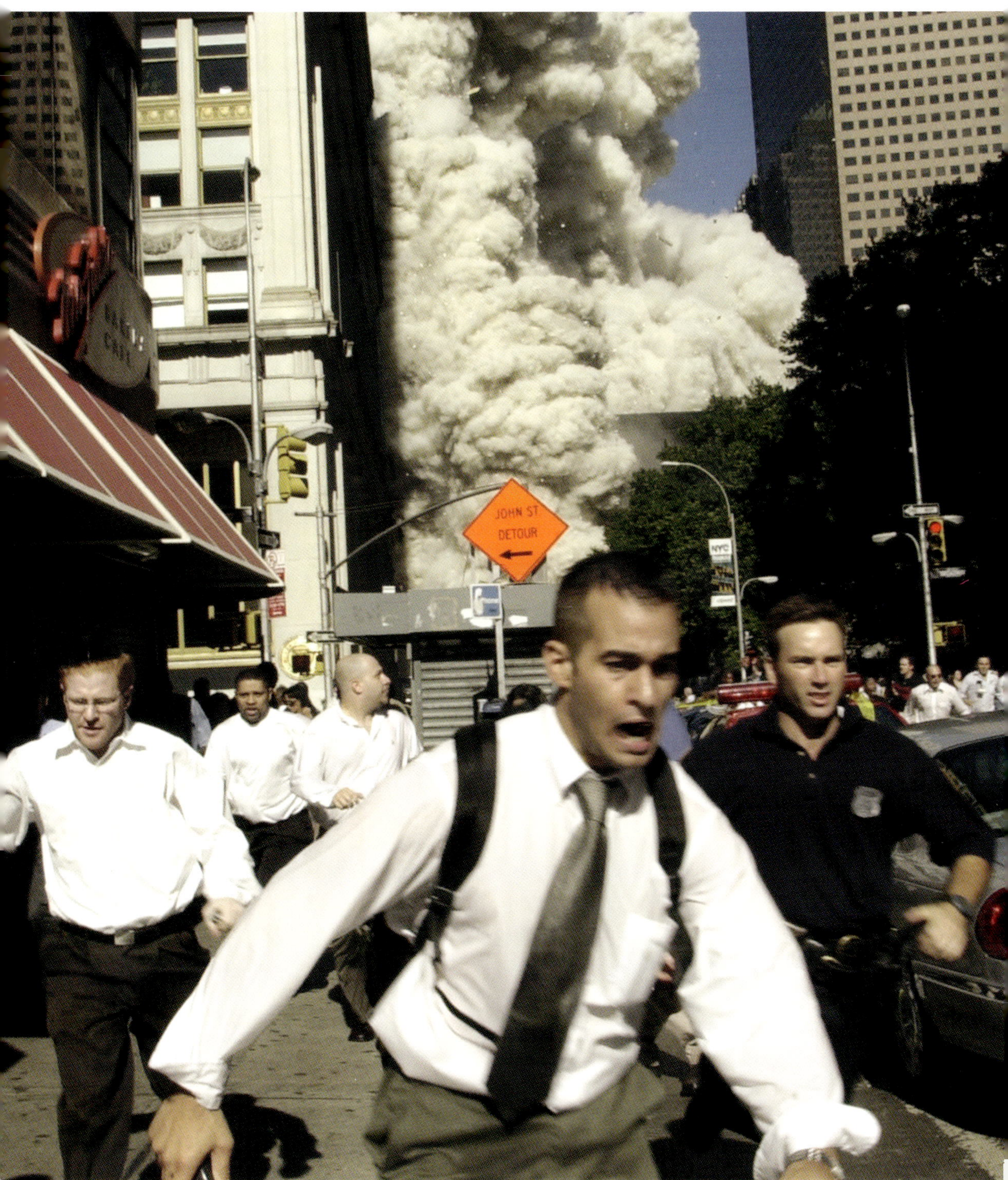
JOHN ST
DETOUR

Lynsey Addario

American

Governor's Compound, Fall of Kandahar

Kandahar, Afghanistan; 2001

Shortly after 11 September 2001, I found myself on a plane to Pakistan. I had never covered war before, but had worked extensively in both Pakistan and Afghanistan and knew that I had to be there to document whatever came next. I made this photo of Afghan men in Governor Gul Agha Shirzai's compound in Kandahar the day the Taliban fell in December 2001, and I have returned continuously for two decades. Much of my work since then has focused on Afghan women: attending school, graduating from university, training as doctors, running for government positions and just generally working – often at great personal risk. And as a single American woman journalist myself, I had to engineer ways to be able to do my own work: sometimes posing as the wife of a male journalist colleague, or photographing through the mesh eye panel of my burka to be as surreptitious as possible. Twenty years after I took this picture, we're now watching the Taliban return and I don't know what that will mean for all of the incredible and resilient Afghan women whose lives I documented over the last two decades.

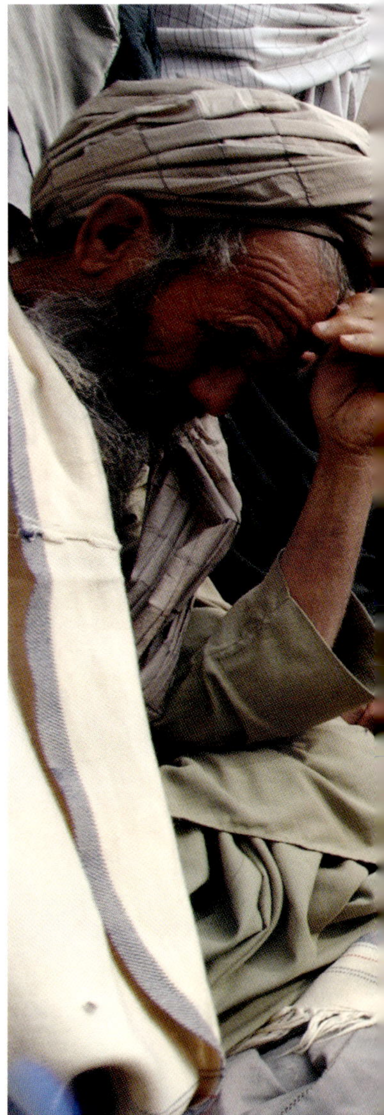

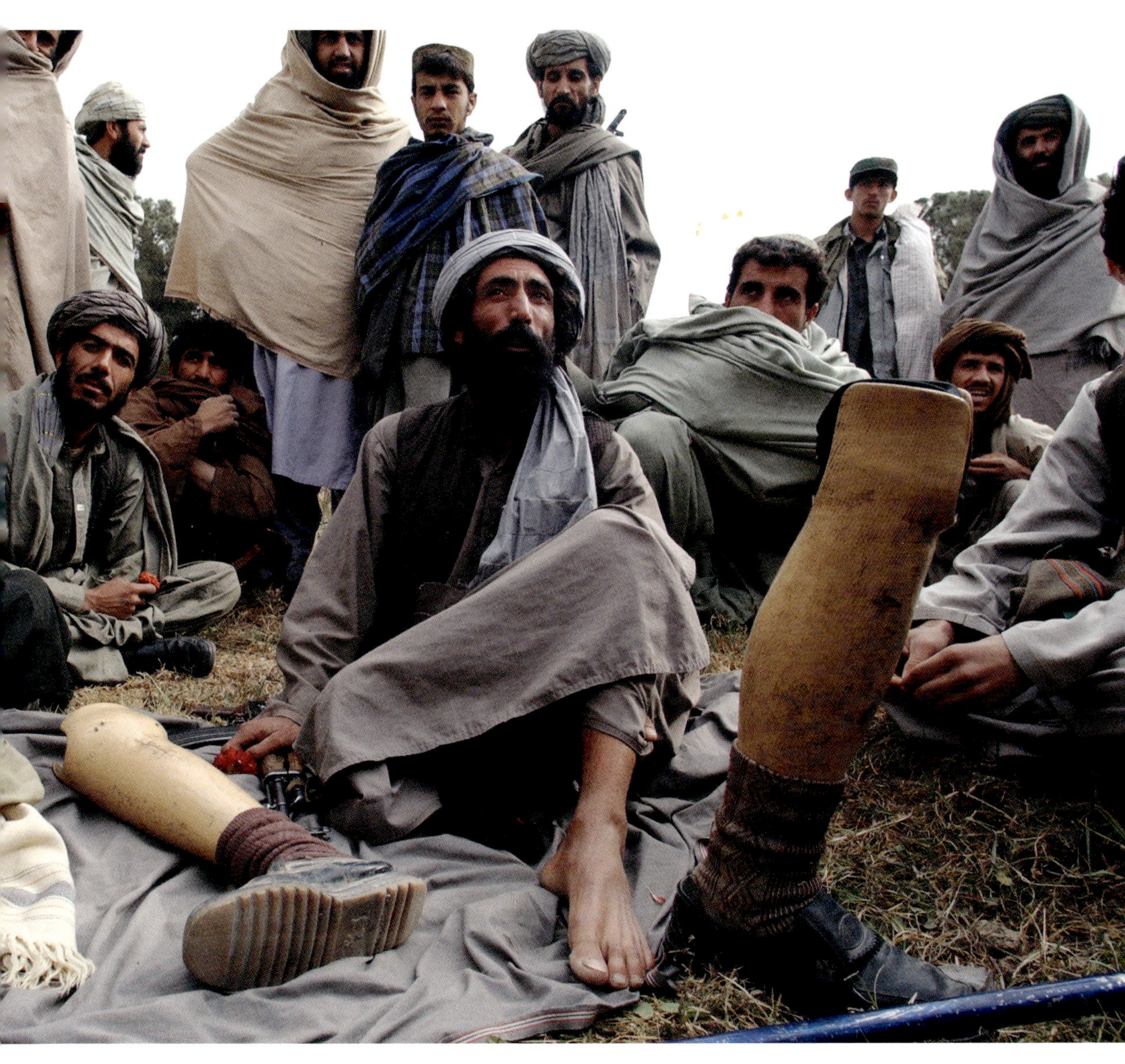

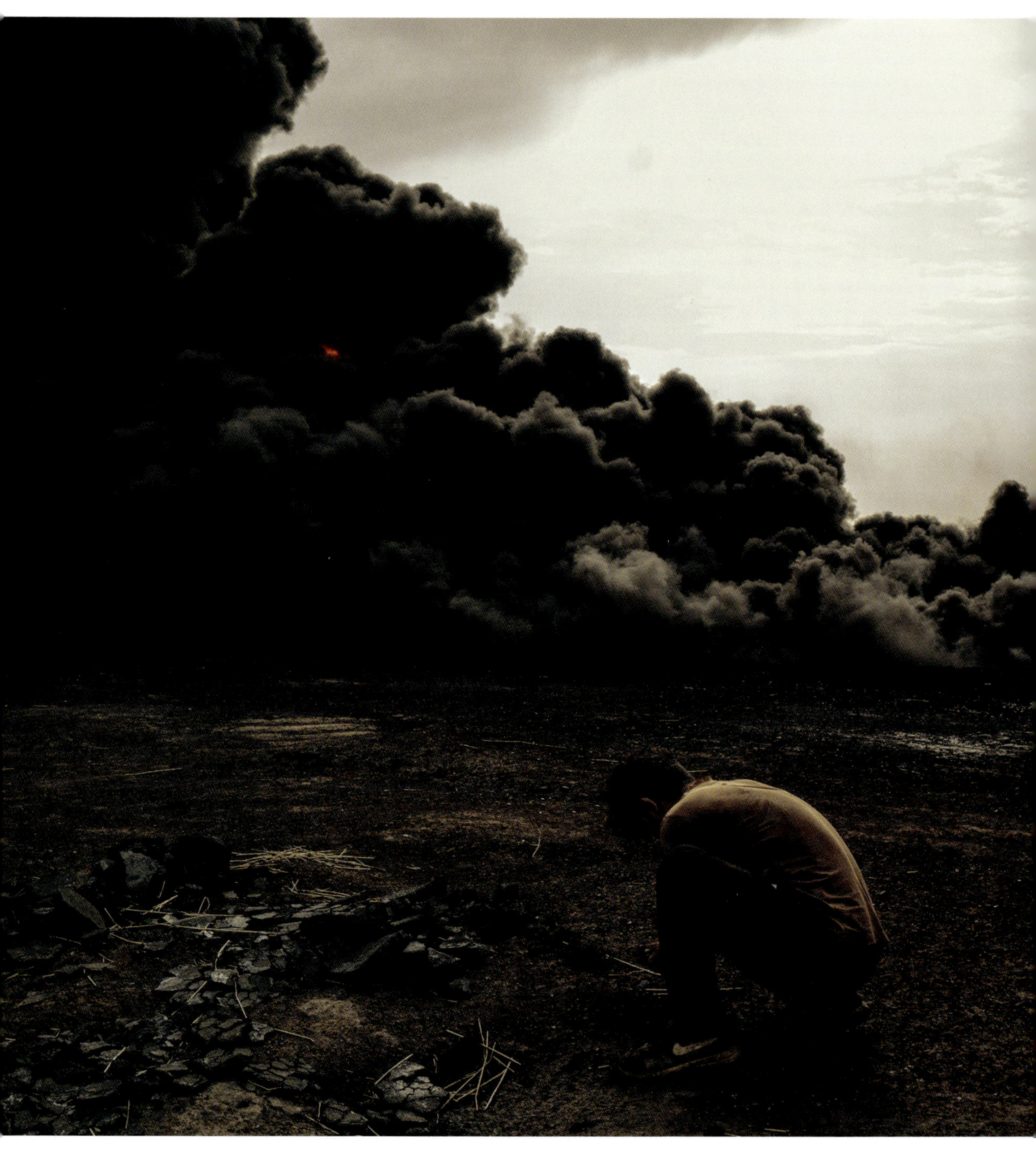

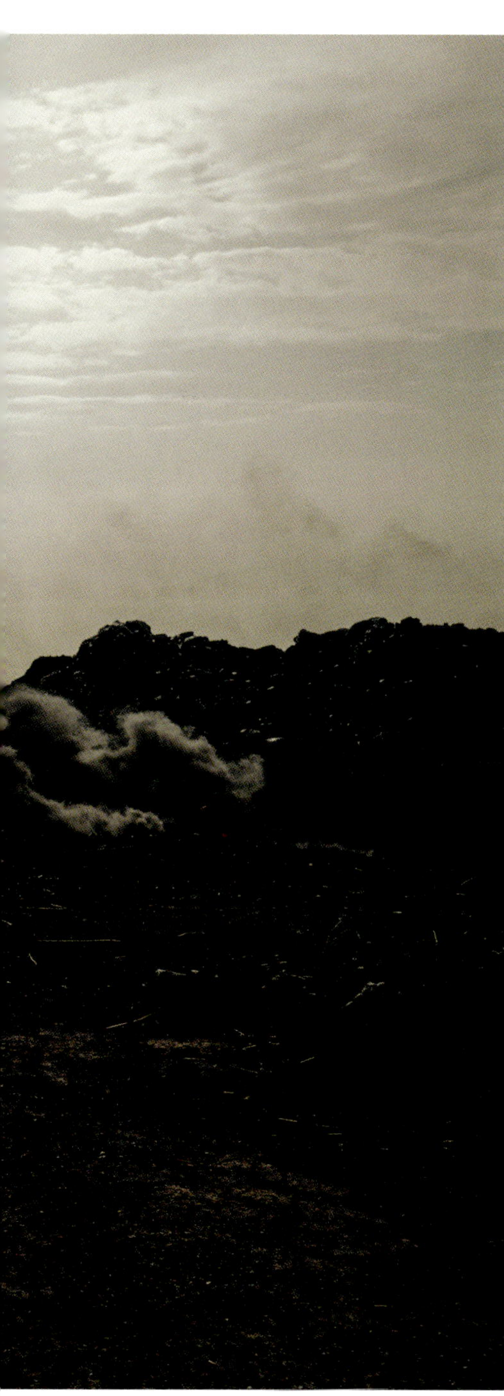

Nicole Tung

American Hong Konger

Haytham in the Oilfield

near Haddad, Syria; 2021

Haytham, who is about 15, uses soil to wash oil off his hands, as smoke from a furnace's burn-off rises in the distance, at a makeshift oil refinery near Haddad in northeast Syria. Haytham says he has been working at the refinery for at least five years. Northeast Syria, and particularly Hasakah province, holds Syria's richest oil fields. The ad hoc nature of the refining process, in which crude oil is made into diesel and other products, causes grave environmental damage, and severely impacts the health of the residents and the workers at the refineries. An economic crisis, a grinding war and few job opportunities push many boys, some of whom are as young as eight, to start working in the refineries despite the extreme hazards. I have been covering the Syrian conflict since 2012, and each time I go, I feel I am witnessing the further deterioration of a country – and its culture, its history – that has been at war for far too long. A generation has passed and the consequences of this conflict and its staggering toll are in plain sight. Yet geopolitical decisions continue to haunt the most vulnerable, and the least powerful.

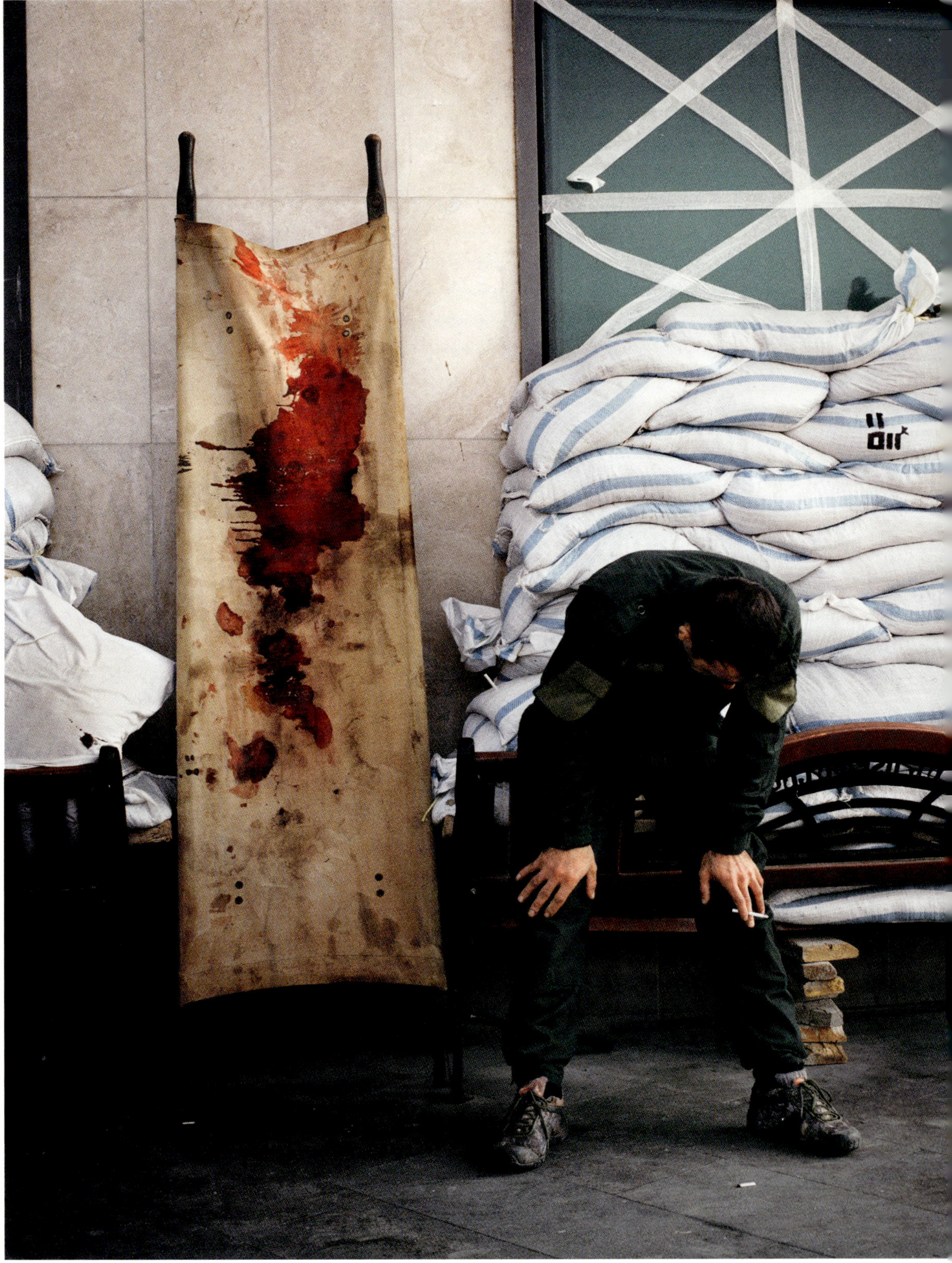

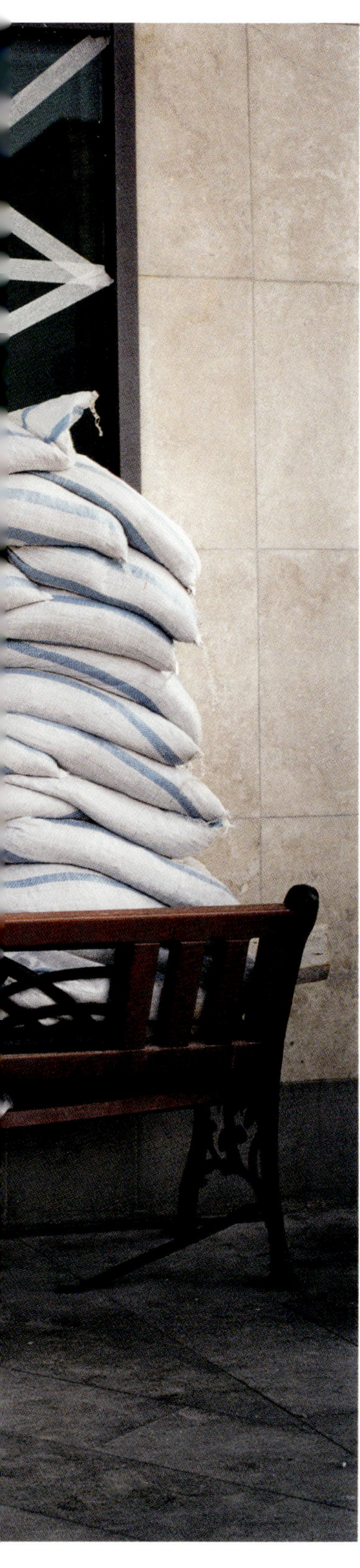

Anastasia Taylor-Lind

British Swedish

Untitled

Nagorno Karabakh; 2020

A man weeps beside a bloodied stretcher outside the emergency department of the Republican Medical Centre in Stepanakert. The war between Azerbaijan and Armenia lasted for six weeks and ended on 10 November 2020 with a Russian-mediated peace deal that left Azerbaijan retaining territory gained during that war and regaining control of districts surrounding Nagorno-Karabakh that Armenia had captured in the 1990s. This was my second time working in Nagorno Karabakh – I had been there almost a decade earlier documenting a story about the region's Birth Encouragement Programme and was able to re-photograph many of the families I had met before. I no longer consider myself a conflict photographer and was not drawn to the region to cover the fighting; instead, I was invested in the lives of people I had met and got to know, and I wanted to see how they were being impacted. This was also during the first year of the pandemic, and medical facilities and workers were dealing with a severe COVID-19 outbreak on top of wartime violence. It was a fraught, scary time for everyone involved. This photo was taken six days before the war ended, and I felt deeply for this man as he was overwhelmed by everything going on around him.

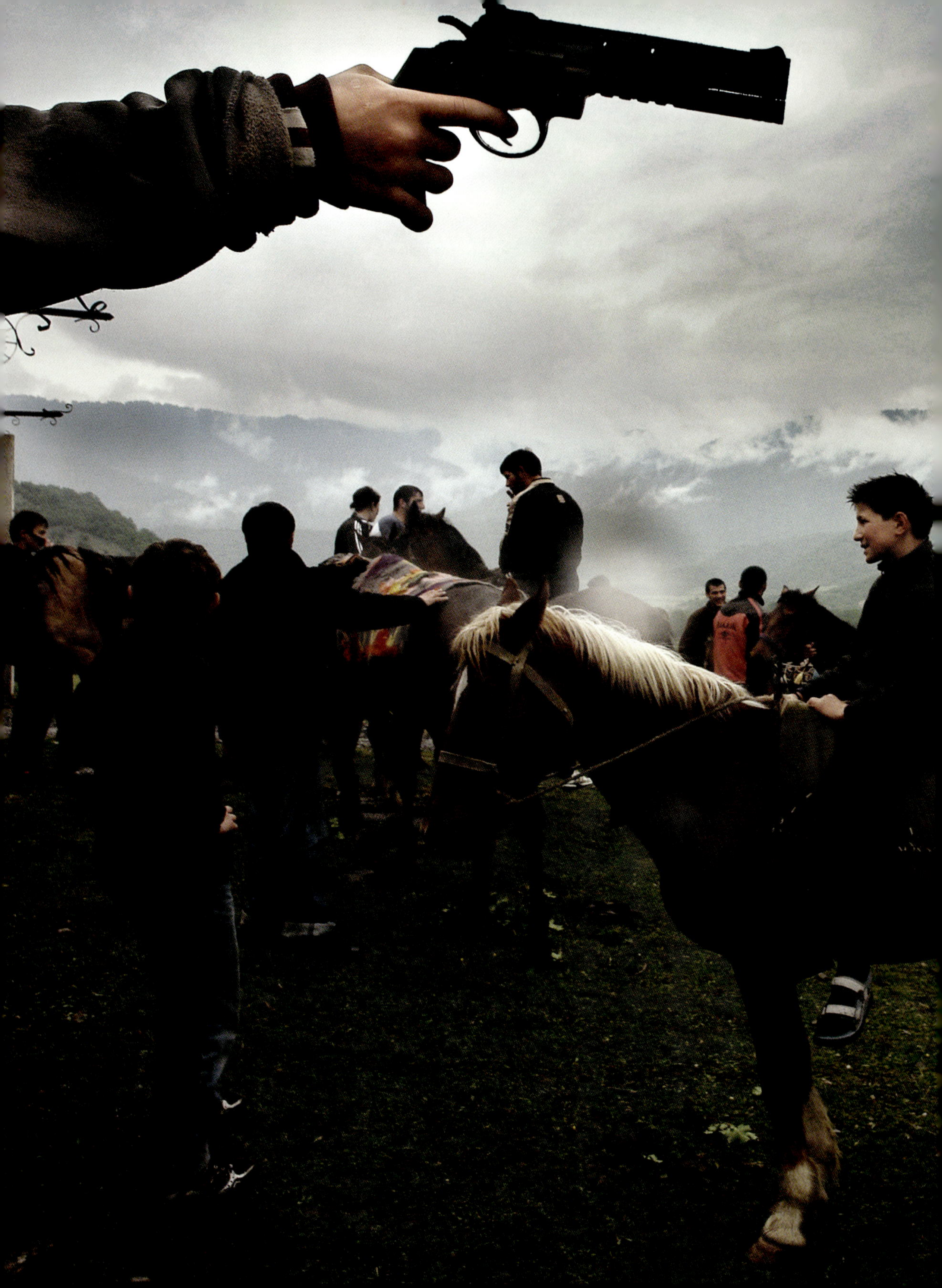

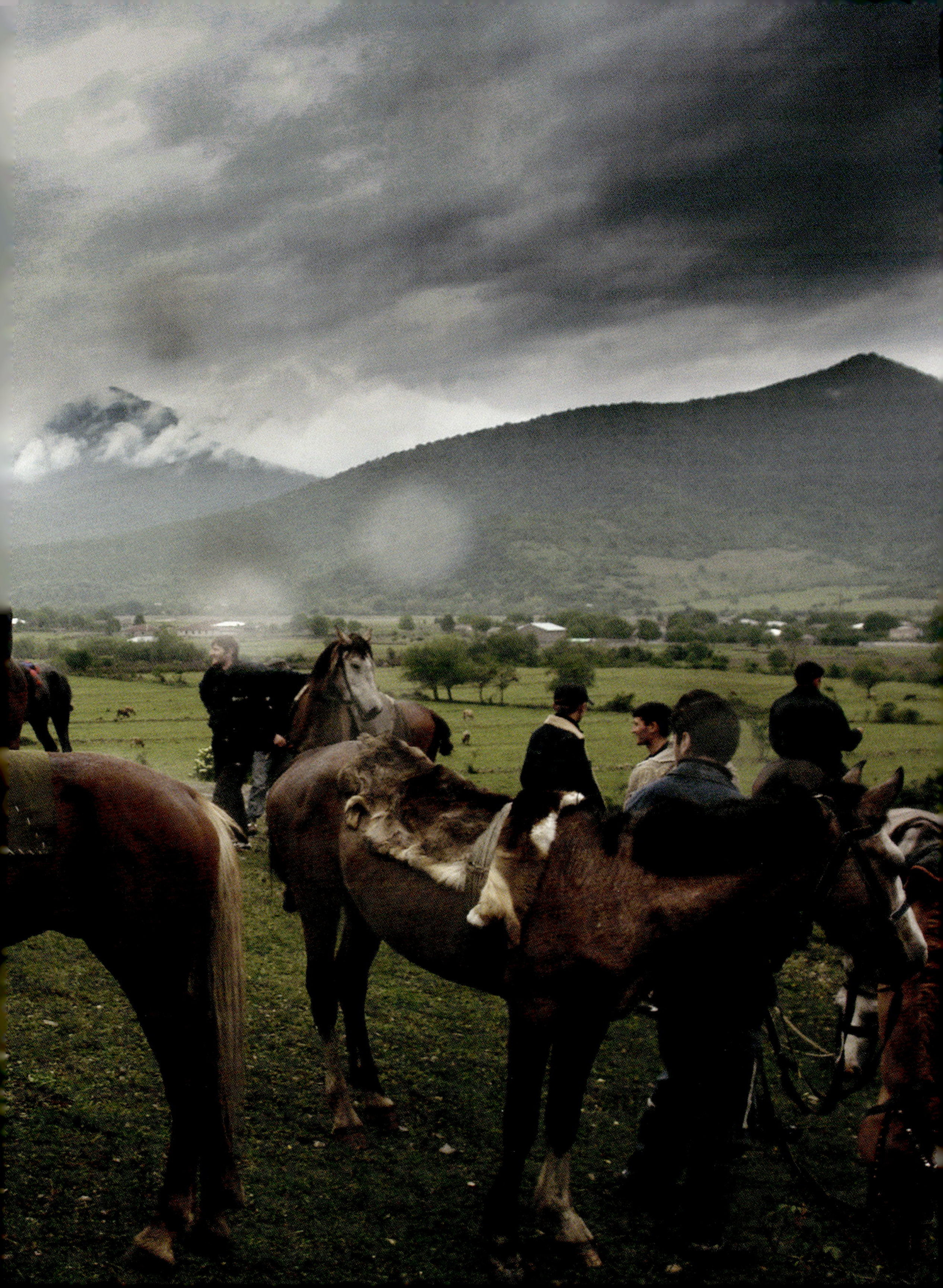

◄◄

Daro Sulakauri

Georgian

Terror Incognita

Pankisi Gorge, Georgia; 2008

This image is a part of my first photo project, Terror Incognita, about Chechen refugees in the Pankisi gorge. At the time I made these photos, it was widely believed that Pankisi was an extremely dangerous place to travel, especially for a woman. My journey was often accompanied by my Chechen uncle, who followed me around like a bodyguard, afraid that I would be kidnapped for a forceful marriage. On this day Chechens were celebrating Independence Day, where, traditionally, children take toy guns and shoot at each other. It was raining. A boy on the left was pointing his gun, I saw the scene coming together and reached for my old Sony camera, the first digital camera I owned, which I had won in a local photo competition. When I pressed the shutter, it released only two long seconds later, so I had always to press the shutter two seconds before I thought the moment would happen. I feel the image represents a moment in history: the gun, the horses, the younger generation and what they experienced when they were growing up in this isolated village. At the time, the word 'Chechen' was a synonym for terrorism. I wanted to destroy this stereotype and show a different perspective, one of ordinary people struggling to have a better life.

►

Kholood Eid

Palestinian American

Sisters Embrace

USA; 2019

In their sunny suburban backyard, I asked the sisters to embrace as I knelt and looked up at them, framing them intertwining in the sky. I worked on a four-part investigative series, Exploited, for *The New York Times* that examines the explosion in online images of child sexual abuse. While I have been commissioned a handful of times to make anonymous portraits for sensitive stories, I often find myself drawn to making them in my own time as a way to explore the world through ambiguity. Garry Winogrand once said that he wanted his pictures to raise more questions than answers, and while that may seem counterintuitive, it resonated with me. Body language, gesture, the relationship of light and shadow and one's relationship to space are elements that move me and inform my portraits. I did not want the survivors I photographed to appear sinister in any way, which can easily happen when the goal is anonymity. I wanted to honour the tenderness and courage I see in those who trust us enough to let us in. The sisters are survivors of the same horrors, and the digital trail of those crimes still haunt them years later. I hope they find strength and comfort in each other.

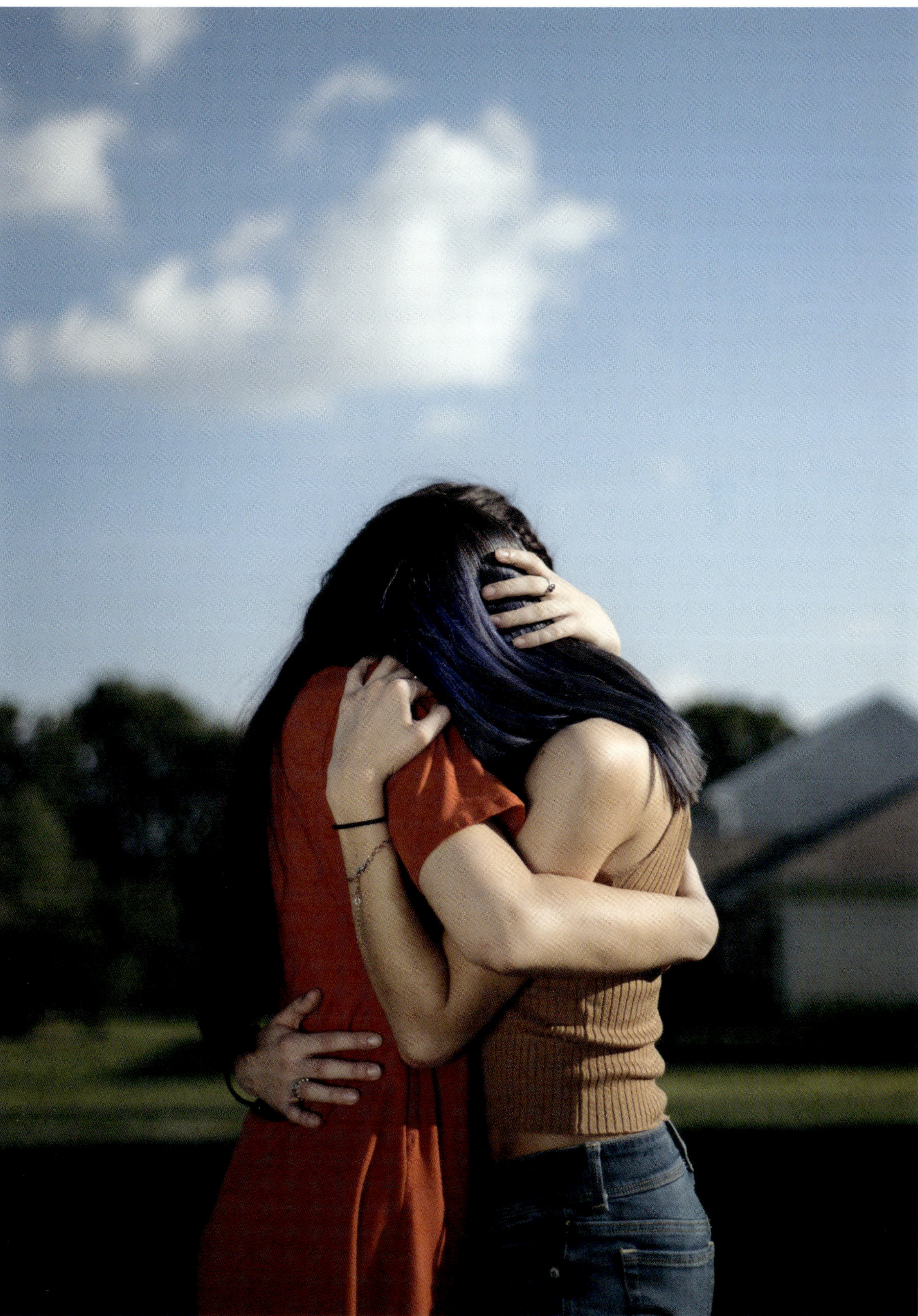

Reclamati

04

on

Many of the photographs in this selection represent an evolution in the medium – the photographer no longer dictates the narrative. Instead, the distinction between photographer and subject morphs into a visual collaboration. In that way, reclamation here is not just for the photographer, but also for those in the photographs themselves: they are being explicitly empowered to dictate the terms and the construction of their own narrative. This makes the images even more powerful: whether through painted mythology or protective nail polish, the agency of storytelling does not belong to the photographer alone.

Yumna Al-Arashi

Yemeni Egyptian American

Northern Yemen

Yemen; 2013

This work was made during my last trip to Yemen, before the ongoing conflict began in 2014. The image was part of a series of photographs that sparked conversation around the ways in which we perceive Muslim women in Western media. I felt the need to ask why Western media always portrayed Muslim women in a negative light, especially hijabi women. This portrayal used women's bodies as a weapon of war, creating propaganda under the usual guise of 'us' needing to save 'them' from their oppressors. I believe women's emancipation does not require women to adhere to any way of dress – whether it is hijab or bikinis. Defining emancipation based on physical appearance is not adhering to the truest form of the word. Woman's emancipation enables a woman to have equal rights in every realm, no matter how she dresses. I sought to photograph women close to me in landscapes and poses that reflect their power. The series was a launching point for my career as a photographer and helped me start to investigate the ways images impact our notions of the world, and why it is so important that we take a critical approach to the work we both digest and produce.

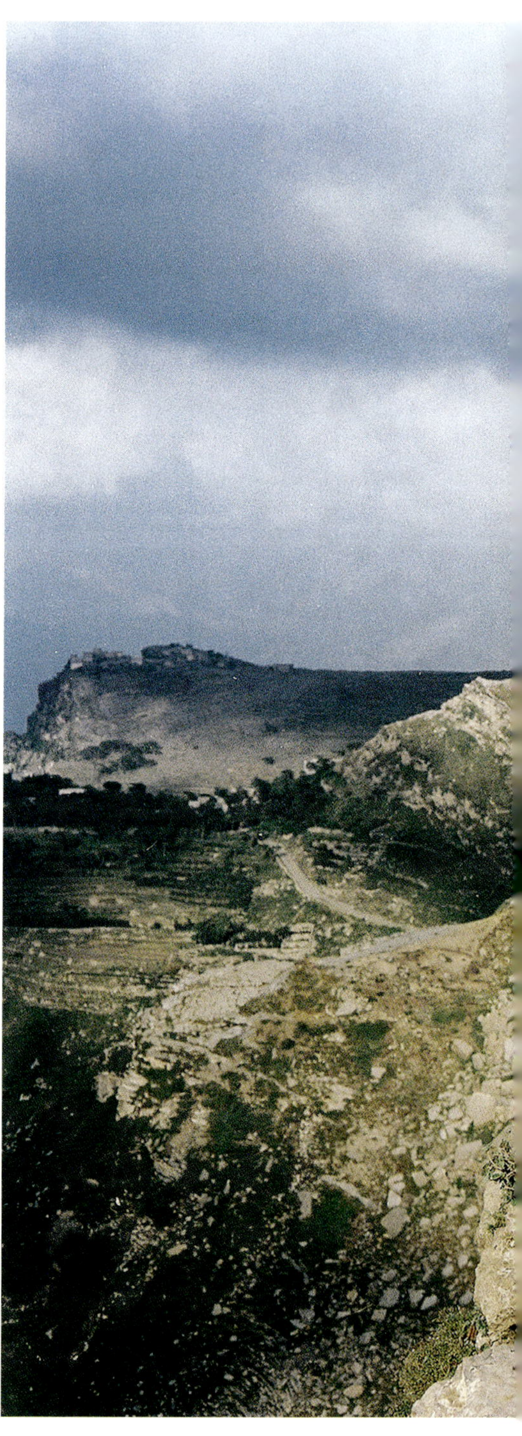

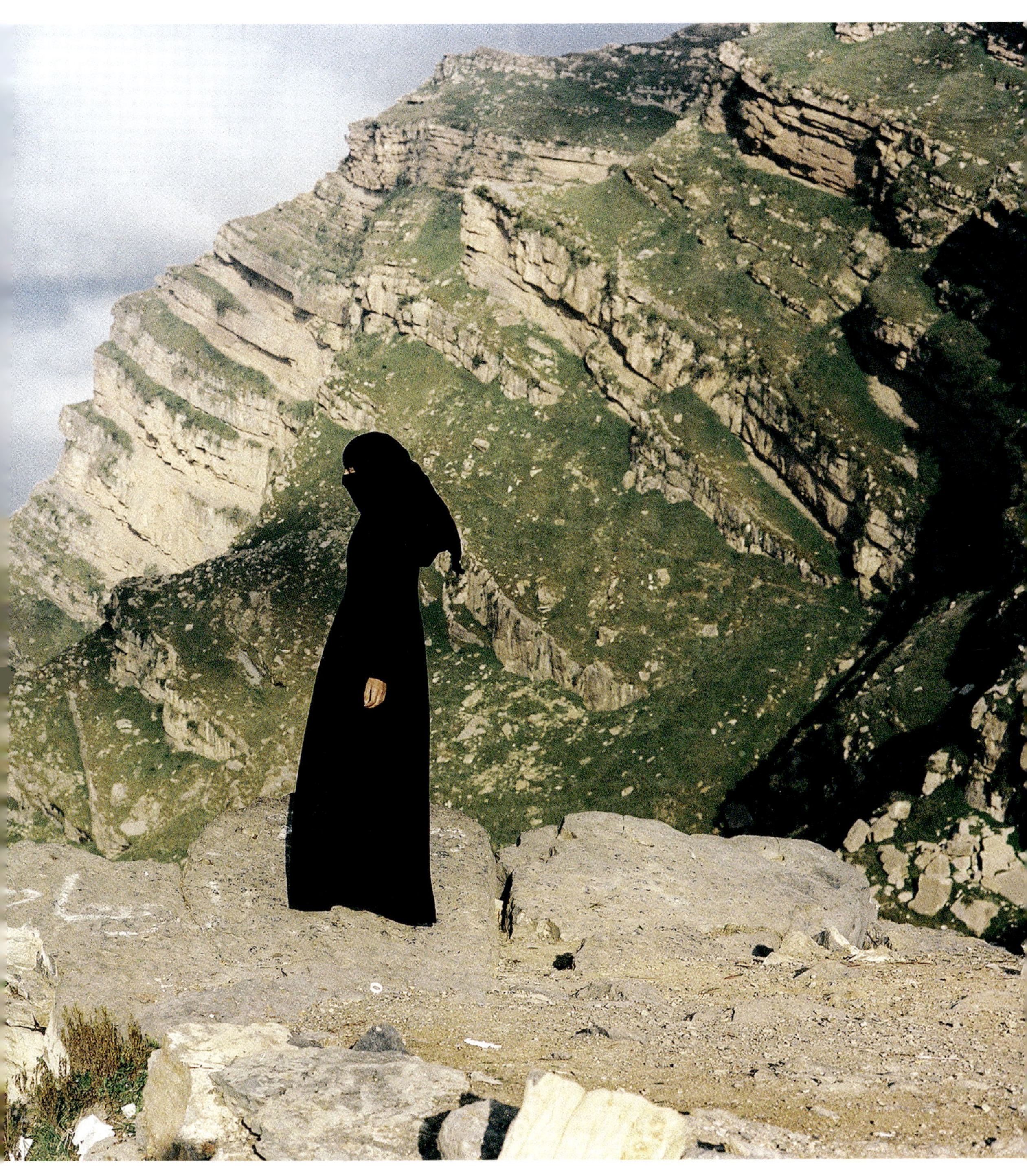

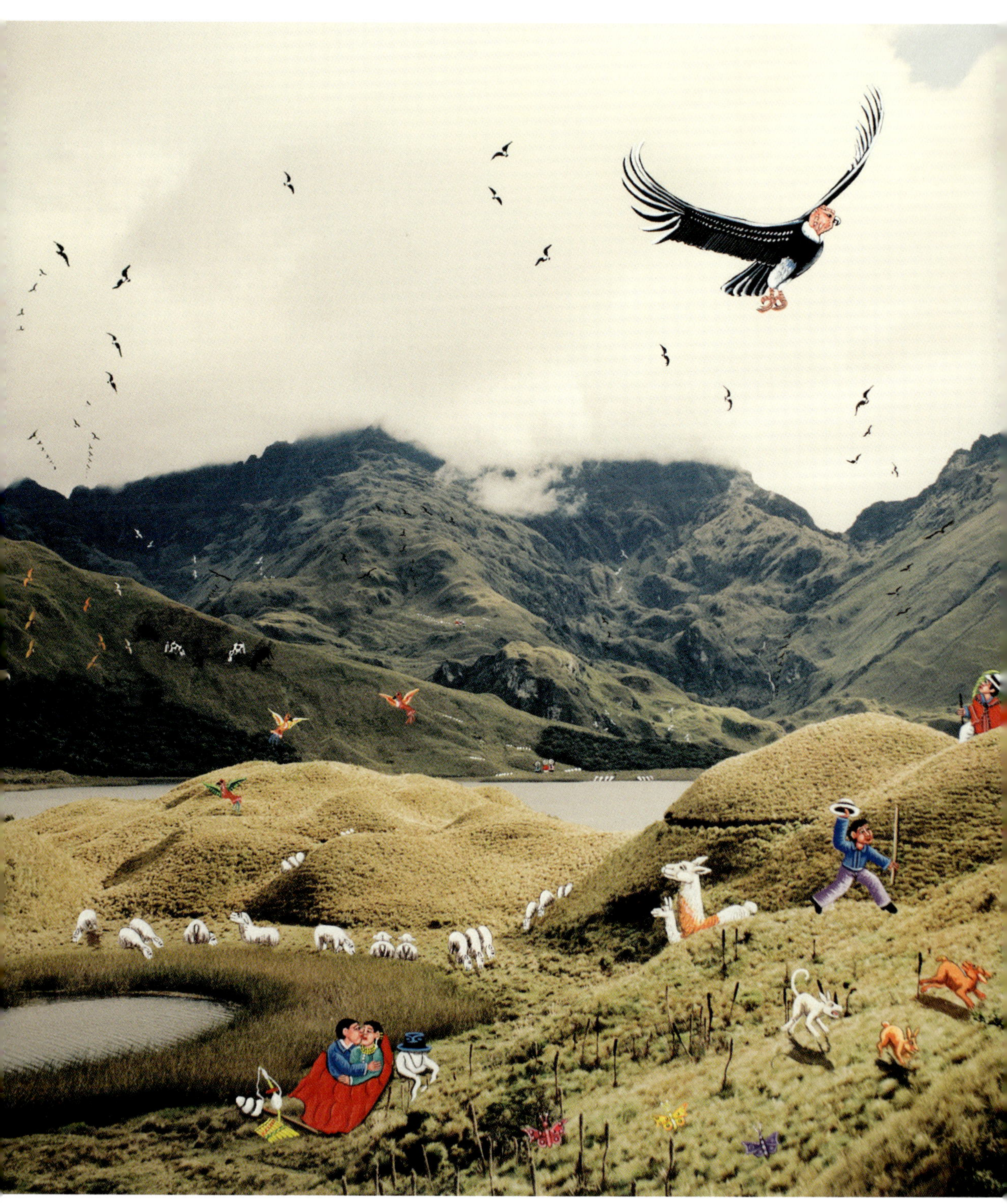

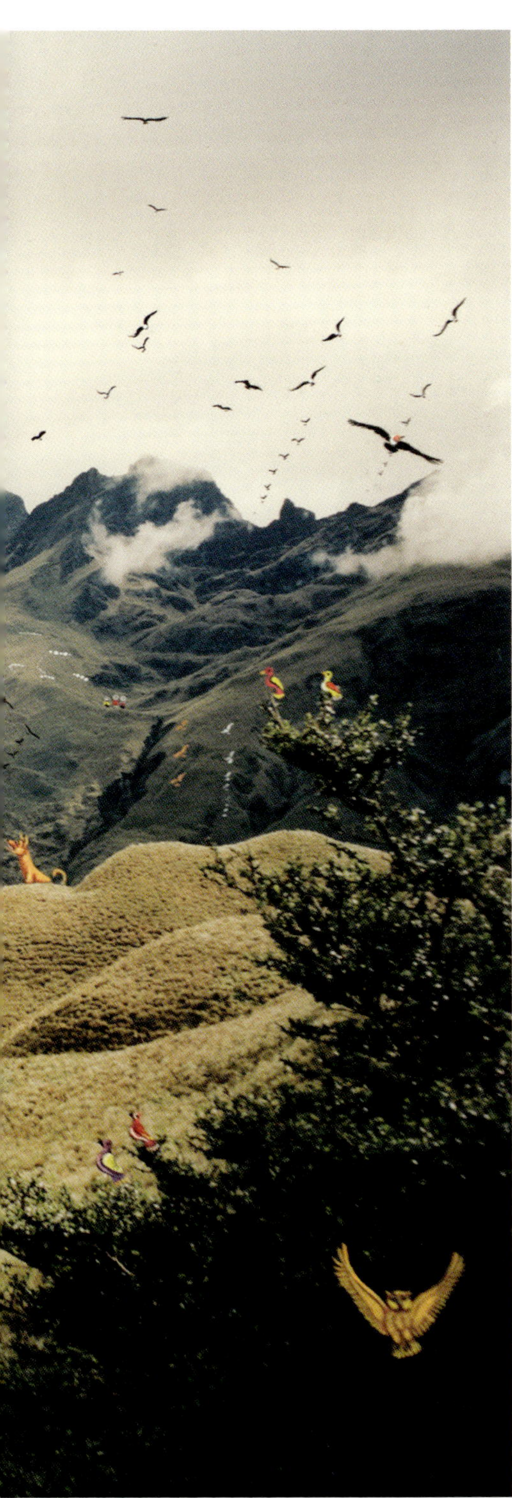

Koyoltzintli

Ecuadorian American

The Spring Time

Andean Ecuador; 2017

My series entitled In the Mouth of the Mountain Jaguar, Everybody is a Dancing Hummingbird, explores fact and fiction in the rural Andes through storytelling, documentary photography and performance with collaboration. I wanted to include interventions from local artists to invite them to interpret my landscape photography. I met my collaborator for this work, Julio Toaquiza, a renowned painter and storyteller, long before we worked together. I knew I wanted to include his understanding and relation to storytelling and place. Each of these interventions carries an Indigenous teaching about the land and her seasons. In the intervention *The Spring Time*, the focus is on growth, creation and romance, the season is pregnant with life and everything is in bloom. Combining Toaquiza's vision with my own was a wonderful surprise; I could not have foreseen what these images would become. His art reveals layers of the land that help us access the way our ancestors view the landscape while blending two forms of storytelling: photography and painting.

Delphine Blast

French

Cholitas, the revenge of a generation

La Paz, Bolivia; 2016

The iconic bowler hat, the long black braids, the adjusted corset and the brightly coloured puffed skirt: the mythical cholitas are a strong symbol of Bolivia and recognized around the world. Discriminated against for generations, they are now a driving force in Bolivia. In contexts that were unimaginable 10 or 20 years ago, nowadays they have real clout in the economic, political and fashion worlds. The cholitas have managed to find their place in modern society without denying their collective past. They are a strong symbol of the success of Indigenous populations, and I wanted my work to capture that dignity through intimate studio portraiture. I first went to Bolivia and became fascinated by the cholitas 10 years ago. I was impressed by their strength and energy, and eventually created a series of 30 portraits. In this series – my first experience with studio portraiture – I wanted to renew insight into Bolivian womanhood and reflect on the social changes of the country. By using traditional fabrics for my backdrops, the series is meant to represent a more personal form of storytelling that moves away from how the cholitas have been documented in the past.

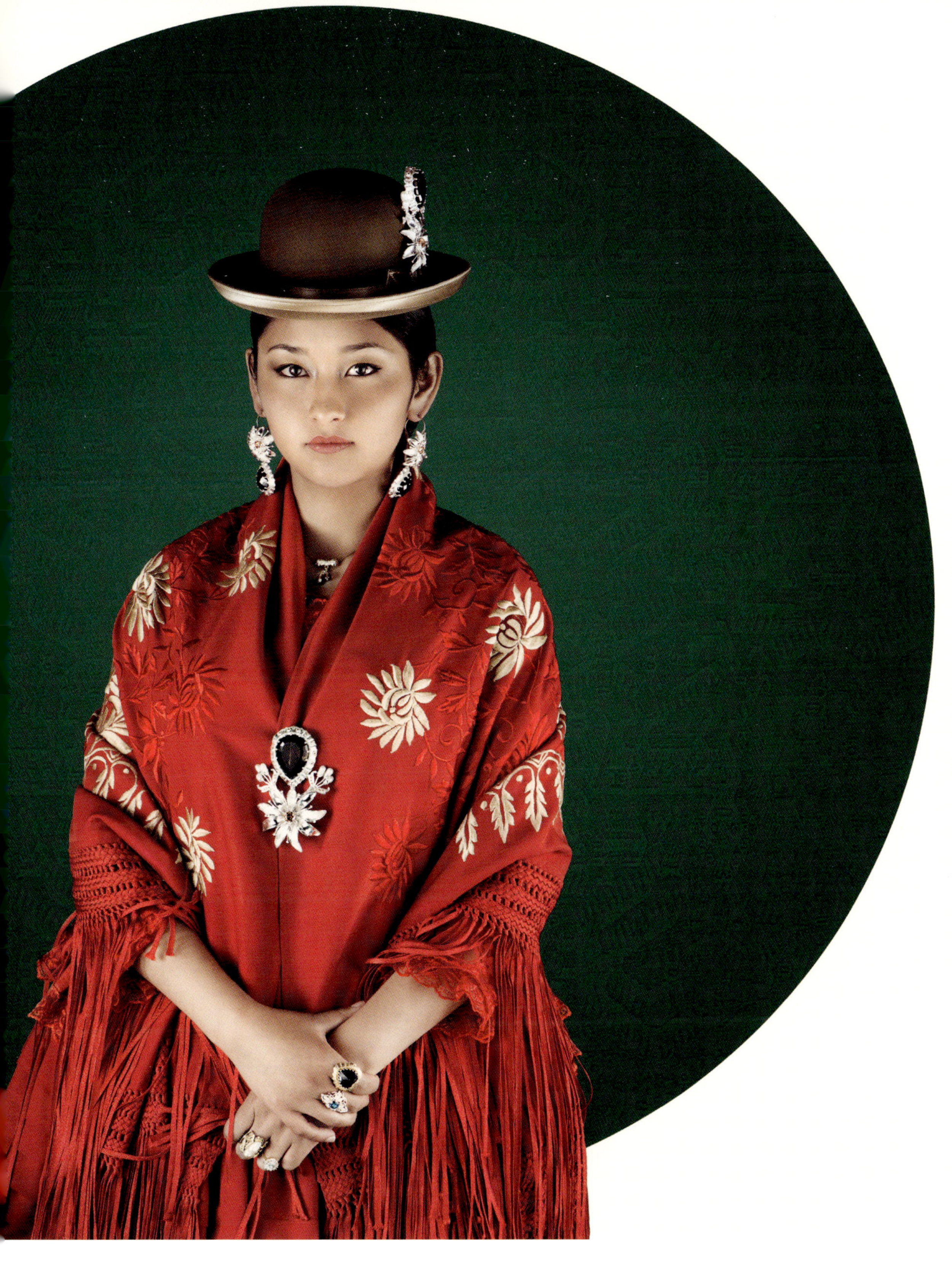

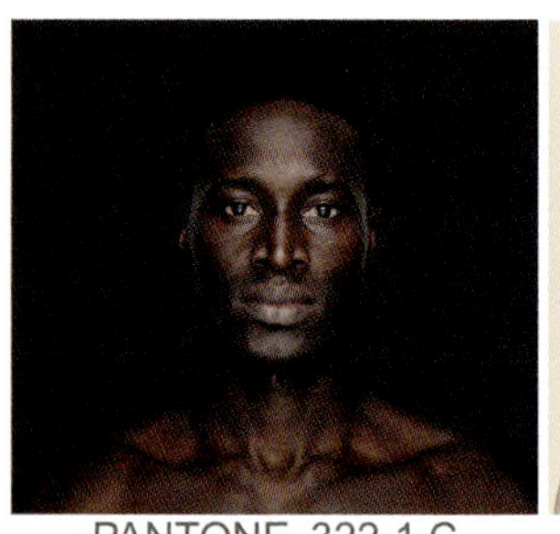
PANTONE® 322-1 C

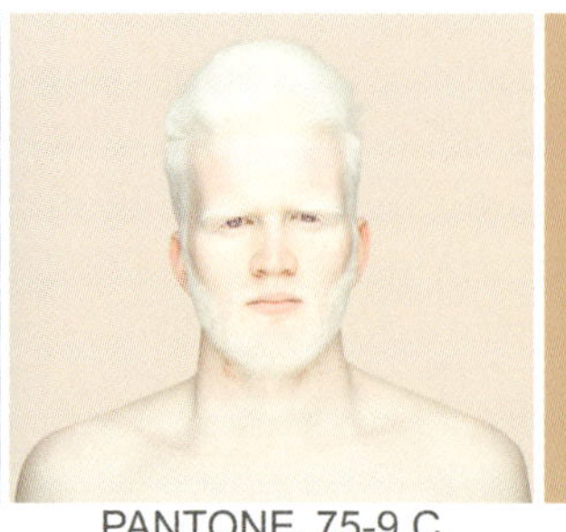
PANTONE® 75-9 C

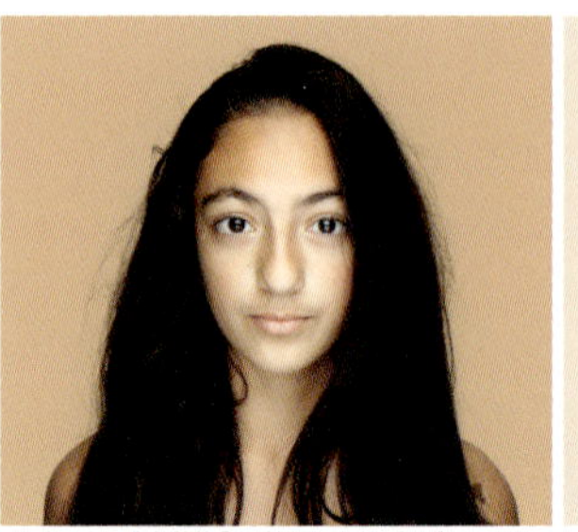
PANTONE® 51-6 C

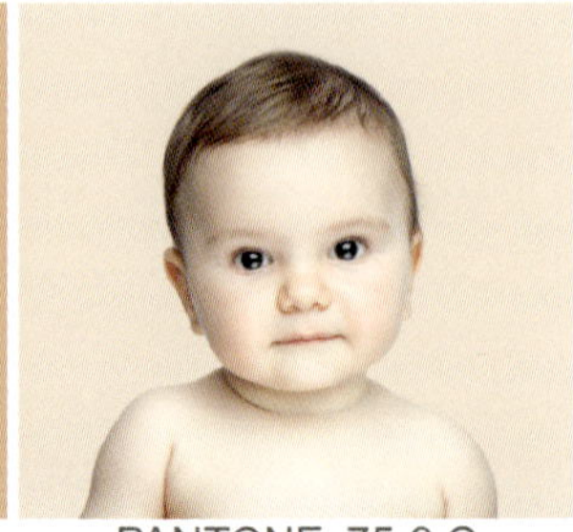
PANTONE® 75-9 C

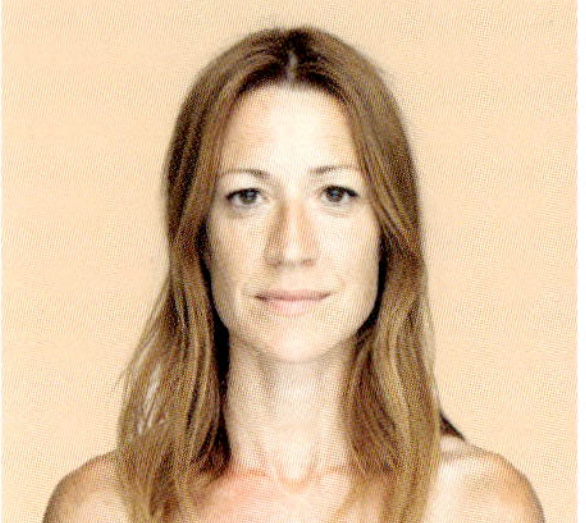
PANTONE® 57-7 C

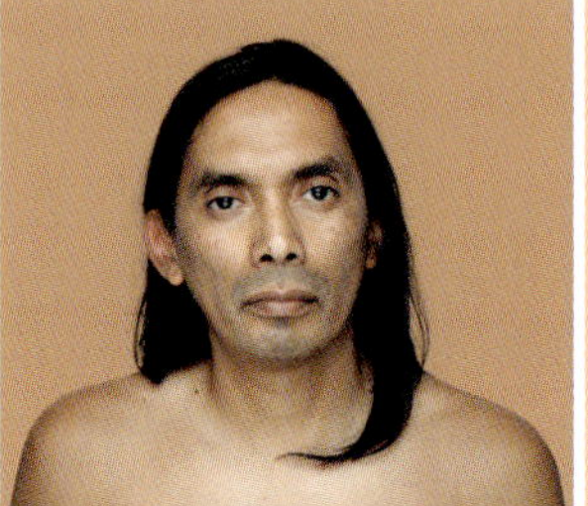
PANTONE® 71-5 C

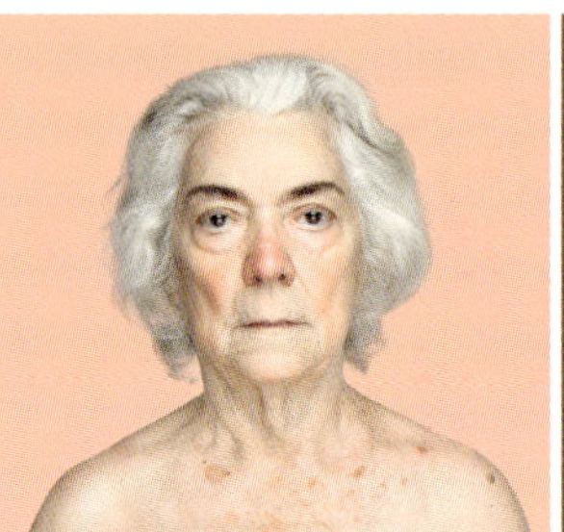
PANTONE® 97-7 C

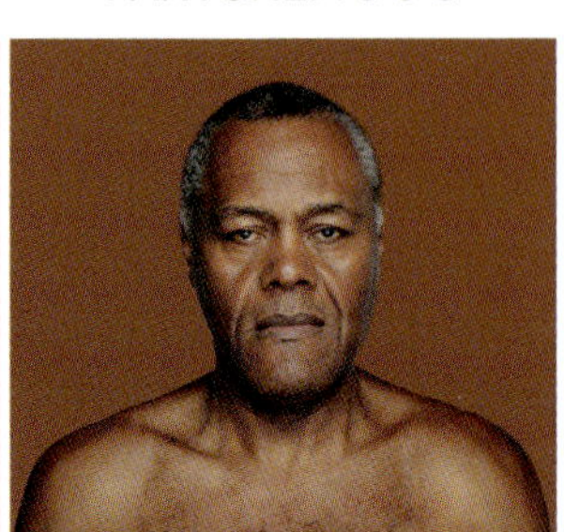
PANTONE® 317-5 C

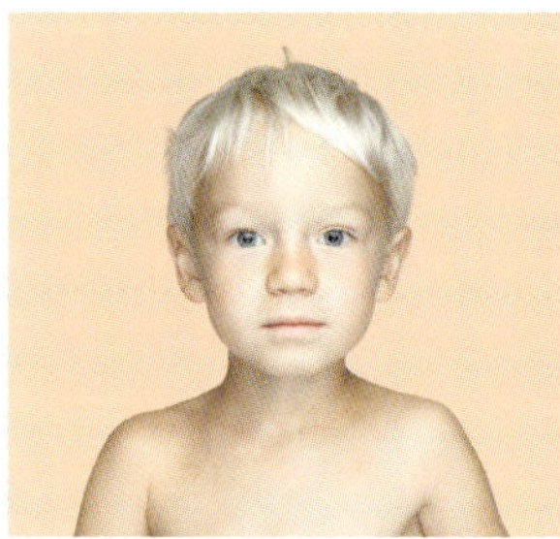
PANTONE® 57-7 C

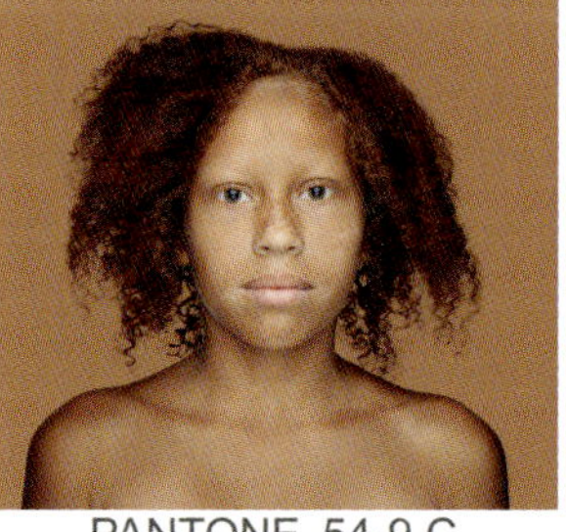
PANTONE® 54-9 C

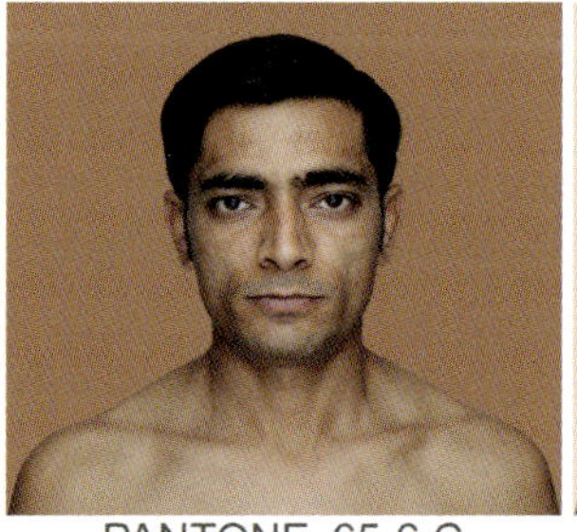
PANTONE® 65-6 C

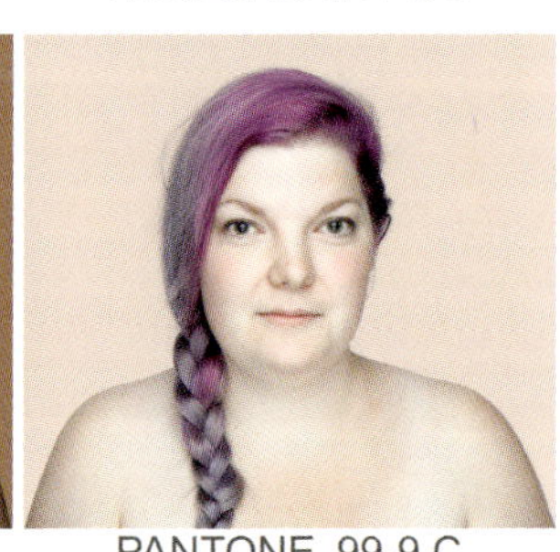
PANTONE® 99-9 C

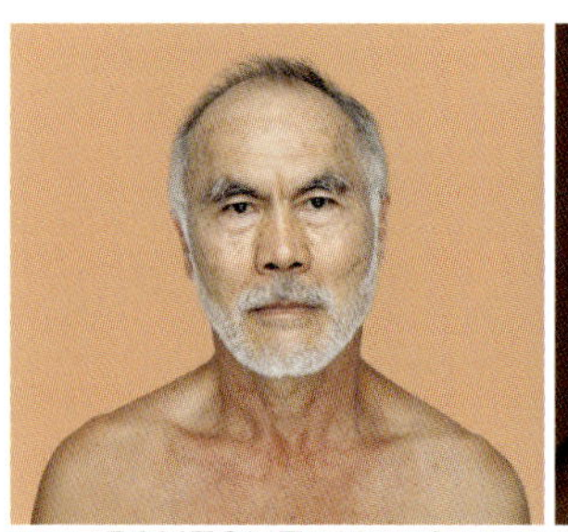
PANTONE® 70-5 C

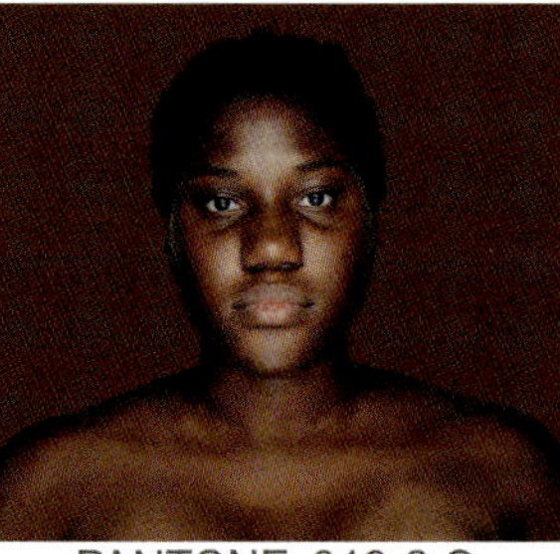
PANTONE® 319-2 C

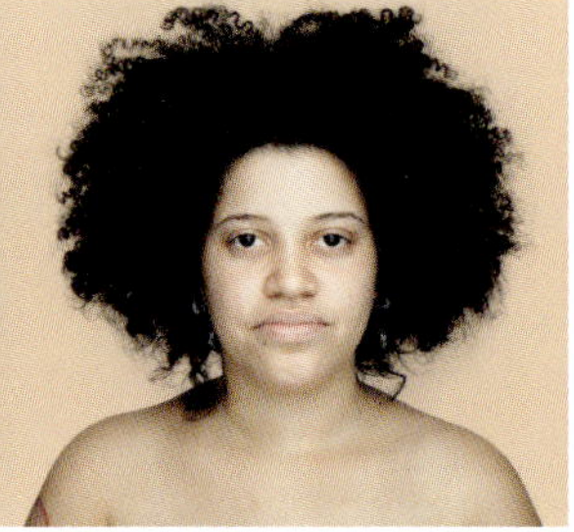
PANTONE® 58-7 C

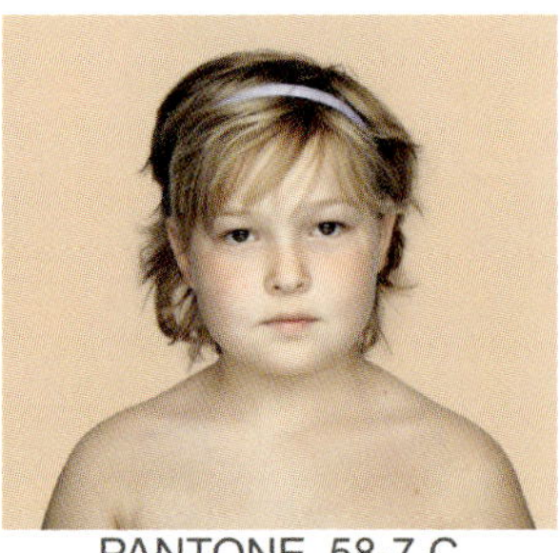
PANTONE® 58-7 C

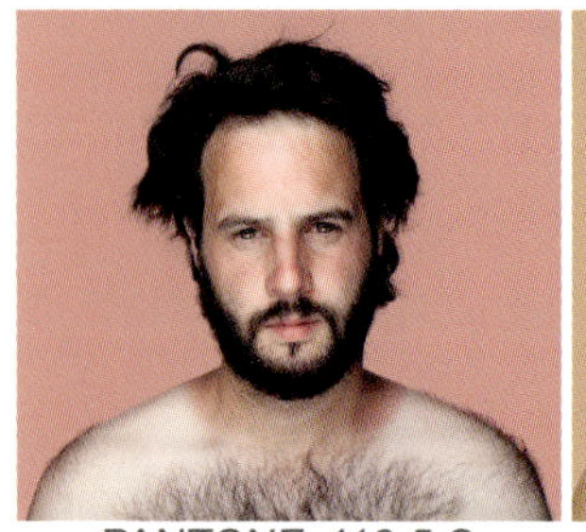
PANTONE® 116-5 C

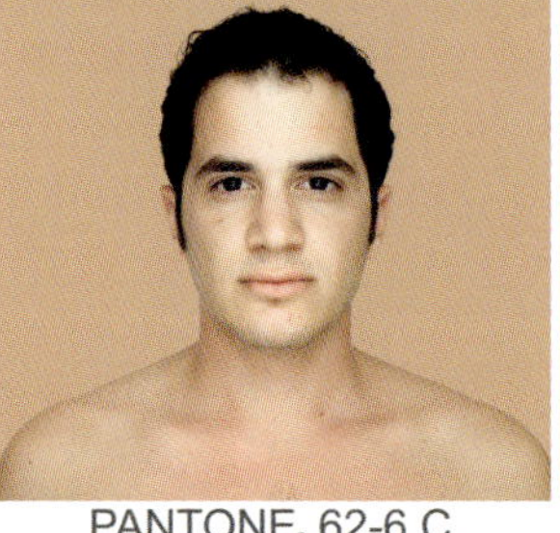
PANTONE® 62-6 C

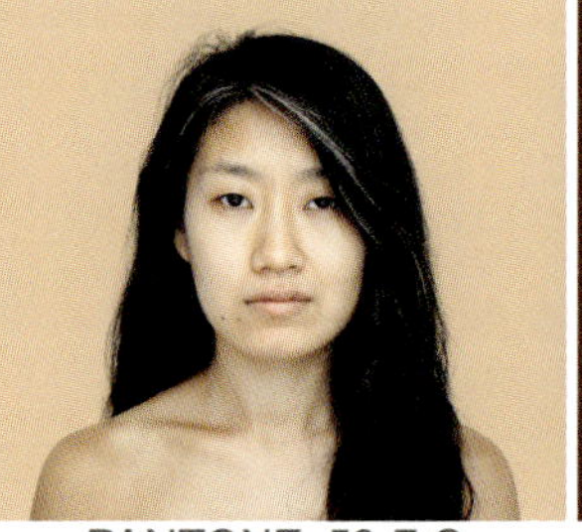
PANTONE® 53-7 C

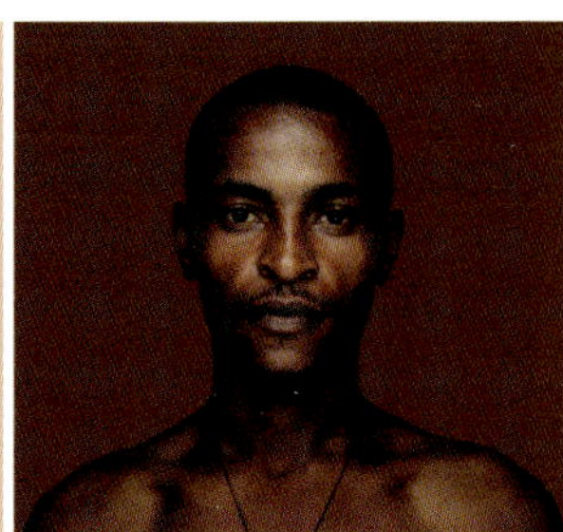
PANTONE® 318-3 C

◀

Angélica Dass

Brazilian Spanish

From the series Humanæ

Global; started 2012

Humanæ is an ongoing reflection on skin colour, and an attempt to document humanity's nuanced colours rather than the simplified labels 'white', 'red', 'black' and 'yellow' associated with race. It also seeks to demonstrate that what defines human beings is our inescapable uniqueness and, therefore, our diversity. The background for each portrait is tinted with a colour tone identical to a sample of 11 × 11 pixels taken from the nose of the subject and matched with the industrial Pantone palette, which, recontextualized, calls into question a spectrum of contradictions and stereotypes related to race. My practice combines photography with sociological research and public participation. I see this project as an activist undertaking, manifested especially in the direct and personal dialogue between me and the public. Humanæ's message is fundamentally educational. I have photographed more than 4,000 volunteers so far across 20 countries and 36 cities around the world. Humanæ is a spontaneous participatory project that has no set end date; instead it acts as a catalogue of the breadth of who we are, without labels.

▶▶

Yagazie Emezi

Nigerian

From the series When Did A Piece Fall Off

London, UK; 2018

This image is selected from When Did A Piece Fall Off, a series of portraits featuring a young woman on a journey of retraced steps and discovery. These images were intended to support a fictional story and allowed me to push beyond my normal space of the outdoors by using a studio provided by PDesigns Studios, in London, with a patterned set design by artist Christina Poku. I wanted to combine my usual documentary approach to photography with something soft and sensitive in regard to the model Favor and the setting. In this bid to try new things, I applied it to the story of Favor, exploring what happens when we leave the old for the new, what is left, what is taken. In addition to the use of fragmented pieces of pattern and glass to build out the story, I also tend to accompany my series with questions and short poems:

What do we leave behind when coming into ourselves?

Looking for lost selves, when did a piece fall off?

Along the way, when you broke down, what part of you did you forget to pick up as you gathered yourself again?

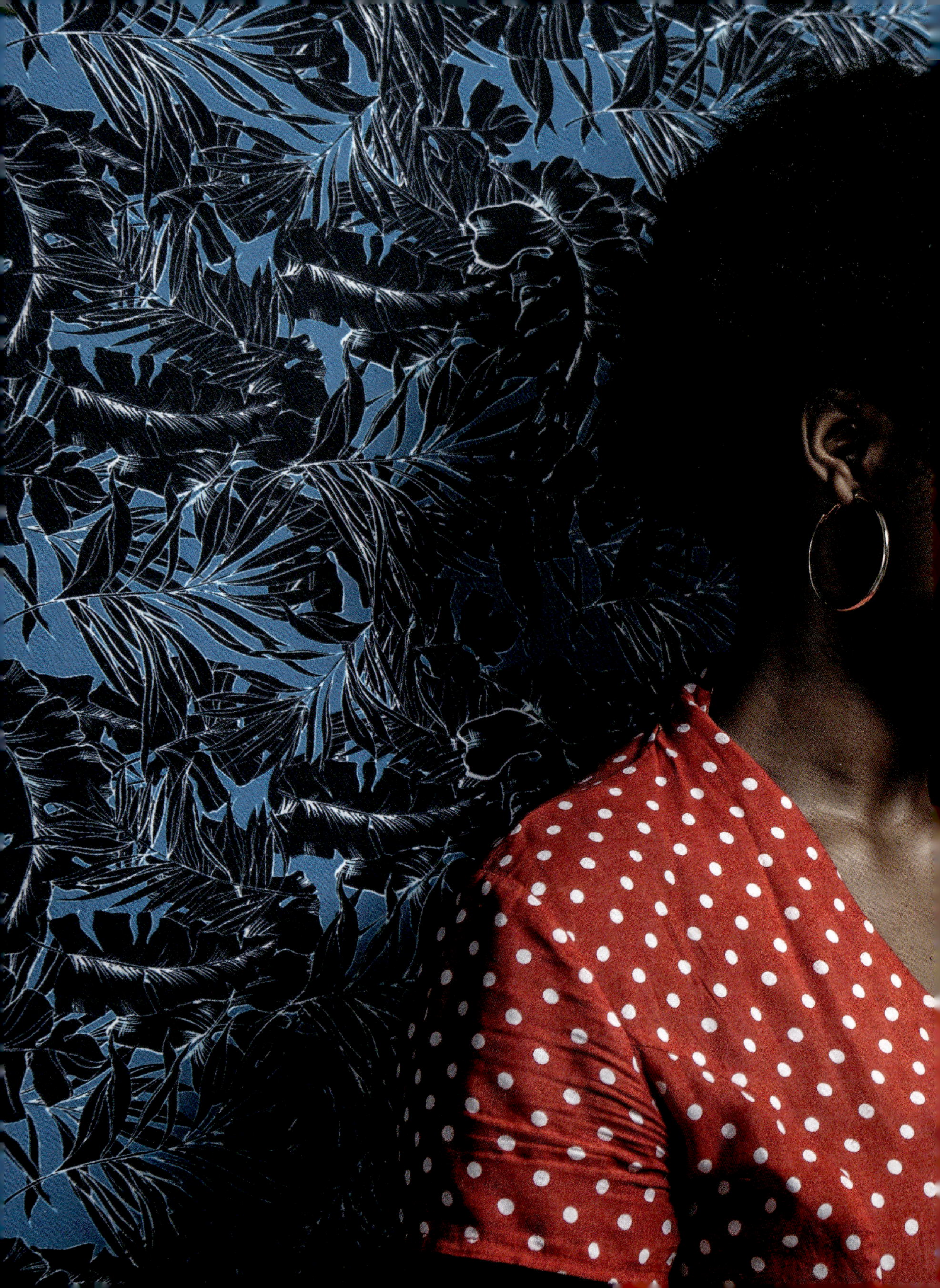

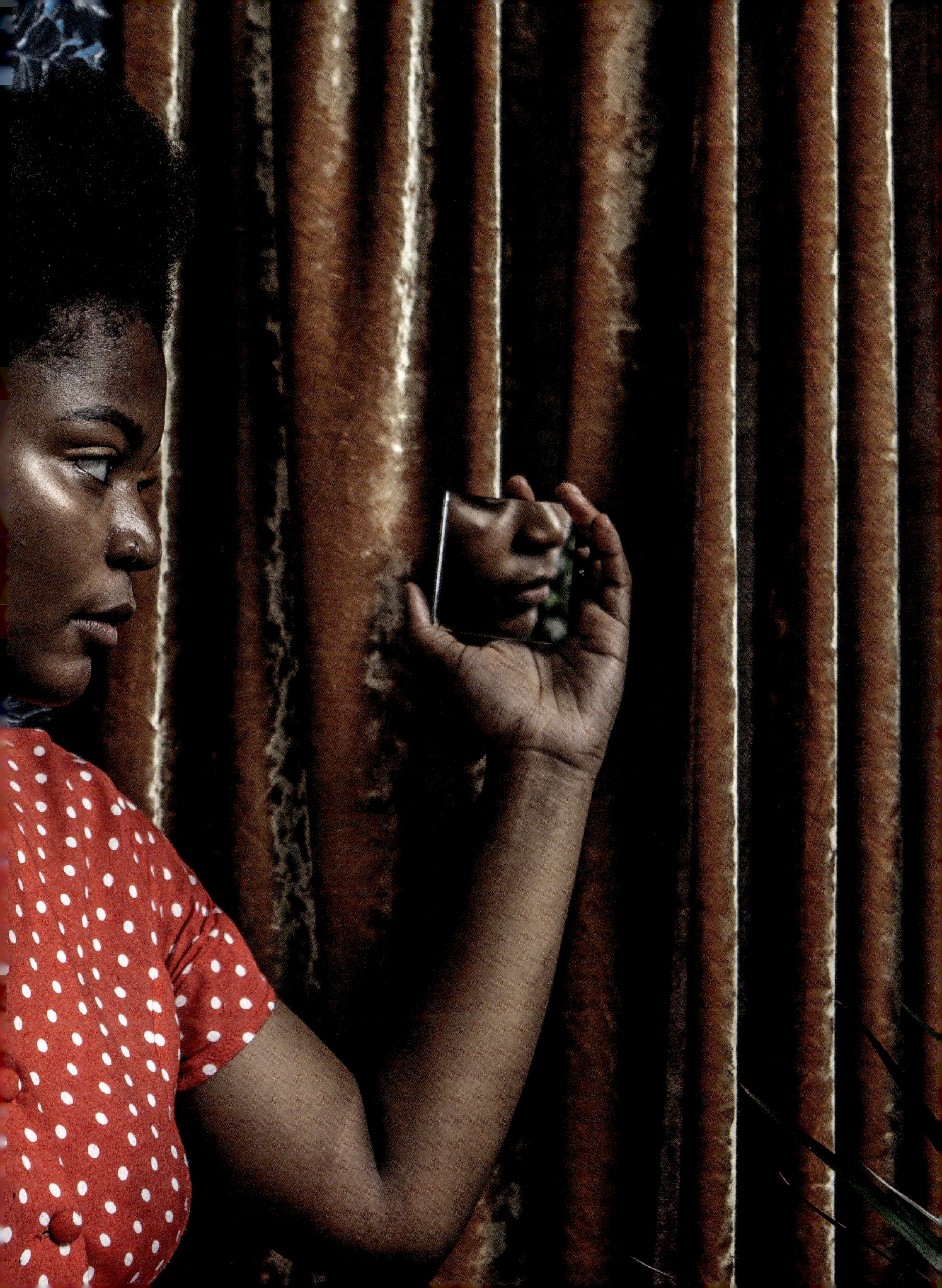

Deborah Willis

American

Carrie in Euro Salon, Eatonville, Florida

Eatonville, Florida, USA; 2004

My photographs explore the relationship between art, literature and other artistic forms – all inspired by the works and words of Zora Neale Hurston. This image focuses on ideas in storytelling using Hurston's hairstyle and dress to link her to the contemporary artist Carrie Mae Weems. My work is always in search of beauty and in search of the storytelling that happens in Hurston's writings. I grew up in a beauty shop and more recently I have started photographing women in beauty shops, including Weems. As a child I used to sit on the floor and listen to women talk about their lives, their hopes and their disappointments. I was a young girl, but I understood that there was something special about that experience and I started noticing a connection in my work to Zora's writing when I considered our shared personal histories focusing on women and Black beauty. This photograph of Carrie Mae Weems in the beauty shop was taken in Eatonville, Florida. The mirrors in the image are central to my work, and connected to not only the search for self-approval, but also the idea of women embracing their own beauty. I am fascinated with the recognition of beauty in our everyday lives.

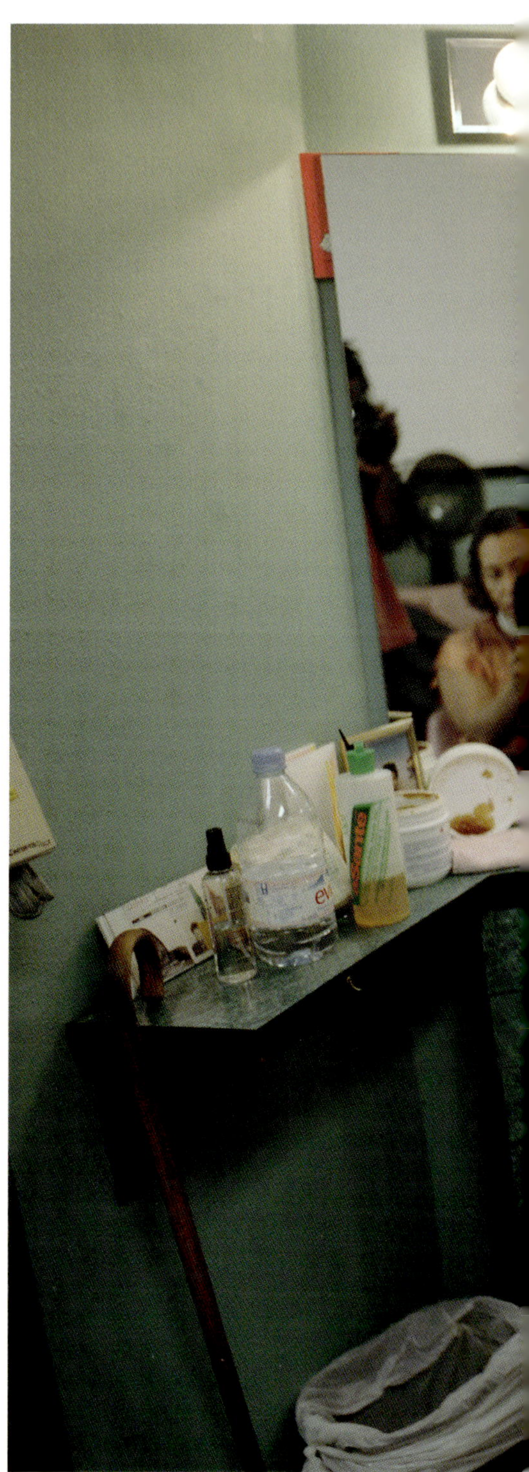

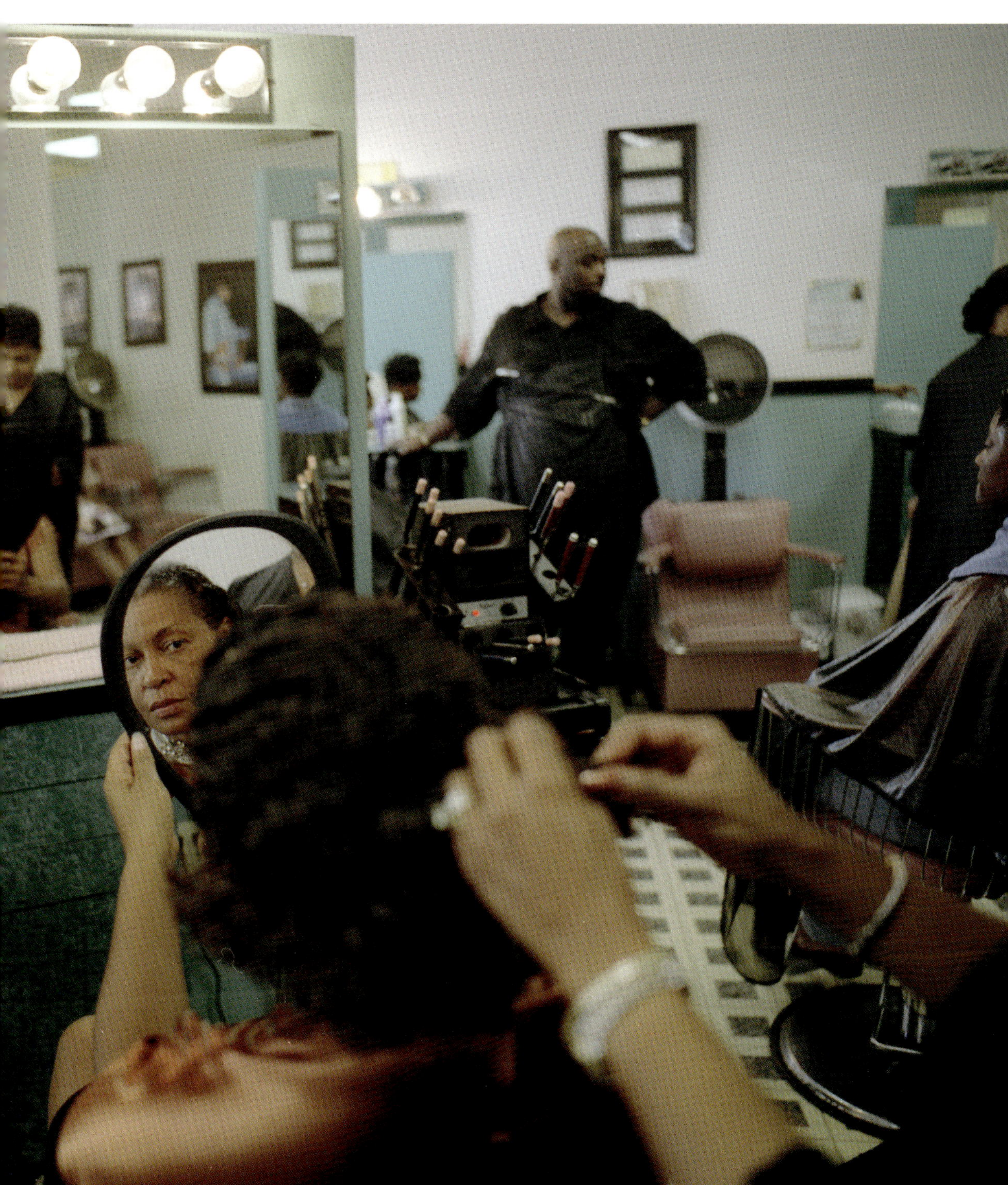

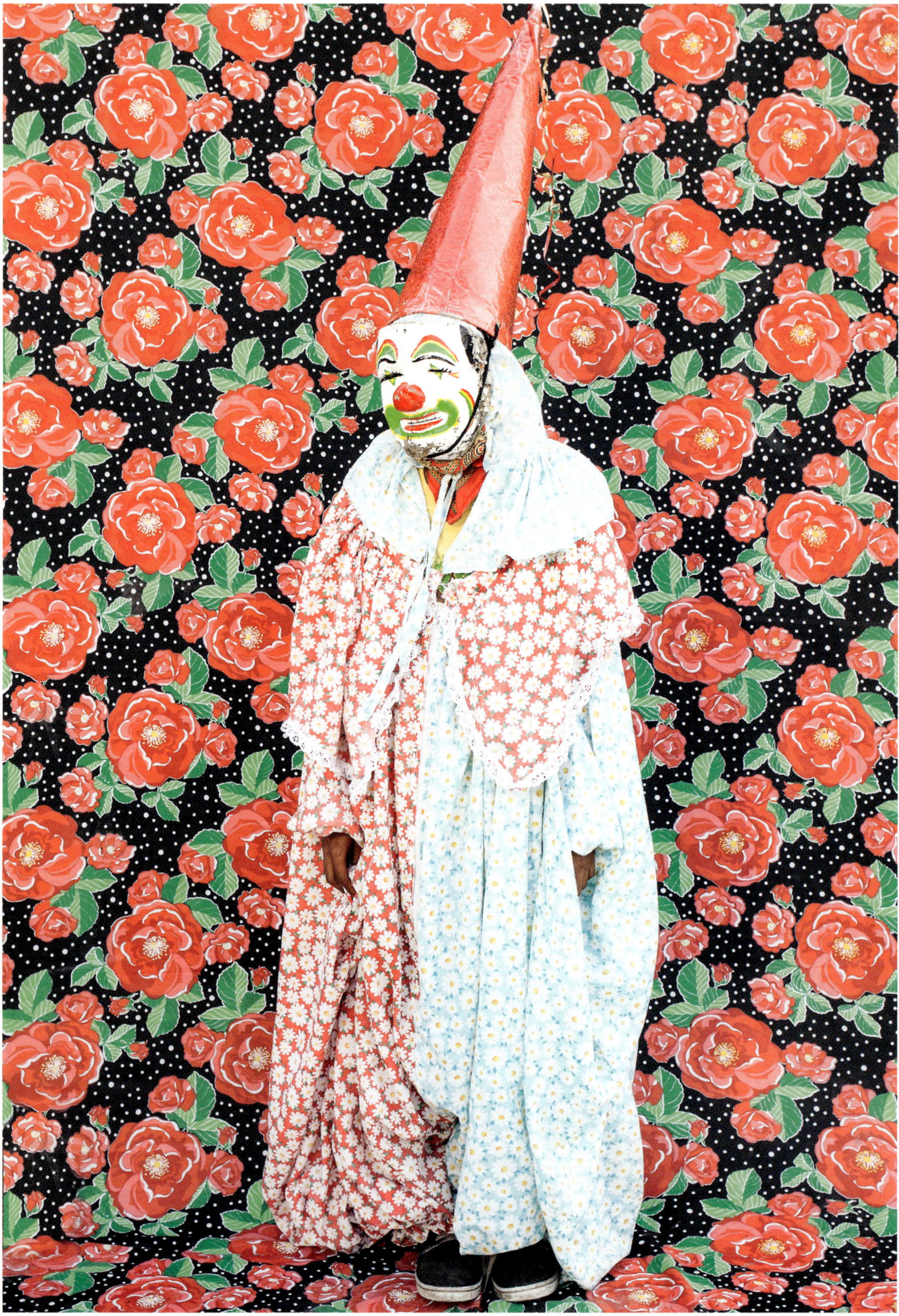

Luján Agusti

Argentinian

Portrait of a dancing clown from the gang 'Cuadrilla de Juquilita'

Coatepec, Veracruz, Mexico; 2016

With the arrival of the Spaniards in the Americas in the 16th century, a process of evangelization began throughout Mexico and Latin America at the hands of colonizers. Among the most effective techniques, apart from the tremendous acts of violence and genocide, were the creation of rituals and festivities that included a mixture of European and pre-Hispanic elements through a process of syncretism. When the colonial period came to an end, many of these celebrations were folded into Latin American traditions and some of them have been revived in recent years. Through this project, ITOTIA: Dancing Clowns I wanted to show the elements of several traditions that take place in different Mexican communities. I set up street studios where the backgrounds were always related to the costume of each dancer and invited the performers to pose for portraits, immersed in a space that highlighted the magic of the celebration. Many of the performers chose not to reveal their identities. Instead, they preferred to remain fantastic beings between our world and some other, deeply connected to the energy that leads them to dance.

Erika Larsen

American

Magda

Peru; 2018

I met Magda during a 14-year exploration of ritual through photography. Fascinated by thoughts of transformation and regeneration, I began to contemplate healing. In time, I came to define healing as the experience of transcending suffering. I realized that healing was simultaneously a subjective encounter and an expression of humanity's wholeness. With that in mind, I searched for people who could share primordial knowledge to help me better understand what it means to be human. This awakened a desire to document ritual, to remember that we are part of nature, and ultimately brought me to a new understanding of time. This journey took me through the Americas and into communities that are deeply intertwined with the natural environment. I met Magda at her home in San Francisco, Peru, where I had met her father and mother years before that. I returned to them several times over the next 14 years. Their daily routines revealed a profound connection to collective memory and a respect for broad interpretations of time. This image is part of my book *Materia Prima*, which is a collection of photographs and poems from this project and includes collaborations with artists Frida Larios and Tsista Kennedy.

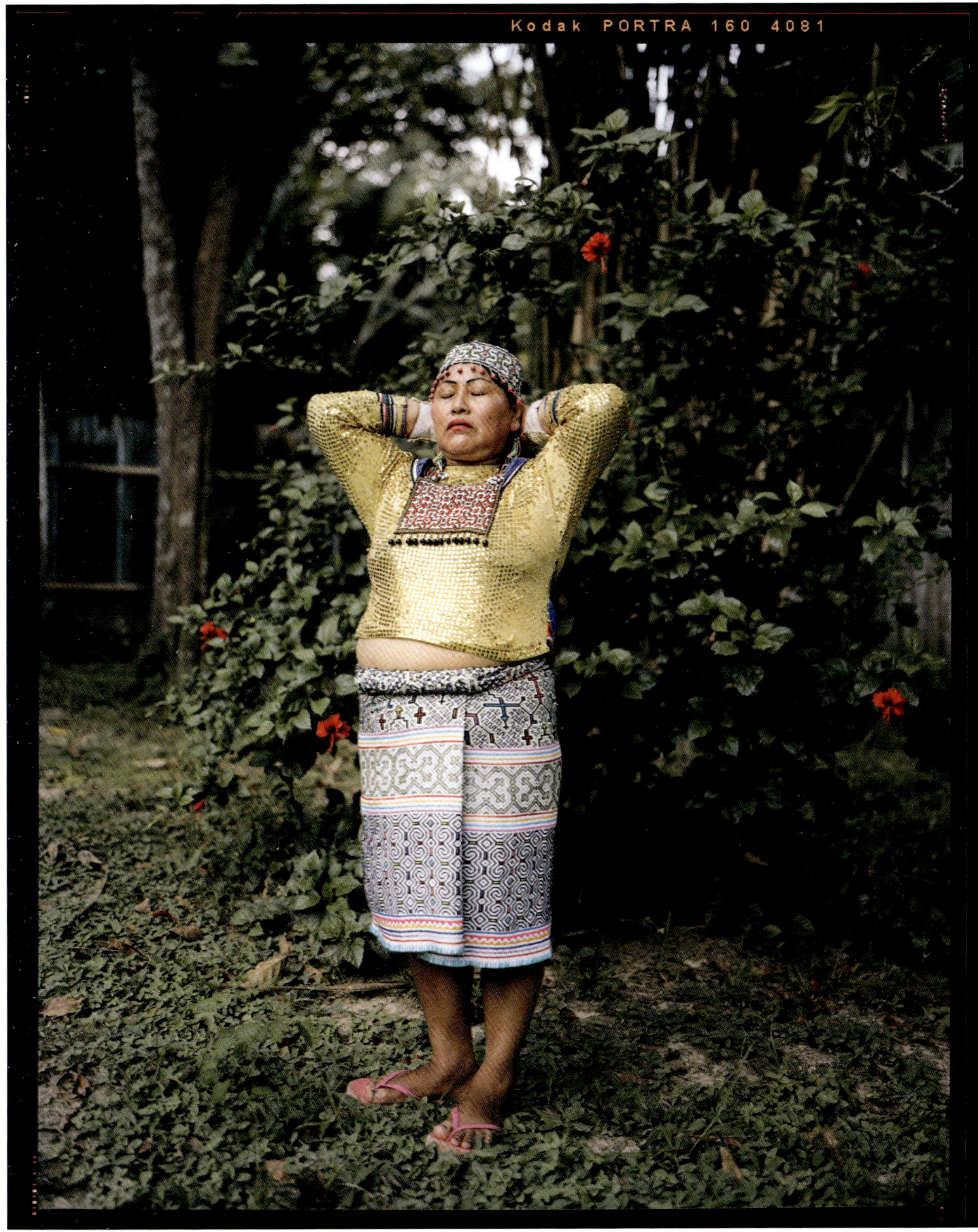
Kodak PORTRA 160 4081

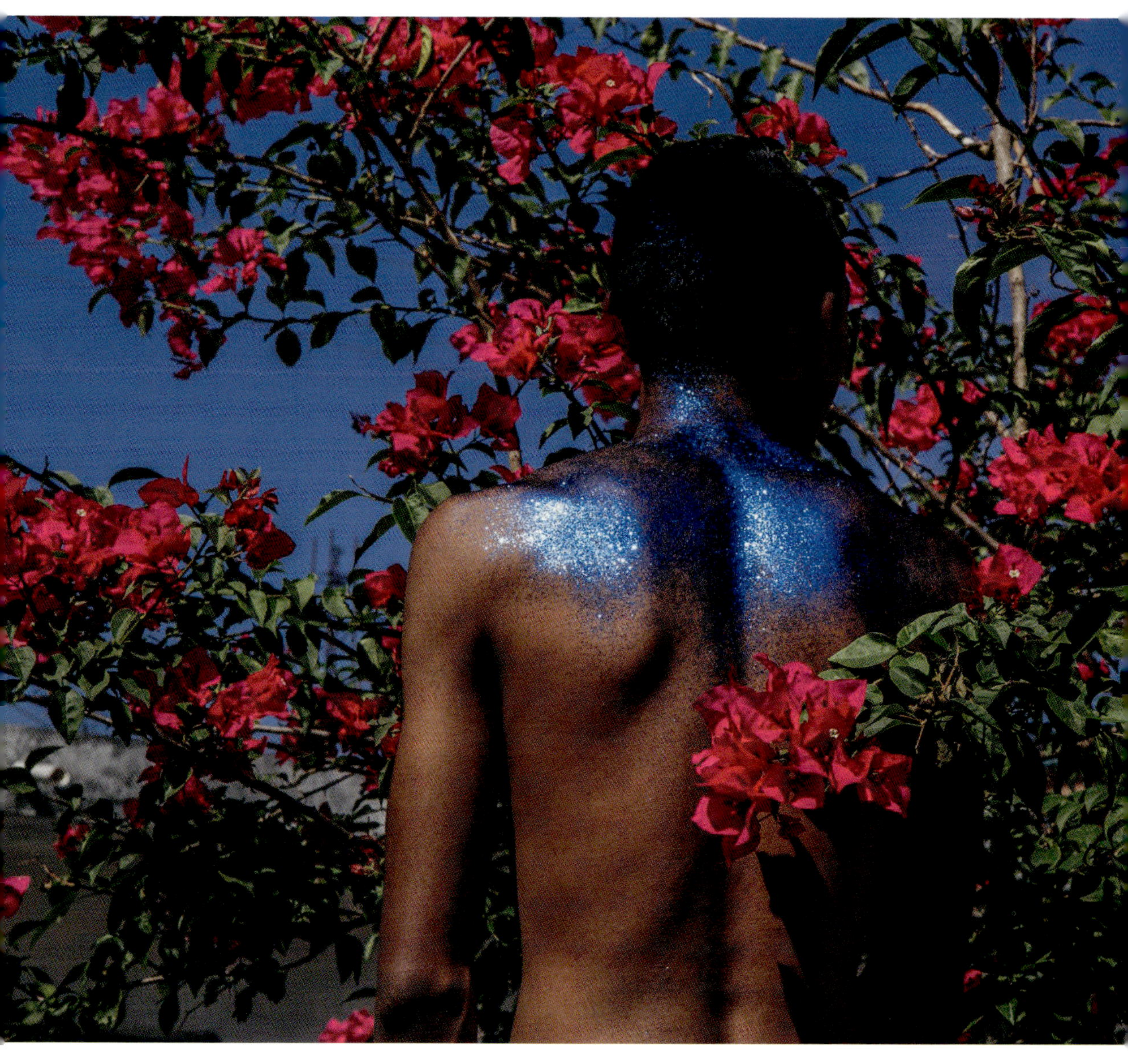

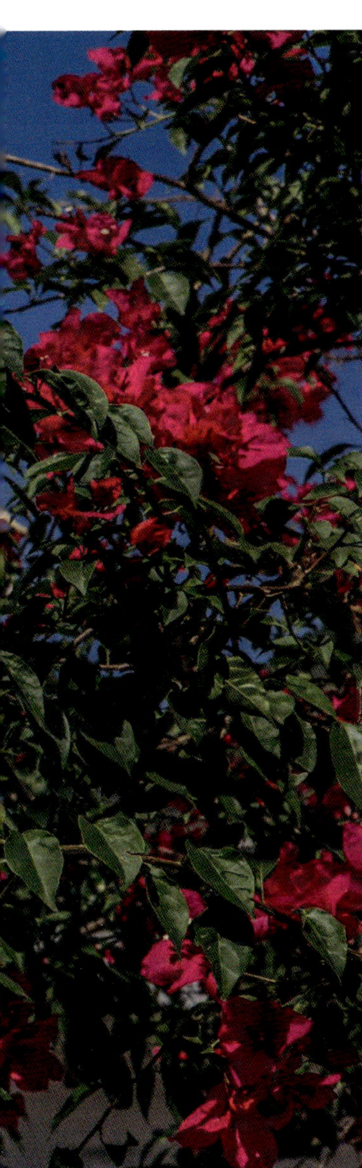

Koral Carballo

Mexican

Yoel's Wishes

Coyolillo, Veracruz, Mexico; 2018

This photograph comes from a larger project that examines Afro-descendance in Mexico. While there is relatively widespread discourse about Mexican identity being rooted in Indigenous and Spanish ancestry, little is said about the Africans who arrived in Mexico by way of slave ships – their history has been largely forgotten and erased. The object of this work is to recognize the daily life, traditions and people of Afro-Mexico through a mixture of documentary photography, collaborative portraits, family photos and visual interventions. Yoel Zaragoza and I worked together to convey his sense of freedom during the Carnival of Coyolillo, a source of pride for the Afro-descendant community. For me, this is a way to take photographs beyond the act of photographing the 'other' – it allows me to create a dialogue and a collaboration through my photography. Hand in hand with this work, I have also been holding workshops in Afro-descendant communities across Mexico to help preserve family photographs and bring those images together to build a cross-cultural archive of our shared experiences and histories. In this way, we are preserving and elevating our own ancestors and their stories, so that they may become a more visible part of our collective Mexican heritage.

Kali Spitzer

Kaska Dena and Jewish

Val Napoleon

Vancouver, Canada; 2018

This image was made on Treaty 7 lands, the traditional territory of the Îyârhe Nakoda (Stoney Nakoda), Blackfoot Confederacy, Tsuut'ina Nations, Ktunaxa and Secwépemc Nations, and Métis Nation of Alberta. Val Napoleon is an Indigenous woman from Saulteau First Nation. She is a grandmother, law dean and self-defined feminist who works tirelessly to amplify the strength of Indigenous women and communities. Her image is part of An Exploration of Resilience and Resistance, a series that was first and foremost for the people with whom I co-created these images. Photography allows for a unique opportunity to reflect back one's strength, resilience, love and self-reclamation. Healing is a prominent part of the co-creative process that we share while making these images. The contemporary images that I co-create with members of my communities represent the healing and power inherent in our communities, rather than the immense hurt that has historically arisen (and too often continues to arise) from the misrepresentation through photography of Indigenous, POC, queer and gender-diverse peoples. Too often, BIPOC and queer communities are not heard or seen, with our stories being narrated for us, rather than by us. Through my photography, I strive to show how we – as BIPOC, queer and/or gender-diverse peoples – narrate ourselves, and live and embody our strength, love and healing every day. Our images bring light to our stories.

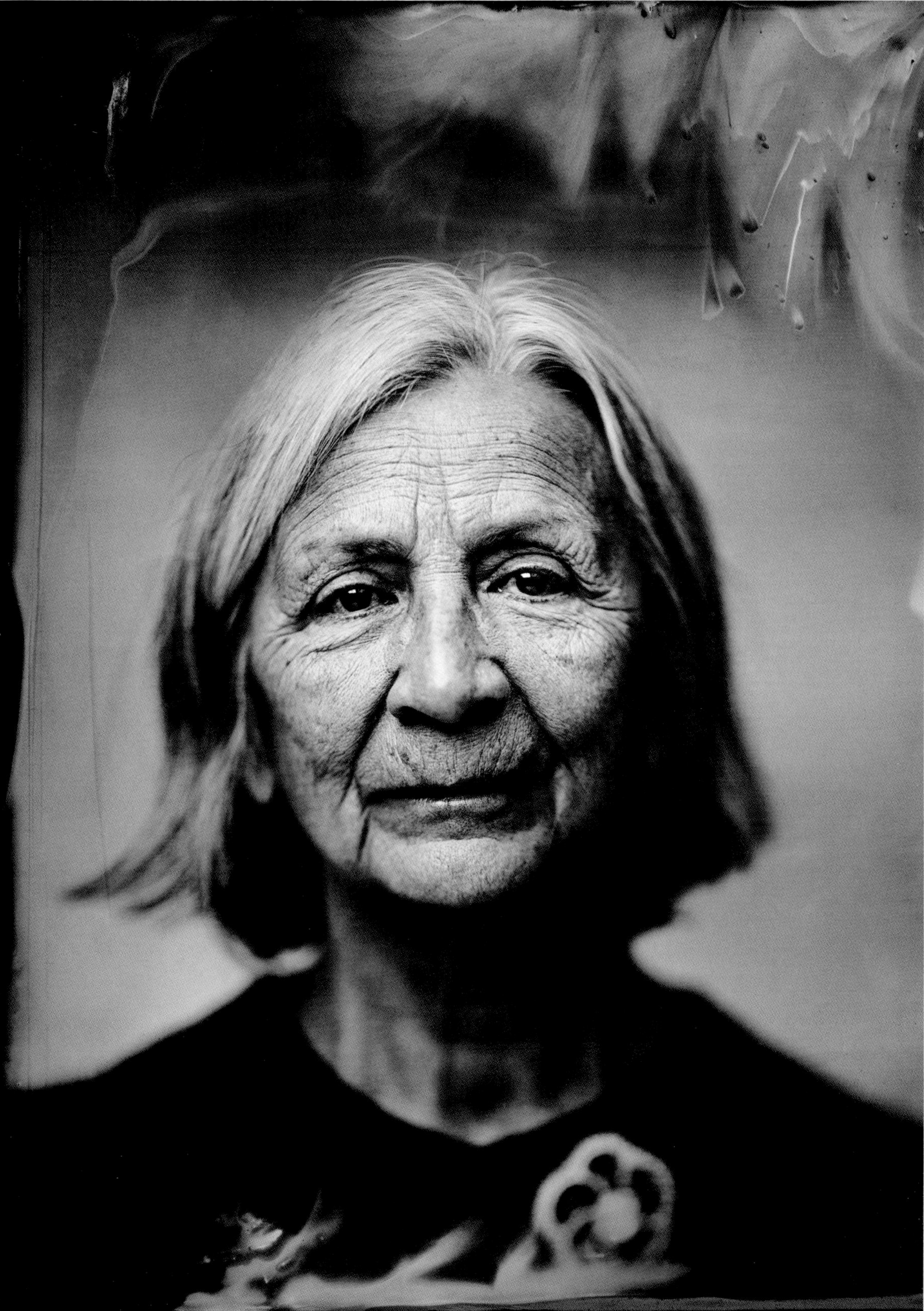

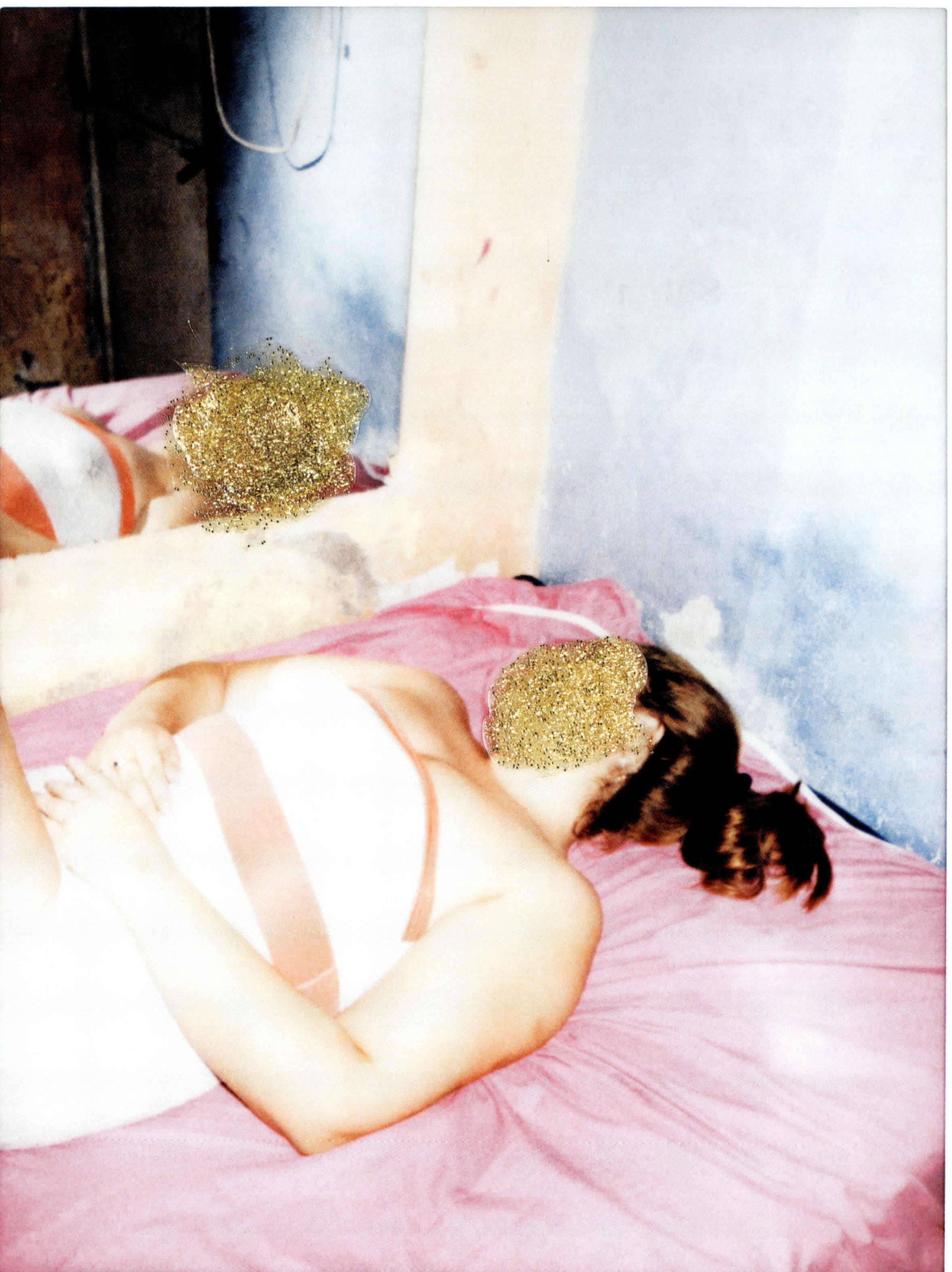

◀

Charlotte Schmitz

German

La Puente

Machala, Ecuador; 2016

I first heard of La Puente, one of the largest brothels in Southern Ecuador, while living in Machala as an 18-year-old exchange student. The brothel stuck in my mind as a place that symbolized the gendered double standards that exist in every society. Hyperaware of, and always bothered by, the inevitable hypocrisy surrounding one's existence as a woman, I returned to La Puente 10 years later to interview and photograph women sex workers, to make sense of their marginalization and misrepresentation all around the world. The majority of sex workers are women, yet most visual projects are authored by men and often fail to provide a deeper emphasis on how sex workers want to be seen. These Polaroids were created in collaboration with the women in La Puente, who chose their own poses and became part of the creative process by applying nail polish to their portraits, in some cases choosing to obscure their faces or otherwise embellish their images. When asking one woman what she was thinking while painting with nail polish on her photo she shared: 'I was thinking that I was enhancing my beauty and covering my identity'.

▶▶

Mariceu Erthal García

Mexican

Waves of the Sea

Veracruz, Mexico; 2017

This image is the result of a physical and photographic immersion I made into the world of Gemma Mávil, a woman who went missing in Mexico after she left her home for a job interview in 2011 and never returned. Through the narrative of this self-portrait, taken in her pool, I reflect on the unbearable pain that the absence of a missing person leaves in their family. For the construction of the story, I began to observe and generate connections with Gemma's spaces. It seemed to me that the territory also speaks, not only people; when a place has gone through stories of pain you can see these scars in it. Touring Gemma's house and her living spaces, I saw her abandoned and cracked swimming pool. It reflected many years of neglect, and there was something in those cracks on a blue sea that moved me. I decided to use a long exposure and began to move through the blue of this space, as a metaphor for the fading of her body and her being. When I started the project, I was the same age as Gemma when she disappeared. I felt a strong connection with her story and her life, a kind of reflection of my own dreams and fears, which is why I decided somewhat intuitively to represent her story using the self-portrait.

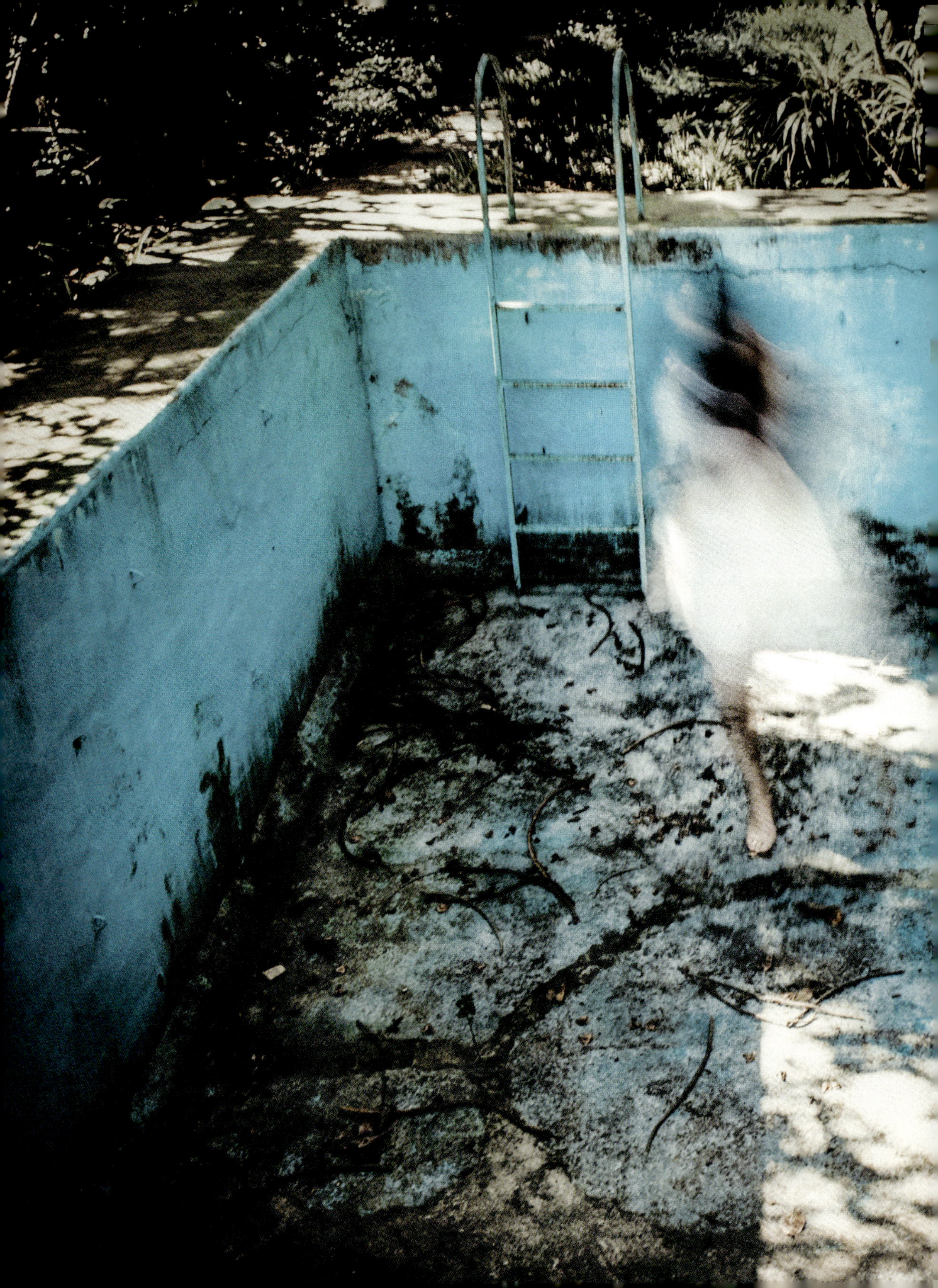

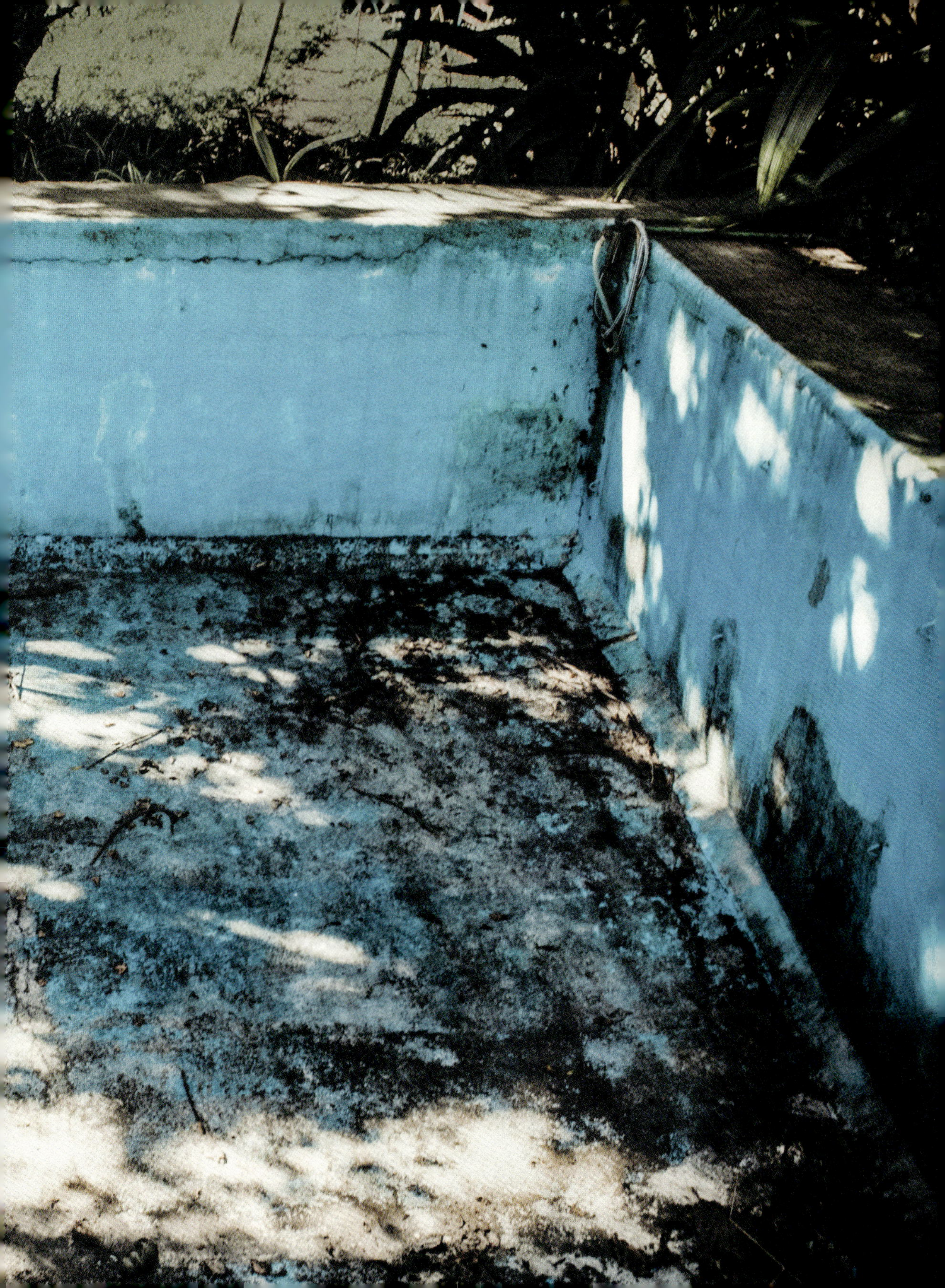

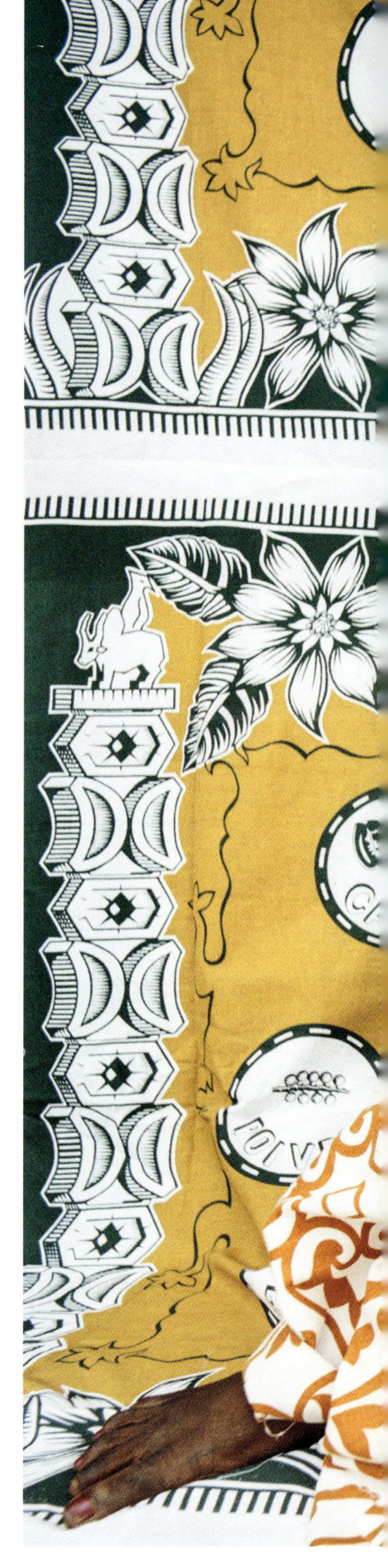

Miora Rajaonary

Malagasy

Hanta

Antanimalandy, Madagascar; 2017

Hanta, a Sakalava woman from Antanimalandy in northwest Madagascar, poses in her *lamba* garment. She wears the Malagasy traditional mask, the *masonjoany*, a powder made from the tree of the same name that grows on the western coast of Madagascar. 'This is my favourite outfit, I feel proud and empowered when I wear it.' My series, LAMBA, is a photographic project intended to show how the *lamba*, this Malagasy garment, serves as a symbol of the island's cultural heritage, pride and tool of empowerment for Malagasy people. Although Western clothing now dominates daily fashion in Madagascar, the *lamba* still accompanies most people at each important step of their lives. For Malagasy women, it remains a symbol of status and cultural pride. For each picture, I used a *lambahoany* as a background (a printed cotton *lamba* typically depicting a Malagasy everyday life scene and featuring a proverb on the lower border of the design). This project, inspired by traditional African studio portraiture, is my tribute to my people, my country and my cultural heritage. As a photographer born and raised in Madagascar, I strive to find new angles and stories on cultural and environmental issues in contemporary Africa through my work.

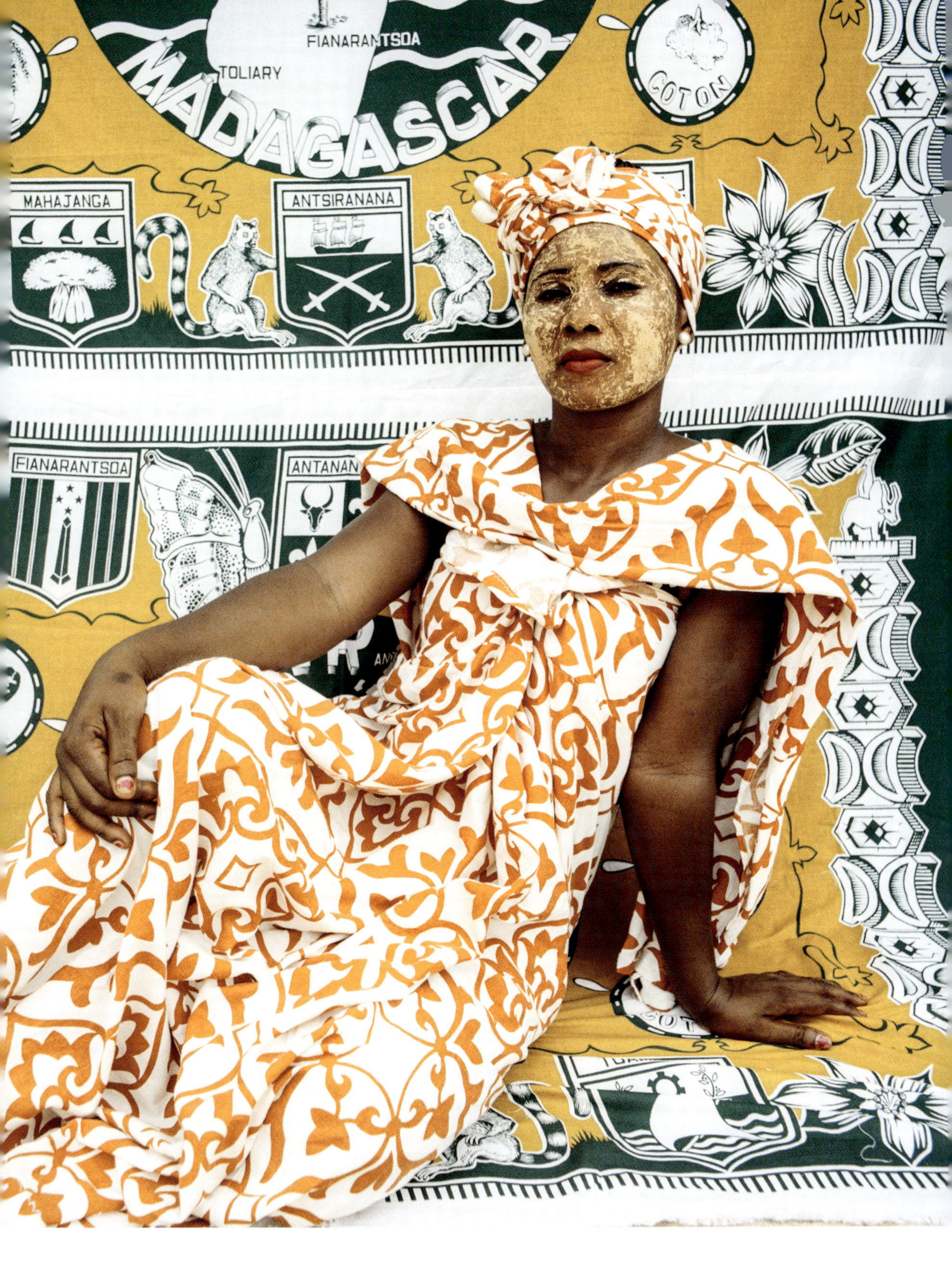
FIANARANTSOA
TOLIARY
MADAGASCAR
COTON
MAHAJANGA
ANTSIRANANA
FIANARANTSOA

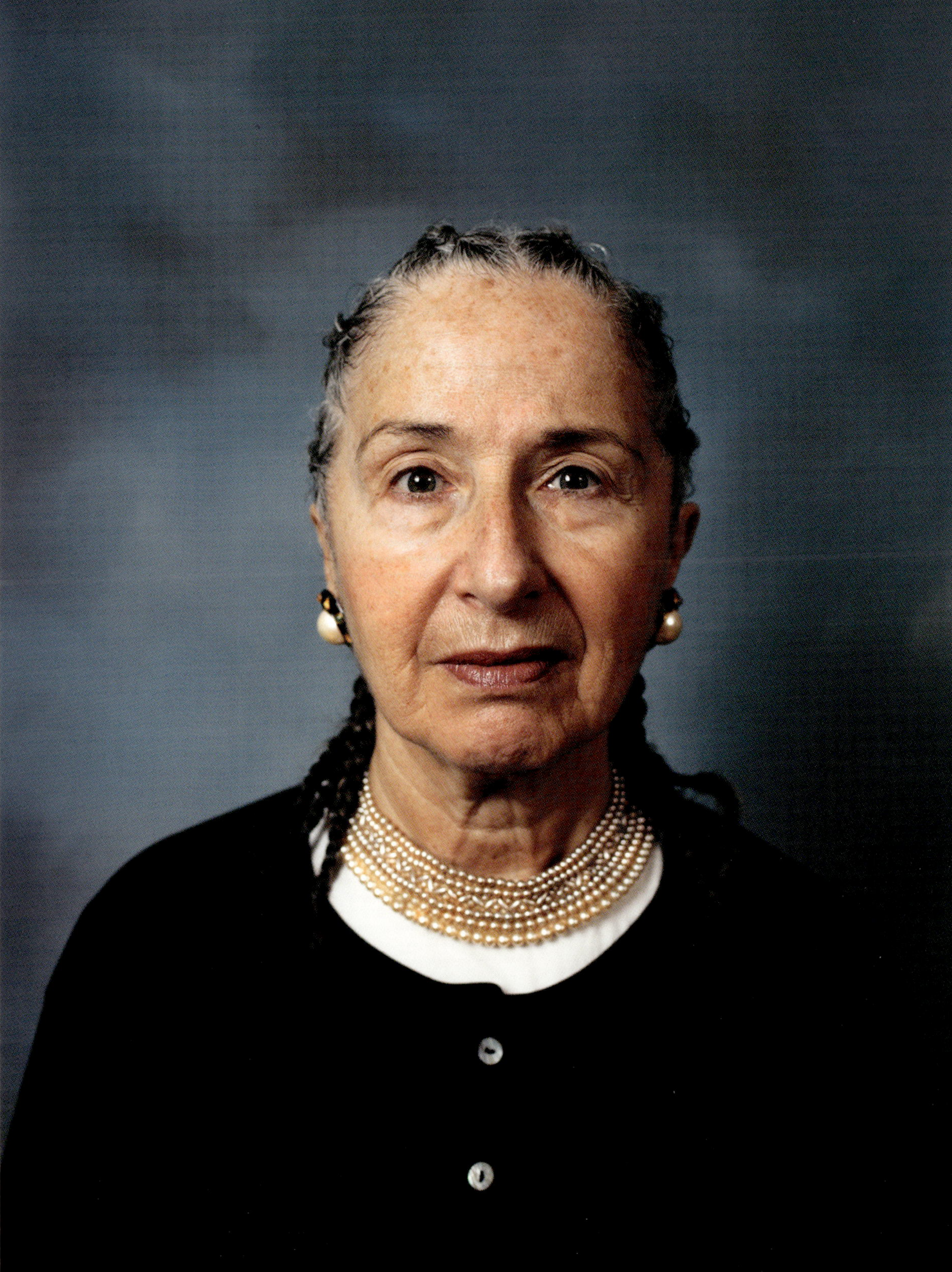

Endia Beal

American

Charlotte

2013

For women, looking 'professional' within a corporate space can be a challenging and frustrating experience – especially for women of colour, who are often asked to downplay or mask certain aspects of their cultural identity. In my photographic series, Can I Touch It? I explore ideas of conformity and race-based hair discrimination through business portraits. I approached white women in their 40s and 50s, some were colleagues and others strangers, and gave them hairstyles typically worn by Black women. Afterwards, I photographed each woman in their business attire against a traditional corporate backdrop. Seen on white women, these hairstyles – all of which I have worn before – challenge us to examine corporate systems that were never designed for women who look like me. As a Black, female photographer, I aspire to create photos that reveal often overlooked and unappreciated experiences unique to people of colour. The women in Can I Touch It? allowed me to make them the 'other' for a moment, in order to highlight the employment barriers facing Black women. Through this project I learned how much all women can relate to these experiences in some way, and I have continued to explore these themes in my work, including the project Am I What You're Looking For?, all of which became part of my first book *Performance Review*.

Bethany Mollenkof

American

Mother

Alabama, USA; 2019

In the media, rural America is almost always equated with white farming communities, but people of colour – particularly Black women – have long suffered from lack of access to prenatal healthcare. I have spent a lot of time documenting reproductive rights, childbirth and motherhood, often focusing on what it is like to be pregnant as a Black woman in the South. This particular portrait of Brianne Moore was created in Alabama, a state with the fewest maternity care providers per capita and one of the highest infant mortality rates in the country. I wanted to photograph someone directly impacted by the collapse of the rural healthcare system and how she was navigating her choices, as one of many women of colour in Alabama working to educate themselves on the safest way to give birth. Trying to solve the maternal health crisis in these rural communities means addressing a web of societal, political and health-related issues that make childbirth or abortion a life-and-death proposition for far too many Black women. As a Black woman born in Tennessee, I try to lend my perspective to create images and stories that offer an intimate portrait and counter narrative of long-ignored, erased and censored communities.

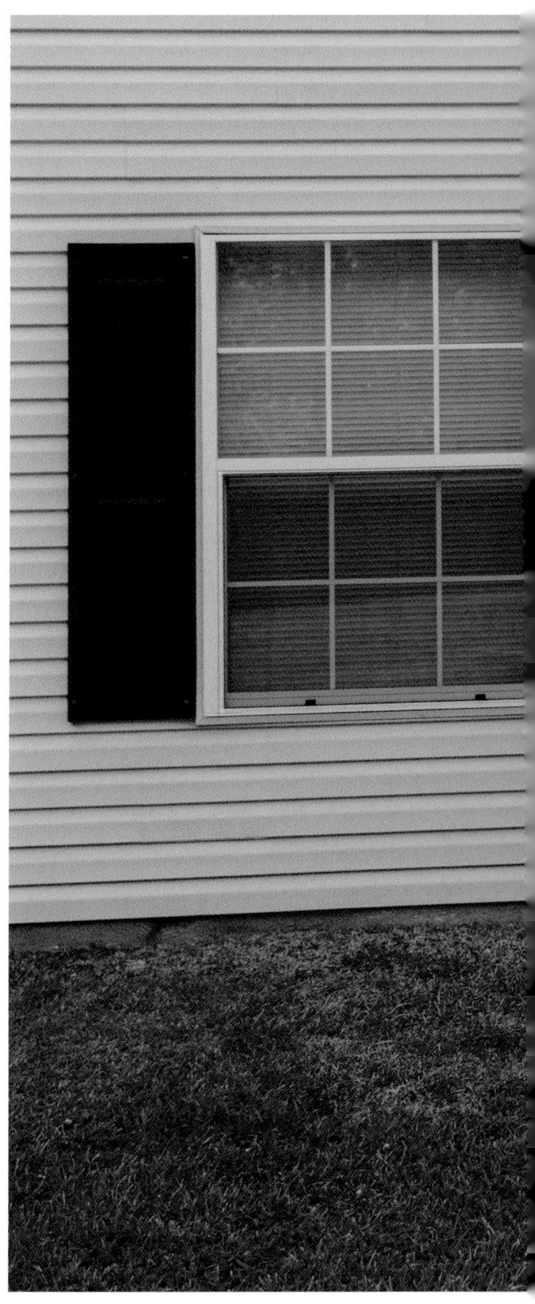

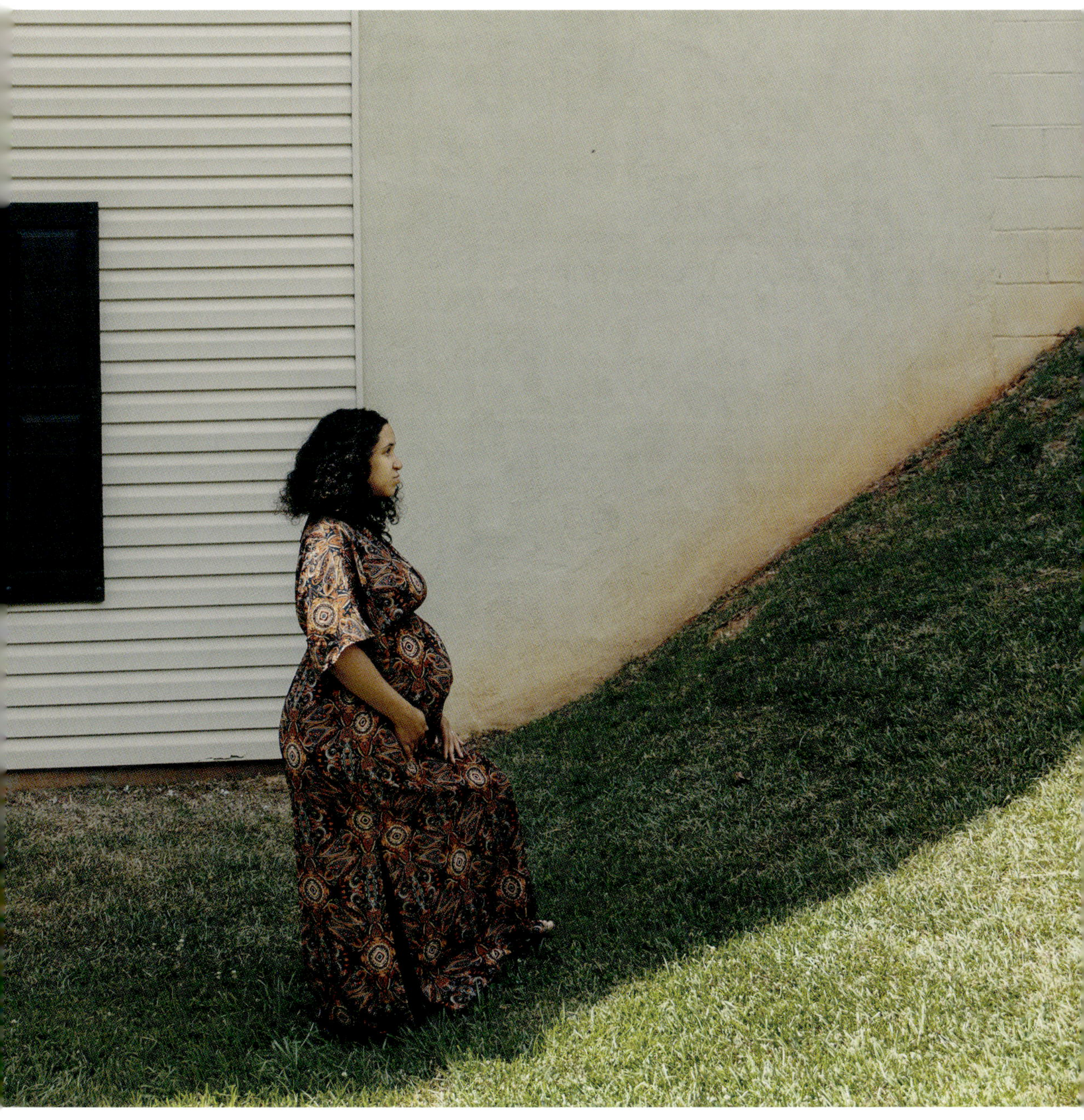

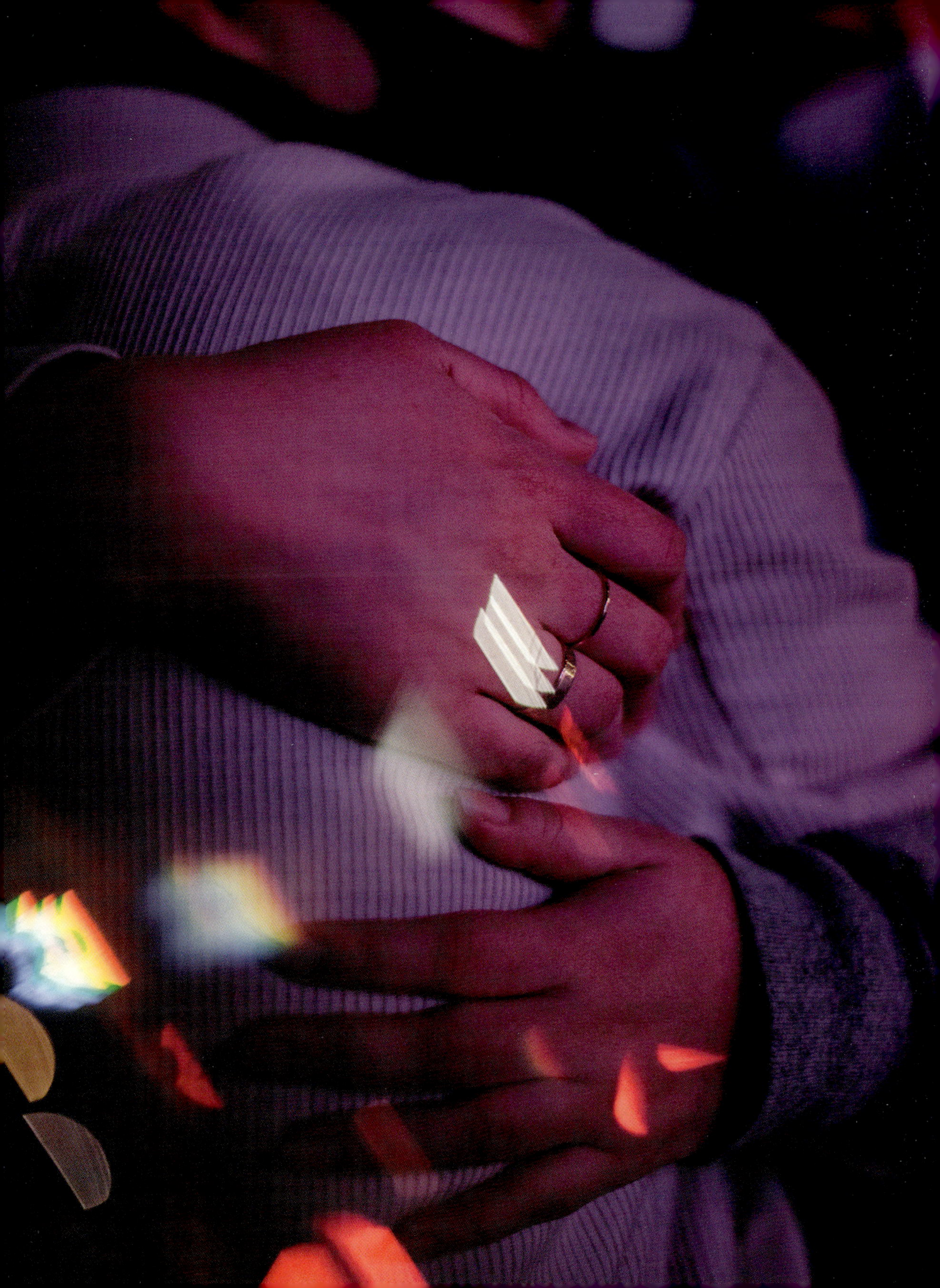

◀

Hannah Yoon

Canadian

A Collective Feeling

Atlanta, Georgia, USA; 2021

In March 2021, *The Washington Post* sent me to Atlanta, Georgia, to document the emotional aftermath of the mass shooting that left eight people dead, six of them being Asian women. When I first heard the news, I was stunned and felt a bit like I was disassociating. Being on the ground and meeting the community that was immediately impacted allowed me to process my own feelings. I connected with a few women who had grown up in Atlanta. We went to the site of the shootings and mainly spent our time grieving together. It was important for me to show the bonds and connections that were being formed in the midst of this tragedy, and affection that can grow out of darkness. I was not sure how this image would make others feel, but my hope is that it stirs up feelings of comfort and reassurance. Later, I decided to put together a small zine. It felt meaningful and empowering to have the images printed and out in the world as a physical item. The impact of this event was huge for many of us Asian Americans, and this was my way of creating a physical record for history's sake.

▶▶

Noriko Hayashi

Japanese

sawasawato

Hamhung, North Korea; 2019

My long-term project *sawasawato* focuses on reconstructing the memories of Japanese wives in North Korea. A large repatriation programme of 93,000 ethnic Koreans from Japan to North Korea took place between 1959 and 1984. Some 1,800 'Japanese Wives' who accompanied their Korean husbands believed they would be able to return to Japan. However, due to political tensions, that has not happened. Since 2013, I have been travelling back and forth between the hometowns of several Japanese wives and where they live in North Korea to document their lives. Here, Akiko Ota looks at a print of her Japanese hometown (which I photographed, printed onto tarpaulin fabric and transported to North Korea) displayed on a beach in Hamhung. Originally, I was going to shoot only one frame, but as I observed how she interacted with the photograph of her hometown – where she has not been able to visit for more than half a century – I decided to keep shooting. It was a touching scene: Akiko's life intersects with the complexities of memory, space and multiple layers of feeling. As a Japanese female, I wanted to shed light on the forgotten existence of these courageous women.

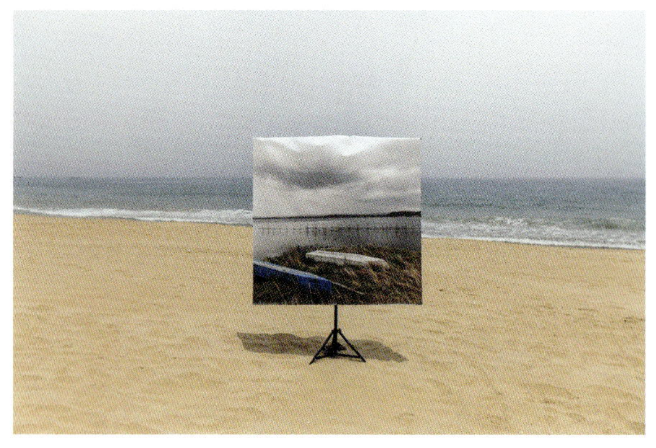
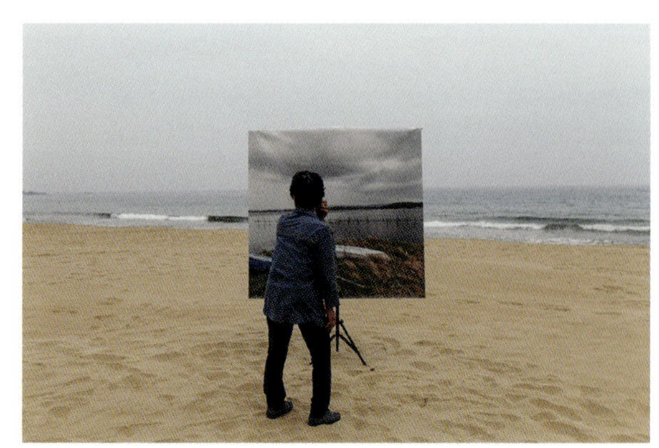
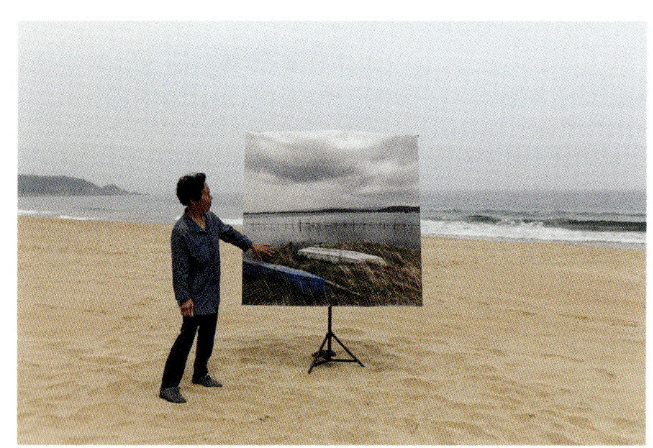
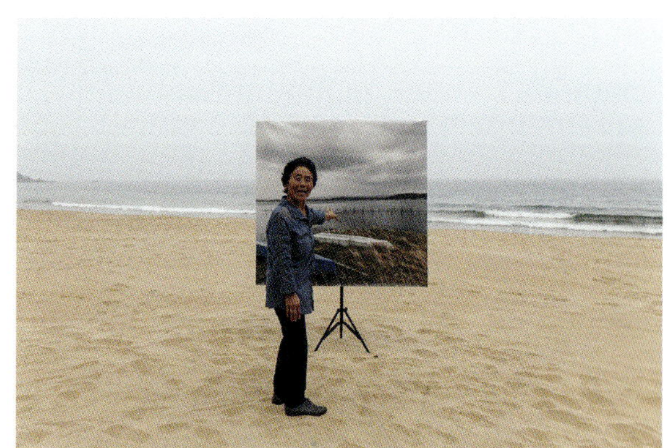
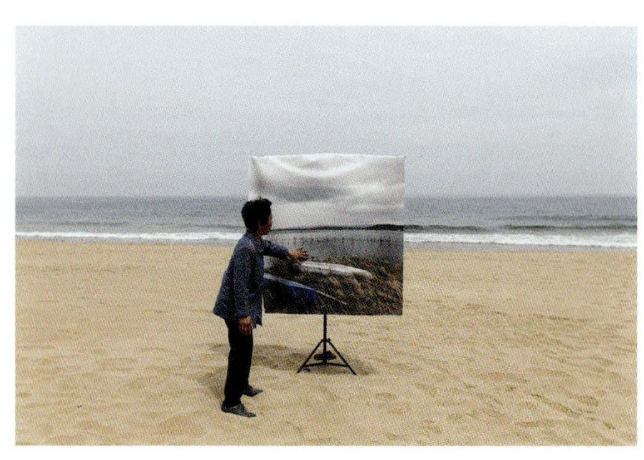
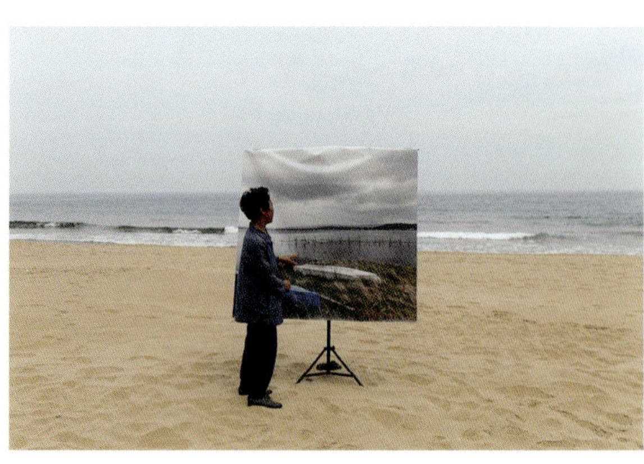

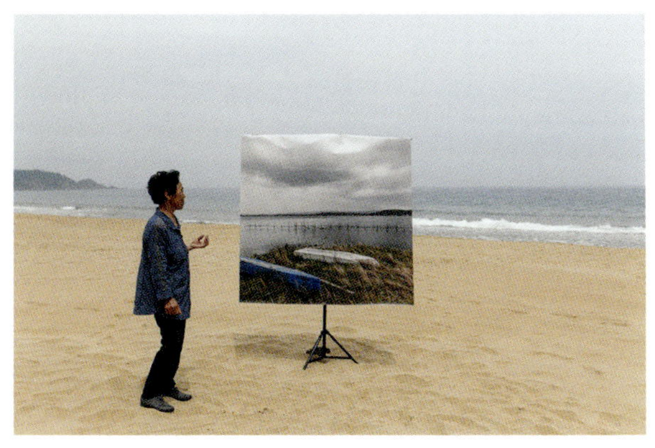
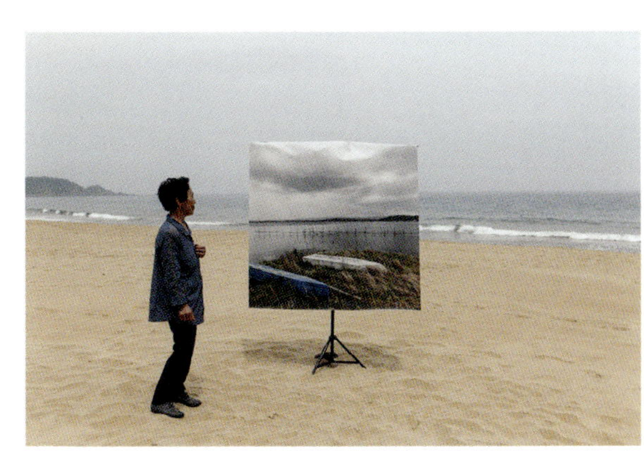
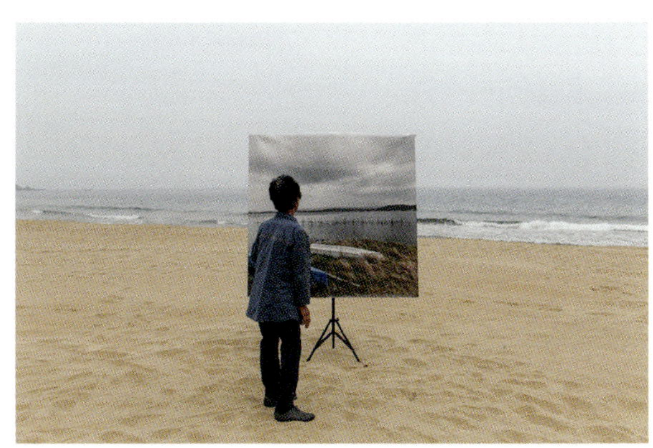
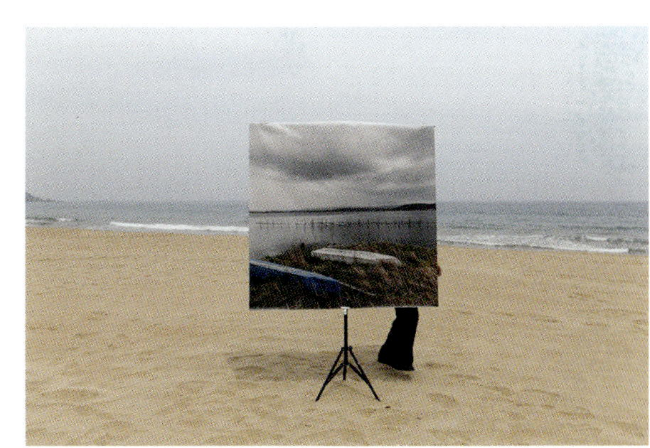
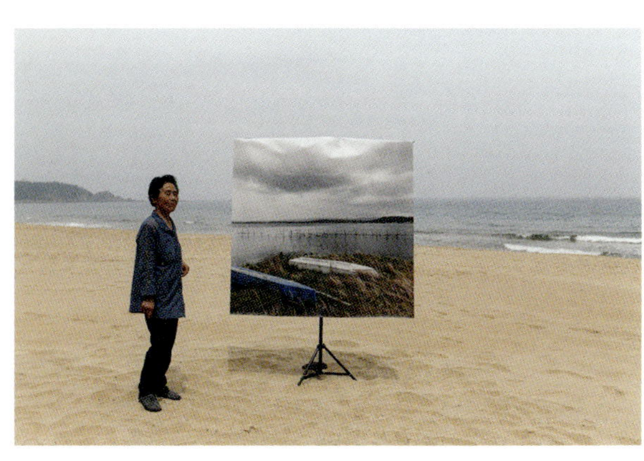
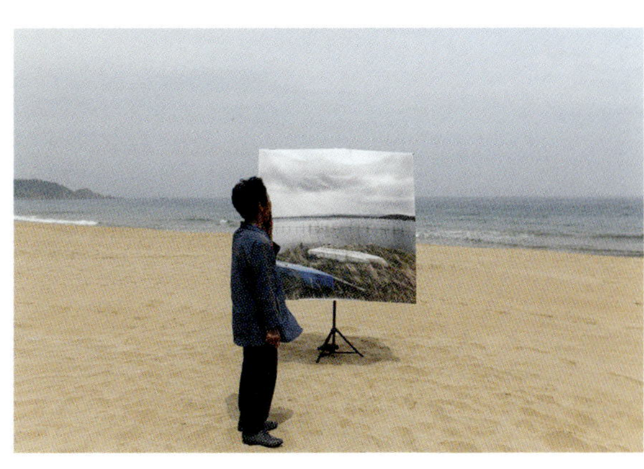

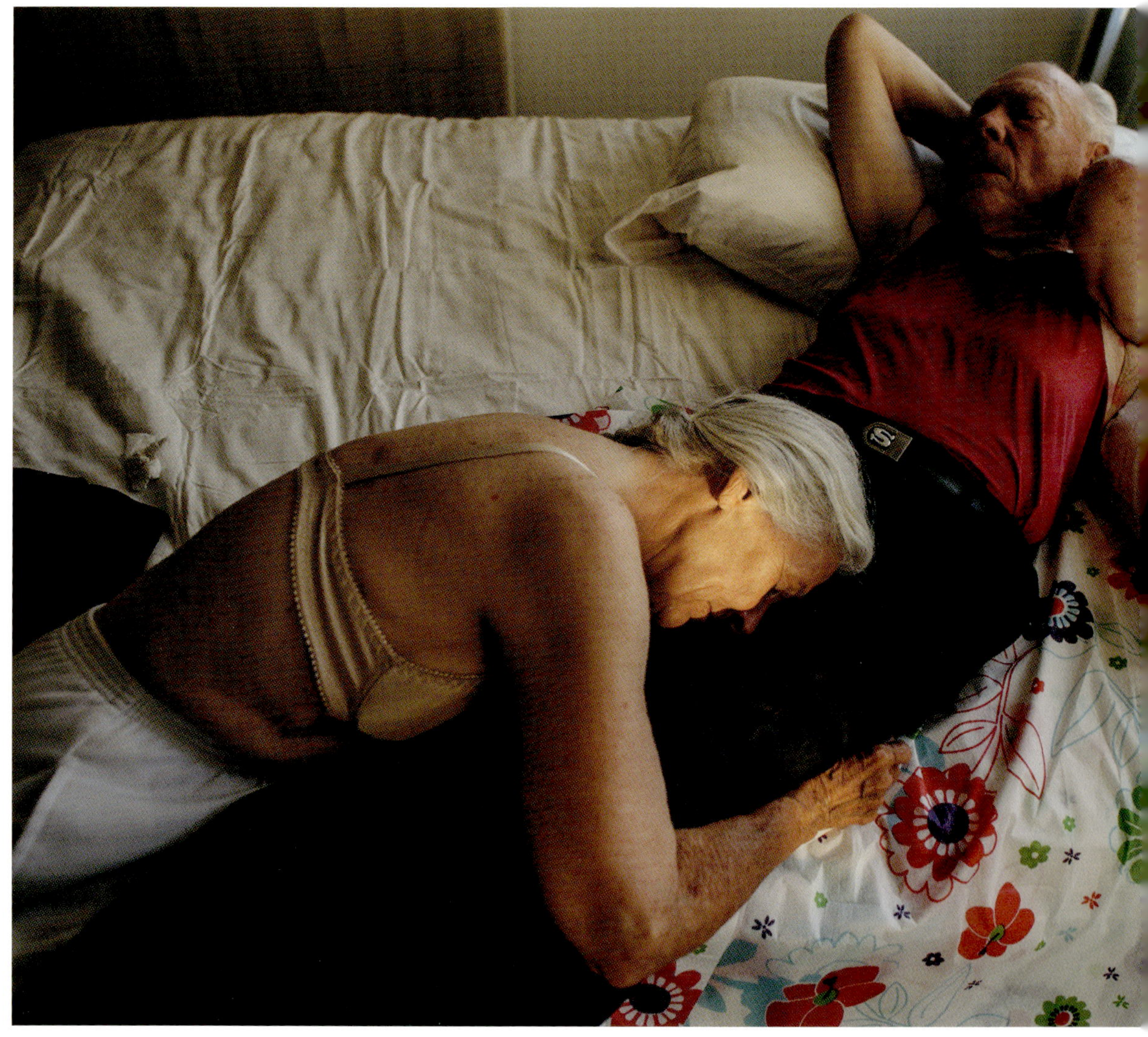

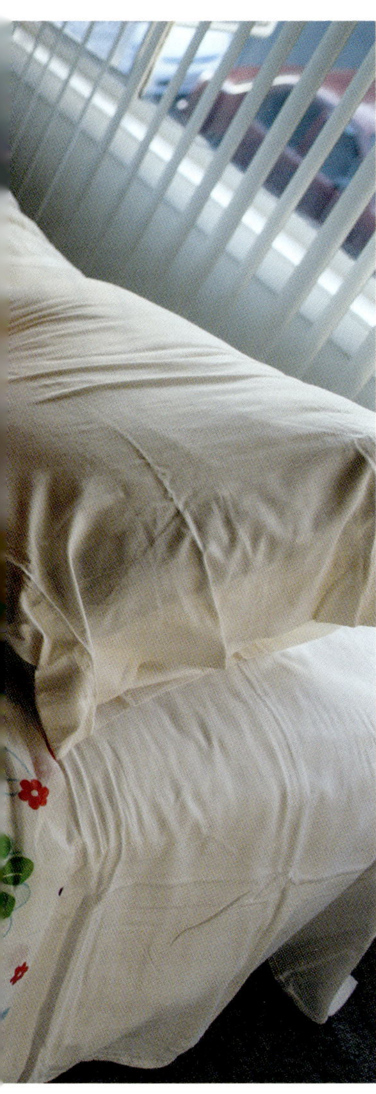

Isadora Kosofsky

French American

Jeanie and William

Los Angeles, California, USA; 2012

This image is from Senior Love Triangle, my long-term photo documentary that shadows three seniors in a romantic conflict. I first met Jeanie, Will and Adina outside a retirement community in Los Angeles and felt an immediate connection to them without knowing the details of their dynamic. Will first formed a relationship with Adina. Then, he moved into another retirement home where he fell in love with Jeanie. Since Will did not want to choose between Jeanie and Adina, they formed a trio. Although there were generations separating us, I was also contending with questions about the fragility and vulnerability of intimacy and romantic connection. All of us have found ourselves in some form of love triangle, whether literally or spiritually. We carry our past loves and heartbreaks into our present relationships. While shadowing them, I experienced longing and remoteness. I have always been drawn to people who experience loneliness even among others. Jeanie, however, saw this chapter of her life as a form of liberation. She could abandon her fears and embrace her sovereignty. Their bond challenges socio-cultural norms about older adults. They break from constraints, while facing ageless desires to be seen and wanted.

Malin Fezehai

Swedish

Eritrean wedding in Israel

Israel; 2014

This image was taken in 2014, of the wedding of two Eritreans who came to Israel as refugees. At the time, they were among about 50,000 African asylum seekers living in Israel, mainly from Eritrea and Sudan. In December 2013, the Israeli Knesset added an amendment to the 'Anti-Infiltration' law, requiring asylum seekers from Eritrea and Sudan to be detained for at least a year and then placed indefinitely in an open detention centre. I was working on a larger project about how Israel's policy towards African asylum seekers pressured them to self-deport or, as the former interior minister Eli Yishai put it, to 'make their lives miserable' until they gave up and let the government deport them. This image is significant for me because it shows a refugee couple getting married and creating a life for themselves, despite living in legal limbo. So often, when people see images of refugees, it is in the more extreme circumstances that most people cannot relate to, and I think it is essential to show the full spectrum of what it means to be a refugee – including the good moments. My image was the first iPhone photograph ever to receive a World Press Photo Award.

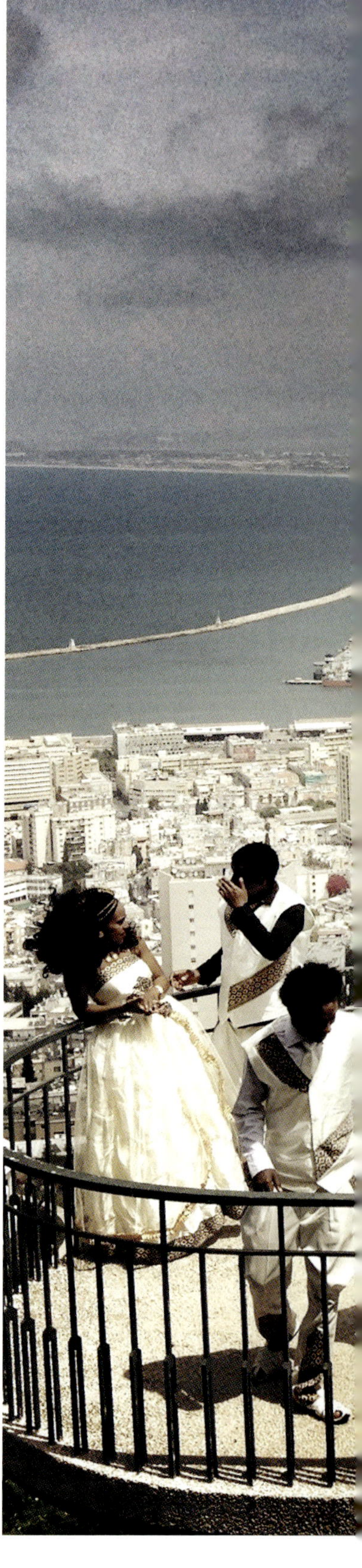

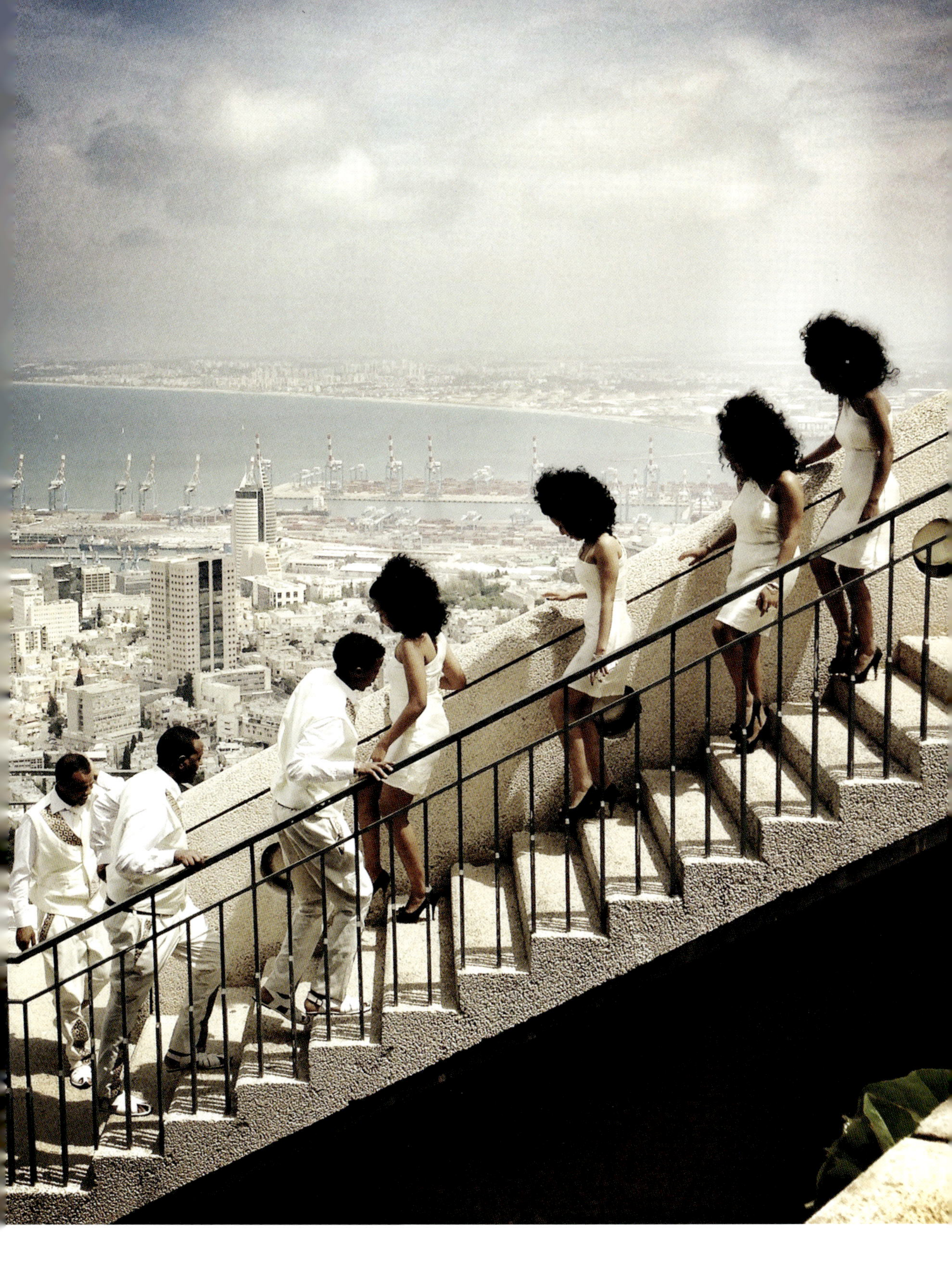

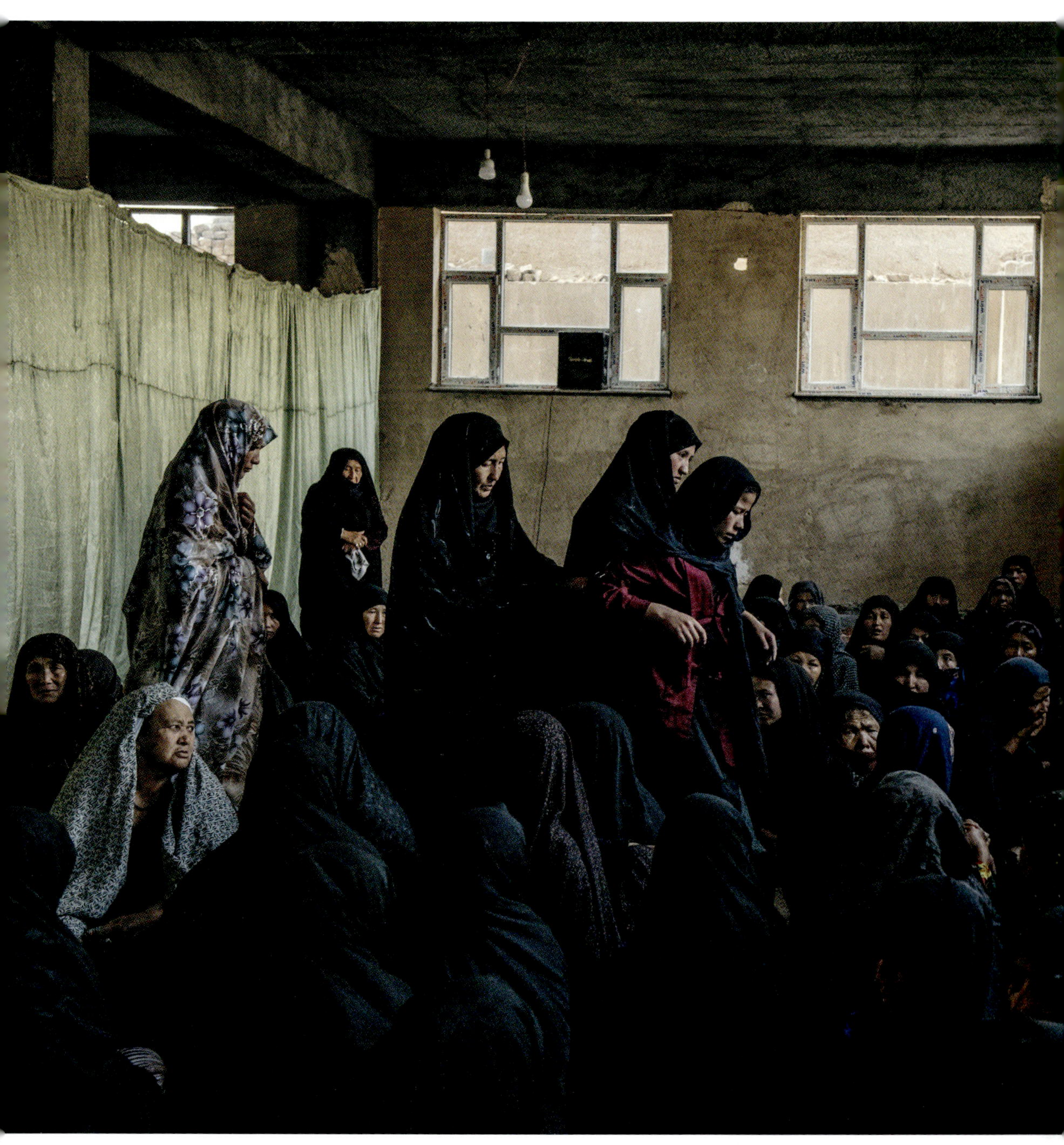

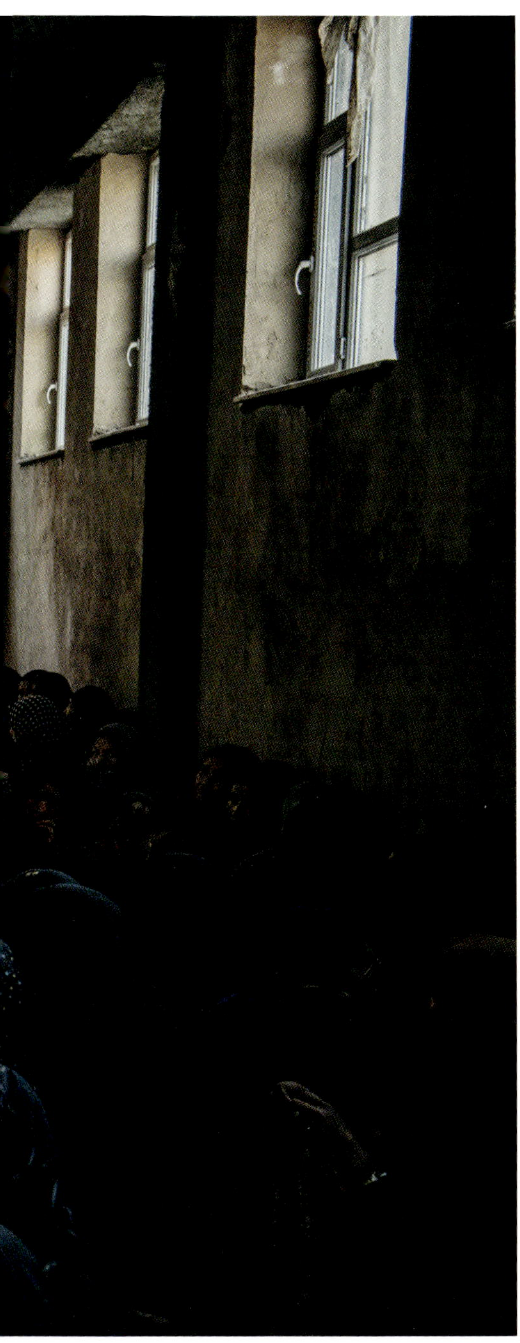

Kiana Hayeri

Iranian Canadian

Mayhem

Kabul, Afghanistan; 2021

A girl was reunited with her mother after a bombing at Sayed Ul-Shuhada school in Kabul, Afghanistan, which occurred about a week after the Taliban's renewed offensive that followed on from the American troop withdrawal. The mother lost a second daughter, aged 13, in the attack, which killed at least 90 people. I have lived in Kabul since 2014 and have covered too many bombings. But this one, outside a school, was probably the hardest. The day before this photo was taken, there was a triple explosion outside a school in Kabul City. Because I am a woman, I was able to enter the space without causing too much distraction. There was a humming sound – the sound of the women crying quietly – but the room was silent otherwise. At this mosque they were burying two girls who were killed the day before. The sister arrived late because she had passed out earlier that morning, so they had taken her to the hospital. The area around the school is one of the poorest areas of Kabul.

Luisa Dörr

Brazilian

The Flying Cholitas

Outskirts of El Alto, Bolivia; 2019

I first encountered the wrestlers while my husband was making a documentary and I saw a short clip of the cholitas in his film. I loved them immediately. Super Barrio wrestling was created in Mexico many years ago around the same time the Fighting Cholitas were born in El Alto, Bolivia. In this image, Elizabeth La Roba Corazones fights against Alicia De Las Flores at a ring in the outskirts of El Alto. In traditional Bolivian dress, the cholitas launch themselves at each other, executing perfect moves in a quest to win. What follows is part acrobatics, part theatrics. They climb the corner ropes high above the ring and 'fly' across the stage, like any Hollywood hero endowed with superpowers; hence their nickname. At first, I was fascinated by the skill – seeing these Indigenous women flying through the air, reclaiming the clothing their community was forced to wear as servants for Spanish occupiers. But then I saw it went beyond the ring. They are fighting for their rights, for recognition, for equality. They are fighting to put a meal on the table for their kids. They're fighting for their lives.

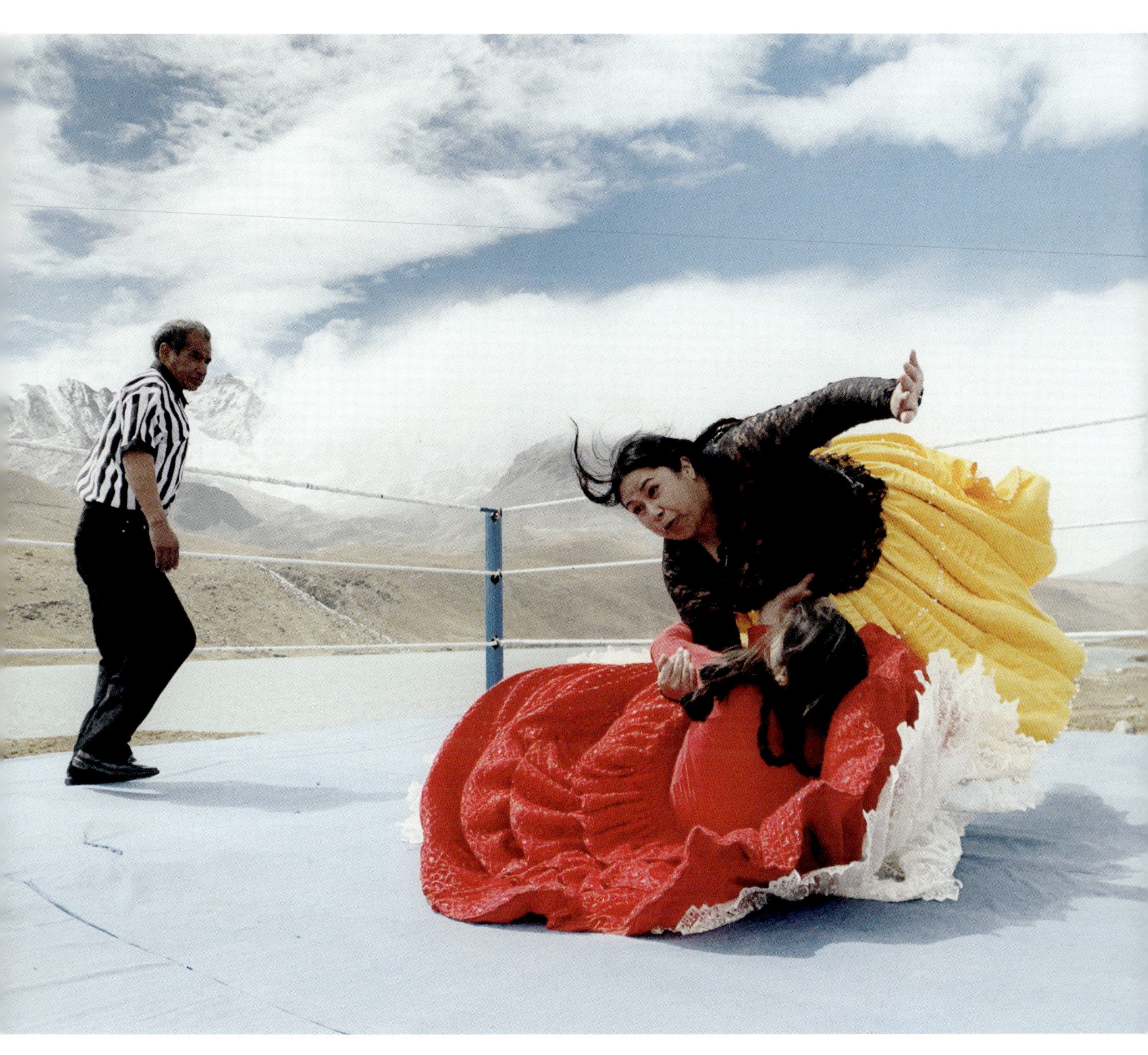

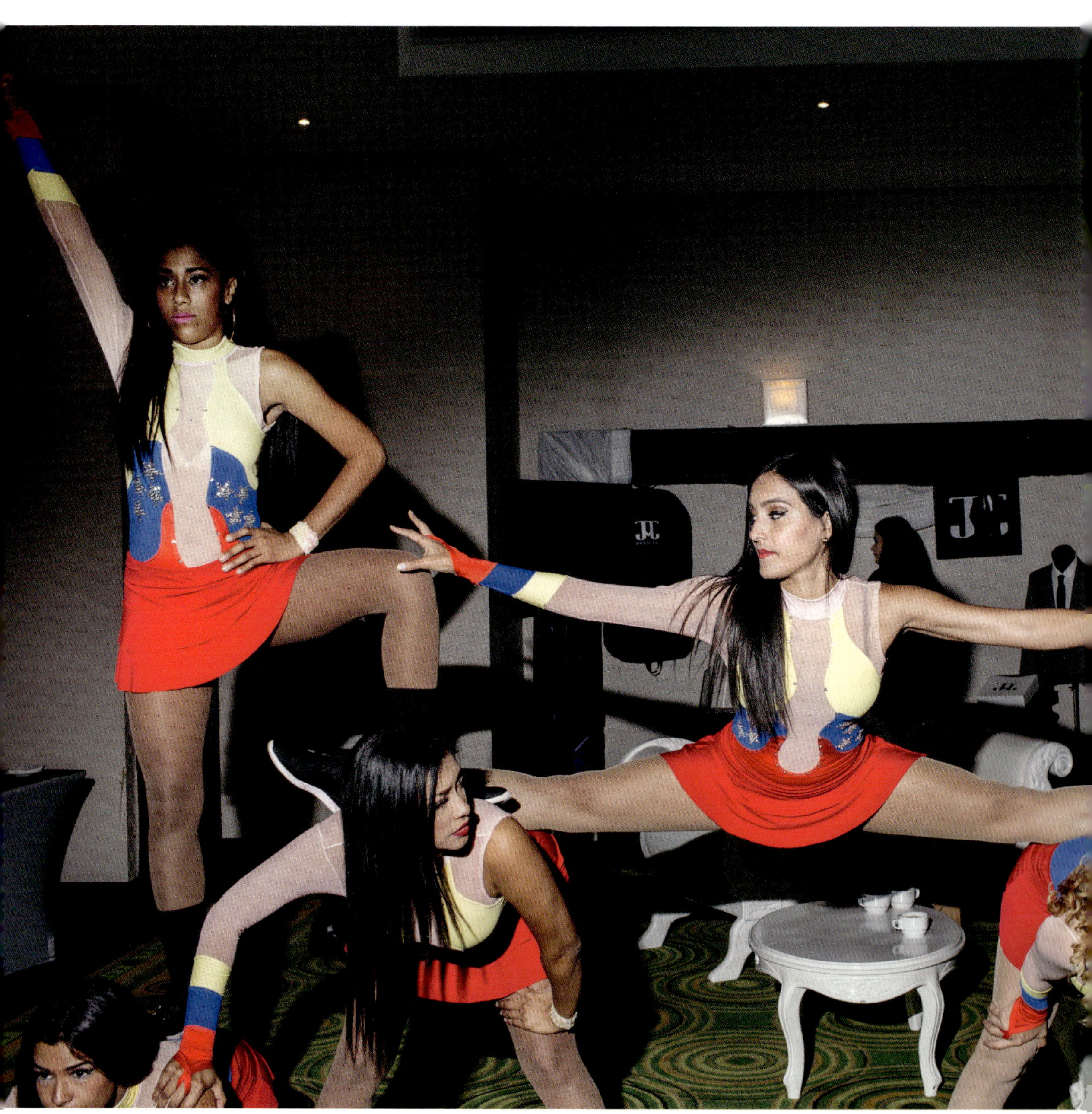

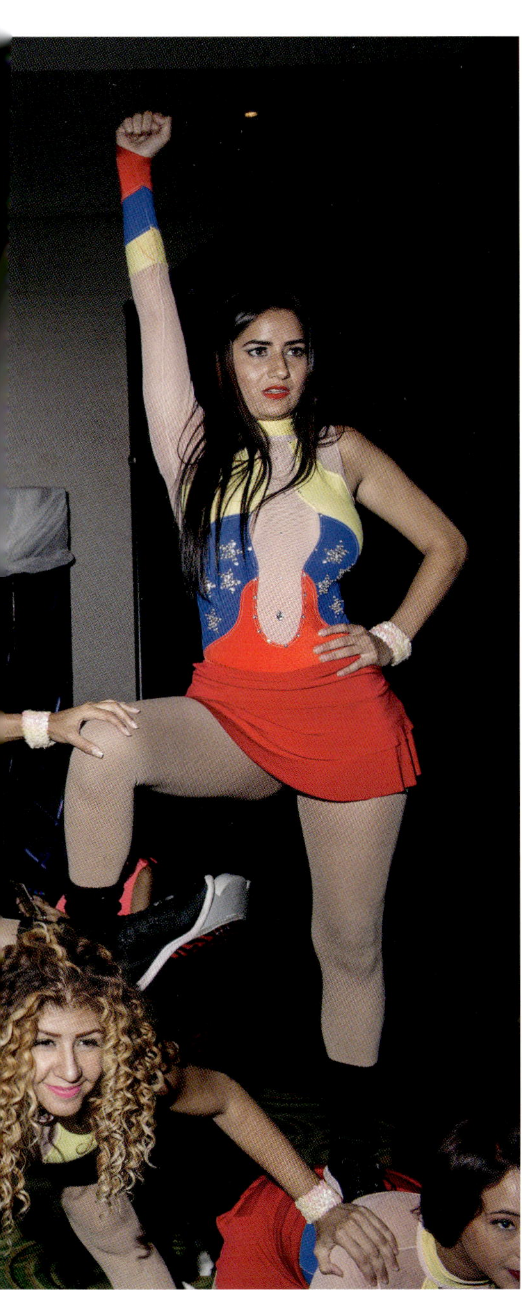

Natalie Keyssar

North American

Seco Cheers at the Bitcoin Conference

Caracas, Venezuela; 2018

I spent weeks following Seco Cheers, a cheerleading team based in Caracas, near the height of Venezuela's ongoing economic crisis as part of my ongoing project about the lives of women amid upheaval. I admire these women for their strength, holding their families and communities together during difficult times. Working with them was an extremely fun experience, punctuated by painful moments of scarcity and insecurity. I have found that the path to understanding often strays from the headline-grabbing events, into intimate moments that help me refine the questions I am asking, as an outsider and student, always searching, while accepting that I shall never quite find the answers. The question here was 'what does it mean to be professionally happy and professionally beautiful as your home is fractured by crisis?' These women taught me about the connection between joy and resilience, the power of sisterhood and the value of talent. Their stories epitomized the surrealism of the moment – the juxtaposition of these women performing at a bitcoin conference at a luxury hotel, at a time when much of the country and some of the dancers were food insecure was hard to grasp. I made this picture as they practised a pyramid formation backstage and marvelled at the layers of symbolism.

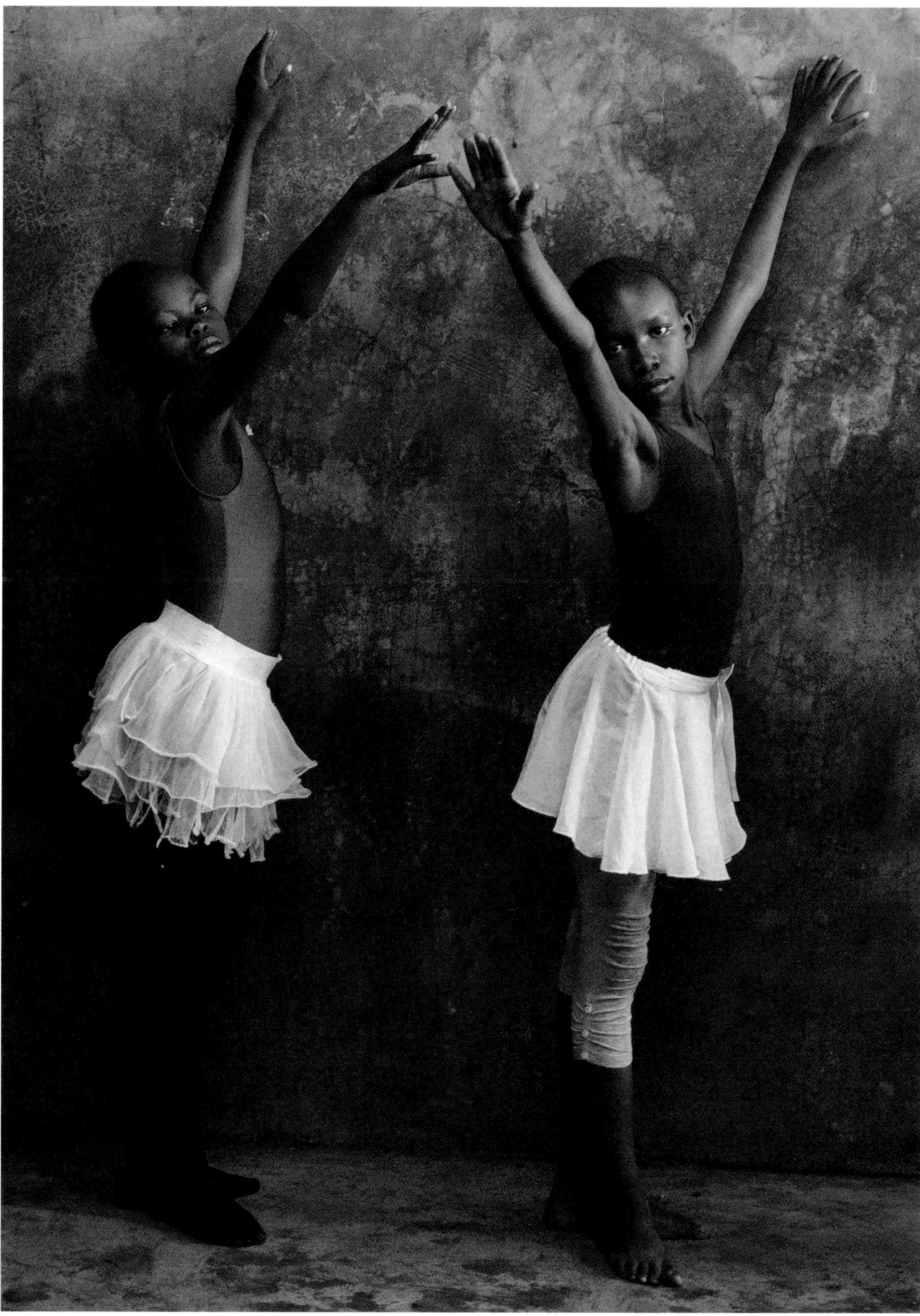

◄

Sarah Waiswa

Ugandan

Last Act

Nairobi, Kenya; 2017

This image is part of my series Ballet in Kibera and was one of the first personal projects I worked on in my career as a documentary and portrait photographer. I have an interest in the intersection between identity and self-expression, particularly new African identities, and strive to highlight social issues on the continent in a contemporary and non-traditional way. I was intrigued by how ballet, often associated with privilege, was being used as a form of self-expression in one of the largest informal settlements in Nairobi. It was also interesting to me how, in that room, the children were allowed to express themselves in spite of their circumstances. I wanted to capture the in-between state of imagination and reality and offer an alternative to the monolithic stereotype of the poor African child from the slum. It was a project that told an African story without centring on poverty, but instead focused on human beings navigating their world. I worked with Annos Africa, a non-profit organization that offered the classes and initially I just watched. For me, it was an important lesson in just how important it is to spend time with your collaborators.

►►

Kendrick Brinson

American

The Aqua Suns Get Into Costume

Sun City, Arizona, USA; 2010

Members of the Sun City Aqua Suns, a synchronized swim team made up of retirees, wait for their cue for a holiday reindeer routine in the pool at the Lakeview Recreation Center. Their performance was part of the Holiday Around the World celebration to mark the 50th anniversary of Sun City, America's first retirement city that remains one of the largest in the world. Since 2009, I have been photographing the more than 40,000 residents 55 and older in this age-restricted city. My two favourite groups to photograph are the Aqua Suns, though sadly the synchronized swim team has now disbanded, and the Sun City Poms, a group of cheerleaders 55 to 89 years old. The lesson I have taken into my personal life after photographing the amazing community groups in Sun City – there are more than 100 clubs for the residents, ranging from tap dancing to pickle ball to weaving to woodworking – is to lean in to doing more creative things outside of photography. I have learned about the joy of doing things that make me feel good and that I do not necessarily have to be the best at them, or even good at them. I have watched these women rehearse and perform and I am inspired.

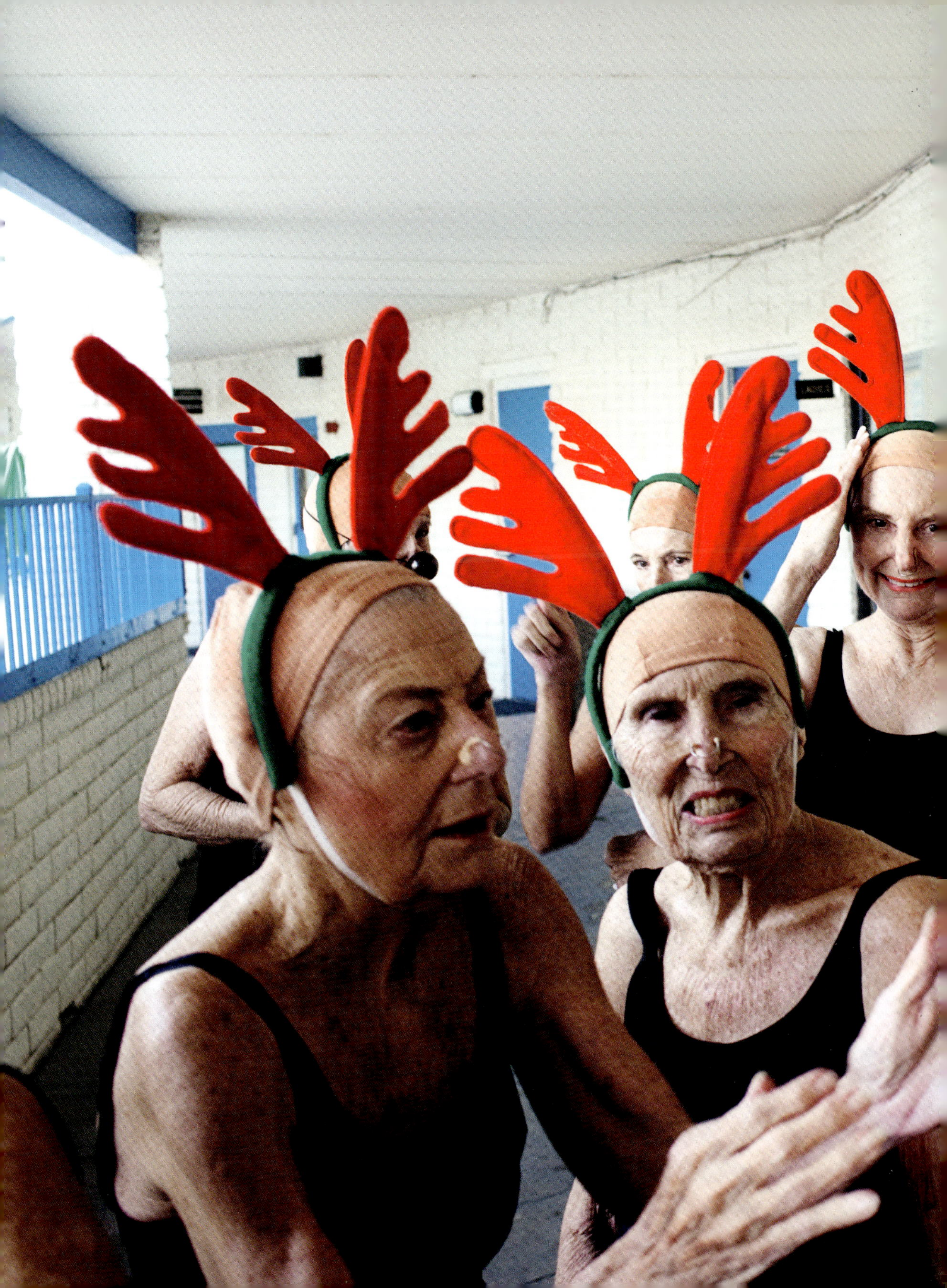

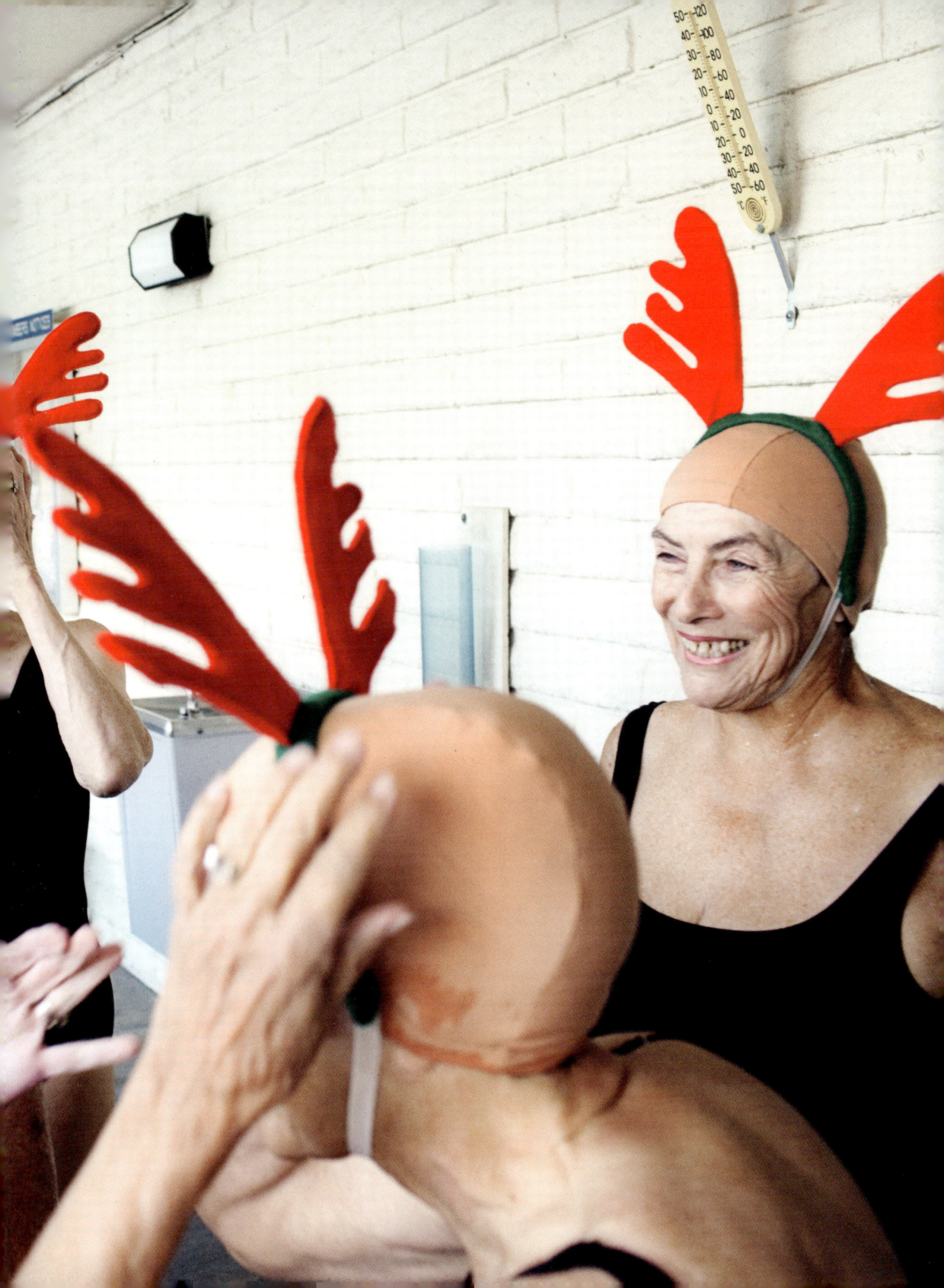

Index

Index of Photographers

Jess T. Dugan pp. 28–29
jessdugan.com | @jesstdugan

Yen Duong pp. 148–149
duoyen.com | @duoyen

Rena Effendi pp. 78–79
refendi.com | @renaeffendiphoto

Kholood Eid pp. 166–167
kholoodeid.com | @kholoodeid

Rehab Eldalil pp. 70–72
rehabeldalil.com | @rehabeldalil

Yagazie Emezi pp. 177–179
yagazieemezi.com | @yagazieemezi

Mariceu Erthal García pp. 191–193
mariceuerthal.com | @mariceu_

Citlali Fabián pp. 12–13
citlalifabian.com | @citlalifabian

Malin Fezehai pp. 206–207
malinfezehai.net | @malinfezehai

Annie Flanagan pp. 38–39
annieflanagan.com | @annieflanagan

Lola Flash pp. 60–61
lolaflash.com | @flash9

Terra Fondriest pp. 100–101
terrafondriest.com | @terrafondriest

Mojgan Ghanbari pp. 88–89
mojganghanbari.com | @mojganghanbari_

Golden pp. 20–21
goldengoldengolden.com | @goldenthem_

Carol Guzy pp. 146–147
@carolguzy

Tanya Habjouqa pp. 83–85
tanyahabjouqa.com | @habjouqa

Nada Harib pp. 74–75
nadaharib.com | @nada_harib

Noriko Hayashi pp. 201–203
norikohayashi.com | @norikohayashi_photo

Kiana Hayeri pp. 208–209
kianahayeri.com | @kianahayeri

Susannah Ireland pp. 149–151
susannahireland.com | @susannahireland

Tailyr Irvine pp. 104–105
tailyrirvine.com | @tailyrirvine

JEB (Joan E. Biren) pp. 106–107
@jebmedia

Lynn Johnson pp. 40–41
lynnjohnsonphoto.com | @ljohnphoto

Mary Kang pp. 80–81
marykang.com | @mary.kang

Natalie Keyssar pp. 212–213
nataliekeyssar.com | @nataliekeyssar

Gulshan Khan pp. 140–141
gulshankhan.com | @gulshanii

Saumya Khandelwal pp. 114–115
saumyakhandelwal.com |
@khandelwal_saumya

Isadora Kosofsky pp. 204–205
isadorakosofsky.com | @isadorakosofky

Koyoltzintli pp. 172–173
koyoltzintli.com | @koyoltzintli

Erika Larsen pp. 184–185
erikalarsenphoto.com | @erikalarsen888

Gillian Laub pp. 22–23
gillianlaub.com | @gigilaub

Nyimas Laula pp. 72–73
nyimaslaula.com | @nyimaslaula

Olivia Locher pp. 94–95
olivialocher.com | @olivialocher

Rania Matar pp. 142–143
raniamatar.com | @raniamatar

Maddie McGarvey pp. 76–77
maddiemcgarvey.com | @maddiemcgarvey

Susan Meiselas pp. 36–37
susanmeiselas.com | @susanmeiselas

Clara Mokri pp. 110–111
claramokriphotography.com |
@claramokriphoto

Bethany Mollenkof pp. 198–199
bethanymollenkof.com | @fancybethany

Haley Morris-Cafiero pp. 54–55
haleymorriscafiero.com | @hmorriscafiero

Rosem Morton pp. 42–43
rosem.xyz | @rosemmorton

Nicola Muirhead pp. 98–99
nicolamuirhead.com | @nmuirhead_photo

Natalie Naccache pp. 92–94
natnacphotography.com | @natnacphotos

Sarah Pabst pp. 102–103
sarahpabst.com | @_sarahpabst_

Oksana Parafeniuk pp. 51–53
oksanaparafeniuk.com | @oksana_par

Laurence Philomène pp. 33–35
laurencephilomene.com |
@laurencephilomene

Tara Pixley pp. 130–131
tarapixley.com | @tlpix

Suzanne Plunkett pp. 156–157
suzanneplunkett.com | @suzanne_plunkett

Charmaine Poh pp. 58–59
charmainepoh.com | @psxcharmaine

Rozette Rago pp. 48–49
rozette.com | @hellorozette

Miora Rajaonary pp. 194–195
miorarajaonary.photoshelter.com |
@miorarajaonary

Hannah Reyes Morales pp. 111–113
hannah.ph | @hannahreyesmorales

Cara Romero pp. 32–33
cararomerophotography.com |
@cararomerophotography

Raphaela Rosella pp. 16–17
raphaelarosella.com | @raphaelarosella

Sumy Sadurni pp. 138–139
sumysadurni.com

Haruka Sakaguchi pp. 90–91
harukasakaguchi.com | @hsakag

Charlotte Schmitz pp. 190–191
charlotteschmitz.com | @_charlotteschmitz_

Camille Seaman pp. 64–65
camilleseaman.com | @camilleseaman

Smita Sharma pp. 144–145
smitasharma.com | @smitashrm

Sim Chi Yin pp. 152–153
chiyinsim.com | @chiyin_sim

Michaela Skovranova pp. 96–97
mishku.com | @mishkusk

Kali Spitzer pp 188–189
kalispitzer.photoshelter.com |
@kali_spitzer_photography

Daro Sulakauri pp. 164–166
darosulakauri.com | @darosulakauri

Anastasia Taylor-Lind pp. 162–163
anastasiataylorlind.com | @anastasiatl

Nicole Tung pp. 160–161
nicoletung.com | @nicoletung

Irina Unruh pp. 86–87
irinaunruh.com | @irinaunruh

Alicia Vera pp. 56–58
aliciavera.com | @aliciavera

Danielle Villasana pp. 29–31
daniellevillasana.com | @davillasana

Ami Vitale pp. 66–67
amivitale.com | @amivitale

Asmaa Waguih pp. 154–155
asmaawaguih.com | @asmaawaguih

Sarah Waiswa pp. 214–215
sarahwaiswa.com | @lafrohemien

Deborah Willis pp. 180–181
debwillisphoto.com | @debwillisphoto

Arin Yoon pp. 44–45
arinyoon.com | @arinyoon

Hannah Yoon pp. 200–201
hannahyoon.com | @hanloveyoon

Etinosa Yvonne pp. 134–135
etinosayvonne.me | @etinosa.yvonne

Patience Zalanga pp. 122–123
patiencezalangaphoto.com |
@patiencezalanga

Adriana Zehbrauskas pp. 132–133
adrianazehbrauskas.com | @adrianazehbrauskas

Credits

Text and image copyright © 2023 belongs to each photographer as listed below, unless otherwise stated; l = left; r = right

Interior: 12, 13l Citlali Fabián; 13r, 14–15 Tasneem Alsultan; 16–17 Raphaela Rosella; 18–19 Xyza Cruz Bacani; 20–21 Golden; 22–23 Gillian Laub; 24–25 Ana Maria Arévalo Gosen; 26–27 Sara Aliaga Ticona; 28, 29l Jess T. Dugan; 29r, 30–31 Danielle Villasana; 32, 33l Cara Romero; 33r, 34–35 Laurence Philomène; 36–37 image © Susan Meiselas/Magnum Photos; 37 text © Susan Meiselas; 38–39 Annie Flanagan; 40–41 Lynn Johnson; 42–43 Rosem Morton; 44–45 Arin Yoon; 46–47 Maha Alasaker; 48–49 Rozette Rago; 50 image © Gabriela Bhaskar/NYT/Redux/eyevine; 51l text © Gabriela Bhaskar; 51r, 52–53 Oksana Parafeniuk; 54–55 Haley Morris-Cafiero; 56–57, 58l Alicia Vera; 58r, 59 Charmaine Poh; 60–61 Lola Flash; 64–65 Camille Seaman; 66–67 Ami Vitale; 68–69 Paula Bronstein; 70–71, 72l Rehab Eldalil; 72r, 73 Nyimas Laula; 74–75 Nada Harib; 76–77 Maddie McGarvey; 78–79 Rena Effendi; 80–81 Mary Kang; 82, 83l Cristina de Middel; 83r, 84–85 Tanya Habjouqa; 86–87 Irina Unruh; 88–89 Mojgan Ghanbari; 90–91 Haruka Sakaguchi; 92–93, 94l Natalie Naccache; 94r, 95 Olivia Locher; 96–97 Michaela Skovranova; 98–99 Nicola Muirhead; 100–101 Terra Fondriest; 102–103 Sarah Pabst; 104–105 Tailyr Irvine; 106–107 Joan E. Biren; 108–109 Rhiannon Adam; 110, 111l Clara Mokri; 111r, 112–113 Hannah Reyes Morales; 114–115 Saumya Khandelwal; 116–117 Tracy Barbutes; 120–121 Nina Berman; 122–123 Patience Zalanga; 124–125l image © Verónica G. Cárdenas/Reuters Pictures; 125r text © Verónica G. Cárdenas; 126, 127l Meghan Dhaliwal; 127r, 128–129 Gabriella N. Báez; 130–131 Tara Pixley; 132–133 Adriana Zehbrauskas; 134–135 Etinosa Yvonne; 136–137 Laurel Chor; 138l text © Sumy Sadurni; 138r–139 image © Sumy Sadurni/AFP via Getty Images; 140–141 Gulshan Khan; 142–143 Rania Matar; 144–145 Smita Sharma; 146l text © Carol Guzy; 146r–147 image © Carol Guzy/The Washington Post via Getty Images; 148, 149l Yen Duong; 149r, 150–151 Susannah Ireland; 152–153 Sim Chi Yin; 154–155 Asmaa Waguih; 156l text © Suzanne Plunkett; 156r–157 image © Suzanne Plunkett/AP/Shutterstock; 158–159 Lynsey Addario; 160–161 Nicole Tung; 162–163 Anastasia Taylor-Lind; 164–165, 166l Daro Sulakauri; 166r, 167 Kholood Eid; 170–171 Yumna Al-Arashi; 172–173 Koyoltzintli; 174–175 Delphine Blast; 176, 177l Angélica Dass; 177r, 178–179 Yagazie Emezi; 180–181 Deborah Willis; 182–183 Luján Agusti; 184–185 Erika Larsen; 186–187 Koral Carballo; 188–189 Kali Spitzer; 190–191l Charlotte Schmitz; 191r, 192–193 Mariceu Erthal García; 194–195 Miora Rajaonary; 196–197 Endia Beal; 198–199 Bethany Mollenkof; 200, 201l Hannah Yoon; 201r, 202–203 Noriko Hayashi; 204–205 Isadora Kosofsky; 206–207 Malin Fezehai; 208–209 Kiana Hayeri; 210–211 Luisa Dörr; 212–213 Natalie Keyssar; 214, 215l Sarah Waiswa; 215r, 216–217 Kendrick Brinson.

Front cover: Nada Harib; Back cover: (top, l to r) Gulshan Khan; Tara Pixley, (middle l to r) Jess T. Dugan; Paula Bronstein; Kholood Eid; (bottom l to r) Koral Carballo; Sarah Pabst.